MUSLIMS IN INDIA

Laurent Gayer is a research fellow at the Centre National de la Recherche Scientifique (CNRS), currently posted at the Centre de Sciences Humaines (CSH) in New Delhi. He is also research associate at the Centre d'Etudes de l'Inde et de l'Asie du Sud in Paris. He has co-edited, with Christophe Jaffrelot, *Armed Militias of South Asia: Fundamentalists, Maoists and Separatists* (Hurst 2009).

Christophe Jaffrelot is research director at CNRS and teaches South Asian politics and history at Sciences Po (Paris), as well as at King's College, London. From 2000 to 2008, he served as director of CERI at Sciences Po and is arguably one of the world's most respected writers on Indian society and politics. His publications include *The Hindu Nationalist Movement and Indian Politics: 1925 to the 1990s*; *India's Silent Revolution: The Rise of the Lower Castes in North India*; and *Dr. Ambedkar and Untouchability: Fighting the Indian Caste System*.

Muslims in Indian Cities
Trajectories of Marginalisation

Edited by
LAURENT GAYER AND CHRISTOPHE JAFFRELOT

HarperCollins *Publishers* India
a joint venture with

New Delhi

First published in India in 2012 by
HarperCollins *Publishers* India
a joint venture with
The India Today Group

Copyright © Laurent Gayer and Christophe Jaffrelot 2012

ISBN: 978-93-5029-546-5

2 4 6 8 10 9 7 5 3 1

Laurent Gayer and Christophe Jaffrelot assert the moral right to be identified as the editors of this work.

The views and opinions expressed in this book are the authors' own and the facts are as reported by them and the editors, and the publishers are not in any way liable for the same.

All rights reserved. No part of this publication may be reproduced, stored in a retrieval system, or transmitted, in any form or by any means, electronic, mechanical, photocopying, recording or otherwise, without the prior permission of the publishers.

HarperCollins *Publishers*
A-53, Sector 57, Noida, Uttar Pradesh 201301, India
77-85 Fulham Palace Road, London W6 8JB, United Kingdom
Hazelton Lanes, 55 Avenue Road, Suite 2900, Toronto, Ontario M5R 3L2
and 1995 Markham Road, Scarborough, Ontario M1B 5M8, Canada
25 Ryde Road, Pymble, Sydney, NSW 2073, Australia
31 View Road, Glenfield, Auckland 10, New Zealand
10 East 53rd Street, New York NY 10022, USA

Typeset in 10.5/13 Garamond Primier Pro
Jojy Philip New Delhi 110 015

Printed and bound at
Thomson Press (India) Ltd.

CONTENTS

Acknowledgements   vii
List of Maps   ix

   Introduction: Muslims of the Indian City. From Centrality to Marginality   1
   Laurent Gayer and Christophe Jaffrelot

1. 'Unwanted in my City'—The Making of a 'Muslim slum' in Mumbai   23
Qudsiya Contractor

2. Facing Ghettoisation in 'Riot-city': Old Ahmedabad and Juhapura between Victimisation and Self-help   43
Christophe Jaffrelot and Charlotte Thomas

3. Ramganj, Jaipur: From Occupation-Based to 'Communal' Neighbourhood?   81
Gayatri Jai Singh Rathore

4. A Minority within a Minority: the Shias of Kashmiri Mohalla, Lucknow   105
Gilles Verniers

5. Aligarh: Sir Syed Nagar and Shah Jamal, Contrasted Tales of a 'Muslim' City   129
Juliette Galonnier

6. Bhopal Muslims: Besieged in the Old City?   159
Christophe Jaffrelot and Shazia Aziz Wülbers

7. Muslims of Hyderabad—Landlocked in the Walled City   189
Neena Ambre Rao and S. Abdul Thaha

CONTENTS

8. Safe and Sound: Searching for a 'Good Environment' in 213
Abul Fazl Enclave, Delhi
Laurent Gayer

9. Marginalised in a Syncretic City: Muslims in Cuttack 237
Pralay Kanungo

10. Kozhikode (Calicut)'s Kuttichira: Exclusivity Maintained Proudly 263
Radhika Kanchana

11. Muslims in Bangalore: a Minority at Ease? 287
Aminah Mohammad-Arif

Conclusion: 'In Their Place'? The Trajectories of Marginalisation 311
of India's Urban Muslims
Laurent Gayer and *Christophe Jaffrelot*

Annex: Hindu-Muslim Riots in Post-independence India 327

Notes 331
Bibliography 383
Index 391
About the Contributors 401

ACKNOWLEDGEMENTS

The present volume is the outcome of a collective research programme housed and financed by the Centre de Sciences Humaines (CSH), New Delhi, a joint research unit of the Centre National de la Recherche Scientifique (CNRS) and the French Ministry of European and Foreign Affairs. The coeditors would like to extend their gratitude to the director of CSH, Basudeb Chaudhuri, for his support to the project all along.

The Centre d'Etudes et de Recherches Internationales (CERI) also supported financially and logistically the programme, most notably by housing the international conference where the first drafts of the papers presented here were discussed collectively in 2010. We would like to thank warmly all the discussants who helped us put each paper in perspective: Véronique Dupont, Chris Fuller, Zoya Hasan, Rubina Jasani, Nida Kirmani, Megha Kumar, Amitabh Kundu, Patrick Le Galès, Filippo Osella, Arvind Rajagopal, Suryakant Waghmore, Vanessa Cam, and Meenakshi Thapan.

The Centre d'Etudes de Inde et de l'Asie du Sud (CEIAS), for its part, gave an opportunity to several contributors to present their preliminary results in the framework of the Centre's research group on 'State, Citizenship, Territories'.

Last but not least, the Maison des Sciences de l'Homme made possible the participation of many Indian contributors to the 2010 Paris conference through its Indo-French exchange programme.

All the maps were prepared specifically for this volume by Bertrand Lefeb-vre (www.ao-seine.com).

LIST OF MAPS

Muslim Population of India	x
Map of Mumbai	27
Shivaji Nagar in Mumbai	34
Map of Ahmedabad	47
Map of Jaipur	90
Map of Lucknow	107
Map of Aligarh	130
Hindu-Muslim Segregation in Aligarh	134
Disputed Sites in Shah Jamal	152
General Map of Bhopal	166
Bhopal Old City	167
Muslim Population in the Municipal Wards of Central Bhopal's Constituency	168
Map of Hyderabad	199
General Map of Delhi	214
Muslim Population in Delhi's Tehsil	215
Map of Jamia Nagar in Delhi	215
Map of Cuttack	246
Map of Kozhikode	270
General Map of Bangalore	296
Map of Shivaji Nagar in Bangalore	296

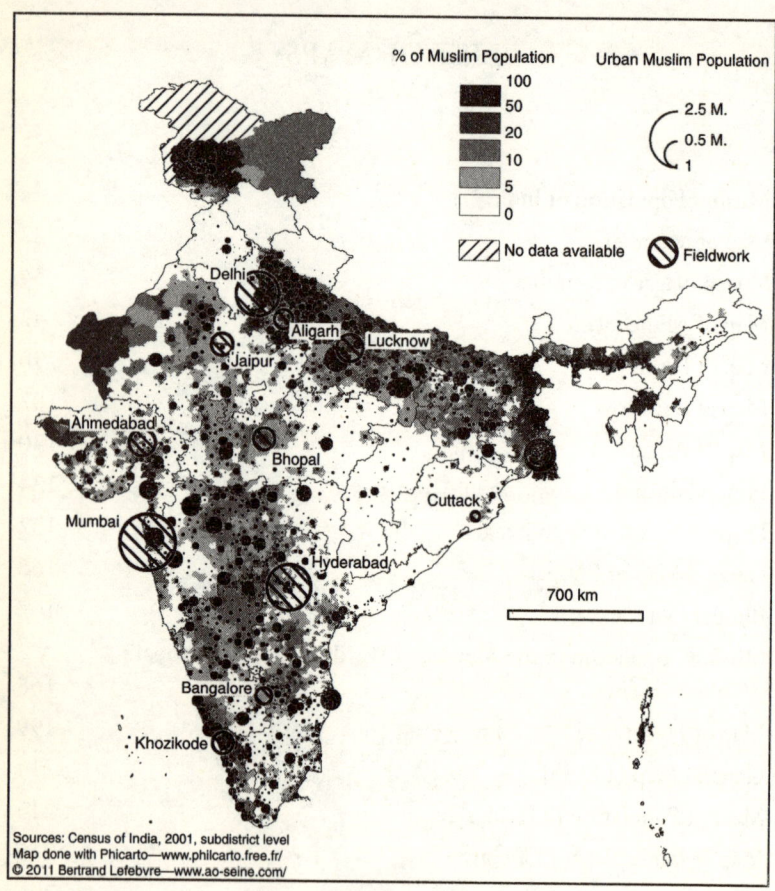

Muslim Population of India

INTRODUCTION

MUSLIMS OF THE INDIAN CITY: FROM CENTRALITY TO MARGINALITY

Laurent Gayer and Christophe Jaffrelot

'In any country the faith and the confidence of the minorities in the impartial and even functioning of the state is the acid test of being a civilized state'.

Justice Rajinder Sachar ('Foreword' to Basant, Rakesh and Shariff, Abusaleh (eds), *Handbook of Muslims in India: Empirical and Policy Perspectives,* Delhi, Oxford University Press, 2010, p. XV).

'In these great cities, where all the passions, all the energies of mankind are released, we are in a position to investigate the process of civilization, as it were, under a microscope'.

Robert Park, 'Human Migration and the Marginal Man', *American Journal of Sociology,* 33: pp. 881–893, 1928.

Indian Muslims are a peculiar minority. First by their sheer number: with 13.4% of the total Indian population according to the 2001 census, they are more than 138 million, making India the third largest Muslim country in the world (slightly behind Pakistan)—and the 2011 Census should give a much higher figure, around 170 million.[1] Beyond their demographic weight, the Muslims of India stand out among the country's minorities for their troubled legacy.[2] The lost children of India's Partition, Indian Muslims bear the stigma of the past. Their forefathers are often—unfairly for certain analysts[3]—perceived as the main culprits in the 'Vivisection of India', and their loyalty has been continuously questioned by sections of the state, of the media and of the political class. Moreover, they are suspected of Pan-Islamist leanings by Hindu nationalists, particularly since the 1980s, which saw the rise of a new fear of 'Gulf money' flooding Indian Muslim localities and religious institutions. And unlike other religious minorities such as the Sikhs, Indian Muslims cannot claim and take comfort in a territorial bastion.[4] Lastly, Muslims largely evade the general rise in their standards of living witnessed by other Indian minorities such as the Sikhs, the Christians or the Buddhists.

In the first section of this introduction, we will assess the situation of the Muslim community in Indian society in socio-economic, educational and political terms, without ignoring the fact that Muslims in India are not one homogenous community, or the differentiation that exists between them.

In the third and last, we will analyse the specifics of the Muslim presence in the cities of India, the framework in which this book is studying the Muslim minority by paying attention not only to the general urban settings, but also to sub-units and localities. As we will see, it is in these cities once ruled by Muslim royals that the marginalisation of Indian Muslims is currently the most blatant, as pointed out by urban Muslims' economic deprivation, by their sense of physical insecurity and by their increasing socio-spatial segregation.

The Muslims of India Towards Marginalisation

Socio-economic and Educational Indicators

For every scholar, activist or policy maker concerned with the current state of Indian Muslims, 'there is a need to consider numbers for here they tell a story that we may not like to confront: the extent to which Muslims are on the margins of the structures of economic, social and political relevance in India.'[5] Though alarming reports had been submitted to the Government of India since the 1980s,[6] the general impression that the Muslim community was increasingly lagging behind gained momentum a decade ago, after the unprecedented wave of communal riots of the 1990s, the rise to power of Hindu nationalist forces in 1998 and the Gujarat pogrom of 2002. In June 2005, one year after the Congress-led coalition, the United Progressive Alliance (UPA), took over from the Bharatiya Janata Party (BJP)-led National Democratic

INTRODUCTION

Alliance (NDA), Prime Minister Manmohan Singh appointed a High Level Committee to report on the situation of the Muslim minority and suggest remedies to its deteriorating condition. This was an unprecedented move reflecting a sense of urgency.[7] The report that was submitted by the committee—which came to be named the 'Sachar committee' after its president—showed, among other things, that only 8% of urban Muslims were part of the formal sector whereas the national average was 21% for Indian city dwellers.[8] This key figure harks back to the marginalisation of Muslims within the formal sector that is well documented by the Sachar Committee Report and other publications.[9] On the one hand a meagre 7.05% of them belong to the public sector, against an average of 18.13%. On the other hand, 68% are part of the informal sector, against about 52% as an average.[10] The 2001 Census points out, in a converging way, that Muslims have the highest percentage of household industrial workers, 8.1%, compared to 3.8% for Hindus.

Muslims are also poorer. The average monthly expenditures of urban Muslims was 800 rupees a month according to the 2004-05 report by the National Sample Survey (NSS), as much as for the Dalits and the Adivasis and much less than for upper-caste Hindus (1,469 rupees).[11] Correlatively, the share of Muslims living below the poverty line was 31% in 2004–05, as against 35% for Dalits and Adivasis, 31% for Other Backward Classes (OBCs) and 21% for the others.[12] More importantly perhaps, the trend is adverse, with Muslims experiencing a relative impoverishment. In 1987, according to NSS data, Muslims' average earning was 77.5% of the Hindus' average earning; in 1999 it was only 75%.[13]

Several chapters of the book edited by Basant and Sharriff—which analyses in details the findings of the Sachar Committee—show that Scheduled Castes (SCs) and Scheduled Tribes (STs) are catching up with Muslims in terms of education. Between the 1999–2000 NSS round and the 2004–05 one, the decline in illiteracy has been much higher in the SC/ST population (9–6%) than among Muslims (4.8%).[14] This development is partly due to a higher drop out rate.[15]

Parallel to the Sachar Committee, the first Manmohan Singh government appointed a National Commission for Religious and Linguistic Minorities (NCRLM) which was notified in October 2004 but constituted in March 2005, and whose report was submitted after the Sachar Committee Report, in May 2007. The NCRLM, which came to be known as the 'Ranganath Mishra Commission' (after the name of its president, a former Chief Justice of India), showed that the Muslim minority had the lowest literacy rate among all Indian communities.¹⁶ In fact, the literacy rate of Muslim males was only one percent above that of Dalit men—67.6% compared to 66.6%.¹⁷ The bureaucrats and politicians interviewed in the framework of the Mishra Commission conveniently attributed the educational backwardness of the Indian Muslims to the *madrasas*.¹⁸ This emphasis on the Quranic schools is puzzling and may well reflect deep rooted prejudices and stereotypes since the Sachar Committee Report concluded, on the basis of data collected by the National Council of Applied Economic Research (NCAER), that only 4 % of enrolled Muslim students go to *madrasas*.¹⁹ It should be emphasised, though, that this figure is only an approximation, as it is not based on Census data and hides important regional variations (with the attendance of *madrasas* being five times higher in the North than in the South, for instance).²⁰

The Mishra report recommended that 'at least 15% of seats in all educational institutions should be earmarked by law for the minorities', including 10% for Muslims.²¹ Similarly, the Committee also recommended that '15% of posts in all cadres and grades under the Central and State Governments should be earmarked' for the minorities, including 10% for the Muslims.²² The Hindu nationalist movement immediately attacked the Sachar Committee Report because of the way it promoted the 'pampering' of Muslims.²³ It may well be the main reason why the Mishra report has not been tabled yet in parliament.

However, in December 2010, on the side of the 19th 'International educational conference' of the American Federation of Muslims of Indian Origin held in Ahmedabad, Veerapa Moily, the Union Law Minister, declared that the Centre was committed to implementing 'all recommendations' of the report by the Committee named after Rajinder Sachar—who, incidentally, attended the conference.²⁴

Towards Political Peripherisation

The Indian Muslims tend to be excluded from three sites of power within the state apparatus: the judiciary, the administration and the police. In 2002, they represented only 6.26% of the 479 High Court judges of India (there was not even one Muslim judge in the Maharashtra High Court), 2.95% of the 5,018 Indian Administrative Service (LAS) officers and 4.02% of the 3,236 IPS officers.²⁵

This marginalisation in the police forces and the judiciary is a factor of the Muslims' vulnerability in the context of anti-terrorist measures resulting in laws of exception. NGOs and the media have documented the way 'a large number

INTRODUCTION

of innocent young Muslims have been and are being victimized by the police on the charge of being involved in various terrorist acts across the country'.[26]

In terms of representation in elective bodies, Muslims are pushed to the periphery of the political system in many different ways. In 1980, their percentage among the Lok Sabha MPs was almost proportional to their share in the population (9% compared to 11.4% of India's total population according to the 1981 Census). Then they experienced a steady erosion which accelerated in the late 1980s until the late 1990s, when the BJP-led NDA (which had not appointed many Muslim candidates) took over power. Things started to improve significantly in 2004 with the electoral defeat of the BJP. But in 2009, the percentage of Muslim MPs decreased again in spite of the electoral victory of the Congress-led UPA. The situation, in fact, is as bad as in the late 1990s when Muslim MPs represented 5.1% of the house members whereas Muslims were 12.1% of the Indian population according to the 1991 Census. Today, Muslim MPs represent 5.5% of the Lok Sabha MPs, but Muslims represent 13.4% of the population according to the 2001 Census. Many important states—including Gujarat, Jharkhand, Karnataka, Delhi, Rajasthan and, last but not least, Maharashtra—do not have even one sitting Muslim MP.[27] Muslims are also under-represented in the state assemblies. On average, over the period 1952–2004, their deprivation rate is below 20%, but it is above 50% in Rajasthan, Andhra Pradesh, Maharashtra, Madhya Pradesh and Karnataka. It is close to 80% (79.27%) in Gujarat.[28]

During the first five decades after independence, the vast majority of Indian Muslims saw in the Congress their natural protector, for its commitment to secularism. Attracted to the party by its ideology as much as by the promises of assembly seats or ministerial portfolios, Muslim politicians joined the Congress en masse. But these Congress Muslims often proved to be men of straw, whose political longevity was conditional to their docility.[29] Moreover, the protection contract between Muslims and the Congress started showing its limits from the late 1960s onwards, with the escalation of anti-Muslim violence and the economic marginalisation of the community, sometimes at the hand of the Congress-State itself, such as during the Emergency (1975–1977). Despite the love lost with the Congress, Indian Muslims have generally been reluctant to form their own political parties, fearing that their political mobilisation on a 'communal' basis would reinforce religious polarisation in the country. The rare exceptions to this rule have been local rather than national. In Hyderabad, the Majlis-i-Ittehadul-Muslimeen (Assembly for Muslim Unity—MIM) emerged in the 1930s with the support of the local princely ruler. It was revived in 1957 and carved a niche for itself in the Old City in the following years, retaining its hold over local Muslims through a mixture of populism and muscular politics. In Kerala, the Indian Union Muslim League (IUML) became an important power broker in the early 1960s and even gave the state its first Muslim Chief Minister, C.H. Mohammad Koya, in 1979. Elsewhere, Muslims have continued to support the Congress by default (save for the 1977 elections, when they massively shifted their allegiance to the Janata party), when they have not thrown their lot with the Communists (in West Bengal) or with regional lower-caste parties such as the Samajwadi Party (SP) or the Bahujan Samaj Party (BSP) in Uttar Pradesh. It should be noted, however, that the Congress remains the largest provider of Muslim elected representatives to the Lok Sabha.[30]

The feelings of insecurity of Indian Muslims have nurtured a minority complex which helps to explain the political inhibitions of this population and, at least until the early 1990s, its support for traditionalist religious elites (*ulama*).[31] In tandem with some Muslim politicians, these *ulama* have been more concerned with the cultivation of Indian Muslims' socio-religious particularism than with the uplifting of the community. The fact that these religious and lay-Muslim elites generally belonged to the Ashraf 'upper castes' only reinforced this trend, with important political consequences in the democratic set-up of post-colonial India. Indeed, self-appointed representatives of these Muslim leaders, keen to build a vote-bank for themselves, have infused in 'their' community a besieged mentality, which has inhibited modernisation. As Zoya Hasan explains, 'Most organizations associated with Muslims in north India and influential sections of the Muslim elite have focused on identity issues rather than education and empowerment, as it shores up their claims to authority and enables them to deliver votes in return for being treated by the state and political parties as the 'representatives' of the community'.[32]

Disaggregating the Muslim 'Community'

The Muslims of India seem to suffer from an unprecedented marginalisation process. They are losing ground in socio-economic and educational terms, and to some extent in political terms as well, as evident from recent reports and surveys. However, this social category does not form a bloc. It needs to be disaggregated, in terms of caste and class as well as in terms of urban/rural divide.

INTRODUCTION

Caste and Class Among Indian Muslims

The Muslim community does not form a homogenous whole in caste and class terms.[33] According to its variant of the caste system,[34] the Ashraf ('nobles')—descending from people originating from Muslim countries (Afghanistan, Iran, the Middle East, Central Asia...) or from converts hailing from Hindu upper castes (generally of Kshatriya status)—represent the elite groups whereas the Ajlaf ('commoners') are mostly descendants of converts from Hindu lower castes. Although Hindu Dalits did not convert en masse to Islam, some of them did so in order to escape the Hindu hierarchies, and their descendants are presently known as Arzal ('despicable'). The affinity of this 'caste' system with the Hindu model is more pronounced at the lower level of the system: if 'upper-caste' Muslims will often abstain from sharing the food of converts from Hindu 'untouchable' castes (sweepers, tanners, musicians), this stratification and the rules of social interaction that it informs are less rigid in the upper echelons,[35] with important regional variations needing to be accounted for.[36] The status of each non-Ashraf 'caste' (*zat*, equivalent of *jati* among Hindus) varies according to its lineage, ethnicity, traditional occupation and physical proximity to the higher 'castes'.[37] However, since this 'caste' system is less rigid than its Hindu variant, there is greater scope for upward social mobility, both at the individual and the collective level.[38] Last but not least, 'there is no social benefit from simply being high caste, unless one has also achieved status through education, profession or income'.[39] Status was here preeminent over lineage and the latter was often adjusted to the former, in a process known as 'Ashrafization'. The role of lineage in this 'caste system' was even attenuated in the last decades of the nineteenth century, following which the notion of '*sharif*' took a new meaning, which 'laid less emphasis on birth, noble lineage and inherited qualities and more on behaviour and achievement'. It is in this context that a new Muslim middle class, characterised by its distinctively industrious ethos and inclination towards reformist Islam, started emerging in the aftermath of the 1857 uprising.[40]

Like Dalit Christians, Dalit Muslims are not officially recognised and, therefore, do not benefit from reservations. The Arzal are enlisted with the Ajlaf in the category of the OBCs. Non-Hindu OBCs—mostly Muslim OBCs—represent 8.4% of the Indian population according to the Mandal Commission Report. Out of 3,743 castes classified as OBCs in this report, eighty-two are Muslim. While the Mandal Commission relied on the 1931 Census, more recently, the National Sample Survey in its 61st round of 2004–05 has pointed out that the OBCs represented 40.7% of the Indian Muslims.

Debates about the inner differentiation of the Muslim community have gained momentum over the last few years. Many scholars have argued that caste differences have become eroded in the course of time. Dealing with Hyderabadis, S. Ali points out that '(C)aste identities have waned in importance over time as they are no longer useful in garnering economic or political resources'.[41] Dealing more specifically with the Ashraf/Ajlaf divide, Satish Saberwal assumes that it has not become as acute as the upper caste vs. OBC opposition one may find among the Hindus. For him, this is due to the absence of 'a scripturally reinforced criterion of purity and pollution', as 'social separations were not as humiliating for the ajlaf as their analogues were for lower-caste Hindus; and Muslim society was somewhat more open socially than the Hindu space'.[42] Indeed, sites of religious power and reform that are not perceived or known for their progressive views appear to be socially inclusive. Thus, if Deobandi *ulama*, have been the flag-bearers of Ashraf supremacy,[43] their *madrasa*—the largest and most reputed in South Asia, founded in 1867—has also been providing Muslims of low extraction with opportunities for upward social mobility—starting with Deoband's 'first family', the Madanis, who claim to be Syeds but were originally weavers.[44] Similarly, 'low caste' Meos 'dominate the number of imams in Delhi mosques (80% according to one estimate)'.[45] Saberwal concludes that 'Religious identity has trumped the caste difference'.[46] This argument is popular among the Ashraf who, like the upper-caste Hindus, would like to submerge caste divisions in religious identities to project an image of 'their' community as united. In fact, inner differentiations remain. But social cleavages opposing the Ashraf and Ajlaf are certainly less marked than similar ones on the Hindu side. This is evident from the figures the Sachar Committee used in its report. Interestingly, this survey showed that non-OBC Muslims as well as OBC Muslims were lagging behind Hindu OBCs in terms of education, even though the Ajlaf, and especially the Arzal, were not as well educated as the Ashraf.

Table 1. Religious sub-groups and education (in percentage)

	Hindu OBCs	Muslim non-OBCs	Muslim OBCs
Level of education			
Secondary	15.0	12.6	13.1
Higher secondary	7.4	5.9	5.1
Graduate and above	3.2	2.4	1.9

Source: NSS 61st round (2004–05).

INTRODUCTION

Once on the job market, non-OBC Muslims do better than OBC Muslims but hardly better than OBC Hindus:

Table 2. Daily wages of salaried people in the public and the private sectors (in rupees)

Sector	Hindu OBCs	Muslim non-OBCs	Muslim OBCs
Public	190	196	176
Private	85	87	79

Source: NSS 55th round (1999–2000).

Moreover, the share of the Muslims is very low in the public sector, regardless of whether they are OBCs or not.

Table 3. Share of three social categories in the public sector (in %)

Institutions	Hindu OBCs	Muslim non-OBCs	Muslim OBCs
Railways	9.3	4.5	0.4
PSUs	8.3	2.7	0.6
University teachers	17.6	3.9	1.4
Non-teaching personnel of the universities	24.9	3	1.7

Source: Sachar Committee Report, op. cit., p. 210.

In 1994, a doctor from Patna, Ejaz Ali, launched the All India Backward Muslim Morcha (AIBMM).[47] He justified this move by citing the way upper-caste Muslims reacted to the demolition of the Babri Masjid when they tried to unite the whole Muslim community behind them in this very tense context: followers of Islam had to be Muslims first and from this or that caste after.[48] The following year, Syed Shahabuddin organised the First Conference on Reservation for Muslims where he argued: 'In my view, the entire Muslim community in the country forms a backward class'.[49]

The fact that Muslims do not form a homogenous community does not necessarily result in conflicts. Indeed Islam carries notions of collective solidarity, which need to be factored in. *Zakat,* or charitable donations, is one of the five pillars of this religion, at least in its Sunni incarnation. The recipient of *Zakat* needs to be a Muslim and cannot be a close relative. According to a recent study, in 2000, such philanthropic donations amounted to 867 million rupees in Indian towns and cities.[50] While the redistributive effect of such donations must not be exaggerated, it should not be underestimated either. Thus, the Jama'at-i-Islami alone (India's prime Islamist organisation, with a limited influence and a membership of only 5,000),[51] budgeted 387 million rupees for its welfare activities in 2007-11.[52] However, charitable activities are not likely, by themselves, to defuse tensions related to inequalities within the Muslim community. This is particularly obvious since a large share of *Zakat* funds go to *madrasas* rather than to the Muslim poor.

Urban Muslims vs. Rural Muslims?

With 35.7% of them residing in towns and cities in 2001, Muslims are the most urbanised religious community of a significant size in India (to the exclusion of Parsis and Jews). While Muslims represent 13.4% of the Indian population, they represent 16.9% of the urban population of India, and only 12% of the rural population. This gap is not new. It was even more pronounced before (in 1991, Muslims represented 16.7% of the urban population of India when they were 12.1% of the population). As a result, more than 50% of Indian Muslims are living in towns and cities in seven states, which, otherwise, are predominantly rural.

Table 4. States where Muslims are more urban than rural (2001 Census)

States	Andhra Pradesh	Chhattis-garh	Gujarat	Karnataka	Maha-rashtra	Madhya Pradesh	Tamil Nadu
% of Urban Muslims	58.1	62.9	58.7	59	70	63.5	72.8
% of Urban population	27.3	20.1	37.4	34	42.4	26.5	44

Source: P.M. Kulkarni, 'The Muslim population of India. A Demographic Portrayal', in Basant, Rakesh and SharifF, Abusaleh (eds), *Handbook of Muslims in India., Empirical and Policy Perspectives,* New Delhi: Oxford University Press, 2010, p. 120.

The urbanisation of Indian Muslims has not followed a steadily linear trend. Their rate of urbanisation slowed down in the 1980s and, more significantly, in the 1990s. While the gap between the Muslim population and the national average remains high in this respect, the decennial growth of urban Muslims remained below one percentage point during the 1990s, for the first time. These figures may reflect a new suspicion of the Muslim community regarding city life at a time when communal riots affected Indian cities more than ever before since 1947.

Table 5. Trends in urbanisation in India, all population and Muslim population, 1961–2001

Year	Percentage of population living in urban areas (urbanisation rates)						Decennial growth of % of urban Muslim	
	All Population		Muslim Population		Differences			
	A1*	B1	A2	B2	A2-A1	B2-B1	A2	B2
1961	18.0	18.0	27.1	27.1	9.1	9.1		
1971	19.9	19.9	28.8	28.8	8.9	8.9	1.7	1.7
1981	23.7	23.3	34.0	32.3	10.3	9.0	5.2	3.5
1991	25.7	25.7	35.5	34.8	9.8	9.1	1.5	2.5
2001	27.8	27.8	35.7	35.7	7.9	7.9	0.7	0.9

*A1 and A2 exclude Assam for 1981 and Jammu and Kashmir for 1991 (two states where census operations could not be held on these years). B1 and B2 include interpolate urban populations for Assam in 1981 and Jammu and Kashmir 1991.
Source: P.M. Kulkarni, 'The Muslim population of India. A Demographic Portrayal', in Basant, Rakesh and Shariff, Abusaleh (eds), *Handbook of Muslims in India.*, op. cit., p. 99.

Not only are Muslims more urbanised than other communities, but urban Muslims are comparatively poorer than rural Muslims, in contrast to the situation prevailing among most other communities. In 1999–2000, the share of urban Muslims living below the poverty line according to the NSS (36.92%) was more than fifteen percentage points higher than the share of urban Hindus living below the poverty line (21.66%) and almost ten points higher than the share of rural Muslims living below the poverty line (27.22%).[53] The Sikhs are the only community with a similar profile because of the economic achievements of the agriculturists of Punjab.[54]

Several of the above listed indicators of the increasing marginalisation of Indian Muslims have cumulative effects at the local level. But one cannot test such hypotheses on the basis of statistical aggregates. Qualitative studies are

Waqfs as resources or bones of contention?

The fact that Indian Muslims are losing ground in socio-economic and political terms does not mean that they are deprived of all collective resource. They can rely on traditional institutions such as the *waqf* (inalienable religious endowments entrusted to a charitable institution; pl. *auqaf*), which dates back to the times of the Prophet. In the words of Abusaleh Shariff, 'A Waqf is defined as a voluntary donation by the owner of the right of disposal of a thing or property and the dedication of the usufruct to some charitable end'.[55] Its main objectives are the financing of educational institutions, scholarships, aid to victims of riots or natural disasters, maintenance of mosques and *madrasas,* support to poor widows, salary of imams and muezzins, etc. In India, this institution, which has been functioning since the medieval period, is affected by many malpractices. As Shariff points out, 'most Waqf properties have neither been demarcated at site nor mutated in revenue records, despite repeated requests and reminders to the revenue authorities concerned. Consequently, many of these valuable properties, often in the heart of a city/town, are either heavily encroached upon or are the subject matter of multiple litigations'.[56] This is due partly to gross negligence confining to discrimination on the part of the state, partly to opposition of Hindu nationalist organisations,[57] partly to the corruption of the Waqf board members, and partly to their lack of technical skills. The Waqf Act 1995 (The Central Waqf Council Rules) has set up guidelines for the administration of *auqaf* proprieties across India except Jammu & Kashmir. But today most of the twenty-four Waqf boards established at the state level (twenty-two of which are being administered by Sunnis and two by Shias),[58] comprise not only persons well versed in Islamic Law but also Muslim MPs and Members of the Legislative Assemblies (MLAs), who may not be competent or with the needed reputation of integrity. As a result, the 4.9 lakhs of registered Waqfs currently spread all over India (they were 3 lakhs ten years ago),[59] whose book value is estimated to be about Rs 6,000 crores, only generate a current income of Rs 163 crores, which amount to a low rate of return of 1.5%.[60]

INTRODUCTION

needed. In India as elsewhere, ethnographic observation is the only way to 'pierce the screen of discourses whirling around these territories of urban perdition' and to 'capture the lived relations and meanings that are constitutive of the everyday reality of the marginal city-dweller.'[61] More specifically, field-work-based studies are indispensable to understand whether all urban Muslims are equally affected and whether all the Muslims of one city are losing ground or whether sub units of a given city—social as well as territorial—need to be identified.[62] This volume is intended to present such an inquiry in a comparative perspective.

Muslims in the Cities of India

Before directly addressing the place of Muslims in India's postcolonial cities, it is indispensable to capture, even in a synthetic way, the place of the city in the history of this peculiar minority and its own contribution to the shaping of Indian forms of urbanity. Then, we will turn to the changes currently taking place in the residential patterns of India's Muslim city dwellers, before clarifying how we understand the increasingly popular but analytically loose category of the 'Muslim ghetto' in the context of India's cities. Advocating a restrictive use of the label, we shall distinguish these 'neighbourhoods of exile'[63] from more benign forms of enclosing.

The City in Indian Muslims' History

The city occupies a central place in the history of Indian Muslims. It is here that Muslim power emerged and consolidated itself from the late twelfth century onwards, in constant interaction with the larger, Hindu-dominated society. These processes of transculturation, noticeable in the realm of ideas and beliefs as well as in material culture,[64] have been nurturing a 'composite culture' *(mili juli/mushtarka/ganga-jamna-tehzib)* which for centuries constituted a contact zone for Hindus and Muslims in the cities of India and later on in its rural areas, to the extent of challenging the very existence of essential 'Hindu' and 'Muslim' identities.[65] But acknowledging these interactions and cultural cross-fertilisations does not imply to engage in a romance with syncretism. Beyond the fact that this shared zone of contact and meaning never precluded conflict, India's 'composite culture' has been receding in most of its cities since the early twentieth century, following the redrawing of communal and national boundaries in the march towards independence and Partition, and more recently after Hindu-Muslim amity came under attack from the proponents of Hindutva.

Going back to the tryst of Muslims with the cities of India, one should recall that the Delhi Sultanate (1206–1526), the Mughal Empire (1526–1857), as well as more localised Muslim medieval principalities such as the sultanates of the Deccan, revolved around towns and cities which were simultaneously seats of power, centres of learning and economic hubs. With the patronage of Muslim rulers, these cities prospered and became the nerve centres of all successive Muslim polities. The expansion of Muslim power to the rural hinterland was a slow process and the first dominions granted by Afghan raiders to their military slaves in North India were simply referred to as 'the town, its neighbouring encampments and suburbs' (*shahr wa qasaba wa muzafat*).[66] Places of opportunity, these cities were also a haven for Muslim elites and commoners fleeing invasions or persecutions in their homeland. Projected by its rulers as the 'sanctuary of Islam' (*Qubbat al-Islam*), the Delhi Sultanate became a magnet for the uprooted elites of Iran, Afghanistan and Central Asia, and the patronage of these emigres by the Delhi sultan made eastward migration an increasingly popular option in the wake of Mongol invasions.[67] From Delhi, these emigres would sometimes proceed further in search of worldly or spiritual benefits,[68] particularly in the Deccan following the de-localisation of the court of the Delhi Sultanate to Daulatabad (1327–34).[69] The consolidation of autonomous seats of Muslim power in the Deccan around the Bahmani Sultanate (1347–1489) and its successor-states (Golconda, Bijapur and Ahmadnagar) was both a product of and an incentive for the circulation of these Persian(ised) elites, with Deccani rulers recruiting soldiers, administrators and artists directly in the Persian Gulf from the early fifteenth century.[70]

The Mughal Empire emerged in the sixteenth century from the same north Indian cities, which had made the fortune and reputation of the Delhi Sultanate (Delhi, Lahore and Agra),[71] but the relation of Babur's heirs to the city as a seat of power was more complex than that of preceding dynasties of Muslim rulers. On the one side, Mughal emperors made their cities of residence the seat and the mirror of their power, rivalling the great cities of Central Asia and Iran. In his memoirs, Jahangir (1569–1627) thus claims that by its number of buildings, Agra was 'equal to several cities of Iraq, Khurasan, and Mawara'a-n-nahr [Transoxiana] put together'.[72] Through awesome monuments and heavenly gardens, and more generally through elaborate town planning (*see infra*), Mughal rulers never ceased to experiment on the city, turning it into a political theatre as much as a site of social engineering. But the heirs of

INTRODUCTION

Babur also feared that their great cities could somehow become greater than themselves. The frequent displacement of their seat of power was not only an answer to the volatile politics of their time, but also partook of a strategy of deterritorialisation and personalisation of imperial authority which located power in the Emperor himself rather than in his capital. Occasional but sometimes prolonged episodes of camp-life, in the course of military campaigns, served to make the point and under Akbar, coins were struck at the mint of the imperial camp. Far from signalling a movement of de-urbanisation informed by some nostalgia for the nomadic past of their Turko or Turkic–Mongol ancestors, these episodes of camp-life (which, in the case of Aurangzeb's campaign in the Deccan, covered two decades) were a testimony to the imprint of urban culture over the Mughals. The emperor's encampment was, in fact, a movable city: 'The massive tents of the imperial encampment, emplaced after the day's march, retained the grandeur and fixed spatial arrangements of a permanent city built of stone'.[73]

The Muslim sultanates, which emerged in Bengal and the Deccan following the collapse of the Delhi Sultanate, were no less urbanised and functioned as city-states, revolving around fortified capital cities. In the Deccan, the successor-states of the Bahmani Sultanate, the most powerful of these autonomous Muslim principalities, resisted the Mughals' claim to hegemony and saw the development of a distinct blend of Indo-Persian culture around cities such as Hyderabad and Bijapur. The achievements of these city-states can be gauged by the flows of Muslim 'men of the pen' and 'men of the sword' to their capital cities all along the medieval period and beyond.[74]

Smaller towns were not immune to these political and cultural transformations. In North India, for instance, the Mughal gentry started acquiring land-rights at the end of Akbar's reign (1556–1605), and from then on started investing in the small market towns known as *qasbas*. They were integrated with surrounding villages—through the collection of land revenue and the consumption of agricultural and non-agricultural surplus—as well as with larger towns, offering a broader canvas of services. This investment was not only material but also affective, so much so that one witnessed the development of a *qasba* culture around these small towns. For the members of the educated and landed Muslim gentry, the *qasba*. was 'the repository of aristocratic and courtly values'.[75] It was also the real locus of their identity, their actual *watan* (homeland). Thus, the dominant castes of the *qasbas* of Awadh often attached the name of their locality to their own, thereby emphasising their attachment to what was much more than their place of residence.[76] This '*qasba* ethos' was explicitly pitted against the supposedly corrupt environment of larger urban centres (although this somehow romantic view of *qasba* society should be nuanced by factoring in the internal differentiations of local elites, which were reinforced by the socio-religious movements of the colonial period).[77] In return, 'the city dwellers poured scorn on the qasbati identity, equating it with rusticity and boorishness'.[78] The decline of their own cities was also lamented by these urbanite elites during the long twilight of the Mughal Empire (1707–1857). This feeling of loss contributed to the development of a specific genre of Urdu poetry known as *shahr-i-ashob* or *ashobia shairi* (lament for the city),[79] a genre in which poets such as Shafiq Aurangabadi, Shakir Naji, Shah Hatim, Mir Taqi Mir and Mirza Rafi Sauda excelled and which 'encapsulates the socio-cultural turbulence of cities in the late Mughal period'.[80] This painful attachment of late Mughal poets to their city of predilection can be grasped, for instance, in these famous verses by Mir Taqi Mir (1723–1810), which he recited at a *mushaira* (public recital of poetry) on the night of his arrival in Lucknow in 1782:

> There was a city, famed throughout the world,
> Where dwelt the chosen spirits of the age:
> Delhi its name, fairest among the fair.
> Fate looted it and laid it desolate,
> And to that ravaged city I belong.[81]

Such 'laments for the city' were not limited to the capital cities of the Mughal Empire but also resonated in the city-states that fell late under Mughal influence. In Hyderabad for instance—a city which had been imagined by its founder, Mohammad Quli Qutb Shah (1580–1611), as a 'replica of heaven on earth'—local poets 'carped and complained about the new administration's sins of omission and commission and invoked the lost historical glory of Golconda'.[82] As Ayesha Jalal has pointed out, this poetry of urban decay is a testimony to the hold exerted by the city over the imagination and identifications of Indian Muslims, for whom the sense of being Muslim was often coterminous with their attachment to a specific city. In other words, for Indian Muslims—or at least for their most literate sections—, cities were the place where a sense of identification to a non-territorial entity (the *Umma*) converged with a sense of belonging to a more circumscribed community (the *qaum,* the *watan*). It was the place where infinite space met finite spaces of belonging.[83] Jalal seems to omit one important fact, though: the *shahr-i-ashob* was first and foremost the swan song of decaying Muslim elites whose 'lament for the city' is inseparable from their resentment at witnessing the emergence of the lower, menial classes. The city lamented by these poets is a world upside down, where the rulers of yore have become destitutes and beggars, where poor carpet weavers wear expensive shawls and shavers of pubic hair compose poetry.[84] Instead of being representative of urban Muslims' predicament, this genre of Urdu poetry is more specifically a testimony to the urbanite ethos of a declining upper class, watching with utter contempt the rise of what would become, after the 1857 revolt, the Muslim middle class.

The Imprint of Muslims on Indian Cities

Muslim royals and their architects/town planners *(muhandis)* were familiar with the model—or, rather, with the myth[85]—of the Islamic City, with its 'concentric arrangement and hierarchical division of the different quarters, topographic partitioning and corporative concentration in commercial districts, and ethnic as well as religious segregation in residential areas'.[86] Even if the imprint of Islamic conceptions of the city over the actual shaping of the cities of medieval India remains a matter of debate among historians of the period,[87] it is undeniable that Muslim rulers and town planners were inspired by conceptions of urban space which put an emphasis on segregation around occupational and ethnic lines. As such, these 'Islamic' imaginations of the city converged with those of Hindus—possibly the result of some 'structural correspondence' between 'Hindu' and 'Muslim' systems of social stratification.[88]

For that matter, Hindu conceptions of urbanism also made their influence felt on early-modern 'master plans'. This was particularly manifest in the planning of Shahjahanabad (currently Old Delhi), the last and probably the greatest capital city ever designed by Indo-Muslim rulers (between 1639 and 1648). The city's plan reflected the influence of the *vastu sastras,* those ancient Hindu treatises on architecture, as well as that of Islamic and more specifically Persian organicist conceptions of town planning. Interestingly, these traditions converged in their attempt to reconcile the microcosm and the macrocosm, man and the cosmos. Shah Jahan and his planners (many of whom were Hindus) borrowed from a rich Hindu corpus the conception of the city as *axis mundi,* or centre of the universe, organised around the person of the king/emperor. Persian traditions of architecture, for their part, made their influence felt in the conception of the city as a living organism, whose head was located in the imperial palace, whose backbone was found in the bazar and whose heart beat in the Jama Masjid. Small streets, for their part, 'inserted themselves in the body proper as ribs and the vital organs—bath houses, schools, sarais, bakeries, water cisterns, teahouses, and shops—developed in proximity to the skeletal center'.[89] This organicist metaphor however omits major institutions of this hybrid city: the mansions of the nobility *(havelis)*, sometimes miniature towns with their workshops *(karkhana)* and quarters for the nobles' dependents and soldiery. The largest of these walled compounds, which replicated the palace/fortress, could house several thousands of people. They 'were the nuclei for the development of the mahallah [*mohalla*] system', which revolved around 'sealed, homogeneous units within the city', named after the locally dominant family or the professional specialisation of the residents.[90] These residential enclaves were generally protected by watchmen *(chaukidars)* paid by the residents, a trend which persists to this day in the middle and upper-class 'colonies' of all South Asian cities.

The Mughals' conceptions of urban space, which mixed religious symbolism with social engineering, were also exemplified by their gardens. In conformity with Islamic traditions, these havens of tranquillity were inspired by Muslim imaginations of paradise *(jannat)*. However, it is only in the late Mughal period that the religious symbolism of these gardens was amplified, when they were sacralised as the abode of the saints, and thus pitted against the vain agitation of the city in a recreation of the traditional *din/dunya* dualism. Until then, these gardens had attended to much more mundane functions, primarily serving as military camps, and in more peaceful times as places of sociability.[91] In addition to public gardens,[92] Mughal cities were dotted with more secluded ones, hidden behind the walls of the princes' and great amirs' residences. Indeed, the *Khana Bagh* (House Garden) was the '*pièce de résistance* [...] of every elite mansion'.[93]

Muslims in (Post-)Colonial Indian Cities

One may nuance the view that 'the major cities of contemporary India are either directly the creatures of colonialism or ripostes to it',[94] in view of the rich social and political history of India's urban settlements, but also because the formation of the colonial economy was originally an indigenous, urban-based phenomenon.[95] Thus, a city like Benares, which in the late eighteenth century was renowned for its capital market as much as for its places of pilgrimage, 'gave an enormous impetus to the British commercial penetration of Gangetic India.'[96] This is not to say that the agents and the capital of the colonisers did not transform the urban landscape of India. The new towns that flourished in North India in the second half of the nineteenth century, such as Kanpur, were to a large extent a by-product of economic changes which found their impulse in British policies, such as the expansion of the army and the extension of the railway system.[97] These economic changes contributed to a redistribution of cards between India's cities. Whereas garrison and railway cities like Kanpur prospered, others were less fortunate, such as Mirzapur, the former 'Manchester of India'.[98]

The second half of the nineteenth century was also characterised by a growing economic and social integration between town and country. Changes in the patterns of consumption in rural areas, as well as the explosion of land disputes, opened new markets for urban-based merchants, industrialists, lawyers and clerks. In the other direction, the *qasba-based* Muslim gentry, Hindu service castes and some Hindu zamindars started sending their sons to the city to complete their secondary education, 'now that examinations had begun to replace patronage as the avenue of professional advancement'.[99] And as historian Chris Bayly has suggested, the strengthening of the bonds between town and country was to play a major role in the transformation of Indian politics in the early twentieth century: 'Teachers, lawyers and the sons of estate managers with experience of both town and country helped mobilise their relatives and dependents for religious and nationalist activity. Small town merchants, now linked more closely to the pace of city bazars, also played an important role in the beginning of nationalist politics in the countryside'.[100]

It is in this historical context, at the conjunction of economic, societal and political change, that the Indian city became this 'dramatic scene of democracy [...] where the idea of India is being disputed and defined anew'.[101] Rather than outdating the pre-colonial triangular relation between market, temple and king,[102] the introduction of a 'proto-democracy'[103] by the British in India in the first decades of the twentieth century reinvigorated it, gave it a new shape and in return fed on it. Thus, in North India, the new Hindu political organisations that would come to dominate nationalist politics were the by-product of a 'corporate urban life' which retained strong links with the religious world of temples and shrines.[104] New Muslim political organisations, for their part, found their primary constituency in the *qasba*, or small town, service gentry.[105] However within the movement for Pakistan, the most successful of these Muslim political organisations, the Muslim League, managed to rally a section of Muslim religious elites and personnel (from *firs* and *ulama* to *maulvis* and *mullahs*).[106] In other words, following Chris Bayly, the origins of India's as well as Pakistan's nationalist politics can be traced to the alliances between the economic and religious elites of two modern, yet distinct forms of urban settlement: the 'Islamic qasbah' and the 'Hindu corporate town'.[107]

The central role of the cities in the vernacularisation of democracy in India was confirmed after independence. Although the bulk of voters came from rural areas, it is in the cities that the new, postcolonial democracy was the most vehemently debated. It is also here that the darker side of India's democracy made a spectacle of itself, the cities being the privileged venues for incidents of communal, and particularly Hindu-Muslim violence. This trend goes back to the early twentieth century, when Hindu, Sikh and Muslim identities were redefined and clashed with each other, in this very city imagined by the coloniser as the 'putative arena of modernity'.[108] Communalism culminated during Partition, which saw mass violence engulf many urban centres (no longer restricting itself to the 'old' parts of the cities), from Bengal to Punjab. Partition also dealt a fatal blow to the 'composite culture' of Indian cities, so much so that far from rejoicing at the prospect of seeing a Muslim state emerge in Pakistan, many Muslim writers and intellectuals lamented these developments. In the years preceding and following Partition, the transformation of the great cities of North India once again became a metaphor for the Muslims' predicament, such as in Ahmed Ali's *Twilight in Delhi*. In this novel, first published in 1940, the co-founder of the All-India Progressive Writers' Movement laments the decline of his city in nostalgic language echoing the *shahr-i-ashob* of the eighteenth century[109]:

> '[...] gone is its [Delhi's] glory and departed are those from whom it got the breath of life. Where are the Kauravs and the Pandavas? Where are the Khiljis and the Saiyyeds? Where are Babur and Humayun and Jehangir? Where is Shah Jahan who built the city where it stands today? And where is Bahadur Shah, the tragic poet and the last of that noble line? Gone they are, gone and dead beneath the all-embracing earth'.[110]

The umbilical cord between the city and Indian Muslims' identities—or at least between the great cities of yore and the courtly ethos of the Ashraf elites— was to a large extent broken by Partition. In independent India, the Urdu poets who had so poignantly sung the city became relics of the past, grieving the death of Urdu and the world in which it had flourished. Anita Desai's *In Custody* certainly offers the most powerful literary evocation of these literati's predicament, through the story of a Delhi-based poet, Nur Shahjahanabadi, reduced to a destitute life in the congested and decaying lanes of Chandni Chowk.[111] The surname Shahjahanabadi (from Shahjahanabad, *i.e.* Old Delhi) tends to suggest a persisting bond of the poet with his city of predilection, a practice which has indeed survived among contemporary Urdu poets, Rashid Banarsi being a case in point. But in Desai's gloomy narrative, this association between the poet and his city is no longer what it used to be and in fact underlines the irreversible decline of both—a communion in decrepitude, so to speak.[112]

In the decades following independence, Indian cities also witnessed a revival of communal tensions, with political dividends and strong spatial repercussions. And the intensification of these urban episodes of communal violence has redefined the geography of many a city during the last two decades, following the Ram Janmabhoomi movement, the destruction of the Babri Masjid, the Mumbai riots of 1992–93 or, more recently, the 2002 Gujarat pogrom.

Ghettoisation among urban Indian Muslim?

These incidents of violence have sustained dynamics of self-segregation among Muslims, who have been searching for safety in numbers. This process has been reinforced by the socio-economic marginalisation affecting Muslims. As the various contributions to this volume suggest, few Indian cities have been spared by this phenomenon. The Muslim-dominated neighbourhoods which have been emerging or expanding in this process of regrouping are increasingly being referred to as 'Muslim ghettos' by India's media, political class and academics alike. This category has even been granted official recognition in the Sachar Committee Report, whose authors claim that 'Fearing for their security, Muslims are increasingly resorting to living in ghettos across the country'. And according to the authors of the report, this ubiquitous process of ghettoisation would have severe effects on the community: 'inadequacy of infrastructural facilities, shrinking common spaces where different SRCs [socio-religious categories] can interact and reduction in livelihood options'.[113] As several contributions to this volume emphasise, this labellisation has percolated amongst the residents of these allegedly religiously homogeneous localities, who are prone to lament their confinement to 'the ghetto', a term which until now has no equivalent in vernacular languages.

If this discourse on the 'ghettoisation' of Muslims in Indian cities is fast becoming part of the common sense of Hindu-Muslim relations in contemporary India, it deserves to be examined carefully so as to construct the 'Muslim ghetto' as an analytical tool rather than a 'folk concept'.[114] Following Loïc Wacquant, we understand a 'ghetto' as 'a bounded, ethnically [or religiously] uniform sociospatial formation born of the forcible relegation of a negatively typed population.'[115] In other words, the notion of a 'voluntary ghetto' proposed in such canonical works as Louis Wirth's,[116] is oxymoronic in nature and misses the principle of exclusionary closure characteristic of these socio-spatial formations.[117] Building upon this basic definition, the concept of 'ghetto' can be further elaborated by pointing out five major characteristics of these spaces of relegation: an element of social and/or political *constraint* over the residential options of a given population; the *class and caste diversity* of these localities, which regroup individuals of different social backgrounds on the basis of ethnic or religious ascribed identities; the *neglect* of these localities by state authorities, translating into a lack of infrastructure, educational facilities, etc.; the *estrangement* of the locality and its residents from the rest of the city due to lack of public transportation as well as limited job opportunities and restricted access to public spaces beyond the locality; the subjective *sense of closure* of residents, related to objective patterns of estrangement from the rest of the city.

This book intends to compare the place Muslims are occupying in a dozen Indian cities sociologically as well as topographically. The overall picture we have just presented suggests that India's largest minority is declining. But is this a linear and general trend? And how does decline manifest itself? To measure it, most of the case studies that follow survey the position of the Muslims among the local elite groups (be they political, economic or legal)—and the rest of society. To locate Muslims in Indian cities and to test the ghettoisation thesis, the contributors to this volume also look at Muslim localities and the way they relate to the rest of the city. Methodologically, this book therefore combines a quantitative approach and a qualitative one, some chapters focusing more on urban sub-units in an ethnographic perspective.

1

'UNWANTED IN MY CITY'—THE MAKING OF A 'MUSLIM SLUM' IN MUMBAI

Qudsiya Contractor

Mehboob Bhai[1] commented looking at me that 'this [Shivaji Nagar] is like living in hell, would you call this living?' pointing towards the sea of garbage that surrounded us. There was garbage everywhere, as far as the eye could see. He pointed to the children playing in it, 'Look, our children even play in garbage, they have nowhere else to play'.

Fieldnotes, 24 January 2010

'It is not because they [Muslims of Shivaji Nagar] are not interested [in upward social mobility] people or because of their lack of commitment, that is really not the problem or that of capability. The problem is that it [Shivaji Nagar] is like a *walled city*. It is a huge area. And they rarely get a chance to go outside. When you don't see things like fancy brands or just the English labels on things or the fancy stores to buy them from, you don't know that is the world you want to aspire for. You are content with what you have. That's what they have learnt from their parents' [emphasis added].

Interview with Kriti Singh, English teacher at a private
English-medium school run by a Shia Trust, 24 March 2010

'Our crime is that we are Muslims (*Hum logon ka jurm yeh hai ki hum Musalman hain*). It is the way we are looked at. We are being pushed behind'.

Interview with Ramzaan ji, 25 November 2010

Shivaji Nagar is a predominantly Muslim slum situated at the periphery of an industrial suburb of Mumbai. It is one of the worst places to live in Mumbai owing to its proximity to the city's largest garbage dump as well as to the economic status of those who live there. However, being a Muslim slum dweller in Mumbai has become not just a socio-economic disadvantage but can also end up as a precursor to peripheral living in a city that was once the panacea to urban aspirations. Based on an ethnography of everyday life in Shivaji Nagar, this paper traces the processes that led to its formation and construction as a 'Muslim area/slum'. I argue that the state, through its violent spatial strategies, and the Hindu right, through its cultural populism and communal politics, have played a crucial role in its construction as a peripheral life space. Furthermore, the paper exemplifies the blurring boundaries between the everyday spatial practices of the state and the Hindu right through the experiences of the people of Shivaji Nagar. Finally, the paper describes how these exclusionary spatial practices are countered by Muslims through everyday claims to the city itself.

Communal Politics as Spatial Politics in Contemporary Mumbai

Historically, Muslims formed a substantial minority in the city with their economic engagements ranging from being traders to constituting the mill workforce in the cotton textile industry (Hansen T.B., 2001a; Chandavarkar, 1994). Muslim localities in colonial Mumbai represented a socio-cultural diversity and their spatial location in the city was closely linked to their position in the city's economy. Parts of the city that had high concentrations of Muslims as early as the eighteenth century are distinctly noted as Muslim areas of the city even today.[2] The 'Muslim quarter' of the city being fairly diverse had *mohallas* associated with caste-like groups or interrelated occupational groups among Muslims that were linguistically and culturally distinct (Masselos, 1977; Chandavarkar, 1994).[4] This included working class neighbourhoods housing the industrial workforce, which were segregated along religious and caste lines as a manifestation of the social organisation of labour in the city.[5] Conforming to broader trends of nationalist politics and communal mobilisation, religious festivals and processions became occasions for contestation and coding of city spaces based on the politicisation of communal identities (Hansen, 2001a; Masselos, 2007a). The 1930s and 1940s saw an incipient isolation of the Muslim working class in the economy as well as spatially in the city, and the process became even more pronounced after independence (Hansen, 2001b).[6] Post-independence, Hindu nationalist agendas, discourse and institutions gradually penetrated everyday life, and acquired a growing, though not uncontested, social respectability in contemporary Indian society (Hansen, 1999; Jaffrelot, 1996). Mumbai was no exception to this and the rise of Shiv Sena in the 1960s marked the beginning of the communalisation of the cultural and political environment of the city (Appadurai, 2000; Lele, 1995).[7] Shiv Sena offered the rhetoric of ethno-religious unity, regional cultural pride and also a solidarity that repackaged older anti-Muslim myths (Hansen, 2001a). The politico-cultural strategies of the Shiv Sena relied heavily on spatial tactics,[8] which included violently rewriting urban space as sacred, national and Hindu space (Appadurai, 2000). The Shiv Sena took to slums and working-class neighbourhoods with its Hindu-Marathi chauvinism in the light of the growing insecurities of urban living (Appadurai, 2000; Heuze, 1995; Sen, 2008). Nationally, the party joined hands with the BJP to further *hindutva* and its agenda for a Hindu nation, which radically transformed the city's geography. The Shiv Sena's spatial strategies widely used public spaces as sites for the display of the Hindu rights violent political strategies and anti-Muslim rhetoric (Hansen T. B., 2001a).[9] Hence, the spatial segregation of Muslims in the city can be attributed to their growing economic, political and socio-cultural alienation as well as violence eventually transforming their spatial location in the city.

The incidents that followed the demolition of the Babri Masjid in Ayodhya on 6 December 1992 (the riots of December 1992 and January 1993, which caused at least 900 deaths, as well as the bomb blasts of March 1993, which made 250 victims) have had a lasting impact on the social geography of the city.[10] Many chose not to go back to their homes in mixed neighbourhoods in the city (Masselos, 2007b; Punwani, 2003; Robinson, 2005). It has been argued that it is the scarcity of housing in Mumbai that translated the explosive violence of 1992–93 into the imaginary of cleansed space, a space without Muslim bodies (Appadurai, 2000). Soon after the riots and as a consequence of the violence, one witnessed the formation of new boundaries around communal identities, defined through a process of naming at the intersection of religious identity, nationality and personal identity (Mehta & Chatterji, 2001). This was the case, in particular, in Dharavi (the largest slum in the city if not in Asia), where the lines of demarcation between Hindu and Muslim-dominated areas were designated as 'India-Pakistan borders'. Other areas with an already sizable Muslim population saw a further influx of Muslims from other parts of the city. In central Mumbai, areas such as Nagpada, Madanpura, Bhendi

Bazar or Mohammed Ali Road, as well as some parts of Wadala such as Kidwai Nagar or Byculla saw an influx of Muslims. In the suburbs, Jogeswari (west), Kurla, Govandi and Mumbra were further concentrated with Muslims. Middle-class Muslim localities such as Millat Nagar, a large complex of apartments off Lokhandwala in Andheri (west) and Mira road, a distant suburb in Northwest Mumbai, have become noticeable and distinct as Muslim localities over the last ten years (Robinson, 2005: 43).

Table 1.1. Population of Muslims in Mumbai and Maharashtra in 2001*

	Total	Muslims	Percentage (%) of the total population
Mumbai	3,338,031	734,484	22.0
Mumbai (suburban)	8,640,419	1,488,987	17.0
Maharashtra	96,878,627	10,270,485	10.6

* Compiled from Census of India, 2001.

In an act to reclaim the city from its cosmopolitan image and to establish its regional credentials, the Shiv Sena-BJP alliance renamed Bombay to Mumbai in 1995 (Hansen T. B., 2001a). Once in power, their spatial tactics through democratic processes/institutions transformed several other landmarks in the city by renaming them after Chhatrapati Shivaji, the Hindu Maratha warrior king and icon of the Shiv Sena. Today several public spaces (including government offices, commercial establishments, lanes, streets, parks and even traffic islands) across the city are marked with the installation of grand statues of Shivaji (mounted on a horse holding a sword) decorated with forked saffron flags. Significant to the institutionalisation of the exclusionary spatial strategies of the Shiv Sena has been its growing dominance in the Brihanmumbai Municipal Corporation (BMC) from the late 1960s through the 1990s.[11] This has even translated into the reorganisation of administrative boundaries in certain suburbs of the city.[12] Furthermore, this is accompanied with a low presence of Muslim political representatives in government. In Maharashtra, out of the 288 Members of Legislative Assembly (MLAs), only eleven (3.8%) are Muslims.[13] The presence of Muslim MLAs in the Mumbai region is slightly better; of the thirty-six MLAs here, six (16.6%) are Muslims. However, of the total 227 Municipal Councillors (Corporators) under the Municipal Corporation of Greater Mumbai (MCGM), only twenty-four (10.5%) were Muslims.[14]

'UNWANTED IN MY CITY'

The following sections are based on ethnographic fieldwork conducted in Shivaji Nagar. I draw from what Hansen (2001a) describes as the 'localised notions of what the locality was' or the 'local phenomenology of locality and space' in the face of the elusive and often unfixable nature of social boundaries in urban space in a city like Mumbai. Through an ethnography of everyday life they describe how exclusionary acts and imposed representations of the state and mainstream society are subverted in ordinary situations by Muslim residents of Shivaji Nagar (Certeau, 1988).

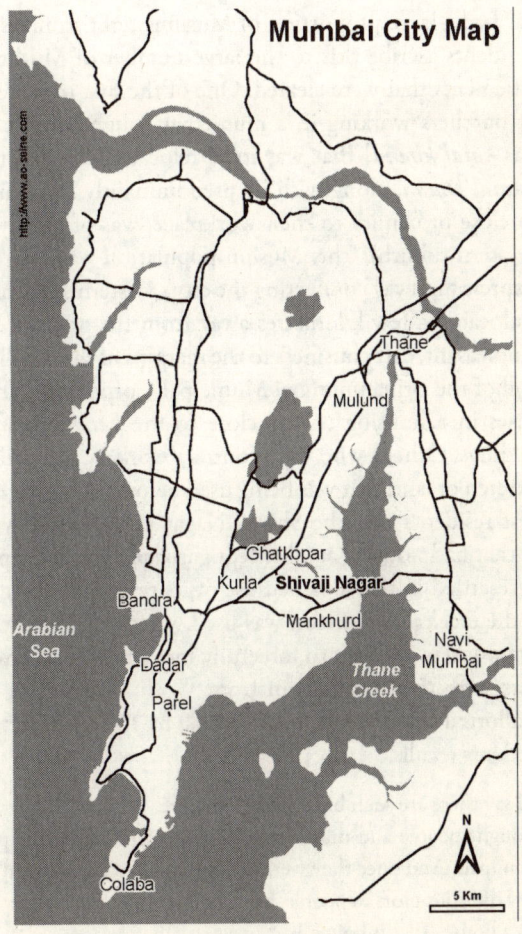

Map of Mumbai

QUDSIYA CONTRACTOR

Garbage dump, human dump

Shivaji Nagar is situated on the swampy terrain of the Thane creek in close proximity to large tracts of municipal land allocated for the disposal of the city's garbage in colonial times, popularly referred to as the 'dumping ground'. The land that it occupies was once a marsh that turned into solid land by the continued disposal of garbage there. Shivaji Nagar came into existence in the early 1970s following the demolition of several slum settlements across the city as part of the state's slum clearance drives. Following the resettlement of slum dwellers from other parts of the city, the population of Shivaji Nagar had a large proportion of Muslims right from its formation. The older residents ascribe this to the large number of Muslims living in the slum settlements that were cleared. One of the first to be resettled was a locality of butchers working in a municipal slaughterhouse (popularly referred to as *katal khana*] that was itself relocated close to the garbage dump. The *katal khana*, along with its predominantly Muslim workforce that lived in close proximity to their workplace, was originally located in Bandra (a western suburb). This Muslim population was evicted to make way for an express highway connecting the city's western suburbs. The *katal khana* was relocated a few kilometres away from the garbage dump, thus moving an unpleasant, dirty business to the margins of the city. The workers on the payroll of the Brihanmumbai Municipal Corporation (BMC) were allotted houses in a housing colony close to the *katal khana*, in multi-storeyed buildings. Others, who were contract workers, were allotted plots in an open stretch of land that was being used before for garbage disposal.

The oldest residents describe Shivaji Nagar in its early days as a large marshy land that had nothing at all except garbage. Not many people were happy to be resettled in this area because of its proximity to the dumping ground and the creek. So coercion was used, which included the burning down of slum pockets in order to forcefully move people to Shivaji Nagar. Slum dwellers were then brought in from Worli, Mahalaxmi, Sewri and Bandra and allotted square plots of land of 10 by 15 square feet. As one of the older residents recalls,

'People would say there are such big mosquitoes here. Who will want to stay here? The BMC brought people and dumped them here. This was a dumping area, so people were dumped. And once they were dumped, they were dumped [*laa ke dala hai*]. Now, they did allot plots to people, but this is still a dumping area (pauses). At least they have a house. That is how it is'.

Interview with Hussein, resident since 1974, 22 March 2010

'UNWANTED IN MY CITY'

Like most squatter settlements in the city, Shivaji Nagar is located on municipal corporation land and hence the residents are tenants who were allotted housing on the submission of proof of residence in the city like ration cards and payment of a deposit amount towards the rental agreement.[15] The area has grown considerably since its formation in terms of the density of population and the area it covers. There has also been an influx of newer residents who have either purchased tenements from earlier residents or rented them.[16] The rents in this area today are as low as Rs. 400–500 per month for a small room. Those who filled in the 'gaps within the squares'[17] came through social or kinship ties with those resettled here, hence further increasing the concentration of Muslims. Their image as 'encroachers' was largely held by outsiders especially BMC officials and even professional NGOs. However, the cause for this influx is seen by the residents as a need for toilers such as themselves to have a familiar, safe and affordable space to live in a mega city like Mumbai.

Communal violence in 1984 and 1992–93

The residents of Shivaji Nagar experienced two major communal riots—one in 1984 and the other in 1992–93—that had a lasting impact on the landscape of the neighbourhood. Although the epicentre of the 1984 riots was the textile and power-loom city of Bhiwandi, it spread to various parts of Mumbai. Shivaji Nagar was among the main troubled areas in Mumbai, where the Shiv Sena with the help of local goons attacked Muslims (Engineer, 1984).[18] Several Muslim residents attempted to flee from the area or sought refuge in neighbouring slums. The area was put under curfew for ten days with the military being called in to put an end to the violence. Immediate action from the state to restore law and order instilled a sense of safety in the residents of Shivaji Nagar. The communal violence led to the out-migration of Hindu residents in the area and localities became more segregated. Some Hindu residents of the surrounding middle-class housing colonies consider the 1984 riots as one of the causes for Shivaji Nagar becoming a distinctly Muslim-dominated area. However, it still remained a mixed locality with some proportion of non-Muslims continuing to live there.

Following the demolition of the Babri Masjid on 6 December 1992, Shivaji Nagar was reportedly one of the major sites of violence in the city. The detailed sequence of events has been reported in the Srikrishna Commission report (1998) as well as the Indian People's Tribunal (1994), two main reports that documented evidence. The trouble in the area reportedly began with

Muslim mobs committing acts of violence and attacking public transport (BEST) buses, a local BJP activist and two temples in the area. Muslims in large numbers gathered in public areas within Shivaji Nagar to protest the demolition of the Babri Masjid wearing black armbands. These acts of public and, in certain cases, violent protests resulted in a violent conflict between Hindus and Muslims living in Shivaji Nagar. The situation intensified with the police opening fire on mobs, killing more Muslims than Hindus. This incident caused a major dent in the relationship between Muslims of Shivaji Nagar and the police. Then what followed was the killing of two police constables by a mob of Muslims during a violent conflict between them and the police.

'On 7th December [...] a mob of Muslims attacked the police during the course of which two policemen were killed. There was a picket of nine constables near a temple in Padma Nagar. The mob overran the police picket and attacked the two police personnel despite eighteen rounds fired by the police. The police were outnumbered and had to retreat. One police constable was killed and the other died on his way to the hospital. Thirteen Muslims were killed in the incident and six were injured'.

(Report of the Srikrishna Commission: An inquiry into the riots at Mumbai during December 1992 and January 1993, 1998; pp. 82–84)

This followed with a violent battle between the police and the residents, with Muslims bearing most of the loss and damage. The evidence presented before both the commissions pointed towards a nexus between the Deonar police station and the Shiv Sena. In some areas, the police had attacked people and burnt their houses along with the Shiv Sena. In other cases, policemen themselves shouted slogans such as *'Jai Shree Ram'* and *'Jai Shivaji'* while they were attacking the victims (Indian People's Human Rights Tribunal, 1994). Thereafter, the military was called in to restore law and order with the area being put under a curfew that lasted for three months.

Table 1.2. Loss of lives and property due to communal riots in Shivaji Nagar during December 1992*

	Hindu	*Muslim*	*Others*	*Total*
Number of persons killed	6	44	–	50
Establishments subjected to damage and looting	665	1006	2	1673
Arrests	11	129	–	140

* Compiled from the Srikrishna Commission Report (1998).

'UNWANTED IN MY CITY'

Muslims in certain pockets within Shivaji Nagar in turn negotiated with some individual policemen to perform the Friday *namaz* in the open areas in order to restore their spatial claims to the locality. During the curfew, Muslim women provided the army and policemen with food and water. This was done with the hope that it would lessen the hostility and antagonism owing to the death of the policemen. Hence, peaceful coexistence between the police, Hindus and Muslims had to be negotiated.

Nearly seventeen years after the incident, the recollections and memories of the riots are part of the history of Shivaji Nagar that residents still feel uncomfortable talking about. The demolition of the Babri Masjid was usually described in terms of martyrdom, a frequently used phrase being *Jab Babri Masjid shahid hogayi...* [When the Babri Masjid was martyred...]'. They offered detailed descriptions of incidents and the environment of fear and terror that gripped the entire area as well as the city. The already appalling living conditions in the peripheral areas of Shivaji Nagar worsened as unidentified bodies were being dumped in the dumping ground. The familiarity of the locality and neighbourhood provided a sense of safety, though:

'Even today if someone mentions '92 it feels like it happened only yesterday. We have seen what happened. So that scene is still fresh in our minds (pauses) as if it happened today, why even yesterday. [...] Any sound at night used to startle us. We somehow managed to pass time in the day sitting at home. At night...we could not sleep. If there was a sound coming from anywhere, we would feel they have come. This would scare us'.

Mehboob, 20 November 2009

'When bullets were fired we used to feel scared. There used to be the sound of shutters being pulled down. There was a house in front of ours on a *mala,* (mezzanine floor) it was a [Muslim] family, they also had kids. We moved into their house. [...] Even today, when someone pulls down a shutter I feel scared'.

Heena, 8 May 2009

'*Goli ruki yani* normal *hua*. *Goli ruki nahin to bahut hua* (It was stable/normal if the bullets/firing stopped. If the bullets did not stop, a lot of violence happened). We could not go out of our homes. Everyone used to tell us, stay here, stay here, don't go out. Keep yourself away from the eyes of the police. If you stay you will be safe. If you go out, there is a possibility that someone might get stuck somewhere or somebody might kill you or do something else to you (pauses) some others may kill you. That is why [you should] stay here. If you want to be safe, stay at home'.

Munira, 25 November 2009

Several residents of Shivaji Nagar chose to flee from the city during the riots after the demolition of the Babri Masjid. Among those who chose to leave were both Muslims and Hindus. A Muslim resident narrated an incident of a Muslim man who fled with all his belongings but was looted before he got on to the train to reach his hometown. Hence it made sense not to leave the locality. Some residents persuaded others (both Hindus and Muslims) not to leave and even accommodated the influx of more Muslims, who were fleeing from neighbouring slums like Sion, Dharavi and Ghatkopar.

'We stopped many people...would leaving the place have solved the problem? What if somebody is caught on the way? If the person is from UP, he has to go for at least 1300–1400 kms. On the way he has to cross Maharashtra and other states. *To yeh 1992 ka lafda India level ka lafda tha. Kisi ko bhi maar sakte the* (the 1992 riots were an all-India level riot. Anyone could have been killed.) So a person was only safe at his location. What if he is killed by the time he reaches VT [Victoria Terminus now renamed as Chatrapati Shivaji Terminus]? There have been several cases like this'.

Mehboob, 20 November 2009

'H: A lot of people sold their rooms and left the area. In our gully there were more Hindus than Muslims before the riots. After the riots, the Hindus sold off their rooms and those were bought by Muslims. Although not a single Hindu was touched in our area. Muslims were killed and nothing happened to the Hindus, but they chose to leave.

Q: Why did they leave ?

H: We don't know what might have come into their hearts (*unke dil main kya aya*). They probably must have thought that if nothing happened to us this time, what if something happens to us in the next riots'.

Heena, 8 May 2009

Most of the relief and rehabilitation work post-riots was carried out by non-state actors in the area. Relief camps were set up in the area by the local *jama'ats* and mosques after the riots. Several mainstream elite Muslims including film actors from the community visited Shivaji Nagar and distributed relief materials. Muslim youth in the area were involved in the distribution of food grains. After the riots several NGOs (headed by progressive middle-class Hindus) got involved in relief and rehabilitation work in the area. Some of these, who had been working there, took their activities to the interiors of Shivaji Nagar and much closer to the dumping ground. In the absence of state facilities, they have continued with the services they provided before the riots such as primary health care, education and sanitation. These have also been a source of employment for Muslim men and women from the area. In the absence of state services in the interiors of Shivaji Nagar, NGOs are functioning as an interface between the state and the people. Some have been engaged in creating a cultural space to reinforce the message of communal harmony through the involvement of youth and children. Post-riots, these organisations have extended their work to poverty reduction through self-help groups and micro-credit programmes. Some have adopted the rights-based approach to development[19] venturing into addressing gender-based violence and nurturing women's community participation. However, their interventions are largely based on a somewhat limiting premise that poverty reduction (through self-help) and religious reform (focusing primarily on Muslim personal law) are keys to improving the condition of Muslims living there. This, coupled with the failure of the state to deliver justice and its general neglect of the area, has often left the residents with self-blame and victimhood as the only means to negotiate survival in the city. In spite of their limitations, the involvement of NGOs in relief and rehabilitation work as well as their continued presence in the interiors has been able to restore connections with the city at large, including trust in the mainstream city's progressive Hindus efforts at bridging a divide that deepened with the riots.

Peripheral Living

Shivaji Nagar is situated in the M (east) ward of Mumbai, which has one of the highest proportions of slums in the city, including the largest number of slum resettlement colonies.[20] According to the Mumbai Human Development Report (2009), M (east) has the lowest Human Development Index (HDI) at 0.05, much lower than the city's average of 0.56. M (east) ward (including Shivaji Nagar among other areas) and has a population of 673,871 according to the 2001 Census. The population has increased to 759,613 in 2008 and 771,177 in 2009 according to the BMC estimates. However, the unofficially estimated population of Shivaji Nagar itself is six lakhs, of which Muslims constitute more than two-thirds.[21] The rest comprises of excluded 'others' such as those from outside Maharashtra, Christians, Dalits etc.[22] The residents present a fair diversity in terms of language, caste, sect and occupation. One can find people from almost every state and linguistic background, but a large proportion of them are from Uttar Pradesh and Bihar.

According to municipal records, Shivaji Nagar is divided into two areas known as Shivaji Nagar I and II, both of them distinct and quite a contrast to each other. Shivaji Nagar I comprises of organised plots and has a network of roads[23] that connect these plots that originally had 150 households each. With the influx of more people and constant need for accommodation, many residents have built additional rooms that they rent out to these new entrants. Hence, each plot in Shivaji Nagar now holds approximately 250–300 households each. Shivaji Nagar II is fairly unorganised, closer to the garbage dump and comprising of newer migrants. The residents of Shivaji Nagar I are mostly Shias, economically better off, most of them are small entrepreneurs and some also work in the municipal corporation. They dominate the economy of Shivaji Nagar and their businesses often employ those from Shivaji Nagar II. The main market, banks, most of the schools in the area (both municipal and private), the government health centre, post office, political party offices (such as those of the Congress, Samajwadi Party and Shiv Sena) are located in Shivaji Nagar I. Each plot here has a common toilet and garbage dump. The roads are much wider and clean. The houses in this area are referred to as '*chawls*' by local residents. Some of the houses here look well maintained and some even grandiose with large ornate wrought iron gates that were painted black and gold. Some houses have doors a few feet above the ground with small steep staircases that lead up to them. Some have walls lined with fancy ceramic tiles and large sliding windows. The windows are heavily curtained, blocking the view of the passers-by, unlike the general milieu of a slum where privacy is a privilege the poor do not possess.[24] The Muslims in Shivaji Nagar I are also well connected

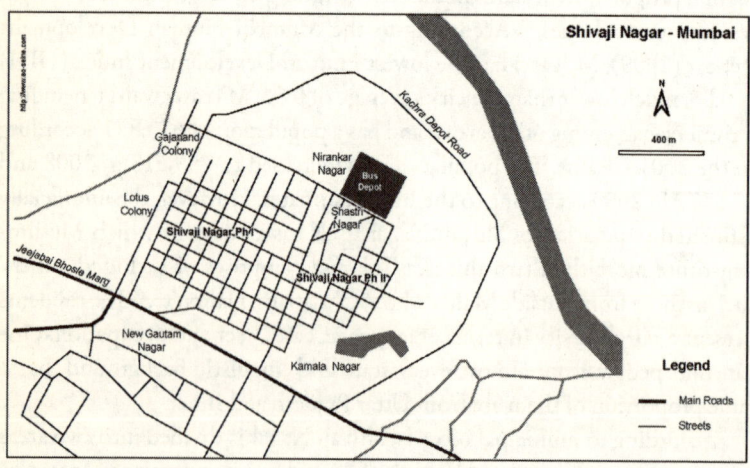

Shivaji Nagar in Mumbai

to the Muslim elite (especially Shias) in the city, which has made its presence felt through business and trade links or through charity-related activities (*zakai*). Some are also involved through charitable trusts which run schools in the area or provide educational sponsorship.

The living conditions in Shivaji Nagar II are appalling due to the proximity to the dumping ground. It has very poor infrastructure and suffers from a complete lack of state services. The houses here are much smaller and separated by congested narrow lanes that gives the entire area a feel of a dense, complex labyrinth. The majority of the Muslims living here are Sunnis. Most of them are skilled workers (such as tailors, weavers, *zari* workers, carpenters, plumbers, drivers etc.), small entrepreneurs or casual labourers. A significant proportion lives off the garbage dump either as ragpickers or involved in the resale of sorted garbage (*bhangar*). The area is always enveloped in thick black smoke emitted from the garbage dump due to the burning of garbage by those involved in sorting and sifting through it. Several women and children are engaged in the collection and sorting of garbage. Islam Bi has been living in Padma Nagar since the last eight years as a tenant. Her husband is a casual labourer and she works as a rag picker at the garbage dump. She earns sixty-seventy rupees for sifting and sorting garbage nine hours a day. The garbage dump is also the only 'open' space available to the residents of Shivaji Nagar II and is used as a playground and grazing ground for cattle and goats.

Despite being a resettlement site for some years now, Shivaji Nagar has been at the centre of housing and slum resettlement speculation because of the city's booming real estate market. Certain pockets have also been under the constant threat of demolition from the state due to their 'unauthorised' or 'illegal'[25] status. In 2008–09, 114 hutments in Sanjay Nagar, 300 in Rafi Nagar and 130 in Indira Nagar (all situated in Shivaji Nagar II) were demolished by the BMC.[26] There is a perception that Shivaji Nagar being a 'Muslim area' makes it more vulnerable to frequent demolitions. Municipal authorities also deal with the demolition of localities in Shivaji Nagar differently and harbour the perception that they are swarming with criminals.

'Whenever the names of our areas come up they feel different. Whether it is the municipal authorities or the police, they feel these areas are dangerous. Why they feel these areas are dangerous I don't know [pauses to answer a phone call]. Perhaps it shows somewhere that this is a Muslim community. These are not good people, more crime happens here. More criminal-type people stay here. This is the message they get'.

Interview with Shaheed, local resident and housing rights activist,
8 November 2009

The scarcity of water is another issue that the residents associate with the demographics of the area such as the influx of more people as well as a disproportionate supply to begin with because of the skewed consumption patterns in the city that favour the elite.[27] The water problem is more than a decade old and is also perceived to have come about soon after the 1992–93 riots. Some however maintain that the water problem started in 1997, after a Shiv Sena corporator in the area was voted out. In official documents of the local municipal office, the short supply of water in the area is attributed to its physical location, specifically describing Shivaji Nagar as a 'fag end' to connote its distance from the main water supply reservoir that is located closer to the non-slum areas of the municipal ward. Dealing with an acute scarcity of water is a part of the everyday life struggles for survival in Shivaji Nagar. Jameel (20 years), who lives closer to the dumping ground, has been fetching water from a neighbouring slum since he was ten years old: 'I have been fetching water my entire life. First my father used to fetch water, now I have to do it too'. His family has to pay Rs. 5 per gallon (3.7 litres), which could go up to ten or even fifteen rupees in situations of acute scarcity. The daily consumption of water per household varies according to economic status and size. For instance, some have a different arrangement, where a monthly water charge of Rs. 300 has to be paid in order to get a supply of water at one's doorstep limited to fifteen-twenty minutes in the morning. Instead of addressing the problem, the lack of political will, apathy of municipal authorities and the police has left the residents no choice but to purchase water.

'What is the purpose of such an independence (*Kya faeda aisi azadi se*)? The government is not even giving us water. You think yourself, 10 rupees for a gallon of water? When the cost of a Bisleri bottle is 5–10 rupees, (pauses) We buy a gallon of water for 10 rupees. [...] When people from Shivaji Nagar go to neighbouring slums to get water carrying their water cans they are confronted by the police, their cans are broken and bicycles are confiscated. These neighbouring slums like Gautam Nagar, Shastri Nagar etc., there is a lot of excess water flowing from the pipes there'.

Interview with Ramzaan ji, 25 November 2009

Shivaji Nagar as a 'Muslim Slum'

Despite a sizeable non-Muslim population, outsiders often label Shivaji Nagar as a 'Muslim area'. However, this image largely held by outsiders is also accompanied by strong associations to the undesirable presence of poverty, garbage and butchering-related activities (due to Shivaji Nagar's proximity to the slaughterhouse [*katal khana*]). To the outsider, mountains of garbage visible from a distance make up Shivaji Nagar's skyline. It carries with it notions of being a forbidden territory associated with all that is foul and undesirable. The slaughterhouse and its association with non-vegetarian food cultures of Muslims—and more specifically the consumption of beef—feeds into its negative image as an undesirable cultural life space, peripheral to the mainstream. Once, an autorickshaw driver—a Hindu OBC migrant from UP, who lives in a slum in Kurla—told me that he usually never takes passengers from this area: 'if the person says Deonar-Shivaji Nagar I generally refuse. There is a slaughterhouse where they cut beef (*bade ka mutton*). It smells so much. Once I took three passengers from here and the whole rickshaw was smelling foul (*pura rickshaw bas mar raha tha*)' (Fieldnotes, 2 January 2010).

On entering Shivaji Nagar, what is visible is a landscape marked by the presence of mosques, temples and Buddha Vihars, some of which are older structures that came up during its formation and some that are recent. Though there is a significant number of Dalits, the number of temples is not representative of the number of Hindus living in the area now. After the riots in 1992–93, several temples stand abandoned or locked but are looked after by the local Hindu residents. The largest mosque in the area is located in Lotus colony and is the only mosque located on a main road. The other mosques are located in the interiors of Shivaji Nagar, some of which are currently under construction, awaiting donations from *jama'ats* and the Muslim elite to be completed. Lanes and market places are also at times lined with green paper flags (a colour associated with Muslims) or streamers put up during the celebration of Muslim festivals such as Eid-ul-fitr and Eid-ul-zuha (also known as Bakra Eid). During weddings, these lanes turn into community kitchens where food for the *dawaat* (feast) is cooked in the open and the aroma fills up the air as do the beats of the latest Bollywood music.

Hansen (2001a) gives us a detailed account of the historical trajectory of the Muslim *mohalla* in Mumbai and its metamorphosis into social spaces that today evoke connotations of crime, prostitution, gang war and the myth of the Muslim *badmaash* (rogue). Shivaji Nagar is no exception to this image. Due to the incident of two police constables being burnt and its notoriety for criminal activity, illicit liquor manufacturing and drug peddling,[28] Shivaji Nagar's image as a breeding ground for the 'rogue' Muslim became reason enough for police atrocities during 1992–93 and hyper surveillance afterwards. At the time of the riots, Shivaji Nagar was under the jurisdiction of the Deonar police station that was located at quite a distance from it. There was neither a police station nor a police beat (outpost) in the vicinity. After the riots, a police station was built right next to the entrance of Shivaji Nagar. Five police beat *chowkies* were constructed within the area. Most of these remain closed today, though a police van with six to eight police constables patrols the area at least twice a day and at times even more. There are police outposts located in public spaces like market places, which are either in close proximity to temples or have been named after them. One of the police outposts situated on the main access road into Shivaji Nagar is located right in front of the local Shiv Sena *shakha*. Amongst the residents, the Mumbai police are considered the real threat, being notorious for their anti-Muslim sentiment and actions: 'they encourage crime in the area instead of curbing it and keep asking for bribes from those who commit crimes in return for keeping them out of jail'.[29]

Most public places such as the post office, police stations, health posts and health centres are marked with pictures of Hindu gods and goddesses. The only indication in state institutions of Muslims living in the area is in the municipal schools where notice boards in Urdu (a language associated with Muslims) can be seen, as it is also one of the mediums of instruction. This denotes the gap between the social worlds of those working for and heading state institutions and Muslims in the city. This deep-rooted chasm can also be seen in their attitudes towards Muslims. A woman resident doctor at a local government facility in Shivaji Nagar said:

'I don't know. This doesn't happen in our [Hindu] families. They [Muslim men] are illiterate, they don't work. All they want is more children. It is all about pleasure. That is all they want. They are not responsible towards their families'.

Fieldnotes, 15 April 2010

The myth of Shivaji Nagar being a 'Muslim area' is much more than simply a label based on a significant Muslim population but is understood as a demographic aberration by state institutions, non-residents and the mainstream city. The production of this myth is an important element of the social spatialisation[30] and cultural discourses that positions local working-class Muslim neighbourhoods socially as well as spatially marginal (peripheral) to the mainstream city. Furthermore, the sensory connotations (visual, i.e. garbage and olfactory, i.e. smell) to the spaces occupied by working class, lower-caste Muslims as well as the criminalisation of Shivaji Nagar contribute to its image as a lawless forbidden territory.[31] In the following section I look at how the Muslims of Shivaji Nagar counter the processes of exclusion and how this involves contestations and negotiations in everyday life.

'UNWANTED IN MY CITY'

Acts of Naming and Counter-naming

Shivaji Nagar, named after the Maratha king by, unsurprisingly, the BMC, is a place at odds with its composition and history. All those people resettled from different parts of the city were allotted different locations and plots; these localities have now become distinct neighbourhoods. Some of these have been named based on the plot numbers allotted by the BMC. Others bear associations to the original locations from where the residents were resettled. The first inhabitants of Shivaji Nagar were resettled from Worli into an area that is now known as Lotus Colony. Rafi Nagar was named after Mohammed Rafi, the famous playback singer in Bollywood whose death in 1980 coincided with resettlement in the area. The Bandra plots are where those resettled from the *qasai wada* in Bandra were relocated. In certain cases the names of localities are based on their past use. Local residents refer to a large part of Shivaji Nagar II as Baiganwadi, as the land was earlier used for agriculture specifically brinjal farming (*baingan* meaning brinjal in Hindi). Similarly, Zakir Husain Nagar came up at a site where a factory once stood owned by a person by that name. Others have been named after slumlords such as Baba Nagar, Kamla Raman Nagar and Raman Mama Nagar. It is the residents of Shivaji Nagar who make associations of the present to the past by naming their localities or in the narratives of their histories. The multiple institutions of the state may not recognise this in their own nomenclature of these areas, effectively disconnecting the present from the past histories of the residents.[32]

Individuals through every day practices also engage in the naming and marking of spaces in order to counter the denationalisation of 'Muslim areas'. Arif Sheikh works as a physical instructor in a municipal school and is a resident of Shivaji Nagar since 1994. He took the liberty to name the *gully* (lane) he lives in after Shaheed Abdul Hamid, a soldier with the Indian army who died during the 1965 India-Pakistan war. He was also the first and only Muslim to have been awarded the Param Vir Chakra by the government.

'Our people have sacrificed their lives. But there is not a trace or sign of our names anywhere. Isn't that true? What has Lokmanya [Tilak] done? He celebrated the Ganpati festival. [...] There are areas, roads and lanes named after others (names a few leaders). Why are they not named after our people? Do you know who this lane is named after? Shaheed Abdul Hamid. I have named it. How will anyone know about him? Arif Sheikh [i.e. Muslims like him] knows who Ram and Ganpati are, but does he know about Abdul Hamid even if he is from his own caste?'

Interview with Arif Sheikh, 24 January 2010

Arif Sheikh has also registered a welfare society with other members of the neighbourhood by the same name that looks into the maintenance of the gully he lives in (such as garbage disposal, sanitation, repairs etc.) with limited success. Sheikh sir (as he is popularly known) is originally from UP and lives in one of the several localities closer to the mountainous heaps of garbage. His house imitates those seen in Shivaji Nagar I with its painted walls, tiled flooring, and sliding window with a few potted plants opening into the narrow gully. Inside, the room had a television, a bed in the corner and a small aluminium folding table. A newly constructed wall in order to make a separate kitchen had divided the small area. A small glass shelf in the corner had two flower vases and a recent picture of Sheikh sir in a military-like uniform, taken in a studio. He has undergone paramilitary training at the National Defence Academy in Pune and completed an MA in Hindi from Mumbai University. He was unable to make it into the army so ended up as a physical education teacher. Sheikh remarked that he was living in this place out of financial and familial compulsions. He supplements his meagre salary by working part-time in a private school. But he pointed out to me that in spite of living in such a filthy place he was doing so in style, 'It is by Allah's grace that we even live here like this (*Yeh Allah ka karam hai ki apun yahan bhi is tarah se rahte hain*)'. He pointed to the tiles and newly painted walls. Then he told me that he does not consider himself any less than others.

Being a municipal school teacher, Sheikh takes a lot of pride in his knowledge of the state system and in his fluency in English and Marathi, for which he is also respected locally. He has registered another welfare society under the name 'Al Hind Friends Group' that is meant to engage in social work for the needy. The letterhead of the society has a logo on the right hand side that comprises of an enlarged map of India juxtaposed on to an image of the globe positioned exactly over and covering up that of the United States of America. Within the map are two hands clasped in a handshake along with an abbreviation of the name of the society, AHFG. Around this image is a byline in capitals that says, 'Only patriotism. Proud to be an Indian'. The entire lane is marked by such patriotic symbols put up by Sheikh sir such as a board that bears the name of Shaheed Abdul Hamid Welfare Society and of all the residents and their house numbers in English, a common letterbox with the postal address and a notice board again bearing the name of the society in English and Urdu. At the entrance stands a flag pole where the national flag is hoisted on 15 August and 26 January with a gathering of local residents. A tattered banner also stood at the entrance that bore the pictures of Hemant Karkare and fifteen other police and army officials who died during the terrorist attacks at the Taj Mahal Hotel in Mumbai on 26 November 2008 and stated in Marathi, 'A great salute to the brave police men who were martyred fighting against terrorists'.

Sheikh sir's case illustrates that formal citizenship in the nation-state is increasingly neither a necessary nor a sufficient condition for substantive citizenship (Holston & Appadurai, 1996). And this seems especially true for low-status Muslims who enjoy formal citizenship, but who are de facto deprived of their citizenship and, more specifically, of their rights to the city. The acts of naming represent the blurring boundaries between state institutions and the agendas of the ruling elite who can manipulate bureaucratic procedures to demand their 'democratic' share of public resources (or more than that). However, even the poor, low-status and weak can sometimes benefit from their own manipulations of political and administrative systems, pragmatically trying to deal with them rather than striving to resist them (Fuller & Benei, 2001). Sheikh sir's act of 'counter-naming' can be understood as an act of mainstreaming or countering segregation by making links with notions of nationhood and patriotism. It counters the notion of Muslims as anti-national by invoking nationalist imagery through symbols from within the Muslim community that are forgotten.

Conclusion

In view of the processes that have led to the formation and construction of Shivaji Nagar as a peripheral life space, some parallels can be drawn here from the perspectives on racial and ethnic ghettos in the west. The complexities surrounding the multiple processes that have both transformed and maintained 'Muslim' slums such as Shivaji Nagar may not be totally explained by adhering to existing nomenclature and classification concerning spatial segregation of racial, ethnic or religious groups elsewhere. However, the case of Shivaji Nagar does point towards possible trends of social cleansing, especially as far as poor urban Muslims are concerned. Despite the specific context of Shivaji Nagar owing to its location (proximity to the city's largest garbage dump), the processes of spatial exclusion and discrimination experienced by Muslims residing there are representative of the condition of slum dwelling Muslims anywhere else in the city. The history of communal politics in its violent outbursts as well as everyday forms of socio-cultural exclusion has resulted in the formation of what Wacquant (2008) refers to as 'neighbourhoods of exile' born out of the forcible relegation of a negatively typed population, which in this case are poor, low-status urban Muslims. The representation of Shivaji Nagar as a culturally deviant (at times anti-national) urban disorder creates the need for it to be 'dealt' with by the state and the mainstream city at large to bring it back into the realms of the (Hindu) nation-space. In doing so, the nation-state engages in the production of local subjects within the locality by creating a wide array of formal and informal techniques for the nationalisation of all space considered to come under its sovereign authority (Appadurai, 1995). Countering these processes of exclusion involves an everyday negotiation with the state as well as society in general, not only for the Muslims of Shivaji Nagar but for those of Mumbai at large. The context of its history and demographic composition augment the complexity of not just these struggles but also the larger question of the right to the city itself.

2

FACING GHETTOISATION IN 'RIOT-CITY'

OLD AHMEDABAD AND JUHAPURA BETWEEN VICTIMISATION AND SELF-HELP

Christophe Jaffrelot and Charlotte Thomas

'Shahpur, Bapunagar, Juhapura, Jamalpur—Muslims cannot live anywhere else in the city' (A Muslim interviewee cited by Arvind Rajagopal, 'Special political zone: urban planning, spatial segregation and the infrastructure of violence in Ahmedabad', *South Asia History and Culture*, 1:4, Oct. 2010, p. 544).

'This is Navangpura, we have no Muslim here. We have cleared the area of Muslims. This area is clean. You are obviously a visitor and do not know much about this city. You must leave this place as soon as possible' (A Hindu hairdresser to Rubina Jasani in her chapter 'A potted history of neighbours and neighbourliness in Ahmedabad', in E. Simpson and A. Kapadia (eds), *The Idea of Gujarat. History, Ethnography and text*, Hyderabad: Orient Blackswan, 2010, p. 153).

'In 1969 we lived in Saraspur [eastern Ahmedabad]. When the riots started we had to escape. We went on a train going to Prantji. On the first stop my husband was pulled off the train and stabbed to death. I went back to our village, near Prantji. For seven years I raised my four sons and two daughters by myself. My youngest son was a baby. For five years we managed with the compensatory money I received from the government. But then we returned to Ahmedabad in search of a job. We settled in Garibnagar and started working in a plastic factory. We have just started our lives again and this happened [the 1985 riot].

If the government wants to kill the Muslims they should get them together and just throw a bomb'.

(Interview with an anonymous woman resident of Indira Garibnagar near Anand Flats, Aman Chowk relief camp, 'The 1985 Ahmedabad Riots', video documentary, cited in O. Shani, *Communalism, caste and Hindu nationalism,* Cambridge: Cambridge University Press, 2007, p. 125).

Introduction[1]

Ahmedabad, as evident from its very name, carries a distinctively Muslim legacy that the ruling party in the city and in the state, the Hindu nationalist BJP, tries to conceal by using more and more often the name 'Amdavad'[2] or even Karnavati. It was built by a Sunni ruler, Ahmed Shah, in 1411, and remained the capital of the sultanate of Gujarat that he ruled until 1422. Located on the eastern bank of the Sabarmati River, Ahmedabad was soon surrounded by walls and closed by several gates to protect the city from foreign invaders. It was organised around places such as the Badhra Fort and the Jama Masjid, which were the city's political and religious centres.

Being the capital of the Sultanate, Ahmedabad was more a political city than an economic one. Most of the dignitaries and administrators of the state were Muslims. But in 1817 Gujarat was taken over by the East India Company and British bureaucrats started to replace or dominate Muslim ones to rule the state.

Ahmed Shah is known in history for having been one of the most intolerant rulers of Gujarat, be it against Hindus or against Shias, including the Bohra community. He destroyed several temples and replaced them with mosques. He is believed to have converted many Hindus by force and imposed *jizya*[3] on the others. At the same time, Ahmed Shah and his successors appointed Hindus in the state's administration, whereas Muslims monopolised the upper layers of the army. And more importantly, Hindus and Muslims used to pay allegiance to Sufi saints and meet in the local *dargahs,* the shrines and tombs of these saints.

In fact, Ahmedabad was not, traditionally, a communally-sensitive place. There was no riot at the time of Partition—even though there were communal incidents in 1941 and 1946. Things changed gradually but in a rather systematic manner in the 1960s–70s, so much so that Ahmedabad became a truly riot-prone area. With 1,119 victims of Hindu-Muslim riots between 1950 and 1995,[4] Ahmedabad ranked just behind Mumbai (1,137 dead) until the 2002 pogrom, when it became the most affected Indian city in terms of casualties of communal riots. So far as the local Muslims are concerned, this is certainly the most distinctive feature of the city, which goes on a par with the marginalisation of this community within the local elite and the development of Muslim ghettos like Juhapura—where, however, promising initiatives are noticeable today as a result of the regrouping of Muslims of all socio-economic backgrounds.

An Ethnic Mosaic: Three Cities, Hundreds of *Pols, Chawls* and Housing Societies

Ahmedabad today amalgamates three urban universes which are themselves—still, but less and less—subdivided into numerous smaller socio-cultural units.

Fort Walls

The first city, the urban core, is naturally the original walled city, also called Fort walls, which has retained this name even though most of the fortifications have disappeared.[5] The distinctive character of the Old City is still attested, though, by the 12 gates through which people used to enter in the past.

The walled city was traditionally divided into *pols,* a distinctive residential pattern inherited from the Pathan architectural and urbanistic traditions of its founders. As Harish Doshi puts it, 'Ecologically, a *pol* is a residential street. It has well-defined boundaries demarcated through a main gateway, sub-gates and a cluster of houses'.[6] While this gathering of houses is grouped around one main street, it comprises also many ramified lanes (*khanchos*) and small squares (*chowks*). This typical housing gathered a maximum of 500 houses and was built to protect inhabitants from attacks, the main gate—that was closed every night until the 1950s—being carefully guarded by a watchman, the *polio*. This residential pattern was overdetermined by occupation. Each *pol* was therefore relatively homogenous in terms of castes and communities. This is evident from the *pols*' names themselves: Ganchi-Pol, Patel-Pol or Jain-Pol, for example. But caste groups and communities lived in a rather promiscuous way since Brahmin pols, Baniya pols, Patel pols, Dalit pols and Muslim pols were next to each other. Mosques and temples also sometimes stood close to each other and were in any case part of the same locality. In Fort Walls the number of *pols* increased from 356 in 1972 to about 500 in the 1980s,[7] but at the same time, the population of the walled city decreased by more than 20% between the 1971 Census and 2001 because of the growth of other parts of Ahmedabad. In fact, if the walled city is experiencing a decline in absolute numbers since the 1970s only (from 480,735 in 1971 to 398,410 in 1991), its share of the total population of Ahmedabad is diminishing since independence, from 44% in 1951 to 12% in 1991.[8]

The Industrial Belt

Ahmedabad started to change a lot with the industrialisation process in which the city, known as the Manchester of India, played a pioneering role. In 1861 the first textile mill was opened and three years later the creation of the railway line between Ahmedabad and Mumbai fostered the former's economic development. In 1870 Ahmedabad attained the status of a municipality as its growth continued. In 1900 there were twenty-seven textile mills, fifty-one in 1920, seventy-seven in 1939 and eighty-three in 1941. This industrialisation took place mostly east of the walled city where villages such as Asarwa, Saraspur, Gomtipur were transformed into industrial townships. By the 1920s, the mill owners started to build *chalis* or *chawls* out of the walled city, in the industrial area, in order to provide the workers with some housing. *Chawls* were rows of rooms with or without sanitary conveniences, which became the most common pattern of urbanisation in the eastern part of Ahmedabad during the 1920s–40s. Most of the *chawls* were inhabited by migrant workers coming from the villages of Gujarat and neighbouring provinces or states. The large majority of this labour force was made of low caste people, Dalits and Muslims but '[i]n the chawls, for example, Muslims and Scheduled Castes lived in separate rows of rooms'.[9]

Between 1861 and 1914, the number of daily textile workers grew from 63 to 32,789, and from the 1920s onwards to the mid-1970s, 60 to 80% of Ahmedabad's population worked in the textile industry. However, most of them were socially integrated through associations based on Gandhian philosophy. Among them, the Ahmedabad's Textile Labour Association (TLA), founded in 1920, was the biggest, since it amalgamated several unions.[10] Each professional unit was dominated by a single community (caste- or religion-based) and as a result, the organisation promoted the cohabitation of different groups which were all represented. In any case, the union's identity was labour- (and even

FACING GHETTOISATION IN 'RIOT-CITY'

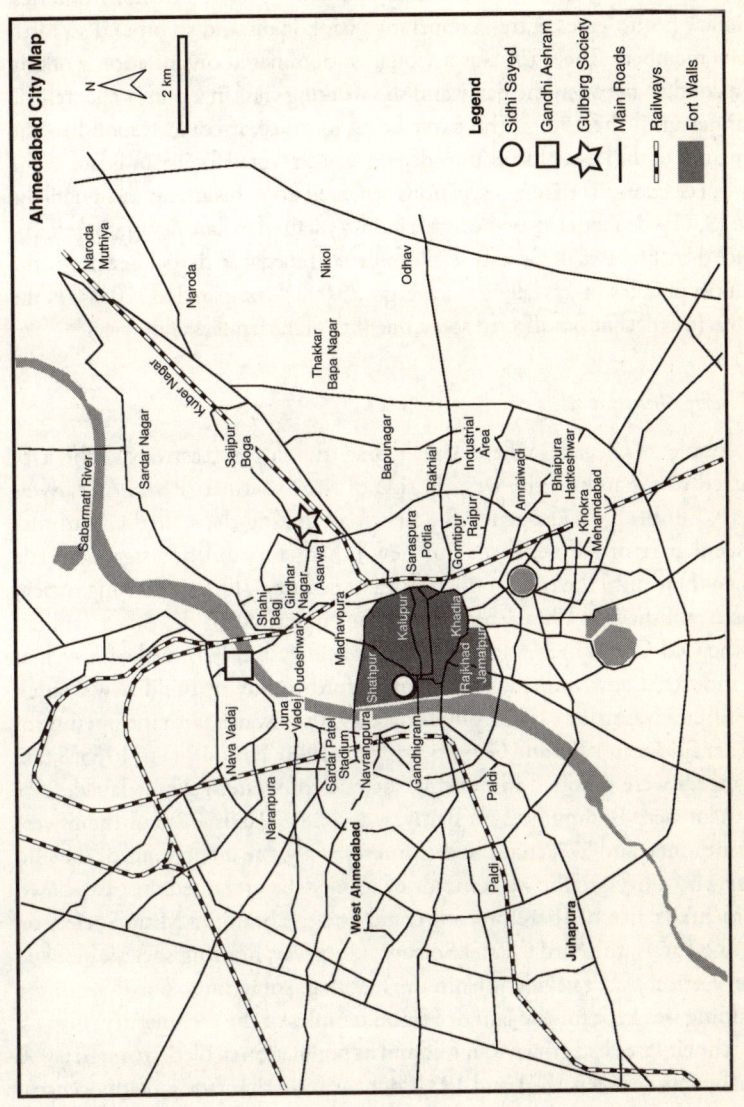

Map of Ahmedabad

class-) oriented.[11] Until the early 1980s, when the TLA still claimed a membership of 135,000 members—about nine-tenths of the textile mill workers—the organisation was a kind of counter society providing libraries, primary health care centres, cooperative bank loans and so on and so forth to its members. The TLA was a Congress-dominated organisation working as a conduit between the party and the working class in a purely clientelistic manner until the 1980s. The party being in office, it could respond to the demands of the labour forces, provided the workers voted for its candidates at the time of elections. The Congress patrons benefited from this arrangement until the late 1970s when the crisis of the textile industry started to have devastating effects. Since then, fifty-two of the sixty textile mills of Ahmedabad have closed down, the number of mill workers falling to a meagre 25,000,[12] compared to 170,000 in the 1980s (this decline has affected about one-fifth of the families of the city).[13]

Western Ahmedabad

A couple of decades after Ahmedabad developed eastwards, the city started to expand on the western side of the Sabarmati River. As early as 1870, Ellisbridge had opened the first road linking the walled city to that nascent part of Ahmedabad. But new inhabitants did not start to settle down there until the turn of the twentieth century. The first housing society was established in 1924. That part of the city attracted the richer families of the Old City which wanted to flee the congested Fort Walls (as well as its industrial environment) and could afford to buy or build new houses. This trend was made easier from the late 1930s onwards with the opening of Sardar Bridge in 1939 and Gandhi Bridge in 1940. From 1941 to 1965, 8,502 members were enrolled in housing societies of western Ahmedabad. 28% of them were Brahmins, 24% Baniyas, and 28% Patels. 27% of them were businessmen and 57% in services.[14] Interestingly, the inhabitants of the Old City who moved to the western side of Ahmedabad retained the caste-based residential pattern. Therefore, one could find the Brahmin Mitra Society or, for the Patels, the Sardar Patel Society.[15] In a way, housing societies looked like 'vertical *pols*', as evident from the fact that, sometimes, one floor of the building was kept for the Jain or Hindu temples of the community.

The city area had grown four fold and its population trebled to over 310,000 inhabitants between 1871 and 1931. But the most dramatic growth occurred during the following decade, when the city almost doubled its population in less than ten years. With the westward expansion, the city limit expanded by 22 sq km, an increase of about 73%. This development accelerated further after

Table 2.1. Evolution of the population of Ahmedabad, 1901–2001

Year	1901	1911	1921	1931	1941	1951	1961	1971	1981	1991	2001
Population	185,889	216,777	274,007	310,000	591,267	863,590	1,193,875	1,731,116	2,396,171	2,925,344	3,694,974
Growth rate (%)	–	16.62	26.40	13.14	90.73	46.06	8.25	45.00	38.42	22.08	26.31

Source: Gujarat Census Office (Gandhinagar).

independence, when the Ahmedabad Municipal Corporation was created (1950), on the east as well as on the west. On the east, in 1958, the city expanded by 21 sq km (an increase of 39%) with the creation of the industrial area of Bapunagar next to the national highway. On the west, the residential growth was boosted by the establishment of Gujarat University in 1952 in the Navrangpura area. The growth of the western part of the city was sustained by the opening of the Nehru Bridge in the early 1960s.

Between 1961 and 1971, the city area did not expand, but its population increased by 38%. Similarly, between 1971 and 1981, the area of AMC remained almost unchanged (+ 5.5%) but the population grew by 30%.[16] In fact, most of the demographic increase was absorbed by new slums which were concentrated around the mills in the eastern part of the city, beyond the railways.[17] Between 1961 and 1971, 45% of the growth of households in the city resulted from the development of such slums. So much so that in 1976, 22% of the population of Ahmedabad consisted of slum dwellers.[18] By the 1960s, the beginning of the industrial crisis that affected the textile mills (mostly the cotton mills) resulted in the impoverishment of the inhabitants of *chawls,* among whom many became jobless and 'Gradually, the *chawls* became more like slums'.[19] In the mid-1970s, about 40% of the population of Ahmedabad lived in such *chawls* or 'proper' slums.[20]

To sum up, Ahmedabad can be disaggregated into three cities: Fort Walls, the original core where all castes and communities have traditionally cohabited in juxtaposed *pols*; the industrial area on the eastern side of the city where low caste people, Dalits and Muslims used to live in similarly juxtaposed *chawls*; and the western bank of the Sabarmati, a residential area where upper-caste and/or rich Hindus (with a small number of Muslims) started to migrate from the walled city in the inter-war period and established housing societies. In each of these areas, the organisation of space was structured by caste- and community-based considerations: *pols, chawls,* slums and housing societies were homogeneous in terms of caste and religious community. This segregation harks back to the roots of the caste system, but also has something to do with customs (like the vegetarian/non-vegetarian diet of some groups) and rituals (like the animal sacrifices observed by the Muslims and by which the non-vegetarian Hindus are indisposed).[21] But it was a relative form of segregation, mixed neighbourhoods giving the city a mosaic-like structure. As Rubina Jasani points out, 'Ahmedabad has always been divided on caste, community and religious lines' and any 'nostalgia' for communal mixity is irrelevant.[22] But the divisions of the past did not result in the making of large blocs. Moreover, she admits that in the *chawls* 'Muslims and Dalits lived separately but in close proximity'.[23]

FACING GHETTOISATION IN 'RIOT-CITY'

Muslims of Ahmedabad

Ahmedabad has traditionally been an 'Islamic city' in the sense of de Planhol,[24] yet, despite the number of mosques and dargahs, Muslims have never been represented in large numbers. However, they were more numerous in the city than elsewhere in Gujarat: while Muslims, with 4,592,854 people represented 8.7% of the state population in 2001, their proportion was about one-third more in Ahmedabad.

In 2001, out of 4,525,013 inhabitants of the Ahmedabad Urban Agglomerations, there were 3,736,916 Hindus and 562,192 Muslims, that is 12.42%.[25] Traditionally, Muslims have been concentrated in some *pols* of the walled city. Each of these Muslim-dominated *pols* was identified with one *jama'at*, an occupation- and status-based group. For example, the Qureshi Jama'at, whose members were butchers by profession, were especially dominant in Mirzapur. Within these *pols* caste life was regulated by a Panch, a chief who adjudicated any kind of dispute; and within each *pol*, different Muslim *jama'ats* used to cohabit, some of them of a higher status than others and some of them richer than the others.[26] Which meant that right from the beginning the Muslim urbanisation pattern shared one common feature with typical (self-)segregated areas where the rich and poor of an ethnic community share some common neighbourhood. But for decades this 'ghettoisation' was relative in the sense that Muslim-dominated *pols* coexisted with Hindu-dominated ones. These mixed neighbourhoods gradually disappeared after Muslims became the main victims of communal riots, which have gone on a par with their growing socio-economic marginalisation.

Riot-city

Ahmedabad was not a communally sensitive area until the 1960s. Interestingly, few people left for Pakistan in 1947–48. One may attribute such remarkable developments to the legacy of Mahatma Gandhi since Gujarat was his home state and Ahmedabad the Indian city where he established his first ashram. But the Gandhian impact on Gujarat—or the impact of Gujarat on Gandhi— also had a clearly conservative dimension. Most of the Gujarati lieutenants of the Mahatma who joined him during the freedom struggle and who ruled over the Congress in the 1940s–70s, were averse to social reform. From Vallabhbhai Patel to K.M. Munshi, they came from the upper or dominant castes. They were rather conservative Hindus and felt no inclination towards

Table 2.2. Population of Ahmedabad by religion and mother tongue, 1961–2001

	1961	1971	Increase 1961–71 in %	1981	Increase 1971–81 in %	1991	Increase 1981–91 in %	2001	Increase 1991–2001 in %
Total population	2,210,199	2,910,307	+31.67	3,875,794	+33.77	4,801,812	+23.89	5,816,519	+21.13
RELIGION, dates for Ahmedabad District:									
Hindus	1,859,816	2,450,163	+31.74	3,286,744	+34.14	4,101,817	+24.80	4,921,747	+19.98
	84.14%	84.18%		84.80%		85.42%		84.61%	
Muslims	242,561	320,646	+32.19	423,776	+32.16	516,142	+21.80	662,799	+28.41
	10.97%	11.01%		10.93%		10.74%		11.39%	
MOTHER TONGUE, data for Ahmedabad Urban Agglomeration:									
Gujarati	NA*	1,202,889		1,765,926		NA		4,481,914	
		41.33%		45.56%				77.05%	
Hindi	NA	186,666		306,121		NA		721,784	
		6.41%		7.89%				12.40%	
Urdu	NA	192,236		248,794		NA		298,770	
		6.60%		6.41%				5.13%	

NA: data non available.
Source: Census Office of Gujarat, Gandhinagar.

the upliftment of the lower strata of society.[27] That was also due, probably, to the fact that Gujarat has remained one of the states where the Dalits are not politically organised. Neither the RPI, nor the BSP have made any inroads there over the last fifty years.

In this context, Hindu nationalism could develop more easily than the traditional antagonism between this movement and Gandhi would have naturally suggested, especially after the Congress broke in 1969. Then Indira Gandhi gave the ruling party a progressive and a populist agenda which was not to the liking of the 'old leaders' of the Congress, including Morarji Desai who became the most prominent figure of the rather reactionary breakaway faction that was the Congress (O). This party won as many seats (11) as Indira Gandhi's Congress (R) in the 1971 Lok Sabha elections. In fact Gujarat, which gave 11 of its 16 MPs to the Congress (O) was clearly its stronghold. The Hindu nationalists then concentrated more and more of their attention on Gujarat, and particularly on Ahmedabad. Their activities contributed to make it the most riot-prone city in India. Every ten years or so, some of the most deadly riots of Indian history until then occurred in Ahmedabad, until the most deadly riot of all occurred in 1969.

1969, When Hindu Workers Killed Muslim Workers or the RSS's Exploitation of the Textile Crisis

The 1969 riot was the most deadly unleashing of Hindu-Muslim violence since Partition. Officially, 660 people were killed (including 430 Muslims)—unofficially 1 to 2,000[28]—1,074 injured (including 592 Muslims), over 48,000 lost their houses, and property worth 42 million rupees was destroyed in Ahmedabad alone, including 32 million belonging to Muslims.[29]

The 1969 riots have been attributed to socio-economic factors by several analysts, including Ashutosh Varshney.[30] Indeed, from the mid-1960s onwards, the textile industry entered a crisis that has lasted well into the twenty-first century. Entrepreneurs turned away from Ahmedabad's big mills to Surat's small units, which were a much better fit with the new way of production. Consequently, Ahmedabad's under-qualified workers—among whom Hindus were overrepresented compared to artisans-turned-workers Muslims—were hit by a first wave of unemployment.

But the riot had political roots too. It started in the eastern part of Ahmedabad where the RSS had established its local strongholds, so much so that it was the place M.S. Golwalkar selected for organising a massive three-day rally between 27 and 29 December 1968 in Maninagar. This meeting prepared the ground for the riot, which almost happened in March 1969 when a policeman made a copy of the Koran fall from a handcart stacked with books. It was triggered off six months later when another police officer who happened to be a Muslim accidentally dropped a copy of the Ramayana while dispersing a Ramlila audience. RSS leaders then formed a Hindu Dharma Raksha Samiti (Committee for the protection of the Hindu religion) which organised demonstrations in which objectionable slogans were heard.[31] The Jana Sangh leader, Balraj Madhok came to Ahmedabad in this context to make a rabid speech on the 14th and 15th of September. The final spark came from a typical incident: Muslims entered the Jagannath Temple to protest against the disruption of one of their processions by cows belonging to the temple. Immediately, Hindu nationalists orchestrated not only protests, but also attacks. The first targets were the Muslim-dominated *pols* of the walled city: Dariapur, Shahpur, Mirzapur, Kalupur, Khadia, Raipur, Gheekanta and Khanpur where 118 people were killed officially and 1,979 shops destroyed. But the most affected area was the industrial belt where the Muslim-dominated *chawls* were singled out by the assailants: 712 people were killed officially and 3,891 properties destroyed in the labour localities of Maninagar, Behrampura, Gomtipur, Rakhial, Chamanpura, Sarangpur, Vatwa, Bapunagar, Naroda, Asarwa, Amraiwadi, Narol, Sardarnagar, Jamalpur and Khokhra-Mehamdavad.[32] A distinctive feature of these attacks was that Muslim *chawls* were targeted by Dalit neighbours who, like in Gomtipur for instance, used to maintain peaceful relations with Muslims but, all of a sudden, killed and raped Muslims. A Muslim woman who narrowly escaped gang rape confided to Megha Kumar—whose PhD is a remarkable inquiry into sexual violence in the course of communal violence in Ahmedabad— 'We were betrayed by people who we lived with all our lives'.[33] This betrayal persuaded Muslim families inhabiting Hindu-dominated localities to migrate to Muslim-dominated places. This impulse was to be reactivated by similar riots every ten years or so.

From 1981 to 1985, From Caste Conflicts to Communal Clashes—The Muslims Lose Their Dalit Allies

The 1985 riot was a sequel to the one which had taken place in 1981, opposing Dalits and upper-caste Hindus because of the government reservation policy. In 1980, the Congress leader Madhavsinh Solanki won the state elections thanks to a strategy of plebeianisation of the party's electoral basis that harked

FACING GHETTOISATION IN 'RIOT-CITY'

back to Indira Gandhi's socialist mottos. He built a new social coalition made of OBCs from the Kshastriyas (his own caste), Harijans (or Dalits), Adivasis (or Scheduled Tribes) and Muslims. To solidify this 'KHAM'group, he introduced in late 1980 new quotas in favour of the Dalits in the medical colleges to which the upper-caste Hindus (mostly Brahmins, Rajputs and Baniyas) and the dominant caste of the Patels (12% of the population) objected to in the streets. The unleashing of violence in late 1980 and early 1981 resulted in heavy losses for the Dalits who had then benefited from the help of the Muslims.

1985 was somewhat of a repeat of 1980. Two months before the state elections, Solanki announced a new quota in favour of the OBCs. Immediately, upper-caste students demonstrated in the streets and attacked Dalits—more than OBCs, probably because they were an easier target and were already doing better because of reservations, disturbing the old social order. But the course of the agitation changed after a few weeks, on 18 March. On that day, Solanki had bowed to the students' demands, but instead of letting the agitation die, the student union of the Sangh Parivar, the ABVP, relaunched it in the Old City on different, anti-Muslim, grounds. The objective of the Hindu nationalists was obviously to repair the damage done to Hindu unity in the course of the anti-reservationist campaign by transforming the Muslims into scapegoats for the upper castes as well as the Dalits. The fact that the riots were preplanned is evident from the fact that the only houses which had been burnt were that of the Muslims, the others were marked 'Hindu' in white.[34] The Muslims of Naginapol were attacked by Hindus of Vadigam who shouted that 'Muslims should go', and 'This is a Hindu Raj—come out and bow down'.[35] A similar scenario unfolded itself in the slums further east.

Not only did the Sangh Parivar reunite the Hindus against the Muslims, but it also made it a point to include Dalits in the Rath Yatra (in which they had not taken part so far)[36] and to help the Dalit families which had been affected by the previous riots—including in terms of legal aid.[37]

In most of the cases of mass violence which occurred in 1985, the police not only did not come to the help of the Muslims who asked for their protection, but they either fought the Muslims themselves, or literally brought the rioters to the places to be attacked.

The areas which had been the most affected were all in the Old City and in the industrial area. In Fort Walls, the epicentre was Dariapur where a Hindu locality, Vadigam, and a Muslim locality, Naginapol (a traditional *pol*), fought each other, before the turmoil spread to neighbouring places (Dagbarward and Kalupur). Other affected places were Astodia, Shapur, Gheekanta and Khadia.

55

In the industrial area, the most affected places were Saraspur, Rakhial and Bapunagar. In the communal violence, 220 people were killed, including 100 Muslims 'only', if one goes by the official report. But 12,000 of them had been rendered homeless since 2,500 houses had been destroyed and 900 Muslims had been arrested.[38] The 1985 riots made the Muslims of Ahmedabad realise that they were socially fully isolated, the Dalits themselves—whom they had helped in 1981—turning against them.

Megha Kumar points out: 'Billboards proclaiming Hindu-dominated areas as "Hindu Rashtras", usually erected by the local chapters of the VHP, started appearing across Ahmedabad. These boards read, for example, "Hindu Rashtra's Gomtipur Village welcomes you" or "You are now entering Saraspur Village of Hindu Rashtra".[39] Many Muslims left the walled city. Partly for that reason, partly because Hindus shifted to west Ahmedabad, Fort Walls declined from 474,223 people in 1981 to 398,410 only in 1991.[40] Muslims also left the industrial belt. As one survivor from Saraspur said: "Hindus say that they don't want Miyan bhai [Muslims] in the *chawli*. This time we barely managed to save our lives. What if they attack us again? Now I will accept living on the streets, but will never go back"'.[41]

While the vote share of the Jana Sangh had never reached 15% in Ahmedabad during state elections, the BJP won 20.2% of the votes in 1985 and 43.2% in 1990. Two years after the 1985 riot, the BJP won the municipal election in Ahmedabad, preparing the ground for the transformation of the city into some Hindu Rashtra. Indeed, soon after, the VHP 'circulated a map [of Ahmedabad] with saffron and green markers (the former signifying the Hindu and the latter the Muslim areas) and pressurised these families to evacuate their property and relocate to Muslim-dominated areas'.[42] Many Hindu nationalist candidates who had been actively involved in the 1985 riots were elected in 1985 to the municipal corporation and the state assembly in the mixed areas where Muslims were in a minority, like Khadia, a Hindu-dominated area of the Old City where Ashok Bhatt has been returned as an MLA without any interruption from 1980 until he died in 2010. In 1985, he had been charged with conducting a mob of Hindu rioters and the assassination of a policeman. He was acquitted in 2006.

1992: Shock Waves of the Ramjanmabhoomi Movement

The 1992 riot was not an isolated event like the 1969 and 1985 ones. It was part of the cycle of violence which was triggered off by the demolition of the

FACING GHETTOISATION IN 'RIOT-CITY'

Babri Masjid on 6 December of that year. But in Ahmedabad, the number of casualties was bigger than in most of the other riot-prone areas, partly because peace was not restored until mid-January. According to press reports, 134 people were killed—no official figure could ever be ascertained since the Commission of Inquiry that had been appointed under Justice Chauhan of the Gujarat High Court was disbanded by the Vaghela government in 1996 before it could finalise its report. Once again, violence erupted in the Old City where the Sangh Parivar had done social work amongst the Dalits.

While in places like Mumbai, riots were fostered by Muslim attacks on public institutions in protest against the demolition of the mosque in Ayodhya, in Ahmedabad, the assailants were Hindu nationalists. Groups of 200 to 1,000 men, armed with tridents, swords, spears, petrol bombs... shouted slogans like '*Musalman ko kato maro*' [Cut and kill the Muslims] and attacked buildings which were not marked (the others were identified as Hindu houses or shops). Once again, their targets were located in the walled city (in localities such as Kalupur, Dariapur and Jamalpur) and in the industrial areas (in localities such as Rakhial, Gomtipur, Danilimbda, Shahpur, Astodia and Behrampura).

As with previous riots, this wave of communal violence contributed to the electoral successes of the BJP, and the polarisation of voters along communal lines, leading the Hindu majority to regroup behind the Sangh Parivar. In 1995, the BJP not only won the local elections—including the Ahmedabad ones—but also the state elections, for the first time. In the late 1990s, riots multiplied once again in the walled city (curfew was imposed in Dariapur, Kalupur, Saraspur, Gheekanta, Dagbarwad and Vadigam in 1999) and in the industrial area (Karanj, Gomtipur, Shalam and Jamalpur met the same fate). But this violence was nothing compared to what was to come in 2002.

2002, A State-sponsored Pogrom to 'Clean' the Hindu Rashtra

The 2002 communal violence cannot be analysed the same way as the incidents mentioned above. It was not a riot, but a pogrom,[43] which did not remain confined to a city, but spread to many others and even to the countryside. Twenty-six towns in all were subject to curfew. But once again, Ahmedabad was the first and the most badly affected.[44] On 28 February, in the Naroda Gaon and Naroda Pattiya areas, an armed hoard of several thousands attacked Muslim houses and shops, killing 200 people. Six other neighbourhoods in the city were subject to similar attacks, like in Khadia—where Ashok Bhatt, now health minister of Modi, was still the MLA—Gulberg Society and Saraspur in the industrial area. The affected areas included parts of western Ahmedabad, like Paldi or Judges Bungalow, where middle-class Muslims were attacked for the first time.

Everything went according to a military-like plan.[45] The troops were perfectly disciplined and incredibly numerous: groups of attackers often included up to 10,000 men. These squads generally arrived in the Muslim neighbourhoods in truckloads. They wore a basic uniform—the RSS khaki shorts and a saffron headband—and carried daggers and pitchforks as well as bottles of water to quench their thirst en route. The lists that the ringleaders had in hand attested to the premeditated nature of the assault: these lists indicated Muslim homes and shops, some of which bore Hindu names, thereby proving that investigation had actually been undertaken beforehand to ascertain the owner's identity. These lists—on computer printouts—had partly been drawn up on the basis of voters' registration lists.

The state partiality also appeared blatantly in the treatment inflicted on the Muslims who took shelter in refugee camps. At the height of the violence, there were as many as 125,000 refugees in these camps. Officially, they still numbered 87,000 in April 2002, 66,000 of them in Ahmedabad alone. In three months, the government registered the return home of 73,500 refugees (52,500 in Ahmedabad) to pretend that law and order had been restored and that elections could be held. In any case, the authorities never took the necessary steps to help the refugees: most of the aid came from NGOs.

The 2002 pogrom was unprecedented on two grounds at least, first the intensity and savagery of anti-Muslim violence, and second, the way it affected middle-class neighbourhoods like Paldi or housing societies like Gulberg. The different nature of the 2002 pogrom, as Rowena Robinson has noticed, was also evident from the fact that this time, in contrast to previous riots, the places of worship that had been destroyed have not been rebuilt.[46]

Three conclusions can be drawn from the characteristics of Ahmedabad as a riot-prone city:

1. The political context is fundamentally against Muslims, because of the growing importance of the Sangh Parivar in the city—where the number of RSS *shakhas* doubled from 150 to 305 between 1998 and 1999[47]—and also because of the communalisation of the state apparatus (including the police), and the ambivalence of the Congress (O) and then Congress (I), a party where senior leaders like Shankar Sinh Vaghela come from the RSS.
2. The Muslims are socially isolated since their allies of the early 1980s, the Dalits, have been won over by the Sangh Parivar. Undoubtedly, the lack of

political consciousness among the Dalits is largely due to the absence of any significant Ambedkarite movement, something one may relate to the impact of Gandhi over the state.[48]
3. Most of the riots took place in the Old City and the industrial area in a very tense socio-economic context due to the decline of the textile industry. The Muslims were especially affected in the *pols* and *chawls* where they were in a minority.

Recurring riots reshaped the residential pattern of Ahmedabad in two ways.

First, it made *pols* and *chawls* more homogenous in communal terms. In the *chawls*, to begin with, migration of workers followed a regional pattern: for example, 'Chamars, Vankars, and Muslims with the same regional background were living together in the same chawl'.[49] This is what has changed, as Ward Berenschot—who has studied closely two riot-prone areas, Khadia in the Old City and Gomtipur in the industrial belt—points out; and since Hindus and Muslims were no longer living in the same *chawl*, they had less and less interests in common.[50]

Second, not only did the *pols* and *chawls* become more communally homogenous because of migrations within the walled city and the industrial belt, but some Hindus left these two areas to settle down in western Ahmedabad and Muslims went even further to more remote places like Juhapura to be safe. Before turning to this pattern of ghettoisation, we need to assess the role of the Muslims among the elite groups of Ahmedabad.

Social Marginalisation, Spatial Ghettoisation

Dipankar Gupta recently argued that the 2002 communal violence in Ahmedabad has affected the local Muslims more than similar events in Mumbai partly because the elite groups of this community were weaker there. 'The Muslim elite of Ahmedabad are not of the same stature as their counterparts in Mumbai, and their impact on Gujarat and the city's politics is marginal, or at best, supportive'.[51] This assessment can be interpreted in two ways. It may mean that the Muslim elites were almost non-existent or that they did not dare to help their co-religionists.

Muslims Among the Local Elite Groups

Muslims used to be present in all the elite groups of Ahmedabad, but they are now marginalised, no matter what the criterion we use.

In the judiciary, the under-representation of the Muslims is especially striking in the apex body of the state legal apparatus, since Muslims represent only 3.9% of the Gujarat High Court Bar Association. Certainly, this is not an institution of Ahmedabad, but it is worth mentioning the under-representation of Muslim lawyers in this court because the most significant judgements are made there or dealt with on appeal there, be they related to communal violence or terrorist acts. After the terrorist operations of Akshardam Temple (near Gandhinagar) in 2002, the assassination of Haren Pandya (who was Modi's Home Minister in 2002) in 2003 and the Ahmedabad blasts in 2008, many Muslims have been arrested. In 2003, all the 240-odd persons detained under POTA in Gujarat were Muslims.[52] To bail them out or make sure that they got a fair trial, dedicated lawyers are needed. Their families can certainly rely on Hindu lawyers, but they would turn towards Muslim lawyers more spontaneously, and this is one of the many reasons why the quantity and quality of the Muslim lawyers matter. Now Muslims are under-represented in most of the judicial bodies, except the Ahmedabad Criminal Court Bar Association.

Table 2.3. Muslims among the Judiciary in Ahmedabad

Courts, Judges and Bar Assocations	Total number of members	Number of Muslims	% of Muslims
The Ahmedabad Bar Association and Small Causes Court Association	2,383	151	6.4
The Ahmedabad District Bar Association	626	48	7.7
Coop. Bar Association	88	1	1.2
The Ahmedabad Criminal Court Bar Association	987	128	13
The Gujarat High Court Bar Association	1,139	45	3.9
The Income Tax and Sales Tax Bar Association	271	3	1.1
The Labour Laws Practitioners Association	192	16	8.5

Source: Compiled on the basis of Rajesh Joshi, *Ahmedabad Advocates Directory—2007,* Ahmedabad, 2007.

FACING GHETTOISATION IN 'RIOT-CITY'

Not only are there not many Muslim lawyers, but those who are fighting cases involving Muslim youth argue that those who dare to defend their co-religionists are even fewer.[53]

On the economic scene, Muslim communities played a significant part in the early development of trading activities in Gujarat, along with Jain and Parsi communities. Muslim traders consisted mainly of two Shia communities, the Khojas and the Bohras, and one Sunni community, the Memons.[54] They took advantage of Gujarat's big coastal interface to develop trade with the rest of the world, the region developing the most important harbours on the Spices' Route. However, this economic dynamism was mostly concentrated in ports, the most famous ones being Cambay and Surat.[55] Compared to these cities, Ahmedabad had very few Muslim traders. Being the capital of the Sultanate, it was better known for its aristocratic ethos, the nobles and military personnel who ruled the state acting as the patrons of the bulk of the community made up of artisans (weavers in particular).

Muslims' participation to the industrialisation process of Ahmedabad was rather weak too. The only Muslim-owned factory opened in 1912, and was shut eight years later. The biggest Muslim-owned firm in Ahmedabad is the Maniar Company. It was established in 1946 and exports equipments worldwide. Shafi Maniar, the son of the founder, is the sole Muslim member of the Gujarat Chamber of Commerce and Industry and the only Muslim industrialist for Gujarat in the Confederation of Indian Industry.[56] This is the only international Muslim company in Ahmedabad. The other ones are small or medium-sized. Their scope is limited to Ahmedabad and Gujarat, and for a handful, it extends to North India like Excell Impex Private Limited, a cosmetics company created in 2003 and which exports to nine Indian states. According to Raju Biman, the chairperson of the company, Muslim businessmen are mainly involved in automobile, cosmetics and construction.[57] So far as construction is concerned, because of communal tensions in the city, Muslim contractors work only in Muslim areas.

Besides the small number of businessmen and the limited scope of their enterprises, the Muslim community suffers from three other liabilities so far as its economic elites are concerned. First, riots affect the Muslim business milieu recurrently. Shafi Maniar and Raju Biman considered that Muslim companies—including theirs—lost 50 to 60% of their incomes in 2002 (like the Hindu business houses in the affected neighbourhoods) and that things returned to normal only in 2003. Second, the Muslim business class of Ahmedabad, like in the rest of Gujarat, is fragmented into three groups: the

Memons, who seem to play a dominant role, the Khojas and the Bohras. Third, these economic groups which are better off than the rest of the Muslims are not prepared to do much for them, at least not openly. They fear social and/or economic boycott. Bohras sometimes do not even feel part of the Muslim community. A small number of them, for instance, do not register as 'Muslims' in the Census, but as Bohras.[58] The chief of the Bohra community, Sayyidna Muhammad Burhanuddin, who took over from his predecessor in 1965 and who is based in Mumbai has become controversial because of his very conservative style. He opposed, for instance, the attempts at reforming the community that intellectuals like Asghar Ali Engineer undertook. Engineer, the son of a Bohra amil (priest) from Udaipur initiated a socio-religious reform movement within the Bohra community in 1972 in Udaipur. He was elected General Secretary of the Central Board of Dawoodi Bohra Community in 1977.[59] But he was under constant attack by Sayyidna Muhammad Burhanuddin, who was not only a conservative leader, but also adopted a low profile vis-á-vis the BJP. In Gujarat, he never expressed any protest against Modi and the 2002 pogrom. In fact, he tried 'to appease' the Chief Minister.[60]

This attitude is not peculiar to the Bohra community. In 2009, Shabbir Ahmed Siddiqui, the imam of the Jama Masjid of Ahmedabad, declared that 'Muslims too have an opportunity to prosper in the peaceful environment that the Modi government has created. Modi has provided an atmosphere which is conducive for those who want to do business in Gujarat'.[61] In the same way, in January 2011 Ghulam Mohammad Vastanvi, vice-chancellor of the Darul Uloom *Madrasa* of Deoband—a post he was to be removed from in July—stated that in Gujarat, there would be 'no discrimination against the minorities in the state as far as development there was concerned'.[62] This was reported by the *Times of India* and created a controversy among Muslim clerics to know whether G.M. Vastanvi should resign his function or not—which so far he has not done. These stances reflect the deep divisions among the Muslim community. Some of our sources analysed these attitudes as a way to protect one's own interest, at least among the businessmen.

On the political scene also, the Muslims are under-represented, even though the constituency-based electoral system allows them to have municipal corporators and MEAs returned in the pockets where they are concentrated. In 2010, the Muslim municipal corporators were thirteen out of 129, that is 10% of the total, not far from the share of the Muslims in the general population. But this percentage was declining (sixteen Muslim corporators had been elected in 2000) and almost half of them came from Muslim-dominated wards. In the walled city, the three corporators of Raikhad (ward no. 5) were Muslims, the three corporators of Jamalpur (ward no. 6) also, and two of the three corporators of Kalupur (ward no. 2); two of the three corporators of Daryapur (ward no. 3) as well as one out of three in Shahpur (ward no. 4) were Muslims too. Out of 13 Muslim corporators, 9 came from the Old City. The 4 others came from Rakhial (ward no. 29), Gomtipur (ward no. 30), Rajpur (ward no. 31) and Behrampura (ward no. 39) in the industrial eastern belt. No Muslim municipal corporator has been elected on the western side of the Sabarmati River in the last ten years. Besides, none of the office-bearers of the municipal corporation has been a Muslim for at least ten years, which is not so surprising since the BJP was in office.

So far as the MLAs are concerned, out of the 9 to 11 MLAs returned in Ahmedabad city, there have been between one and three Muslims since 1967—the 1962 elections, the first one for the newly created state of Gujarat being an exception: there was no Muslim MLA elected at that time, but there were just three constituencies. The Muslim MLAs were very few even when the Congress won most of the seats in the 1960s and 1970s (there was only one in 1972 when the Congress won all the seats). But since the 1980s, they have been in smaller numbers when the BJP swept the poll—like in 1995— and in larger numbers when the Congress staged a comeback. In 2007, the Congress won four seats, including three held by Muslim MLAs. Two seats have traditionally been held by Muslim politicians, Kalupur and Jamalpur, that have always been won by a Muslim candidate since 1967. Once again, the Muslims are confined to their pockets of the walled city. None of the MLAs elected in the rest of the district was a Muslim, even though there were large concentrations of Muslims at the periphery of Ahmedabad, like Juhapura.

None of the sitting municipal corporators and MLAs seems to be recognised as the leader of the Ahmedabad Muslims, even though some of them have been in the political arena for a long time. Among the MLAs Farooq Shaikh has been elected three times in the constituency of Kalupur and Shabir Kabli two times in Jamalpur.[63] Both of them are struggling with the authorities to get basic amenities like a drainage system, electricity or running water for their voters. But their party affiliation (both are from the Congress) and their religion make things very complicated. As S. Kabli puts it: 'It is very tough for us to get the work done because it is a BJP/RSS majority.'[64] For that reason, they do not rely on public resources only. In veiled terms, both of them acknowledged that they help Muslim people of their area in their personal capacity. For example, they provide poor students with books or uniforms and use their influence to get them admissions in good schools, probably with an eye on the next elections.

F. Shaikh and S. Kabli have two different approaches to their role as community leaders. When asked about what he can do for the Muslims, S. Kabli replied that he is just working for people of his area and wants to 'keep [his] voice low'. S. Khabi, on the contrary, considers that '[the Muslim MLAs of Ahmedabad] have to work a lot for the Muslim community because we are only three'. In 2002 he was the sole Muslim MLA of Ahmedabad and got actively involved in helping the victims. Although there were no casualties in his area because Kamalpur is mainly Muslim[65] he got a lot of calls from victims outside and tried to rescue them. In addition, the 2002 riots occurred during the Haj pilgrimage. Thus he helped people who were coming back from Mecca to cross the city and reach their homes safely. He also collected food, clothes and medicines in his area to support victims in the camps. The contrast between Shaikh and Kabli illustrates the increasingly marked difference between the Muslim leaders who prefer to keep a low profile and those who articulate the grievances of a community which is also their vote bank—Shaikh does not look at himself as a politician interestingly.

Regarding the poor state of the political opposition to the BJP, a growing number of Muslims have been voting for the pro-*Hindutva* party since 2002. Obviously they do not share its ideological views but this appears to be a political strategy to get something in return for their vote, such as new or improved amenities. Moreover, the 2010 local elections proved that the BJP has been changing its attitude to win the Muslim electorate. The party wooed it by appointing twelve Muslim candidates state-wise and moderating its anti-Muslim speech. For example, Vijay Rupani, MP and general secretary for the BJP in Gujarat, declared that 'we are clearly pro-Hindu, but we are not anti-Muslim. We believe in appeasement for none, justice for all. We will take nationalist Muslims with us in our path to development'.

The only local politician who could have played a leading role among the Muslims of Ahmedabad was Ahsan Jafri. Jafri was a freedom fighter, a leftist and a literary person. He joined the freedom movement in the 1940s while he had become the editor of the Urdu magazine published by his R.C. High School in Ahmedabad. Influenced by communism, he became a labour union leader and was jailed in 1949 for one year because of his 'calls for revolution'.[66] When he was released, he became the General Secretary of the Progressive Editor's Union and completed his law degree. He then started to practise as attorney in Ahmedabad. In 1969, his house in the old Ahmedabad was burnt by Hindus during the riot. His family had to stay in a relief camp. He rebuilt his house almost at the same place and even created a Bohra society, Gulberg Society of fourteen houses. But this event led him to get involved in the promotion of secularism. Attracted by Indira Gandhi's brand of socialism, he joined the Congress and became president of the Ahmedabad branch of the Congress (R) in 1972. He became MP of Ahmedabad in 1977 with 50.6% of the valid votes at a time when the Congress (R) was so unpopular that it reached an unprecedented low number of MPs (ten out of twenty-six). No Muslim had been elected MP of Ahmedabad before him and no Muslim could be elected to that position since then. He never contested elections again but remained involved in public affairs, even though literature (including Urdu poetry) took more and more importance in his life. He published eight books during his lifetime, including *Qandeel* (*Lantern*) in 1996. In 1986, the Gulberg Society was attacked again, but Ahsan Jafri could ask the Chief Minister, Amarsingh Chaudhury for help. In 2002, he was one of the most vocal opponents of the way Modi was exploiting the Godhra incident for political mileage. On 28 February, one day after, he was one of the first targets of the Hindu rioters. A huge number of people besieged his house. He telephoned officials, the police, old friends—including Muslim personalities who had shifted to the BJP.[67] But his calls for help were in vain. When he realised that the attackers may set fire to his house, killing his family and those who had rushed to him for safety, he went out. He was immediately slaughtered in the most savage way. This targeted killing was a reconfirmation of the status of Ashan Jafri as a local Muslim leader. One of his achievements, so far as the defence of Muslim interests is concerned, pertained to the protection of the Bohra Amil of Ahmedabad, Abde Ali who, apparently, was not targeted in 1985 because of him.[68]

The local dons sometimes appear as the leaders of the Muslim community, not only because they protect their co-religionists physically, but also because they are involved in social work. This pattern is well known in Mumbai where Dawood Ibrahim is a case in point.[69] In Ahmedabad, the most accomplished Muslim don who approximated the role of a *neta* (leader) was probably Abdul Latif. This bootlegger who—like many others—benefited from the prohibition of alcohol in Gujarat, first helped one of the local MLAs (Muhammad Hussin Bareija) in the 1985 elections.[70] Then he developed an intense activity of social work in favour of the Muslims, distributing food and medicines, and providing financial support to widows during the 1985 riots. Finally, he was elected from five wards of the Old City as a municipal corporator in 1987 (even though he contested the elections from behind the bars). Latif took part in the preparation of the Mumbai blasts of 1993 that had been engineered by Dawood Ibrahim. He followed him to Dubai and was arrested when he came back to India.[71] He died mysteriously in his cell and nobody has taken over from him, so much so that the Muslims of Ahmedabad have no don to whom they can turn the way they did towards Latif.

A Tale of Two Ghettos: The Old City and Juhapura

In many Indian cities, the marginalisation of Muslims has resulted in this minority becoming insulated and besieged within the urban centre; the old cores of the cities are gradually losing their past vitality because of general neglect. The Ahmedabad pattern is different. Certainly, parts of the walled city are crumbling down.[72] But besides this decline of the core, Muslims from the centre are pushed out of the city into new ghettos like Juhapura.[73]

What Urban Core?

The Old City of Ahmedabad is steadily declining. The city has lost some of its traditional functions and has emptied itself from the inside. Certainly, the Central Business District remained in the Old City, 'but following the completion of the infrastructure of the new capital city of Gandhinagar in 1970, commercial establishments increasingly began to be located in the west, along the Sarkhej-Gandhinagar or S.G. Road'.[74] The symbol of the expansion of the city towards the west and of the emptying of the Old City from within has been, in 1994, the relocation of the stock exchange.

This trend has resulted in a profound division between western and eastern Ahmedabad, a summa division that has blurred the old trifurcation, the river becoming a major frontier, and the railway line losing its significance. The mental geography of Ahmedabad reflects this evolution. The opposition between the two banks of the river is more and more expressed in cultural terms. As Rajagopal points out:

'Over time, the old city grew into a symbol of dysfunctionality in Ahmedabad and at the same time provided a rationale for new developments that strangely left the problem untouched. It was as if the old city enclosed a form of moral pollution that had to be preserved as a way of underlining the relative purity of the remainder of the city.'[75]

This purity-related opposition between the two faces of Ahmedabad (which harks back to the values underlying the caste system) translates itself in the division of the city into 'gastronomical zones',[76] as meat and eggs are not openly available in the western part of the city.

This 'dividation' (a term used by one of Rajagopal's informants)[77] of the city reflects the fact that the eastern part has become more and more Muslim. This process started in the 1960s when middle-class Hindus crossed the river to establish housing societies in less congested residential areas. Middle-class Dalits who had benefited from the reservations partly took their place, until the 1985 riots which persuaded them to go back to the mill areas where most of them had come from. This move resulted in the eviction of Muslim tenants in order to make room for the newcomers. To resist this evolution towards more segregation, the Congress-led municipal corporation of Ahmedabad passed an emergency regulation—the Prohibition of Transfer of Immovable Property and Provision for Protection of Tenants from Eviction from the Premises in Disturbed Areas Act (1986).[78] But it hardly made any difference and the flow was repeated anyway after the riots of the 1990s. According to another act that was passed in 1991, the sale of property in the 'disturbed areas' had to be endorsed by the administration. But those who wanted to leave found ways and means of transferring their property without actually selling it.[79] After the 1992 riots, for instance, Hindus left Danilimda which became a Muslim-dominated area, also because of the inflow of Muslims from Shah Alam.

However, Muslims also left the Old City. As early as 1969, some Muslims left places like Khadia and then after the riots of the 1980s, places like Teen Darwaza. Around the same time, rich Muslims crossed the river to settle down in Muslim housing societies in Paldi and Navrangpura.

The 2002 pogrom was of such magnitude that, this time, Muslims left in larger numbers, not only from the walled city, but from other parts too. In the walled city, two of the most severely affected targets were the markets of Palij Kuan and Kalupur which were so badly damaged that they had to merge. But the area that was hit even worse was the eastern mill area where Muslims and Dalits had continued to cohabit in large numbers for technical reasons. Indeed, in the *chawls*, the Mumbai Rent Control Act kept rents low and made properties non-transferable even after the mills shut down. According to a recent survey, 'just before the riots, the Muslim population share in mill parts was 23% and in non-mill parts was 11%.'[80] This high level of mixing between Hindus and Muslims resulted in a higher degree of violence, most of the Muslim casualties happening in the mill areas.[81]

Some Muslims left the Old City, the mill area and the housing societies which were targeted too. Those who stayed behind were locked in an even more clearly ghettoised central and east Ahmedabad. First, those who lived there belonged to different social classes and had primarily religion in common—a characteristic of the traditional Jewish ghetto.[82] Second, the Muslims of the Old City were not welcome on the other side of the river, some of them being arrested by the police when they went there—hence the removal of any Islamic sign from their rickshaws by the local drivers.[83] The ghettoisation process also curtailed mobility within the city.

While parts of East Ahmedabad have therefore become a Muslim ghetto, many of those who left these places took part in the making of another ghetto, Juhapura.

Juhapura: What 'Little Pakistan'?

With about 240,000 Muslim residents, Juhapura represents between one-third and half of the Muslim population of Ahmedabad according to different estimates.[84] This is why this unique concentration of Muslims in India is called 'little Pakistan' by most of the Hindus who know about the place. This is the phrase the taxi drivers will invariably use when they take an outsider to the place—with great variations of intonations reflecting, alternatively, hate, reluctance or fear. But Juhapura, though it is a Muslim ghetto—or because it is a Muslim ghetto—is building a new kind of society.

The Initial Utopia

Forty years ago, Juhapura was a village at the periphery of Ahmedabad, a few kilometres away, southwest of the city. Today, it has one of the largest concentrations of Muslim people in India, connected to the city via the Dalit-dominated area of Vasna in the southwestern part of Ahmedabad. In fact 'Juhapura' is the label that is used in common parlance to designate eight amalgamated localities: Juhapura, Maktampura, Fatehwadi, Makaraba, Sarkhej, Okaf, Vejalpur and Gyaspur. While Muslims represent 100% of the population of Shahwadi, Fatehwadi, Gyaspur and Maktampura, they form 30 to 40% of the population of the other areas.[85]

The development of Juhapura really began in 1973 after a heavy flood occurred on the Sabarmati River banks and devastated the houses of 2,250 Ahmedabad slum dwellers, 'the two predominant religious groups [being] nearly equally represented' among the victims.[86] The Ahmedabad Study

FACING GHETTOISATION IN 'RIOT-CITY'

Action Group (ASAG), a city-based NGO dedicated to human resettlement and poverty alleviation, decided to relocate the affected people in Juhapura. The idea was not only to provide victims with houses but to empower them through their active participation in the housing project. Kirtee Shah, an architect and the founder of ASAG, wanted them to select the place of their house, to design it and to choose their neighbours. He enforced this project with both public and private partners such as the Municipal Commissioner and the Housing and Urban Development Corporation Limited (HUDCO), the national housing finance agency[87] on the one hand, and some NGOs like the Saint Xavier Social Service Society on the other. The only available and affordable land was located in Sankalit Nagar, a very small locality within Juhapura, which at that time was not yet considered a part of Ahmedabad. It was more than eight kilometres away from the city, where the flood-affected slumdwellers used to work. Hence there were many kinds of infrastructure and amenities that had been planned initially in the relocation project in order to link this new township to the rest of the city and allow people to continue their income-generating activities.

Victims were involved at every stage of the project and especially during the houses' allotment phase. Sankalit Nagar, the first colony of Juhapura, was composed of 2,700 houses[88] where the majority of resettled people deliberately chose to live within mixed-religion societies—the choice of one's neighbours was motivated more by personal affinities or economic relations than religious considerations. Initially, Juhapura was therefore a promising project of communal harmony and development-cum-resettlement. But problems appeared very soon. Yaqub, who has been living in Sankalit Nagar since 1973, explained that the houses were very small and that dirty water often went out of the drainage lines which were open air and built between the houses.[89] Besides, almost none of the planned infrastructure and amenities were actually built. People got stuck in this remote area and could not easily work anymore; indeed they had to walk a huge distance to reach Ahmedabad or to pay fares for private transportation which dramatically impacted their income. As a result, the resettled people began to leave Juhapura.[90] Yaqub told us that 'out of 100 persons, only ten stayed. The others went back to the river banks and sold their house'. Poorer people—Hindus as well as Muslims—bought them, with Muslims probably representing then a slight majority.

The area really began to grow after the 1985 riots. From that time on, each communal clash resulted in migrations of Muslims from central and eastern Ahmedabad to Juhapura. Most of these newcomers were poor people from the Old City and the industrial area. However, after the 1992 and even more after the 2002 events, middle-class Muslims—including (ex-) IAS, IPS and IFS officers, advocates, professors, doctors, businessmen...[91]—have started to look for safety in Juhapura too.[92] They left their previous localities, even though many had been living there for generations. They told us that during each riot, their houses and businesses were looted, thus the fear of living in the midst of Hindu localities also grew among them, even if they were not physically attacked until 2002. One of them, Nadeem Jaffri, an MBA-graduate and creator of Hearty Market, the first supermarket in Juhapura, admitted that earlier, he would have never thought about living in 'a ghetto', but in 2006, he moved from Paldi to Juhapura for security reasons.[93] Several of Juhapura's middle-class inhabitants, such as Ghazala Paul, considered the locality to be 'unnatural [because] there is only one religion'.[94] Most of the middle-class Muslim inhabitants feel compelled to live in Juhapura. Living in Juhapura is 'not a choice, it's a coercive thing because a lot want to live in mixed areas'.[95] For Mr. Gena, the principal of the FD School located in Maktampura:

'I would like to live in the University area but it's impossible because security is the main concern; and that's why this area is more and more a ghetto. If I get the chance [to leave] for another area I will take it, but still, there is a question of security'.[96]

After the post-2002 riots-related inflow of Muslims in Juhapura, Hindus who live in neighbourhoods next to Juhapura have built a wall between this locality and their own.[97] This wall reflects the mutual fear among Hindus and Muslims of the area. Both communities refer to it as 'the border'.

Juhapura has become a Muslim ghetto in the true sense of the word for three reasons. First, it gathers together people who have mostly one thing in common, their religious identity, irrespectively of their socio-economic and socio-cultural status. Second, it is insulated from the rest of the city, not only because of one wall, but because no bus connection had ever been established. Buses cross the area on the main road, but not a single one goes inside the locality. People are compelled to use private means of transportation like autorickshaws or scooters which are much more expensive. Third, the area has not benefited from the same kind of attention from the state as other parts of the city. But, paradoxically, this ghettoisation process has been to some extent a positive thing since the newcomers have been in position to initiate development projects.

A Deprived Locality Ignored by the State and 'Developed' by Its Inhabitants

Darshini Mahadevia argues that Juhapura is not a ghetto any more, but a city, like in Shah Alam, an area representing about one-fifth of the Muslims of

FACING GHETTOISATION IN 'RIOT-CITY'

Ahmedabad: 'Around the housing, markets have come up. There are boards announcing the starting of schools and kindergartens. Every thing that a new city requires! (...) Thus, Juhapura is emerging as a self-sufficient Muslim city in Ahmedabad'.[98] Certainly, the sheer size of Juhapura and the fact that it is situated at the periphery of the city do not fit with the classic notion of the ghetto as a limited enclave. But Mahadevia ignores the fact that not only is Juhapura populated with Muslims looking for safety irrespective of caste and class, but that one cannot find 'everything that a new city requires': the state is missing.

Since its creation in the mid-1970s the area of Juhapura has been totally neglected by the authorities, whatever the ruling party may be. This was partly due to the fact that the area was not part of the Ahmedabad Municipal Corporation (AMC), but divided into five *panchayats*: Vejalpur, Maktampura, Shah Vali, Sarkhej and Gyaspur under the authority of the Ahmedabad Urban Development Authority. In 2006 it was merged within the vast constituency of Sarkhej-Lambha and has become part of the AMC under the administrative name of 'New West Zone'. But this change made little difference since this new unit is overwhelmingly Hindu. Thus one of the largest concentrations of Muslims in India is represented by a BJP MLA (Amit Shah)[99] and a BJP MP (Solanki Kirit Premaji) for whom the development of Juhapura is not a priority.[100]

Besides frequent episodes of load-shedding, Juhapura also misses gas, a pipeline having been deviated from Vasna to avoid the area. Apart from Sarkhej Road there are only sand- or gravel-paths (*kaccha*) within Juhapura, but not one secondary tarmacing road (*pakka*). As a result, most of the time, one has to walk in the mud after the monsoon. It is the same regarding drainage or running water systems.

Since the AMC does not build crucial infrastructures, either they result from private initiatives when people can afford them, or they are tremendously lacking. For example, a lot of inhabitants are still using pump systems to get drinking water which is sometimes contaminated and brings diseases to inhabitants.[101] This could be explained by the fact that the area of Juhapura is surrounded by several wastewater treatment facilities plants which smell very badly and whose dirty water seeps underground. Regarding the lack of health infrastructures in general, Dr. Kherala, who has been working in Juhapura since 1974, considers that 'People are treated like stray dogs'.[102] There is no public hospital or public campaigns to inform people about safe health habits. But Dr. Kherala states that inhabitants lack this awareness, whatever their socio-economic background may be. The sole hospital is a private one, the Iqraa Charitable Hospital, founded fifteen years ago by the Pir Mohammed Shah Trust. But it is 'poorly managed, without adequate medical facilities and has no equipment for diagnostic and surgeries'.[103] Otherwise patients have a narrow choice between the fourteen private cabinets of the area or the dispensaries and mobile health centres run by local NGOs or associations like the Gujarat Lokhitseva Trust. According to Dr. Kherala, there are around a hundred dispensaries 'but 90% of them are run by unqualified people'.[104]

In terms of education, the area is lagging behind too. There are only twenty-seven primary and secondary schools in Juhapura. All of them are registered with the Gujarat Board of Education but only four are run by the government and, therefore, do not ask for fees. A survey conducted by the NGO Samerth[105] points out that there are more than 6,000 new six-year-old children to send to school in Juhapura every year but the government schools can only provide education to 10% of them.[106] Moreover the government is not running a single college or technical education institution in the area.

However, the worst living conditions are in the relief colonies that have been built by Islamic NGOs after the 2002 pogrom to give transitional shelters to Muslim families whose houses had been destroyed.[107] 1,745 riot-affected people live in one of the seven relief colonies of Juhapura:[108] Arsh Colony, Ekta Nagar I, Ekta Nagar II, Gupta Nagar, Javed Park, Siddikabad Colony or Yash Complex. These societies are located in the remotest areas of the locality. Some of them being closed by gates, they look like inner enclaves and are even more neglected by the state than the rest of Juhapura. Almost no facilities have been built, while inhabitants are not able to afford those scarce amenities, like running water, since their revenue has significantly declined because of the pogrom. Rachida,[109] who lives in Ekta Nagar, told us, for instance, that her household income has dropped from 10,000 to 3,000 Rs a month. The few things people get there result from the Islamic trusts or from a legal decision. For example the High Court forced the Gujarat government to provide tanks of drinking water to the relief colonies. Islamic trusts continue to help them but less and less because of financial problems and a diversification of their actions now that the rehabilitation and resettlement phases are over.[110] Thus relief colonies' inhabitants think that 'now [the Islamic trusts] don't care about [them]'[111] anymore. Besides, they still refuse to give the ownership of the houses built in the relief colonies, another reason to generate anger among inhabitants.

FACING GHETTOISATION IN 'RIOT-CITY'

Islamic 'purification' and self-help

Dealing with the Muslim victims of riots in Mumbai, Thomas Blom Hansen points out that they had the choice between two options only: either 'community purification' through Islamic reform or 'plebeian assertion' through a closer association with low caste-oriented political parties.[112] In Juhapura, the second option does not exist because such parties are very weak. The first one remained. On the basis of her fieldwork in Juhapura in 2003–04, Rubina Jasani, in a seminal article, suggests that the Muslims who had been affected by violence have followed this alternative. While studying 'the growing influence of Islamic reformism in Juhapura between 2002 and 2004',[113] she focuses on the work of the Jamiat-i-Ulema-i-Hind, the Jama'at-i-Islami (and its relief wing, the Islamic Relief Committee) and the Tablighi Jama'at in the relief colonies to observe that:

'Each group (...) engaged in "community purification" through running regular *ijtimas* [gatherings] for both men and women in the newly established resettlement colonies. This was done in most cases by playing upon a sense of guilt and relating the conditions of riot survivors to their neglect of prayers and having become *gumraah* (lost), by getting caught up in worldly desires'.[114]

This attempt at re-Islamising the Muslims was also supported by the building, in some colonies, of mosques and *madrasas*. The form of Islam that was propagated this way confronted the traditional worship of Sufi saints and none of the tombs of saints which had been destroyed during the pogrom—including that of Shah Wali Gujarati—were rebuilt. The Tabligh which, so far, had only one mosque in the Old City, in Gomtipur, mostly for UP migrants, created seven new ones in Juhapura after the 2002 pogrom, plus two *madrasas*.[115] The Tabligh was especially strong in the relief colonies it had started, but not only.[116]

We came to similar conclusions as Jasani after doing fieldwork in Juhapura relief colonies in 2006.[117] But the residents' state of mind has started to change in the post-trauma phase and the relief colonies represent a very special milieu anyway—whose members are largely depending upon the Islamist organisations. The other inhabitants of Juhapura do not necessarily share the views that some of them communicated to Rubina Jasani in favour of Islamist purification in 2003–04. Interviews and fieldwork indicate that it took almost two years for people to start recovering from the riots, the activity of the first six months being totally paralysed. As Alamder Bukari, the joint editor of the *Gujarat Today* newspaper, puts it: 'after 2002 and until 2004, it was a trauma because [the community] needed time to recover [from the riots].[118] Since 2004, residents have been going back to what they call 'a normal life'[119] namely earning their life in a decent way whereas those who had their own business looted had to deal with insurance companies which delayed the payment of compensations. Once people stopped worrying about their day-to-day survival, the priority became education.

In 2010, most of the middle-class newcomers we interviewed considered that it was high time to open a new chapter and argued in favour of the rapid modernisation of the community. Some of them went so far as to describe the 2002 pogrom as a 'blessing in disguise'. A.A. Khan, the general secretary of the Sarkhej Area Welfare Organizations Federation, said: 'in a way, the government is helping us because it puts us in such a situation that the Muslim community is compelled to develop'.[120] Everybody agreed that after the 2002 violence, the Muslims realised that they could rely only on themselves. Bukari Fakuna, the principal of the Anjuman Islami English School of Kalupur sums up this general point of view:

'We want to fight back [those who attacked us] by education. Education awareness is growing because, owing to our educational backwardness, we suffered a lot. So even poor parents try to educate their children in the best schools'.[121]

According to a large part of respondents, the Muslim community was attacked because of its backwardness. No matter how correct or incorrect this analysis may be, what is most important is how Muslim people perceive this situation, and how it drives them towards education. As Karim Lakhani, a wealthy chartered accountant, sums it up:

'Lack of education is the big thing; we don't have education [...] education makes the difference; now due to 2002, education is growing within the community. Because of our education, we can fight them, we can fight for our rights; without education we have to rely on goons only, but now, we are quite aware of our rights and duties also'.[122]

Interestingly, activists in the Islamic trusts share this point of view too. Javed Sayed, a Tablighi in charge of education in the Gujarat Savarjanik Welfare Trust (GSWT) states that:

'once people take education it helps in many ways of life: upliftment, understanding what is right and wrong; they can approach problems with education [...] if they want to start a business, they have to know how to count...'[123]

For that reason, the GSWT started training classes to prepare Muslim students who wanted to join the administration.

However, the main proponents of education are willing to keep Islam at bay. A case in point is the development of new schools in Juhapura by the F.D. Education Society. Established in the Old City in 1961 by two Muslim notables, A.A. Shaikh and F.M. Shaikh, a businessman and a civil servant, this society is run by a managing body of twenty-one persons among whom at least eighteen have a Muslim name—including Shafi Maniar. While it had remained confined to the Old City for decades, after 2002 the F.D. Education Society expanded in Juhapura.

All the students we met in the Juhapura higher secondary school seem to be Muslims too. But Islam is not mentioned anywhere in the brochures that are given in the Juhapura schools or in the interviews with the faculty members or administrators. The brochure, in fact, eulogises scientific knowledge and excellence more than anything else, suggesting that this is the only way out for the Muslim youth. The box called 'Our vision' is very telling in this respect: 'Well-educated, well-versed [sic], disciplined and dedicated students possessing merit have bright prospects in the progressive world of excellence and competition of the day to become the corner-stone of a good society, a good nation'. Below, one reads:

'Application of computers has solved manifold problems that mankind faced. It has opened new doors of progress. Today, therefore, emphasis is on technical or professional knowledge. It is the merit now that counts whatever the discipline or faculty'.

This obsession with excellence (the box 'Our motto' says: 'Achieving excellence') and merit reflects an existential anxiety and hope: if the Muslims are well educated, they will be part of a 'good nation'. This is why education must be given to everybody, including girls. The brochure mentions that 48% of the students are girls, and our visits of the school make this figure plausible.

The F.D. Education Society runs thirty-three institutions ranging from primary schools to colleges. The first ones were established in Jamalpur, in the Old City of Ahmedabad, where twelve schools are still functioning, but in the 1980s new buildings were constructed in Juhapura where there are now four primary schools, one high school, one higher secondary school and one industrial training centre. The principal of the higher secondary school points out that after 2002, English has become the medium of education for some classes, as a result of the inflow of middle-class people and the pervasive desire to foster the modernisation process among the Muslim community.[124] Nevertheless, teaching through English medium is still at the beginning.

The Crescent Primary School of Juhapura was created in 2008 along similar lines. It is very well equipped with computers and 'intelligent class', namely digital blackboards. It welcomes 700 students from three to eleven years old, mostly from well-off families. Asifkhan Pathan, one of the trustees of the school, told us it was very complicated to start the school because they were asked for bribes and the government harassed them in an attempt to prevent the creation of the school.[125]

Meenakshi Thapan has studied another Muslim school, which has moved from a Hindu-dominated neighbourhood of Vejalpur to Juhapura after the 2002 pogrom. She emphasises the absence of any explicit Muslim culture in the school and even the presence of many Hindu symbols. For instance, all the school's houses are named after Hindu heroes. For her, all this 'is indicating a preference for the projection of a Hindu nationalist ideology into the development of the child as a citizen of India'.[126] If this analysis may be too radical, the Muslim promoters of modern education in Juhapura are definitely playing down their religious identity, as if that was the price to pay for being recognised as a full-fledged Indian citizen. Taken to its logical conclusion, this process of cultural occultation will seal the fate of India's multiculturalism.

In Juhapura, the will to educate children is not limited to regular education in school. Since 2002, NGOs and local associations have developed informal classes. They are dedicated to the education of adults, like the computer classes of the Gujarat Lokhitseva Trust for example. Other organisations work on education and formation of women like the Gulshan-e-Maher charity trust of Dr. Chandibibi Sheikh.

Besides education, the arrival of richer Muslims in Juhapura also brought some new kind of activities and shops like supermarkets, petrol pumps and banks which were lacking less than four years ago. Even some fancy brands like Havmor, the ice cream producer, are now investing in Juhapura because these new customers can afford their products. Indeed, 'in post 2002 some Muslims wanted to shift in this safe area, even educated and cosmopolitan people; the problem is that people came here but there were no basic amenities in this area, so people have to go outside to buy their things'.[127]

For that reason businessmen or entrepreneurs like Nadeem Jaffri, who established the first supermarket of the area, 'found a good opportunity to open a business'.[128] The inflow of middle-class Muslims in Juhapura resulted in many new self-help initiatives. Welfare organisations and citizen associations were set up, dedicated to education but also to the upliftment of the backward members of the community.[129] They provide cheap medical services through dispensaries and financially help poor people during religious festivals, mourning times, and so on. These activities are mostly handled by middle-class and high-caste notables like Shafi Maniar, the well-known industrialist who is involved in several charity trusts. For him, 'a share of our income should go to the poor; they [the middle classes to which he himself belongs] think that to live one's life for one's sake is worthless'.[130] One could object that Shafi Maniar's dedication to poor people is not only philanthropy-oriented. But whatever his motivations may be—including the quest for prestige, rewards in the Hereafter and power over the community—he contributes to the upliftment of the community, which was not the case before 2002. Although the philanthropic organisations are mostly charity-based, financed through *Zakat* and donations, they ask more and more for some payment of minimal fees (ten rupees per year for tuition for example). They also tend to promote micro-credit. The Ahmedabad Muslim Women Association (AMWA) has been doing this since 2003 to help widows to recover after the riots and become self-sufficient. This new modus operandi is well in tune with the sense of merit, self-help, and entrepreneurship of the new middle class.

Things are not different so far as the development of the area is concerned. Well-off Muslims build amenities within the societies they live in, such as roads, drainage systems, running water. For example, we observed in January–April 2010 that Asifkhan Pathan was supervising some works to bring running water and electricity to the Crescent School, because the state was not doing it. This is new. For a long time, middle-class Muslims did not pay attention to the poor of the community. They mostly gave them money as their religious duty. But since 2002, they have been more directly involved in the development of the community.[131]

The improvement of living conditions in Juhapura being mainly due to private initiatives, it can be considered as a self-developed area. But its inhabitants are not resigning themselves to the absence of the state and their second-class citizens status. As Bukari Faruna points out, 'people are stronger in 2010 than in 2002'[132] and more aware of their rights. Therefore, citizen associations have lodged complaints to have their basic needs fulfilled. For example, Nadeem Saiyed, an activist living in Juhapura, registered a Public Interest Litigation at the end of 2009 to complain against the AMC about the poor state of drinkable water facilities. After all, inhabitants pay taxes to the AMC without getting any services back.

At the same time, Juhapura's inhabitants feel proud about the way they are developing their area since 2002. Asifkhan Pathan proudly told us that now Juhapura was 'a label'. Imamkhan Pathan, president of the NGO Gujarat

Lokhitseva Trust, argues that 'now Juhapura is becoming a place for good people: doctors, IPS, IAS, judges, businessmen, advocates'.[133] Interestingly, this assessment is also made by Tablighis who have definitely turned their back to the victimisation cum purification discourse. It is widely admitted among the community that 'compared to 2002 [the situation of the community] has improved a lot: economic upliftment, education, etc. [even if] it is still not sufficient'.[134] Thanks to this evolution, people we met told us that Muslim people are less and less dependent on the goons and that criminality in Juhapura is decreasing.[135] As Karim Lakhani noted, 'now the models for the community are Shah Rukh Khan or Abdul Kalam, not Latif or Dawood Ibrahim.[136]

Conclusion

Community-wise, the original pattern of the Ahmedabad urbanisation process resembles the one we can observe in most of the Indian cities founded by Muslim dynasties, in the sense that the Muslims occupied the historical core of the walled city, where most of the mosques, schools and other Islamic places of importance were located. But Ahmedabad represents a very specific case for many reasons. First, this urban core was organised around *pols* which were associated to caste groups and religious communities but coexisted in a very intermingled way, a cultural mosaic that was reproduced in the *chawls* of the industrial area. Second, partly because of the strength of the Hindu nationalist movement and the Hindu traditionalist leanings of the local Congress, Ahmedabad has been the city of India that has been the most affected by communal riots. Muslims, who have been the first victims of this violence have been partially removed from the walled city and have increasingly migrated to safer places at the periphery.

Communal violence and migrations have been one of the main reasons for the marginalisation of Muslims within the local elite groups in different domains such as the economy, the judiciary and the political scene. Discrimination has been an additional decisive factor too.

Communal violence and discrimination have resulted in an unparalleled fragmentation of the city's space along communal lines. The multiplication of boards signalling the 'borders' of mini-Hindu Rashtras and concrete walls have been symbols of this evolution. After the 1985 riots, a high wall was built between the property of a Patel and a Muslim neighbourhood in the Old City; after the 1990s riots, 'almost all dalit *chawls* in the industrial area had erected high walls around them';[137] in 2002, one more wall appeared in

Juhapura, as mentioned above. But in addition to these boards and walls, invisible frontiers multiplied and hardened between the Hindu space and the Muslim space. The making of 'gastronomical zones' and of no-go areas for the Muslims has also shaped immaterial ghettoes, as evident from the insulation of east Ahmedabad and Juhapura.

However, the ghettoisation process and sheer violence have had unintended and not so negative consequences. First, it has enabled Muslims to be in a majority in constituencies where they could elect their representatives. Whether these men could help their community or were willing to do so is another question. Secondly and more importantly, the regrouping of Muslims from different backgrounds in a place like Juhapura has endowed the local plebe with a new elite, middle-class people in quest of safety who initiated self-help based development, including schools. The local plebe was aspiring to such a modernisation of the Muslim community via education after the riots and the 2002 pogroms had shown them that this minority could only rely on its own forces. This is the third unintended consequence of communal violence which shows that the victimisation discourse and the craze for Islamic purification represented only a post-traumatic phase that was mostly confined to the relief camps. Paradoxically, unprecedented communal violence and ghettoisation have prepared the ground for a modernisation whose symbol lies in education, English medium. Whether this new way towards prosperity will bear fruit remains to be seen. Discrimination may frustrate high expectations, but Muslims may also benefit from the growth on the basis of their new skills. Whether they will downplay their Islamic identity in order to be more acceptable to the majority community is another question.

Last but not least, the Hindu nationalists have failed to eliminate the Muslims from the centre of Ahmedabad. The walled city remains a Muslim-dominated area. More importantly, in some mixed neighbourhoods, the Hindu-Muslim relations retain their ancestral quality. A case in point is Ramrahim Nagar, a locality situated on the eastern bank of Sabarmati River south of the walled city, whose name combines that of a Hindu god and one of the names of Allah. Since 1969, Ramrahim Nagar has not been affected by any of the Gujarat riots, including the 2002 pogrom, an achievement which led Sonia Gandhi to award the elders of the place the Indira Gandhi Award for National Integration.[138]

3

RAMGANJ, JAIPUR

FROM OCCUPATION-BASED TO 'COMMUNAL' NEIGHBOURHOOD?

Gayatri Jai Singh Rathore

Built in 1727 by Sawai Jai Singh, Jaipur is among the first planned cities in North India. Following the disintegration of the Mughal Empire, the city was founded as a spearhead of princely political control in Rajputana. In an atmosphere of stability, the city flourished as one of the premier trade centres in the subcontinent. It attracted Hindu bankers, jewellers and traders as well as Muslim administrators and craftsmen from Delhi, Multan and Afghanistan. While interaction across the occupational groups[1] was stratified and limited to an extent, the city lay over an interweaving of Hindu and Muslim coexistence, a way of life which the city's residents nostalgically refer to as the '*ganga-jamni*'[2] or '*mushtarka*[3] *tahzeeb*'. This harmony was largely preserved in everyday life until the riots of 1989. In the 1990s, with the cultural revival and the development of a nationalist consciousness among Hindus, the latent opposition between elements of the two groups transformed itself into open hostility in the form of riots, changing the landscape and composition of many neighbourhoods. With the exception of a few elite families, the alienation of the Muslim population was intensified by the gradual decline of economic activities amongst the working class in the aftermath of the 1990 Gulf war.[4]

In the current setting, Hindu-Muslim relations tend to revolve around accounts of suspicion and distrust. Two features increasingly characterise Muslim localities in Jaipur. First, these neighbourhoods face spatial exclusion. Second, with the exception of localities such as Kidwai Nagar and Mansarovar (inhabited by elite Muslims such as retired civil servants and professors), most Muslim neighbourhoods are ridden with poverty and underdevelopment. Recently, however, a new emerging elite from various Muslim *biraderis* has been dedicating itself to elevating the cultural and economic status of its community and has been making its presence felt in the constant negotiations and disputes that define everyday survival in the Muslim areas of Jaipur.

The first part of this chapter discusses the historical background, outlining the development of Muslim presence in Jaipur until independence. The present socio-economic condition of Muslims is detailed in the second part. The chapter concludes with a case study of a Muslim-dominated *mohalla* of Jaipur, Ramganj.

Muslims in Erstwhile Jaipur

There are no reliable aggregate figures on the city's population prior to the nineteenth century. Nonetheless, estimation by Boileau,[5] an officer of the Survey of India, suggests that the Muslim population was about 17% of the total in 1835. Brahmins then constituted one-fifth of the city population.[6] Baniyas, made up of a bunch of castes (Maheshwari, Saraogi, Oswal, etc.) of local merchants and bankers, also constituted one-fifth of the city population. Other castes of equal demographic importance, Rajput and Jats, were more specific to the state.

Elite Muslim inhabitants, who served as ministers in the Jaipur court, comprised a mixed group of *hakims* (physicians), intellectuals, and administrators of the Mughal empire. Sufis advised the rulers in spiritual matters and received state patronage in return. The subaltern group of musicians and lower-caste artisans comprised the bulk of the Muslim population. They were mostly involved in cloth weaving, with 700 families of weavers (*julaha*). Other important Muslim groups were the ivory bracelet makers (*chooregur*) and horse doctors (*salotree*). In order to streamline the activities of the occupational caste groups, 36 state *karkhanas* (factories) were opened within the palace complex in the Mughal mode. The *karkhanas* provided state patronage to the courtly classes and artisans, helping them to train and produce a steady output in terms of art and culture. By 1901,[7] the Muslims' share in the city's population had grown to 25%. They were divided socially and notions of high (*ashraf*) and low (*ajlaf*) lineage were deep-rooted. The 1931 Census of India classified the city's Muslim elites into different castes—namely Sheikh (90,400), Pathan (35,078), Syed (10,462) and Kayamkhani[8] (16,573). Theologically, they were Sunnis, Shias and Bohras.

Town Planning and the Formation of Muslim Mohallas in Jaipur

The city was planned according to Shastric texts, following a 'pattern of settlement of people according to caste or *jati*'. Town planning was 'more than a matter of mobility and geometry. It relates to the system of social distribution, nowadays more commonly known as the *mohalla* system'.[9] Hence, at the time of its foundation in 1727, Jaipur was made up of seven rectangular *chowkri* or wards: Purani Basti, Topkhana Desh, Modi Khana, Visheshwarji, Ghat Darwaza, Topkhana Hazuri and Ramchandraji. Each was attributed to a particular caste group based on its lineage and ranking. While the Brahmins were settled in Purani Basti, Marwari and Jain merchants occupied Modi Khana and the Ghat Darwaza area; *chowkri* Topkhana Hazuri[10] and Ramchandraji were reserved for the subaltern castes of Hindu and Muslim artisans. The latter areas initially belonged to the unplanned parts of the city. They grew rapidly and in a haphazard manner and today they comprise the bulk of Muslim labour workforce in the city. Together, Chowkri Ramchandraji and Topkhana Hazuri house 50% and 40% of the city's total Muslim population respectively. Although a particular residential space in the city was allotted to each caste group, the ruler enjoyed the liberty to bestow personal favours on people close to the court. As a result, certain Muslim elites found a place in the vicinity of the palace, a place normally reserved for the Brahmin caste. Thus, the Prime Minister of Jaipur in the court of Ram Singh, Nawab Faiz Ali Khan, lived in a *haveli* bordering the palace complex at Tripolia Gate. The royal *hakim*, Salim Khan, was for his part allotted land near Johari Bazar.

Structurally, *mohallas* were identified by the professional groups that resided there. In some cases these *mohallas* or streets were known by the names of influential men who resided there, as in the case of Geejgarh Thakur ka rasta, Thakur Pachewar ka rasta, etc. With a few exceptions, the artisan tradition required the use of apprenticeships in which master-apprentice relations were limited by the barriers of religion and caste. This meant that the social life of most people functioned within frameworks of extended kinship and religion. Each *mohalla* therefore represented an extended ethnic group, homogenous in terms of caste and religion. Administratively, the *mohalla* acted as a governing body with a formal role, with spokespersons organising themselves for collective activities such as processions, marriages and neighbourhood-based religious traditions. Nevertheless, at the same time, the unifying character of the *mohalla* stressed its exclusiveness and the rigidity of the ethnic boundaries it delineated.

Throughout princely rule, the occupational castes were considered as inferior groups and were tied by client relations to higher castes, often represented by the feudal lords, merchants or bankers. They were dependent on local upper castes not only for patronage but also to sell their produce. This vertical patronage and the occupational pattern left little room for trust-based interactions between individuals across religious lines. Hindus and Muslims lived side by side, but interactions between them were limited.

Muslims Under British Paramountcy

In 1818, the British established another kind of patron-client relationship with the state of Jaipur through a treaty of 'subordinate cooperation'. Yet, it was not until the reign of Madho Singh (1880–1922) that Jaipur actually integrated administratively with the British Empire. Owing to his faithful allegiance to the crown, the Prince largely managed to pursue his and his state's interests without much interference from the empire. As a result, the city was more or less insulated from the events of British India and even the growing nationalist movement did not affect the city until the 1930s.

The first significant incident of the Muslims of Japiur affirming their identity took place in 1939, when they organised a protest march demanding the expansion of the staircase of the city's Jama Masjid. A week later, colonial authorities ordered firing on the mosque during Friday prayers, killing twenty-two people. Nationalist Muslim leaders linked this incident to the wider nationalist Muslim unrest against the British administration by labelling it a 'Second Kanpur'.[11] The protest even received a mention in Jinnah's speech for the Lahore Resolution in 1940. For the first time, the Muslim *mohalla* became a site for political performances that contributed to the construction of its religious identity.

Much later, in 1942, Maharaja Sawai Man Singh appointed another Muslim elite, Mirza Ismail Khan, as the Prime Minister of Jaipur without the approval of the British. Like the Prince himself, Sir Mirza was regarded as a

Congress sympathiser and anti-Muslim. He undertook many urbanisation projects. M.I. Road today stands as a testimony to his contribution to the development of the city. Sir Mirza had an important role to play in determining the political landscape of Jaipur. First, sensing the democratic wave in the country, he was supportive of the Praja Mandal (People's Council) formed in 1938 by members of the Brahmin and Baniya castes, and even encouraged the participation of its cadres in Jaipur state's politics. As a result, he paved the way for the merger of the Jaipur court with the Congress Party. Second, he used the Praja Mandalists to keep the peasant movement, led by the Kisan Sabha (Peasant's council) in check. As such, he widened political support for the Praja Mandal, which accepted the rural peasantry, particularly the Jats, into its folds. Third, he initiated wide-scale legal reforms to abolish the *jagirdari* system, a task that was completed only after the merger of Jaipur into the Indian Republic in 1949. He also appointed a committee on Constitutional Reform (1942) in order to create a Legislative Council and a Representative Assembly in 1944.

Following the elections of 1945, power passed into the hands of the Brahmins and Baniyas of the city. While the Rajputs were given separate electorates, Minas and Jats were still dependent on Praja Mandal for their representation. The Muslims were not only denied a separate electorate such as the one they had enjoyed in British India since the Morley-Minto Reforms of 1909, they were also excluded from the Praja Mandal's constituency. While the number of seats reserved for Muslims was in proportion to their population in the state (7%), the success of their candidates largely depended on the support of Baniya and Brahmin elites. Among the state's poorest and least educated people, Jaipur Muslims were therefore sidelined by the constitutional reform.

Jaipur Muslims After Independence

With the Partition of the country in 1947, Muslims were further marginalised in demographic and social terms following the migration of a significant number of their elites to Pakistan. When the Princely State merged with the newly-founded state of Rajasthan in 1949, the Congress Party filled in the vacuum left by the departure of these elites with leaders belonging to Hindu upper castes (Brahmins, Marwaris and Jats). Lower-caste Hindus and Muslims were absent from the leadership of the party.

Yet, in the initial years of state politics, Muslims had faith in both Congress and Jana Sangh (earlier formation of the right wing BJP). The Jana Sangh initially entered politics with the help of feudal landlords who received ample support from the Muslim population. For example, the Johari Bazar constituency in

Jaipur, though prominently a Muslim area, returned a Jana Sangh candidate (S.C. Agarwal)[12] thrice in succession in 1957, 1962 and 1967. In cases where the Jana Sangh adopted a more Hindu nationalist ideology, Muslims turned to other political options. In the Vidhan Sabha elections of 1952, Shah Alimuddin Ahmed of Congress was elected from Jaipur Shahar constituency. From the 1970s onwards, the Muslim population voted more for Muslim candidates in the Johari Bazar seat: Muzaffar Ali of Samyukta Vidhayak Dal (SVD) in 1972, G. Mohammad of Janata Party (JP) in 1977, Takiuddin Ahmed of the Indian National Congress (INC) in 1980 and 1998.

Communal Politics and the Transformation of Muslim Localities

Latent Hindu-Muslim tensions developed because of the rise of Hindu nationalism in the state in the 1980s. The first overt change in the relationship was witnessed during the *Ramshila Pujan* (1989) in Jaipur. Backed by the Hindu bourgeoisie (Brahmins, Baniyas and Rajputs), the state population made the largest donation and contributed about 20,000 bricks for the construction of the Ram temple (Mayaram, 1993). The first communal skirmish in the city took place in October 1989, followed by a second violent incident on 27 November 1989.[13] The third and deadliest riot occurred in October 1990, following Advani's arrest during the *rath yatra*. In contrast to previous riots, this one was more lethal as 100 to 120 people were killed (90–95% of the victims were Muslims). The violence was not limited to the Old City but extended to residential areas such as Shastri Nagar and Rishi Ghalav Nagar (the latter was the scene of a three-day-long massacre of its Muslim residents).[14] The army had to be called in to control the situation and the loss of property was estimated at 1 billion rupees. On the Muslim side, violence was organised and executed through *biraderi* (clan) structures, while Hindu nationalists mobilised lower-caste Kolis, Banjaras and Dalits to perpetrate killings. The local media and the police played a key role in these outbreaks of violence. Far from containing the violence, which was systematically instigated by Hindu nationalist activists, the police and the paramilitaries of the Rajasthan Armed Constabulary (RAC) took an active part in the killings of Muslims. The last major episode of communal violence in Jaipur took place in December 1992, after Muslim youths started assembling in Ramganj to protest the destruction of the Babri Masjid. The police and the RAC responded by firing on the crowd and around eighty people were killed—again, mostly Muslims.[15]

RAMGANJ, JAIPUR

The Aftermath of the Riots: From Profession-based Mohallas to Religious Localities

Although spatial segregation based on professions already existed in the city under princely rule, as detailed at the beginning of the chapter, this violence reshaped boundaries around communal identities, making segregation much more pronounced. In this section, I focus on the reshaping of the cityscape after the riots, with particular emphasis on Ramganj, my principal field site.

The process of spatial segregation based on religious lines evolved in various phases. It started in the early 1980s with the wave of urbanisation under the Jaipur Development Authority (JDA). New neighbourhoods developed in and around the city were given either Hindu or Muslim names, depending on the religion of the predominant population. For instance, Sita Rampuri colony in the Hida ki mori area of the walled city is Hindu dominated; Muslims inhabit localities named after Muslim or Islamic personalities: Kidwai Nagar, Karbala, Hasanpura, Madeena Masjid, Haji Abdul Rehman Colony. A Hindu working class neighbourhood is increasingly referred to as '*basti*': banjara basti, harijan basti, etc. The act of naming neighbourhoods on religious lines was in itself a way to restrict a certain population within rigidly demarcated boundaries, thus making its identification easier.

Second, the riots reinforced the institutional segregation of the JDA. Overall, due to fear of violence, Muslims moved out of Hindu dominated areas after the riots to settle in Muslim-majority localities. Many mixed neighbourhoods have turned into all-Muslim and/or all-Hindu localities. For instance, Rishi Ghalav Nagar, a residential area outside the walled city, which developed in the 1980s and housed a sizeable affluent Muslim population, had hardly any Muslim houses left after 1990. Middle-class Baniyas and Brahmins now occupy this locality.

Besides Rishi Ghalav Nagar, Ramganj and Ghat Darwarza were also badly hit Muslim neighbourhoods. The Muslims who had moved to other residential areas situated outside the Old City walls came back to the already crowded walled city after the riots, like in Hyderabad a decade before. This development affected middle-class Muslims too. For instance, one of the respondents, Anwar Shah, who currently runs a Muslim girls' school, moved to the Char Darwaza area of the Old City from Gopalbari, an upper-class Hindu neighbourhood. Apart from the walled city, Hasanpura and Sikar House located in east Jaipur, areas north of the Jaipur–Delhi Highway saw an influx of Muslims. Shastri Nagar and Bhatta Basti colony have also become Muslim-majority localities in the 1990s.

Today, most Ramganj residents do not move to other areas and if they do so it is in the safer confines of adjacent neighbourhoods such as Amritpuri and Ghat Gate—which, owing to their proximity to the walled city, can be considered an extension of the latter. A sense of community and security prevails in these Muslim settlements. And whereas Hindus live both in the poverty stricken and in the affluent areas of the city, Muslims are generally confined to poor areas (with the notable exception of Kidwai Nagar and Mansarovar). However, the grouping of Muslims in the spatially constricted Old City cannot be completely attributed to a search for security in numbers. The Muslim population depends on the Old City for its economic survival. Being the hub of the semi-precious stone industry and the grain trade, the walled city is also a place of professional opportunities. Moreover Muslims consider the walled city as their own space. The spatial concentration of their community is not always perceived as a disadvantage but also as a strength.

In the case of the walled city, a predominantly Muslim area, outward movement mainly involved Hindus. Thus, Kolis fled *mohalla* Koliyan, currently dominated by Muslims. Amritpuri colony (Ghat Gate), which lies outside the walled city and close to the National Highway no. 8, was a Hindu-majority Balmiki area. In the 1980s, owing to the neighbourhood's proximity to the walled city and its location on the Delhi-Uttar Pradesh route, many Muslims settled down here. During the 1990 communal riots, Hindu Dalits were attacked by Ansari Muslims. Following which, many Dalit and Hindu families sold their houses to Muslims and moved to other locations. The existing houses in the locality are strictly divided on the basis of religious lines. There are a few Dalit lanes, beyond which lay the Muslim area, with the exception of a few lower-caste Hindu houses. Hindus also moved out of another area around Char Darwaza, which is now dominated by Muslim migrants.

Certain mixed neighbourhoods saw the formation of caste and religion-based pockets within their existing boundaries. In mixed areas usually inhabited by lower-caste Hindu and Muslim migrants, the streets or roads between the localities act as borders. Thus, I was often warned by my Hindu respondents not to venture into 'Muslim territory':

'If you listen to me do not go to that side... Muslims live in that area, they are not nice... if something happens to you we are not responsible... these people have no respect for others. If someone harasses you, we will not be able to help'.

(M, 21 years old, Hindu, sweeper)

RAMGANJ, JAIPUR

Muslims Today: Muslim Population & Representation

According to the 2001 Census, Rajasthan accounts for 8.7% of India's Muslim population. Fifteen districts in Rajasthan have 9% or above Muslim population, with Jaipur district at 9–8%. In Jaipur, the growth rate of Muslim population is slightly but consistently higher than that of Hindus. The majority of this population lives in and around the walled city. As 7% of the total JMC population[16] lives in the walled city, the area recorded the highest population density in the city at 58,207 persons/sq km. Some Muslim-dominated areas of Jaipur include Ramganj, Ghat Darwaza, Ramnagar, Jalupura, Bhatta Basti (Shastri Nagar), Hameed Nagar, Chandpur and Topkhana. Jalupura is one of the thickly Muslim populated localities in the city. Hasanpura and Sikar House localities and some parts of Sanganer and Bagru also have an important Muslim presence. There is a growing population of migrant Muslims from Bangladesh and other parts of India and this population has settled in recently developed migrant *katchi basti* (slums) in other parts of Jaipur—Sanjay Nagar Bhatta Basti, Jawahar Nagar Kachhi Basti—and in parts of rural Jaipur.

Table 3.1. Area and population of the walled city

Total Area (sq km)	Total Population 1991 (Million)	Total Population 2001 (Million)	% JDA Population 1991	% JDA Population 2001
6.7	0.5	0.4	26.4	15.0

The 2001 Census data shows that the population of the walled city has declined from 1991. The outward movement of inhabitants is attributed to the violence unleashed in the walled city during the communal riots and to the desire for a better living environment in the new residential colonies being developed on the periphery.

The presence of Muslims in politics and in the administration is not representative of their share of the population. In terms of political representation, Rajasthan has so far elected two Muslims members of Parliament (MP)—both from the Indian National Congress (INC)—but none of them belonged to Jaipur city. The state has had a Muslim, Barkatullah Khan, as Chief Minister. A native of Jodhpur, he first served in the state cabinet as Deputy Minister (1957–62), rising to the ranks of cabinet minister (1962–67) and then Chief Minister (1971–73). None of the six Muslim elected representatives from Jaipur have been inducted into the state cabinet yet. Constituencies in the city continue to be dominated and represented by Hindu upper castes.

Two trends have recently been observed in the municipal elections. First, a fall in the percentage of elected Muslim representatives has been recorded from 15.71% in 2004 to 10.38% in 2009, a deprivation partly attributed to the delimitation exercise. With six corporators, four women and two men, the INC is today the party with the largest number of elected Muslim representatives. Two elected representatives are independent candidates. Muslim votes were particularly decisive in the victory of Congress mayoral candidate Jyoti Khandelwal, who hails from the walled city area.

Official data establishes the under-representation of Muslims in various government sectors. A closer look at Muslim employees in the elite state civil services,[17] comprising the Rajasthan Administrative Service (RAS), the Rajasthan Police Service (RPS) and the Rajasthan Secretariat Service (RSS), indicates that Muslim under-representation is acute. At present, Muslims comprise 2.26% of the officers in RSS, 4.37% in RAS and 3.38% in RPS. The percentage of Muslim judges (past and present) in the Rajasthan High Court

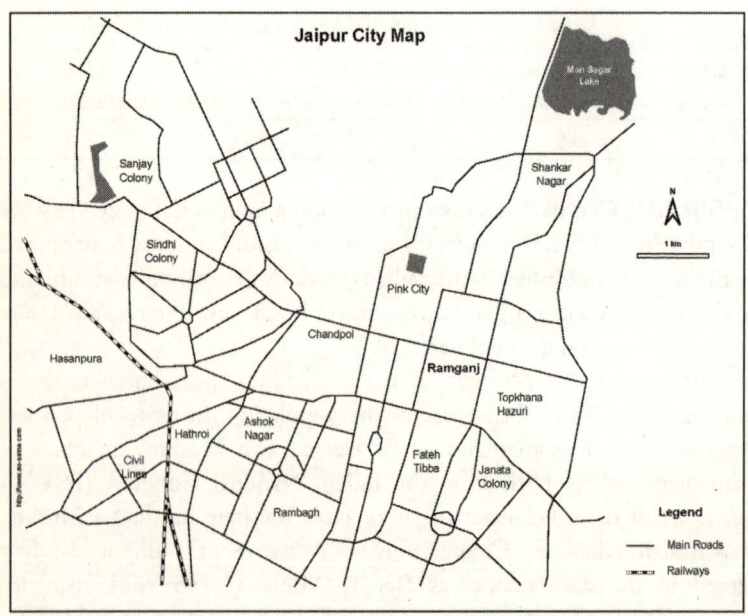

Map of Jaipur

stands at 4.31%. Rajasthan has never had a Muslim as Chief Justice in the High Court. The percentage of Muslim members in the Rajasthan High Court Bar Association is 5–23%.

The Transformation of Ramganj

A late addition to the five bazars initially planned for the city, Ramganj lies on the eastern periphery of the walled city. It sits between the Badi chaupar and the Galta road; its edges are delimited by Johari Bazar to the west and by the ramparts lined with three massive entry gates: Char Darwaza to the north, Sanganeri gate (Suraj Pol) to the east and the Ghat gate (Ram Pol) to the south. At first glance, it appears to be a crowded market area but beneath this chaotic place lies a well-organised and structured city. A city within the city of Jaipur that has its own set of institutions: *madrasas,* mosques, community welfare associations, professions, shops, etc. But Ramganj is also a neighbourhood that is now synonymous with Hindu-Muslim tensions.

The area is predominately Muslim but other religious groups like Hindus and Sikhs also have a limited presence. The Muslim population traces its presence in the city to anywhere between 100 to 300 years. Furthermore, the Muslims are not a homogenous group and can be divided on the basis of sect, caste and class. They are Shias and Sunnis, and are articulate about their beliefs, rituals, and religiosity. In contrast with Sunnis, the Shia minority, which is concentrated near the Char Darwaza area, is well integrated into Jaipur society. Shias are educated and hold important posts as university professors, teachers, government servants, etc. Also, a fair number of migrant Muslims from Uttar Pradesh and other Muslim-dominated districts of Rajasthan like Sikar, Karauli and Dhaulpur, etc. have settled along the fringes of Ramganj and in adjoining areas such as Char Darwaza, Idgah, Amritpuri Colony (a neighbourhood inhabited by traders in the semi-precious stone industry).

Reflecting demographic patterns, there is a somewhat larger proportion of residents with low education and high school drop outs, working in the low-income self-employed sector. The broad occupation categories include unskilled casual labourers (construction workers, labourers in industry, lime and stone quarry workers, daily wage earners); skilled workers (carpenters, painters, sanitary fitters, electricians, carpet factory workers); vehicle drivers (rickshaw-pullers, autorickshaw drivers, cart-pullers, taxi drivers and hotel boys); artisans (gem industry workers, embroidery workers, bangle workers, folk artists, handicraft workers); self-employed workers (shopkeepers, hawkers, vegetable vendors, cycle repairers, garage workers); government employees.

The following survey[18] was carried out in four blocks which fall under the jurisdiction of Ramganj Police Station, namely Chowkri Ghat gate, Chowkri Ramchandraji, Chowkri Ganga Pol and Chowkri Topkhana Hazuri. Muslims there constitute 70% of the population. Hindus and Sikhs make up the rest. In terms of infrastructure, the neighbourhood has main markets, hospitals, a dispensary, a post office, offices of political parties and schools, all within a distance of 1–2 km.

- Chowkri Gangapol: includes ward[19] 49 and 50. The population of this *chowkri* is about 60,000 of which 32,000 are Hindus, 24,000 Muslims and around 4,000 Sikhs.
- Chowkri Ghat gate consists of municipal wards 44 and 45. It has a population of about 150,000, including 75,000 Hindus and 30,000 Muslims. Therefore, Muslims make up 30% and Hindus 70% of the total population. The *chowkri* is home to an affluent Baniya community. Most jewellers have their *gaddi* (headquarter) in this *chowkri*. The Muslims mostly live near the Kharadiyon ki Masjid and Bisatiyon ka Mohallah. The communally sensitive areas of this chowkri include the Ghosiyon ka rasta, Regaron ki kothi, Kawantiyon ki pipali, Chokwri bardar ka bagh.
- Chowkri Ramchandraji is a square shaped area measuring about 2.5 sq km and includes wards 56 and 57. It has an almost equal proportion of Hindus and Muslims—approximately 45% each. The Ghora Nikas Road that runs from Char Darwaza to Ramganj Chaupar houses workshops for gem polishing, shops selling electrical equipment for weddings, cattle fodder and others catering to the daily needs of the residents. Muslims in this *chowkri* are mainly engaged in *varq saji* (silver and gold leaf making) (Singh, 2003).
- Chowkri Topkhana Hazuri, once a place for artillery workers, is now inhabited by workers of the gems and semi-precious stone industry. Spread over an area of 3x3 sq km, it includes wards 46 and 47, linked through squares (about 15) and narrow winding lanes. 90% of the households are Muslim. Most residents work in the gemstone industry.

In this section, I look at everyday activities and experiences of the residents to see what these could tell us about the marginalisation of Muslims living in the historical area of Ramganj. I do this by observing not only inter-ethnic (Hindu-Muslim) relations but also intra-ethnic (Muslim-Muslim) relations, with a particular focus on two occupational groups: artisans (mostly shoemakers, dyers, ironsmiths) and workers in the gemstone industry. Secondly, by analysing state-Muslim relations, I argue that what may appear as the reorganization of social structures within the Muslim community groups in the absence of the state is in fact a state's contribution to the marginality of the Muslim population.

Everyday Life in Ramganj

Everyday life in Ramganj mainly revolves around small-scale industries characterised by low capital investment, increasing prices, absence of trade unions, heavy reliance on middlemen, the uncertain supply of raw materials, earning by the piece, and the difficulty of achieving economies of scale beyond a point. The artisans are part of a multilayered vertical and hierarchical system of production. In the house of Gulshan Bano, a 21-year-old housewife who belongs to the Rehmani (*mochi,* shoemaker) community, the entire family is involved in the manufacture of leather shoes. She was pursuing a Masters in Urdu literature and living with her illiterate parents, a sister and two brothers at the time of the interview. The family starts work at 9 am and except for an hour's break for lunch, work goes on until 6.30–7 pm. Friday is chosen to take a day off work; interviews with this family were generally conducted on Fridays. The women generally prepare the embroidery for the shoe with the help of a machine and then stitch them on to a soft sole prepared by the men. The embroidered part is then pasted on to a rubber or leather sole by the men folk. The men also do the cutting of rubber soles. It takes them a week to prepare a lot of 125 shoes. Occasionally, when there is too much work, a temporary worker is hired. The family makes shoes for children that are sold to a local vendor at 30–40 Rs per piece. There are around 10–12 wholesalers of the Rehmani community and almost everyone sells their produce to them. The vendor in turn sells them to shops in Mumbai and the Gulf countries. When the women are not working on the shoes, they engage in embroidery work on saris and dupattas for local shopkeepers. On average, they make around 500–700 Rs a month through this work. They are nevertheless accustomed to insecurity at the daily level and to periodic slumps in business. Once a year, the men travel to Nainital to sell their shoes at a higher price.

The gemstone industry also occupies a central role in the life of the neighbourhood. Gemstone work was made famous under princely rule and continued to grow until the 1980s. The industry mainly deals with the processing of stones (cutting and polishing) and the setting in jewellery and is characterised by numerous small, fragmented and unorganized players engaged in small-scale craft based production. Many artisan communities (Teerandaz, Mahawat,

Cheetahwallah, Kamnigar, etc.) who lost their traditional occupation at the end of princely rule shifted to the gemstone industry. Others followed, attracted by the prospects of rapid upward social mobility. Figures on the number of workers involved in this industry and their earnings are uncorroborated. Estimates suggest that 85% of gem workers in Jaipur are Muslim, and the remaining 15% Hindu. The industry also employs children, especially in the polishing of stones. Workers earn anything between 50 to 1,000 Rs a day, depending on their skills and experience. The Hindu minority in this trade however controls the industry. Mujahid Naqvi, Media Secretary of All India Milli Council, Rajasthan, points out:

'Although the trade is controlled by Hindus, Muslims also made a lot of money. But after the riots in 1989, our business was affected. There was less trust between Hindus and Muslims. Trust is very important in this sector: the entire business runs on trust. Many Muslim traders then started their own business in other countries, they started going to the Middle East, Bangkok, Brazil, Africa to buy the raw material directly'.

In Chowkri Ramchandra Ji, there are about 150 workshops spread out across the area in groups of twos and threes, mostly involved in cutting and polishing work on emerald, coral and ruby stones. This work does not require a lot of space and is run through cramped, small workshops with usually two to eight workers. Gemstone carving work is also carried out here, but in comparatively bigger workshops and better working conditions. The ratio of Hindu and Muslim workers is 1:3. In Topkhana Hazuri entire families are employed.

'Most gem stone workshops are family-run, like ours, so we work at home, and then we sell the stones to *dalals* [middlemen] at Ghat Gate who sell it to Hindu traders in Gopal jikarasta. This area is a Muslim area, where a lot of skilled craftsmen and families live'.

(Ramzan Bhai, 43-year-old, gemstone dealer)

As one *ustad* (master craftsman) pointed out, 'Muslims have taught this work to the Hindus but Hindus have taken over, as they are more educated than us. Today, many big merchants prefer Hindu artisans to Muslims'.

Poverty and mobility of workers between the informal and the formal sectors is mostly attributed to global economic slowdown following the Gulf War in 1990, which contributed to higher unemployment, poorer working conditions and lower wages. Yet, poverty is not considered as the failure of government policies, though residents mention that the state did not come to their rescue and has not done much to improve their condition. Haji Abdul Jabbar, a 78-year-old resident narrates:

RAMGANJ, JAIPUR

'There is no work since the Gulf War. Those who have been in the business for more than fifty years and the wholesalers are still making money but for people like us there is nothing. My son had to remove half of the labour a few years back and now he has completely stopped working in *nagina* (precious stones). Last year, he opened a dairy booth. This is not our profession, we are skilled people but we also have to feed our family'.

The severe economic pressure in the semi precious stone industry resulted in the emigration of many local Muslims to the Middle East, giving rise to a new elite from the subaltern group since, on their return from the Middle East, they run employment centres, remittance services and visa facilities for the Gulf countries.

The residential patterns of the artisans vary depending on the prosperity of the owner and are not necessarily occupation-dependent, as was the case in the earlier days. The traditional setup of *haveli* structures exists in some parts of the area but the majority has been split due to growing families and divisions between family members. The result then resembles a tall and narrow set of matchbox-like structures, usually consisting of a room with an open or enclosed *verandah* and very likely a latrine on one side. The *verandah* quite often doubles as kitchen, sitting room for the guests and working space. A similar arrangement is found over four to five floors, each connected by a dark narrow stairway and each occupied by a family. Little or no furniture is kept except for some plastic chairs, cots standing up during the day, and trunks and cupboards of storage. However, some newly constructed homes of rich businessmen, built in Islamic style of architecture with carved arches resting on pillars used in colonnade, have a separate room or floor which works as *karkhana* or factory. The house may become elaborated with the multiplication of floors, rooms, and a courtyard guarded by high walls with large iron gates and fancy cars parked inside. With the use of Islamic architecture for Muslim houses, a relatively new feature in the neighbourhood, Muslims try to claim their own legitimate space alongside the already existing *haveli* structures in the region.

The grip of religion on the Muslim population is certainly growing. It is primarily among the adult generation between the ages of 20 and 30 that a renewed interest for the teachings of Islam is developing. The *madrasas* and mosques are increasingly making visual and social claims on the public space. These places doubled up as space for political expression and the reaffirmation of civic rights, especially in the wake of the elections held in April-May 2009 where community and religious leaders urged Muslims to vote for a particular candidate or party and to enrol for the census count. Many assemble and socialise in the mosques, which are considered ideal places for social networking and public awareness. In the words of Anwar Shah, the Director of Al Jamea tul Aaliyah Girls school:

'A whole social group develops in the mosque. As you know, Friday prayers, *johar namaz*, is very important for the Muslims, every Muslim attends this prayer. If I have a scooter problem... there is a mechanic, I will ask him to help me. We also use this occasion to educate people through *khutba* (address), tell them about various government policies and schemes concerning them. Regarding education, we have informed them about scholarship programmes. Recently, we asked them to enrol in the population census, identity card scheme, etc. As women cannot attend mosques, they are educated through their men who come here for prayers'.

Social Order in Ramganj

To begin with, the *mohalla.* emerges as a set of contact zones between various occupational groups. My fieldwork coincided with the monsoons, and the hues of red, blue and orange dyes which mixed in the overflowing drains not only indicated the geographical location of the *nilgar* (dyer) quarters, *nallah nilgaran,* but also gave an idea of the colour patterns and dyes each dyer specialised in. Similarly, a particularly synchronous beating sound around 5pm would indicate the *mohalla* Pannigaran (silver foil maker). In Topkhana Hazuri the sound of machines used for cutting and polishing gemstones can be heard. It is then important to draw attention to the social ordering of various groups in the area. This social fragmentation does not only occur along religious lines but also along lines of caste, kinship, clan, class, etc. However, it should be emphasised that social hierarchies are not static. Among Muslims, collective attempts at upward social mobility take the shape of 'ashrafisation', through which subaltern castes claim a higher status than their actual one by invoking a (largely imaginary) prestigious genealogy.

Thus, butchers (*khatik*) and metal beaters (*paledar*) designate themselves as 'Qureshis' (members of the tribe of the Prophet), weavers as 'Ansaris' (descendants of the hosts of the Prophet in Medina),[20] quilt-makers (*pinari*) as 'Mansooris', shoemakers *(mocha)* as 'Rehmanis'[21] etc. Here as in the rest of India, alleged Arabic origins are seen as a vehicle towards collective upward social mobility.[22] Nonetheless, an inquiry into the adopted names reveals a contrasting story. Most people are not aware of how the name change came about. They have internalised the Islamic names to such an extent that it appears as a natural identity that has existed for generations. According to others, name change is a recent trend which took place around twenty to thirty years ago to organise and distance themselves from the migrant and former elite groups. As a member of a prosperous Muslim dyer family pointed out:

'With economic prosperity and growing fame of our community, migrants from the regions of Bihar and Bengal started to come in. They learnt our work and opened their own firms. They started to call themselves *nilgar*. It was necessary to distinguish ourselves from the outsiders; it was also necessary to protect our girls. How can we marry our girls to someone from outside ? Thus, we organised the *nilgars* and formed the Rangrez[23] society'.

Secondly, the artisan castes started to organise themselves socially by reviving the *biraderi*[24] system which is based on the principle of submitting a certain amount of one's individuality for the community. These parochial structures have tremendous influence on the social and economic life of its members. There is very little mixing between *biraderis*, a *manihar* (banglemaker) once told me:

'Though the government pays up to 50,000 rupees to encourage inter religion marriages, even today, 95% of people marry within their *biraderi*. I think it [the government policy] is very good for national unity but we do not encourage this policy. We will be ostracised by the community' (*Humara hookah-paani band ho jaayega*).

In the wake of the economic slowdown, this system contributes to a relative homogenisation of products within each *biraderi* ensuring employment for everyone without eating into the earnings of another. Today almost every family specialises in one style or pattern. For instance, if one *Rehmani* (shoemaker) family makes *nagara* shoes for children, another family would probably make the same for adults; also the type of embroidery used by one family would not be similar to that of another family in the same profession. It is the same for the *Rangrez* (dyer): if one family specialises in dyeing *dupattas* and scarves, another would specialise in tying of threads around the scarves which forms the base pattern for dyeing. Also, the type of dyeing and the choice of material dyed vary from one family to another.

These *biraderis* gave birth to *biraderi panchayats* or welfare committees. These are not only the guardians of Islamic values and morals but also work as an alternative 'social security system'. They are authorised to make and enforce rules binding every person within the jurisdiction of the clan. In some *biraderis* like the Rangrez and Pannigar (silver foil maker) they usually meet once a month, and in others (Lauhar, Rehmani), they meet whenever required, to resolve community matters. Referring to the importance of community structures, 43-year-old Chand Bhai, who belongs to a family of dyers of the Royal family, and is Vice President of the BJP's minority wing and Rangrez society leader told me that:

'Disputes within the group are settled by the *biraderi panchayat*. Why should we go to the police? There has never been a need to call the police. The *biraderi* members often know the people involved in a dispute which makes counselling easier. It also lessens the burden of the police force. They want fewer cases so in a way the *biraderi* is helping the police and the administration'.

A constable from Ramganj Manila Thana confirmed:

'Many times we cannot interfere because the victim does not want to register a case. So, even if it is a murder we cannot do anything, we have to follow the law. We also have instructions to solve cases amicably as far as possible because legal matters involve spending a lot of money and these people cannot afford it. Once the dispute is put before the *biraderi*, they will outcast the person if the person decides to come to the police or go to the court'.

It is not surprising then that political parties collude with the *biraderi* system, making it indispensable to fight a political battle. Furthermore, during the riots of 1990, the *panchayats* were instrumental not only in organising Muslim groups against the Hindus but also in ensuring peace in certain parts of Ramganj.

Interestingly, these structures are mostly present among lower-caste Muslims. The main reason for this trend, according to my informants, would be the will to educate and uplift these subaltern occupational groups. With respect to upper-caste Muslims and new migrant groups belonging to the same religious category, the occupational groups experience constant distancing. As a result, there is a progressive narrowing of their relations not only with the Hindu community but also with other Muslim groups. The upper-caste groups—the descendants of *nawabs* and courtly service classes—on the other hand, reject casteism and promote a more universalist Muslim identity. They characterise the *biraderis* as backward, manner-less, crude, and uncultured. In the words of Arif, an Urdu teacher whose family migrated from Mysore to Jaipur during princely rule:

'In the past years, the artisans have made money. But money does not get *saleeka* (manners). They still do not know how to talk. They speak the "athey-kathey" language (refers to the local dialect spoken in the region). You must have noticed the difference in the way we speak and the way they speak? (referring to their Urdu accent) they will say *"jer-jabar"* instead of *"zer-zabar"*'.

Anvaar Bhai Netaji, a 76-year-old former BJP ward councillor who belongs to the marginalised Silawatan[25] community notes that the animosity is mutual:

'Gone are the days when these nawabs ruled over us. They have exploited us for almost a century, now it's our turn. What do they know about us?'

Finally, as *biraderis* have differing motivations and political affiliations, they fail to unite to form a pan-religious identity. The shift in professions or divergent religious belief has been observed as a point of discord. *Kalals* (former winemakers), for example, are disliked by the *Rehmanis* (shoemakers) as they partly control *nagara*[26] shoe export.

At times, sub-ethnic and sub-sectarian rivalries are intertwined and differences between the communities can operate at both levels. For instance, Ansaris, former weavers, and one of the most prosperous groups among Muslims in Jaipur, shifted to the semi-precious stone business in the 1970s. Today, they control a major part of this trade in the city after the Hindu merchants. They do not let other occupational groups, even Muslims, work in this trade. According to a respondent, 'Ansaris only help Ansaris'. The parochialism attributed to this community has nurtured the resentment of lower-caste Muslim labourers. The Noorani mosque incident in Amritpuri,[27] near Ghat Gate, is a case in point.

Amritpuri is home to the affluent Ansaris, who make up the majority of the Muslim population. Most of them are Barelwi Sunnis. Their allegiance to this particular school translates through visual symbols like green flags hurled atop their houses, green turbans, etc. 'These things were not present fifteen to twenty years back but these *hari pagriwallas* [men with green turban] have changed the ways of Islam', said a local Kayamkhani leader. The remaining Muslims of the colony consist of labourers belonging to other caste groups such as Lauhars, Qureshis, Kayamkhanis, etc., most of which follow the (Sunni) Deobandi creed.

The Noorani Masjid is the only mosque in the area for both sects. On 20 February 2008, during *Johar* (afternoon) prayers violence broke out in the mosque vicinity. Since the regular *muezzin* was absent another person was calling out the *azaan* (call for prayer). A few people objected to this person calling out the *azaan*. This was followed by heated exchanges between the two sects. Muslims who had gathered in the mosque for prayers came out on the roads and hurled stones at each other. Some had come with swords and *tamancha* (knife). Stones were also pelted on the crowd from the roofs of nearby houses and two motorcycles and a few kiosks were torched. Forty people were injured, two of them seriously.[28] The police had to use force and tear gas to control the mob. RAF[29] (Rapid Action Force) was called in for a fortnight to prevent further escalation of violence. Twenty people from both sides were rounded up, though no formal case was registered against them. Later that evening, the police played an active role in reconciling both sects.

The reasons for violence stemmed not only from ideological differences between the two sects but also from the economic rivalry between the different Muslim caste groups found in the neighbourhood. According to some sources, the main reason for the heated exchanges had been the *Itjema.* (congregation) organised by the Tablighi Jama'at at Jamia Hidayat (the largest residential *madarasa* in Jaipur), which was held earlier that week. It is reportedly one of the biggest *Itjema.* in the country and is considered to be second only to the *Haj.* People from all over the country attended the *Ijtema.* Barelwis had reportedly objected to Tablighi Jama'at's sermons at the congregation, while other residents believed that it was a premeditated attempt at threatening the poor Muslims of the area. They even linked their position as victim to the Hindu victims of 1989–90 riots in Jaipur. Abdul Kadir Netaji, a local leader who passed away recently, recounted, 'Ansaris had also attacked *Harijans* of this area during the 1990 riots. They had the support of other Ansaris living in the walled city. All of them had come into the neighbourhood through the *Mori* (gate) to kill the Hindus'. This animosity that appears foremost economic in nature, although not visible in daily interactions, has taken the shape of inter-sect or intra-religious violence in the last few years.

Hindu-Muslim Relations

Irrespective of sub-ethnic identities, Hindu-Muslim relations have led to the creation of an overarching religious identity, that of 'Miyan,'[30] 'Mohammedan' or 'Mussalman', over the above-mentioned distinct *biraderi* identities. *Miyan* is a derogatory term used by Hindus to refer to Muslims. But the ascriptive *miyan* identity has been partly internalised in some parts and often appeared as a self-designation. Many residents referred to themselves as belonging to the 'Miyan' or 'Mohammedan' community.

The increasing physical and social distance between the Muslim populations and the rest of the city also alters the way the Hindu and Muslim groups look at each other. It is not uncommon to meet residents who have travelled to other cities but have never been to other parts of Jaipur. Many residents, especially women, did not know the location of Bani Park, the area where I lived in at the time of fieldwork. While the cordial nature of Hindu-Muslim relations is common knowledge in the older generation, the younger generation would always badmouth Hindus and vice-versa. Among the Hindus, most people interviewed had no or very limited interactions with the Muslims. They did not have Muslim friends. A few had Muslim colleagues at work. A similar situation emerged in Muslim narratives on the Hindus.

'I have studied in the neighbourhood Rehmani School, most students there are from the Muslim community, I have never had Hindu friends. I never got a chance. But it doesn't mean that I do not want to make 'non Muslim'[31] friends. We would like to make some friends but circumstances have never permitted so...'

(Gulshan Bano, 21 years old, Muslim housewife and MA Urdu literature student)

These alterations point to decreasing opportunities for social interaction between the two groups. However, in some cases interaction is unavoidable and need-based, like in the case of the Hindu controlled semi precious stone industry. The everyday communal tensions feed on and nurture stereotypes about the 'other' which are then manifested as problems arising from a growing population and spatial concentration of the Muslim population.

During my fieldwork I was suffering from nasal congestion, which was often received with remarks such as 'Oh that is the reason you do not have a problem going to Ramganj, you cannot smell anything'. Another respondent remarked that it is political and religious issues, rather than economic and social ones, which energise Muslim activism in the country.

'They would do anything for their religion. It is the only thing that motivates them. Take the example of Muslim groups who protested because they do not want their children to sing Hindi prayers at schools, a demand all but unknown among other religious groups. Our [Hindu] children willingly learn 'Our Father' in missionary schools!'

(M, 43 years old, Hindu)

Muslim narratives, for their part, project the community as a victim not only of Hindu conspiracies but also of international campaigns of vilification in the aftermath of 9/11. As Nishat Hussain, a female activist states *'Mussalman ka koi bhala nahi chahta* (Muslims have no well-wishers), 'Muslims have always been harassed'. 'They give a bad name to Muslims. No religion preaches ill of the other religion'. Secondly, these narratives often make a claim to citizenship, by putting forward communal interests through the established channels of civic and political life and at the same time proving their loyalty to the nation. The Muslims feel that Hindus do not welcome them as Indian, but discriminate against them and treat them as second-class citizens. Antique dealer Sadiq had the song *'Saarey jahan se achcha* (a patriotic song promoting a united India where all religious differences are forgotten) set as ring tone to his cellphone. During the interview he repeatedly asked, 'Aren't we Indians?'

'Muslims have played an important role. The *madrasas* were involved in the struggle against the British. Now they are labelled as terrorists'.

(Sadiq, 45 years old, Muslim, businessman)

Narratives of partiality on behalf of the majority Hindus are invoked.

'My son studies in Seedling school. During a class, his teacher asked Muslim students to raise their hands...there were three. The teacher then said that Muslim *badshahs* who ruled the country were the bad guys. The other children laughed. My son was really upset. This feeling of hatred is not only in the Muslims, even Hindus feel it. But since it's your country you would not talk about it yourself'.

'In your culture, cow piss is sprinkled for purification, if you cross paths with a Muslim'. [When I expressed my surprise over it, she insisted] 'Yes, yes, they do it... You live abroad, you would not know these things'.

(Saba Javed, 36 years old, Muslim, housewife)

After 1990, Jaipur figures on the map of communally sensitive cities and the state police is now armed with an anti riot-squad to counter communal tensions. Moreover, policing in violence-affected areas, which also happen to be Muslim areas, has increased. The boundaries of police jurisdiction have been redrawn and the number of police stations and outposts increased. Breaking with the usual tradition, Independence Day celebrations at Ramganj Chaupar is presided over the head of the state police instead of the district administrative head. In this context, local Muslims feel that their religion, culture, language, institutions, etc. are in danger, that they do not have a 'public space' and that whatever public space that exists is monopolised by religious institutions. The only institutionalised public space revolves around the *Shanti Samiti* or the peace initiatives started after the 1990 riots by the Ramganj police station. Although they have been effective in maintaining peace, residents consider them as a way of confining their population. Second, they have helped widen the clientelistic net as committee members are chosen from among opinion leaders, social workers, retired persons, local politicians and businessmen.

Conclusion

Muslims in Ramganj date their association with Jaipur back to its founding years and take pride in their contribution to the city's art and semi-precious stone and jewellery industry. They show a very strong emotional attachment and sense of belonging to the city. However, as detailed in the earlier sections of this chapter, the boundaries of their city are often set around the walled city area and a few Muslim neighbourhoods outside the Old City. Social interaction with other religious groups is limited and problems of hygiene, poverty, education, and unemployment abound, which have earned a bad name for the neighbourhood. Most respondents have been confronted with a negative reputation of their neighbourhood in different aspects of their own lives. The residents live under fear of attack, reprisal and anxiety about being on the outside and isolated. To counter this somewhat bleak scenario the lower-caste Muslims have started mobilising themselves to address issues in the field of education and politics by starting schools and creating their own political party. Though these nascent organisations remain fragile and will have to earn official recognition to exert more than sporadic and punctual pressure, considerable gain has been registered in terms of access to education and political awareness among this community.

4

A MINORITY WITHIN A MINORITY

THE SHIAS OF KASHMIRI MOHALLA, LUCKNOW

Gilles Verniers

Lucknow is a city of hills and dales, where altitude once defined status. The rulers of Awadh, a Shia dynasty that established itself in the city in the late eighteenth century, distributed lands and properties—or *jagirs*—to their administrators and courtiers in the higher reaches of the hills. The commoners, labourers and orderlies of the State and the Court were concentrated in the lower parts, darker, more congested and prone to water logging.

The locality of Kashmiri Mohalla, considered in this chapter, is located at the top of a hill dominating what is now known as Lucknow West. It was founded between 1775 and 1778 by Kashmiri Pandits, who migrated to the city when Asaf-ud-Dowlah, the fourth Nawab of Awadh, shifted his capital from Faizabad to Lucknow. These Pandits, many of whom had originally been brought to Faizabad from Delhi by the third Nawab of Awadh, were highly educated and served as state administrators or tutors to the nobility. They built magnificent *havelis*, or palatial mansions, and gave their name to the locality.[1] They were soon joined by Muslims families, mostly Shias who also hailed from Kashmir, and were directly or indirectly connected to the royal family and its court, or served the Awadh State as high-ranking officials.[2]

Kashmiri Mohalla was a locality where the arts flourished. Poets and musicians were patronised and many Kashmiri Pandits contributed to the development of the arts, especially calligraphy and theatre.[3] The locality has produced renowned poets and social reformers such as Pandit Brij Narain Chakbast, who used to organise in the late nineteenth century *mushairas* ('congregations of poets' or public Urdu—or sometimes Persian—poetry recitations) of national importance. The culture of the Mohalla was in essence syncretic and drew its influences from many traditions. It was a place of exchange of ideas and cultural practices, defined more by shared intellectual and cultural interests than by the ascriptive identities of its inhabitants.[4]

In contemporary Lucknow, the locality of Kashmiri Mohalla and its immediate surroundings is known as a 'Shia ghetto' or is sometimes referred to by many, including some of its inhabitants, as a 'royal slum', where destitute nobilities and Muslims of low economic background live. The locality indeed bears the stigma of under-development, poor or non-existent public infrastructure, and remoteness from the mainstream of an otherwise growing and developing city. As we shall see in a subsequent section of this chapter, its population is socio-economically heterogeneous and shares only faith as a common trait. This commonality of faith gives the locality a sense of closure from the rest of the city, which is reinforced by the local representations about this Shia enclave.

Even if the Kashmiri Pandits left en masse long ago and were progressively replaced by Muslims of various communities, the locality only recently acquired the reputation of a Shia ghetto. An aggregate of seven localities—Hasanpuria, Najaf, Rustom Nagar, Dargah, Kazmein, Noor Bali and Tapewali Gali—all located to the west of Tulsidas Marg and adjacent to Kashmiri Mohalla, account for at least 80% of Lucknow's Shias or more. This Shia pocket is embedded in Sunni-dominated localities, between Chauk in the North, Tikaitganj in the South and Saadatganj in the East.

This spatial concentration is before all, as we shall see, the product of a recent history of dissension between Sunnis and Shias in Lucknow and of repeated episodes of violence between the two communities. Contrary to many other riot-prone cities in India, the city of Lucknow has never witnessed severe open Hindu-Muslim tensions or confrontations. However, the city has witnessed many episodes of Sunni-Shia violence that have greatly contributed to shaping the areas where the Muslims live today.

If these dissensions have existed since the turn of the twentieth century and stretch even further back, they have aggravated in the post-independence context, in terms of scale and consequences. After retracing briefly the general

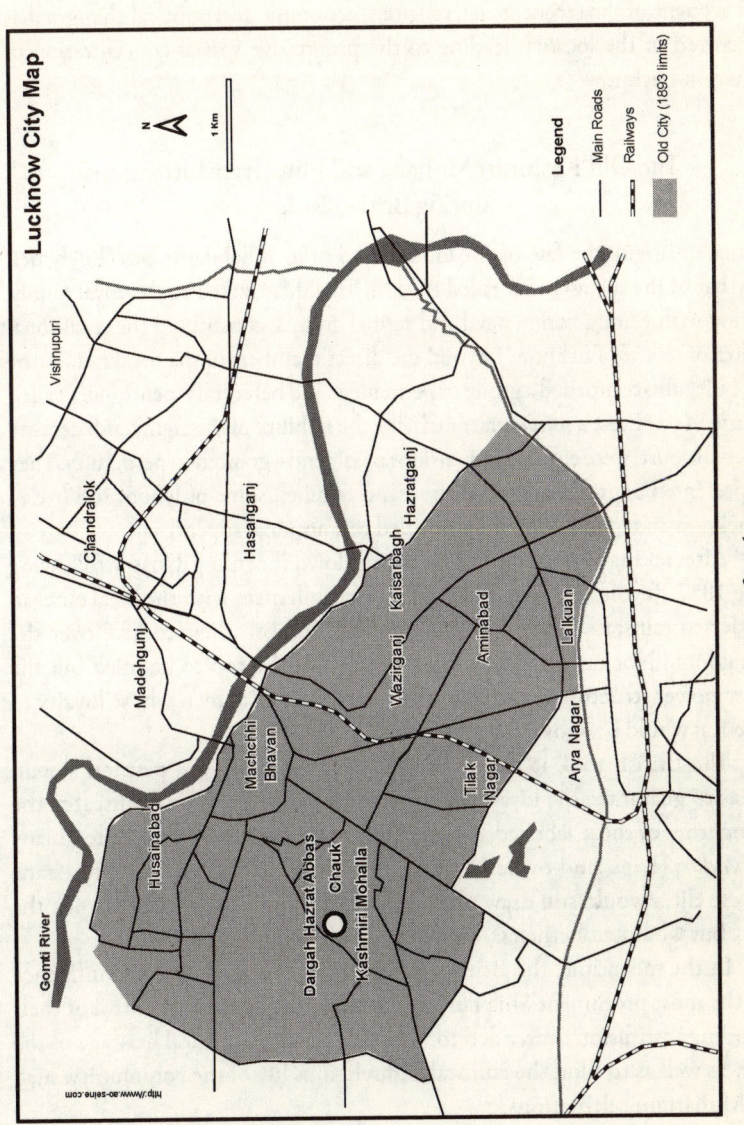

Map of Lucknow

history of the locality and providing a broad picture of the state of the Muslim population in Uttar Pradesh and in Lucknow, this chapter will attempt to give an account of the recent social, religious, economic and political changes that occurred in the locality, leading to the progressive spatial concentration of Shias in Lucknow.

The Old Kashmiri Mohalla and Elite Transformations during British Rule

Since its origin, the fate of the locality and of its inhabitants was closely tied to that of the dynasty that ruled Awadh. The Shias linked to the royal family, along with Hindu commercial and scribal groups, constituted the traditional elites of *nawabi* Lucknow. Beyond the direct members of the royal family, the nobility also comprised a group of permanent and hereditary 'pensioners' called *wasiqadars*. These *wasiqadars,* much like the nobility of the eighteenth century French court, were entitled to pensions or stipends, granted in perpetuity. They represented approximately one thousand families, some of whom still live in Lucknow today and still remain entitled to a nominal stipend.

After taking over the city and bringing down the ruling dynasty, following the 1857 Revolt, the British sought to form alliances with the local elites in order to reinstate peace and stability and establish their control over the kingdom. 'Not only had a political vacuum at the top to be filled but the new power structure required a solid buttress of local men whose loyalty to the Raj would be above question'.[5]

The British took it upon themselves to maintain the pension system so as to guarantee the loyalty of the traditional elites. They confiscated the properties of those labelled as or reputed to be 'traitors' and co-opted many *taluqdars* (large land-owners) as new pensioners or dependants of the state. These elites would still draw revenue from the land they owned outside the city but would, nonetheless, remain dependant on their new rulers.

In the meantime, the British endeavoured to undermine the influence of the most prominent Shia families of Lucknow by taking control of their funding institutions, intended to maintain the architectural heritage of the city as well as to fund the cultural and religious life of the community, such as Muharram celebrations.

The fall of the Awadh dynasty also meant that many of the households from the non-elite groups, who had lived off the profligate lifestyle of the Court, faced a severe diminution, if not a complete disappearance, of their income.

A MINORITY WITHIN A MINORITY

Many cooks, musicians, low-ranked administrators, guards, household servants, clerks, etc. lost their source of income in the great social churning that marked the beginning of the colonial period. Historians have shown that if their large landholdings entitled them to a prestigious social status, they were not necessarily a great source of income for all and were often actually a source of dispute and financial difficulties.

The *wasiqadars* who kept the trust of the British could, for a while, maintain their feudal lifestyle. This position, however, would become increasingly precarious as many of those families were confronted with steadily dwindling resources.

In this context, the Kashmiri Pandits, former administrators of Awadh, quickly adapted themselves to the new regime, switched from Persian to English and continued to serve as civil servants in the new administration. They also offered their services to the British in other parts of the Raj and started migrating from Kashmiri Mohalla. Their educated and trained background equipped them better than the Shias to face the transition and find other avenues of income and professional activity.

In 1877, the Kingdom of Oudh was annexed to the North-West Provinces, dealing a further blow to the influence of the *taluqdars* and *wasikadars* in Lucknow, now a provincial city. Many administrators, lawyers, sought employment in the new capital, Allahabad, or went farther to work in the various nerve centres of the British Empire.

The Slow Demise of Lucknow's Shias

Many prominent Shia families had been able to maintain their lifestyle after the demise of the Awadh dynasty thanks to their landholdings. Their loss and the cost of court proceedings initiated against illegal tenants or to retrieve bits of the seized properties brought many families down to poverty, and in consequence, affected also the income of the number of households that were dependant on their employ. The abolition of the *zamindari* system in 1952 dealt a direct blow to the revenues of the property-owning families who had stayed on in Lucknow. They suddenly lost the main source of their income and lost even more money in court proceedings, attempting to preserve whatever they could from their seized patrimonies. The marginalisation of Shias from state affairs and their inability to create new avenues of wealth generation kept them away from the opportunities created by the new imperial political order.

'Shias were few in the professions and fewer still in trade and commerce. The substantial group of poverty-stricken *wasiqadars* clung to the crumbling remains of their ancestral environs. Most lived in ghettos or in the narrow lanes of the old city of Lucknow and Allahabad.'

(Hasan, 1997, p. 128).

The life of Khan Prince Basharat Husain, descendant of Syed Muhamad Amin and Mirza Faghfoor Jah (Kaisar-i-Hind)[6] is illustrative of the fate shared by many prominent Shia families of Kashmiri Mohalla and its immediate surroundings.

'My grandfather, Prince Emur Jah, lived in a huge mansion, made on twenty bighas,[7] in Triveni Ganj.[8] He used to bear sword and hunt lions with Lord Curzon. We shifted to Kashmiri Mohalla in 1954, when the property was redistributed after the demise of my maternal grandfather Haji Nawab Sultan Ali Khan. This is when we shifted to Farhat Manzil, which covered an area of only three bighas. My mother married his seventh son, Khan Prince Hussain Ali. In those days, the family was very rich and had all sorts of orderlies working for them. Fifty gardeners, one hundred fifty guards (including twelve Nepali guards for Farhat Manzil alone). Fifty women also were working for them. All had their special assigned tasks [...] I grew up surrounded by women, over-protected by our female guards. I stepped out of the house for the first time on my own when I was twenty-five. I never received formal education and spent my days playing the sitar'.[9]

Income-generating activities were considered degrading and were actively discouraged by the community.

'To work was an insult. We were fixed in self-imposed glory. My grandfather had started a pharmacy and lost his status. He then withdrew from the trade and vowed to never leave his house again' ... 'My father had property in Faizabad[10] and spent a huge amount of money after independence in court procedures against illegal tenants. Money started to drain out from the claims of these illegal occupations'.

This did not prevent them however from maintaining their lifestyle and preserving their status.

'When my mother died, in 2000, food was distributed for one month. In 2002, the property was divided among the nine siblings'.

Yet, many families would go to any extent to preserve their lifestyle without overcoming their aversion for labour. Sibtey Hasan Naqvi, a political activist and social worker whose family has been long rooted in Kashmiri Mohalla recalls:

'After the Zamindari Abolition Act, the aristocracy started selling their properties in order to maintain themselves. But they were not able to sell them at correct prices. They were cheated by middlemen. Women would barter their silver-embroidered saris against money and utensils. The saris would be burned in front of their house, the silver melted and collected'.[11]

Kashmiri Pandits left the Mohalla en masse during this period. Their high level of education and the traditional occupation of public administration eased their migration. Many Kashmiri Pandits from this area and their descendants had extremely distinguished career trajectories.[12]

Representation of Muslims in Uttar Pradesh and Lucknow

26% of India's Muslim population lives in Uttar Pradesh. The share of Muslims in this state has grown from 14% to 18% between 1952 and 2009. Though numerically important (they represent more than 50% of voters in six Assembly constituencies, between 40% and 50% of voters in thirteen Assembly constituencies and between 30% and 40% of voters in twenty-five Assembly constituencies), they have—apart from a few exceptions—been under-represented at all levels (see Tables 4.1 and 4.2).

The average of Muslim representation in the Vidhan Sabha is slightly lower than that at the Lok Sabha constituency level, at 8.43% of MLAs (see Table 4.2). This average decreases even further if one does not consider the number of independent Muslim candidates elected to the Vidhan Sabha (thirty-seven independent candidates elected out of a total of 538 Muslims MLAs since 1952).

One can observe that the notable increase of Muslim candidates fielded by parties has not led to an increase in their share of representation. Their percentage of representation dropped throughout the 1990s and regained strength in the early 2000s, but with a lower conversion ratio of candidatures versus seats obtained. Among the possible reasons for this trend, one can quote the dilution of Muslim candidates among the inflation of the total number of candidates, the exclusion of Muslims from the two main political driving forces of this decade—the assertion of backward categories (post-Mandal politics) and the rise of the Hindu right. The combined effect of the polarisation of the electorate along caste as well as communal lines during the 1990s and the distorting effect of the electoral system has led to the relative marginalisation of the Muslim electorate.[13] A lower rate of participation to elections reinforces these phenomena.

The Congress and the successive avatars of the socialist parties have been the main providers of Muslim representatives to the regional assembly. In recent

Table 4.1. Muslim representation in Uttar Pradesh—Lok Sabha constituencies

Year	Number of Seats	Muslims Nominated	Muslim Members Elected	Muslim Independents Elected	Muslim Members Elected %
1952	86	11	7	–	8
1957	86	12	6	–	7
1962	86	21	5	–	9
1967	85	23	5	–	11.8
1971	85	15	6	–	7
1977	85	24	10	–	11.8
1980	85	46	18	–	21.2
1984	85	34	12	–	14.1
1989	85	48	8	1	9.4
1991	85	55	3	–	3.5
1996	85	59	6	–	7
1998	85	65	6	–	7
1999	85	68	8	–	9.4
2004	80	85	11	–	13.7
2009	80	91	6	–	7.5
Total		657	117	1	n = 9.8

Source: adapted from the Election Commission of India and Ansari, Iqbal, *Political Representation of Muslims in India.*, New Delhi: Manak Publications, 2006, p. 71.

years, the Bahujan Samaj Party has become the first party in India in terms of representation of Muslims (it currently accounts for 25 Muslim MLAs in Uttar Pradesh as well as three MPs in the Lok Sabha).

Contrary to their counterparts in Kerala or Andhra Pradesh, Muslims in Uttar Pradesh have never been able to develop a political strength of their own and have always preferred to support parties in power, likely to offer them protection from communal tensions. There were however a few cases of Muslim parties which managed to send some representatives to the regional Assembly. The Muslim Majlis, for instance, founded in 1968 by Dr. Abdul Jaleel Faridi, a former supporter of the Samyukt Vidhayak Dal, managed to get two of its members elected to the 1977 state Assembly, in alliance with the Janata Party. After the demise of its leader and the 1977 success, the party gradually declined and sank into the slump of local politics and alliance building with other Muslim political outfits.

More recently, various fronts (Peoples' Democratic Fronts, United Democratic Fronts, etc.) have been appearing on the eve of campaigns,

Table 4.2. Representation of Muslims in the Uttar Pradesh Legislative Assembly

Year	Total Seats	Muslims in the State %	Muslims Nomitated**	Muslim Members Elected	Muslim Independents Elected	Muslim Members Elected %
1951	430	14.28	138	39	2	9.53
1957	430	14.28	83	29	8	8.84
1962	430	14.63	119	30	-	6.98
1967	425	14.63	122	23	-	5.41
1969	425	15.48	156	23	6	5.41
1974	424	15.48	201	24	1	5.90
1977	425	15.48	104	46	3	11.53
1980	425	15.93	167	46	1	11.06
1985	425	15.93	188	47	2	11.53
1989	425	17.33	242	30	8	8.94
1991	419	17.33	267	16	1	4.05
1993	422	17.33	238	24	1	5.92
1996	424	17.33	224	32	1	7.78
2002	403	17.33	402	46	1	11.66
2007	403	18.02*	432	46	2	11.90
Total			3113	501	37	n = 8.43

* Sachar Committee Report data
* Independent candidates excluded
Source: adapted from the Election Commission of India and Ansari, Iqbal, *Political Representation of Muslims in India,* op. cit., p. 291.

appealing to Muslim unity under a single banner. These fronts, short-lived and electorally unsuccessful, are doomed from the beginning due to internal dissensions, by the sociology of their leadership (many of these front leaders are local or regional clerics or upper-caste Muslims who lack both the experience of political campaigns and the legitimacy to represent their co-religionists) and the fact that few Muslims actually seek a representation of their own, contrary to many other deprived social groups of the state.

It is a fact that Muslims in Uttar Pradesh, a state that has been shaken by communal violence and religious mobilisations from the Hindu Right, have generally tended to vote for the party best positioned to provide them with the protection they aspire to. The Congress was a logical choice during the first three decades after independence since it was the party in power. Growing disillusions and discontent incited them to divide their vote and support the socialists in the late 1960s. In the late 1980s and early 1990s, in the context of assertive religious mobilisation campaigns by the Bharatiya Janata Party (BJP) and decline of the Congress, they started to support the Janata Dal/Samajwadi Party led by Mulayam Singh Yadav, helping the party to govern the state on three occasions.

Over the past decade, the mainstream parties in Uttar Pradesh—barring the Bharatiya Janata Party—have attempted to enlarge their electoral base to the minorities, thus nominating more Muslim candidates. As a result and in a context of great electoral uncertainty, the Muslim vote has recently tended to split among parties. Many seats being won with narrow margins, the importance of the Muslim vote increased. In the 2009 general elections, a fraction of the Muslim vote certainly helped the Congress to win the necessary votes to outstrip the BJP.[14]

Table 4.3. Representation of Muslims in Uttar Pradesh Lok Sabha Constituencies—Party-wise

	1991	1996	1998	1999	2004	2009
Congress	1	1	–	2	–	3
JD/SP	2	4	2	2	6	–
BSP	–	1	3	3	4	3
Others	–	–	1	1	1	1
Total	3	6	6	8	11	6

Source: adapted from the Election Commission of India, op. cit.

The under-representation of Muslims in the Assembly can also be observed in the composition of the state Cabinet. Between 1952 and 1999, on an average, 10.6% of Cabinet members (Ministers, Vice-Ministers of State Secretaries) have been Muslims.[15] Though it is not surprising that the BJP-led governments count the least number of Muslim executive members, it is worth noting that the parties counting on the electoral support of Muslims—notably the Samajwadi Party—do not necessarily distribute more portfolios to this community.[16] The portfolio inflation visible in the late 1990s and in the subsequent years has led to more Muslims being nominated in the Cabinet in absolute numbers, without necessarily increasing their relative share of representation.

A MINORITY WITHIN A MINORITY

Muslim Representation in Lucknow

Muslims represent 36 to 38% of Lucknows total population,[17] 25 to 30% of which are believed to be Shias.[18]

Table 4.4. Evolution of Lucknow's population

Year	1951	1961	1971	1981	1991	2001	2006
Population	459,484	615,523	774,644	947,990	1,619,116	2,185,927	2,490,127
Growth rate	–	33.95	25.85	22.37	70.79	35.00	13.91

Source: Regional Centre for Urban & Environment Studies, Lucknow.

With Partition and the UP hinterland Muslims moving massively to Pakistan, Lucknow saw the arrival of a large number of educated Hindus (70% of the total immigrants), who steadily diluted the Muslim influence in government, business and trade. Their influence was further undermined by the departure of a large part of their elites—mostly Sunnis—for Pakistan. Some Shias also left for Pakistan, but those who supported the National Movement and considered Pakistan as a mostly Sunni enterprise remained.

The city's overall population grew steadily after independence, due in large part to a massive migration from the hinterland of Uttar Pradesh, in majority Hindus, furthering the marginalisation of Muslims.

The city of Lucknow is divided into four assembly seats in which Muslims represent 22 to 28% of the electorate. In Lucknow West, the Shias represent overall 100,000 votes and roughly 70 to 75,000 votes in Lucknow Centre. Their presence in the rest of the city is too marginal to make them politically significant.

Their demographic strength makes them an important variable in the electoral strategies of parties, but has not been enough to ensure a direct representation for themselves. Since 1952, Lucknow has sent only five Muslim representatives to the state assembly (four Congress and one Bharatiya Kranti Dal, in 1969). The only Shia MLA, Syed Ali Zaheer (Congress), has been elected three times in the 1950s and early 1960s (once from Lucknow Central and twice from Lucknow West). The last Muslim to be elected MLA from Lucknow is Zafar Ali Naqvi (Congress) in 1985. Since 1989, BJP candidates have systematically won all four assembly seats because the contests are usually fought between the BJP candidates and a divided opposition.

The Muslim vote itself is far from being united, with the Shias often supporting different candidates from the Sunnis. It is in fact a recurrent accusation of the Sunnis that the Shias are supporters of the BJP, an assertion difficult to assess. There were occasions though when Shias and Sunnis voted together. Shyam Kishore Shukla, the Congress candidate in the Lucknow West 2009 by-election, won with the support of both Shias and Sunnis, as well as with the support of some BJP rebels, breaking the twenty-one-year monopoly of the BJP in Lucknow's Assembly constituencies.

The Lucknow Lok Sabha constituency, from which no Muslim has ever been elected, reveals a similar pattern. The fact that Muslim candidates usually get a smaller vote share than the demographic strength of their co-religionists demonstrates that direct representation is not the prior motive for electoral choice among Muslims. It illustrates the difficulty for Muslim candidates to gather votes outside their community.

The electoral behaviour of Muslims in Lucknow, and of Shias in particular, is not easy to discern. One element that has emerged from the various fieldworks conducted in Lucknow in recent years is that the 'natural' leadership of the communities—their religious leaders—has little impact on their electoral behaviour. In the 2009 general elections, for example, clerics had overtly supported the BSP candidate Akhilesh Das. He was severely defeated, the Shias having chosen to support the Congress candidate, Rita Bahuguna, quasi en bloc.

These glimpses of Lucknow's electoral competition illustrate the difficulty of mainstream parties to find interlocutors and intermediaries within Muslim groups likely to garner support for them. Not knowing to whom they should talk, they tend to address themselves to their religious authorities, perceived as their natural leaders.

The Polarisation of Muslims and the Ghettoisation of Shias in Lucknow

Communal riots have often generated or accelerated existing processes of spatial concentration and marginalisation of targeted communities in India. As far as Lucknow is concerned, the city has known and still knows such processes but with the specificity that the communal violence has been mostly circumscribed within the minority, divided between Sunnis (70 to 75% of Lucknow's Muslim population) and Shias (the remaining 25 to 30%).

Although Lucknow has a long history of Sunni-Shia violence, dating back to the beginning of the twentieth century,[19] three recent major riots have marked collective memories: in 1969, 1974 and 1977. Sporadic violence on a lesser scale has, however, been recurring on a regular basis. If these riots never assumed the scale of larger Hindu-Muslim riots that have occurred in other cities or towns of India—in terms of victims or property destruction—they have had a deep impact on the social, religious and economic life as well as on the political representation of Muslims in general in Lucknow.

Riots

The 1969 riots started after the circulation of a pamphlet urging the Shias to wear green caps and to publicly recite *tabarra*[20] in the case of Sunnis reciting *Madhe-Sahaba*. The pamphlet also called for the creation of a *Tabarra Volunteer Force* whose task was to enforce the pamphlet author's recommendation. Strong reactions and stone pelting during a Shia procession on 26 May 1969 degenerated into full-fledged riots in which six persons were killed and many hurt in the confrontation with police forces. The then Chief Minister, Chandra Banu Gupta, forced leaders from both communities to reach an agreement to tame the provocative practices.

In 1974, the recitation of *tabarra* during a Shia *Chellum* procession sparked protests and degenerated into violent confrontations between the two communities. Eight people died and many more were injured, including members of the police force. Following the riots and confronted with the lack of understanding between the leaders of two communities, the Congress Government, headed by H.N. Bahuguna, banned Muharram processions in the city.

In 1977, on the eve of the general elections, in March, Shias attacked a procession of Sunnis carrying flags bearing the names of the four Caliphs. On 24 March, day of *Nauchandi*, Shias organised an unauthorised procession that generated further incidents and deaths.

The years that followed witnessed sporadic communal tensions, usually related to protests led against the ban imposed by the Government on the Shia processions. The ban, however, was not total. The chest-beatings and the recitation of *majlises* were still permitted. The ban on processions lasted for 23 years and was only lifted by the first Mayawati-led Government in 1997, after a number of students in Kashmiri Mohalla committed self-immolation on this issue.[21]

In 2005, during the tenth day of Muharram, the murder of two Sunni boys triggered strong reactions. The intervention of a prominent Shia Cleric, Maulana Kalbe Jawad, prevented the skirmishes from developing into a full-fledged riot. These tensions erupted in the specific context of a schism within the

All India Muslim Personal Law Board, a group of Shia clerics and notables seceding the organisation to create a specifically Shia Personal Law Board.[22]

The Spatial Impact of Riots

The first and most important impact of the riots that occurred in the late 1960s and during the 1970s was the exchange of populations between Shia and Sunni localities. This process of population exchange was progressive, unorganised and did not occur in massive waves. Family by family, individual by individual, Shias and Sunnis started to regroup in the area where their co-religionists lived.

'The 1977 riots were too big an episode. They started on the day of *Barafat* (the Prophet's birthday). The curfew continued for days. Houses in the adjoint Mohallas were burned. Properties looted. Thousands were jailed. Since then, the interchange of population started'.[23]

At the turn of the 1960s, Kashmiri Mohalla was still a small locality with a landscape dominated by large *havelis*. This is the description that Khan Prince Basharat Husain sketched of the locality:

'Houses around Farhat Manzil[24] were made of mud. The area was sparsely populated. Big palatial houses of Kahsmiri Pandits and other former dignitaries of the Nawabi Court were the only landmarks. The rest was dust and mud. Kashmiri Mohalla in those days was confined to a small geography. There were few people living there since the only source of income came from serving the Pandits, Rajas and Thakurs, former members of the Nawabi Court. There were no companies or other jobs available'.

Kashmiri Mohalla was perceived as a natural rallying point for the Shias as the locality was situated in the immediate vicinity of the Hazrat Abbas Dargah, a replica of the shrine of the eponymous companion of Hussain, flag bearer of his army, who died during the battle of Karbala. The population of the locality started to increase rapidly as it received migrants from the surrounding areas and also from other parts of the city, where Shias lived in small numbers.

Many Shias from Mansoor Nagar, Pata Mullah, Gali Meer Mata, Achuti Gali, migrated to Kashmiri Mohalla. Tanveer Husain alias 'Guddu', municipal corporator representing the Kalbe Abid Ward Part I since 2000, recalls the conditions in which he and his family shifted to Kashmiri Mohalla:

'I was born in 1965 in Sitapur and my parents settled soon after that in Ghulam Husain ka Pul. After the 1969 riots, all my family members had to flee the area and find a place in Kashmiri Mohalla, where we had relatives. All our belongings were burned. We shifted from relatives to relatives for four years until my father could buy some land. The population of Kashmiri Mohalla grew a lot after 1969'.[25]

Once again, this process of shifting populations was peaceful and did not necessarily generate the resentment experienced by collectively displaced population. Maulana Kalbe Sadiq, an eminent Shia cleric and educationist, underlines:

'The cross-migration was a peaceful process. The concentration was also convenient. It facilitated religious life. Riots became rarer and were restricted to limited areas'.[26]

Shias started to invest in the crumbling properties of the nobility and the Pandits and recycled their material to build houses. They used the mosques abandoned by the Sunnis, who did the same with the mosques the Shias had left behind them. The demographic density of the area rose sharply and what used to be an abode of peace and luxury became one of the most congested, densely populated and economically deprived areas of Lucknow.[27]

Similarly, Sunnis who were living in these areas started shifting to Sunni-dominated areas, adjacent to these developing Shia pockets. The localities of Ghulam Husain ka Pul, Balda, Mansoor Nagar, Chawal Wali Gali, Bhawarchi Taula (where the cooks used to live), Akbari Gate, Kachha Pul, Chaupatiyan (located around Abdul Aziz Road, also known as 'Jeddah Road'), among others, became almost exclusively inhabited by Sunnis.

Moving away from Kashmiri Mohalla was easy for these families since most Sunnis in the area were landless labourers. Most of them were tenants of Shia landlords. The image of destitute landowners and former aristocrats that weighs on the Shias of Lucknow did not help improve their relations with the Sunnis, who sometimes refer to them as the 'surplus population'.

Interestingly, the locality seems to have received only few migrants from outside Lucknow, even though Shias from other parts of India (including Hyderabad) and Uttar Pradesh, mostly from the east, have been migrating to Lucknow since long. There could be two explanations for this. The first is that the locality was already seriously congested and migrants preferred to settle in the fast-developing suburban residential areas located around Lucknow. The second, linked to the first one, could reside in the very poor state of public amenities that characterises the Shias pockets of Lucknow West. The non-existent sanitation system, the absence of a garbage collection system, poor energy and water supplies do not make the locality particularly attractive compared to other accessible localities surrounding Lucknow. The scarcity of jobs in the locality could be a third reason.

As a result of this process of spatial polarisation, skirmishes and tensions between Sunnis and Shias are geographically confined to the boundaries between the Mohallas. It thus creates by contrast a sentiment of security within the Mohalla, reinforcing its attractiveness.

Impact on Religious Life

The spatial polarisation of both the Sunni and Shia populations of Lucknow has further institutionalised the perceived differences between the two communities and has contributed to the closure of means of communication and understanding between them. It also provided a context in which collective religious practices would evolve and crystallise around specific identities.

There is also a minority complex at work. Over this period [the post 1977 riots], the influence of the clergy increased. During Muharram, clerics have to be there to recite the *majlis*. Now, the number of *majlis* has increased tremendously, in every *imambara*, every Sunday, Thursday... the practice of *majlis* was always there—when people died, for example—but not with this enormity, or with so much money'.[28]

Possibly because of the sense of insecurity generated by this context of tensions combined with economic difficulties and a general context that disfavours religious minorities, many Shias and Sunnis found solace and comfort in the collective practice of their faith. As we saw in previous sections, religious festivals had been since long instrumentalised by both the clergy and the political class to assert the identity of their flock in the latter case and of their vote bank in the former.

Religious practices also often serve as catalysts for caricatures and stereotypical perceptions of the other. The split within the Muslim Personal Law Board and the creation of the Shia Personal Law Board in 2005, by Maulana Athar Rizvi and other clerics, was the occasion for many Shias to underline the growing influence of specific religious currents—generically labelled as 'wahabbis'—within the organisation.[29]

'There is a book, written by Ismail Syed Delvi in the nineteenth century, which says that all Muslims of the world who don't believe in the philosophy of Ibn Taymiyya,[30] are *kafirs* (infidels); they should be executed and their properties seized and given to the Muslim State. This book is prescribed in the course of Nadwat ul-Uloom. Ali Miya Naqvi, an ex-President of AIMPLB has written notes on this book'.[31]

According to many Shias, there is a clear perception of a growing radicalisation of thought and religious practices among Sunnis. On the other side, there is a common rumour that depicts the board members of the Shia

Personal Law Board as puppets in the hands of the Bharatiya Janata Party and Israel as well as the United States as their allies.[32] Shias are often accused by Sunnis to play the game of the BJP by supporting them during elections. This is difficult to establish since religious leaders rarely if ever urge in the open their co-religionists to vote for the BJP. Even if they did so, the influence of religious leaders on the electoral behaviour of their community, as we have seen in an earlier section, is highly questionable.

It would be simplistic, however, to assert that transformations of religious and cultural practices, and their political and social consequences, reflect the dynamics of two coherent groups sailing in two opposite directions. The fact of being the minority within the minority does not prevent the Shias in Lucknow to be divided among themselves, notably on religious and political issues. Two related cases illustrate this point.

First of all, it has been argued that the creation of the Shia Personal Law Board in 2005 reflected as much the divisions among the Shias than the divide with the Sunnis. The competition between Shia clerics led a large faction to split the Board and create one of their own. Despite constant pressures from the splitting factions, some Shia clerics persist sitting with the All India Muslim Personal Law Board, defying the trend of polarisation between the two communities. Secondly, some emblematic institutions, such as the Shia College, provide another arena for the confrontation of factions of clerics and other notable members of the College Board, who oppose clerics' growing control of an otherwise secular institution.[33]

Despite the Shias' growing religiosity, one should not however exaggerate the scope of the clerics' influence within their community. If they still hold the upper ground in the organisation of the religious life of the community, their influence in other social and political aspects of its members has been dwindling. Many look down at the internecine struggles between clerics with a mix of amusement and despair. Their legitimacy to regulate the social conduct and norms of morality of their flock is more and more contested from below.

After the clerics, politicians are usually blamed for the predicament of the marginalised and deprived sections of society, and those from Lucknow are no exception. Despite a longstanding history of Sunni-Shia enmity, the blame for the violence arising from this divide is generally laid at their door. The manipulation of Sunni-Shia riots by politicians is the chief reason assigned by the interviewees to explain these outbreaks and their regularity. Local electoral politics and gerrymandering indeed plays a role in the polarisation of the two communities.

The Politicisation of Differences

Shias are a divided minority within a minority. They can play a role in state elections merely as a 'nuisance' factor, as evident from the situation prevailing in Kashmiri Mohalla.

In its present form, the Kashmiri Mohalla Municipal Ward covers an area of 4.2 sq km and houses a population of 39,319 inhabitants,[34] of which 95% are Muslims. The two other municipal wards that cover the locality known as Kashmiri Mohalla—Kalbe Abid Ward Part I & II—cover an equivalent area and offer the same population density as the Kashmiri Mohalla Municipal Ward.[35]

Municipal Elections

The municipality of Lucknow is divided into 110 municipal wards, ten of which are almost certain to send a Muslim representative to the Council, having a Muslim population exceeding 50%. Among these ten wards, only two—Kashmiri Mohalla Ward and Kalbe Abid Ward Part I—are predominantly Shias and have sent Shia representatives to the Council on a regular basis.

The civic polls started in 1989. In that year, most of Kashmiri Mohalla was covered within a single municipal ward bearing the same name. This municipal ward also encompassed some pockets from adjacent areas, ensuring a certain degree of social heterogeneity in the constituency. Shias, however, were the predominant voter group. Three main candidates contested the two seats available in the ward. From the Shia side, S.T. Wahid and Raja Corporator contested, opposed to Muhammad Iqbal, a Sunni who had made a fortune in the perfume business. On the eve of polling, a serious riot erupted at Kashmiri School. Polling was disturbed in the locality. The identity factor determined the outcome of the election, Shias supporting S.T. Wahid en masse and Sunnis backing Muhammad Iqbal, the former defeated the latter.

In 1995, the ward boundaries were redrawn and a new ward created. It was named after the famous and influential Shia cleric Kalbe Abid.[36] The domination of Shias in Kashmiri Mohalla Ward was reinforced and the electorate in Kalbe Abid became more mixed, with a slight majority of Sunnis. For the first time that year, parties were authorised to field their candidates in municipal elections. Corporators, who were enjoying until then a mostly honorary position, started to develop some political clout, since some decentralisation policies entrusted them with local executive responsibilities, mainly in the allocation of public funds for the development of infrastructure and amenities. Lucknow being the state capital, they started to enjoy a status otherwise enjoyed only by MLAs.

Kashmiri Mohalla became a reserved ward for women that year and a Shia candidate, Subi Qazmi, a non-resident of the ward, got elected with the Samajwadi Party's support. In Kalbe Abid Ward, the Samajwadi candidate Ali Murtuza (a Shia) was defeated by a very narrow margin by Mohammad Haleem (an Ansari), a Sunni independent candidate. Shias felt betrayed on losing a seat they thought was theirs (the very name of the ward expressed its Shia identity).

In 2000, the Kashmiri Mohalla ward became a general seat again. Haseem Rizvi, who hailed from a traditionally rich land-owning Shia family, contested as a Bahujan Samaj Party (BSP) candidate and won against Mohammad Abbas, an independent Shia candidate. In the Kalbe Abid Ward, the Sunni candidate Mohammad Haleem had campaigned on the theme of changing the name of the ward to Maulana Abdul Shakoor ward, which provoked strong reactions from the Shias and resulted in communal tensions. Tanveer Hussain, alias 'Guddu' (an independent Shia candidate) won against him, by supporting a minor proxy Sunni candidate, Ifhamullah Babu Hakim, who cut the Sunni vote.

The Kalbe Abid Ward was split furthermore in 2005, creating, as a result, two socially homogeneous wards. The Kalbe Abid Ward Part I became almost exclusively Shia and the newly created Kalbe Abid Ward Part II—to which adjacent pockets had been added—became almost completely Sunni. This split was initiated on the recommendation of its corporator, Tanveer Hussain 'Guddu', who saw this as a means to ensure the representation of Shias in the Shia-dominated part of the ward (a representation he sought to ensure in the long run). The municipality promptly agreed to proceed to the split, due to the sheer size of the ward (which, with 18,000 voters, was one of the most densely populated ones of Lucknow) and saw it as a way of preventing communal tensions in the area.

Tanveer Hussain 'Guddu' was re-elected in Kalbe Abid Ward Part I, against the now deceased Shakeel Rizvi. He subsequently joined the ranks of the BSP. Quite logically Sunni candidate Ifhamullah Faiz won in the new Kalbe Abid Part II ward against Mohammad Haleem.

Constituency delimitation, in the hands of the administration and the State Electoral Commission, has been a means for pursuing a two-fold objective: the first one, at the local level, was to create socially homogeneous wards in order to preserve public order; the second, at the Assembly level, less tangible but operative in its effects, was to dilute the Muslim electoral strength at the Vidhan Sabha level by cutting through densely-populated Muslim areas.

Since 1995, and the direct involvement of parties in civic elections, the role and functions of municipal corporators has changed.

Besides representation in the Municipal Council, one of the main roles of municipal corporators today is to supervise the development of public amenities in their constituencies. In the wake of the Sachar Committee Report, which emphasised, in the case of Lucknow, the very poor state of public infrastructure in Muslim-dominated areas, many public works were undertaken in Kashmiri Mohalla, with generous funding from the World Bank. Open-air sewage system and roads were built, and water pumps installed. It is alleged by many in the Mohalla that most of the contractors who were awarded the contracts were relatives of the corporators or their proxies and that a large part of the funds allocated to these infrastructure development projects has been siphoned off.[37] Corporators can make a very lucrative business out of this public attention, hence increasing the stakes of local elections. As a consequence, municipal elections have now become a costly affair and the capacity of local corporators to redistribute resources or to provide access to public resources has become an important factor for their electoral fate.

Poor public amenities and severe economic deprivation are another noticeable features of Kashmiri Mohalla. A closer look at the locality, however, reveals a more complex picture of the socio-economic conditions of its inhabitants.

The Economic Life of Kashmiri Mohalla

The Shias of Lucknow have traditionally drawn their wealth from lands, of which they were massively dispossessed after independence and the Zamindari Abolition Act of 1952. Having practically no experience in any sort of trade, turning to moneymaking ventures proved difficult.

'Many households used to be dependant on the nobility. They had no education and no money to start their businesses. They progressively became labourers, *zardozi* workers, helpers in shops. In order to get out of your place, you need education, skills. Those who had the means shifted to other areas.'[38]

The Kashmiri Pandits, as we saw, could migrate and offer their talents elsewhere. They progressed and prospered in every domain of activity in which they invested their energy and gradually abandoned the locality. Only forty families remain from the thousand families of Kashmiri Pandits that had originally settled in Kashmiri Mohalla.

Today, according to the local trade union, 70% of the Kashmiri Mohalla population is involved in *zardozi* work, a hand-embroidery technique with golden threads particularly popular in Delhi and Punjab markets. Since most Shias faced difficulties in finding work outside the Mohalla, they looked for jobs that could be undertaken at home. Though considered lowly as in the case of other manual professions, it nonetheless provided sufficient income for many households to survive.

'Even *zardozi* became a slur. Those who were rich found themselves offended by this trade. *Zardozans* can't find a match with girls from good families'.[39]

For a long time, *zardozi* remained a Shia monopoly. The position of the Shias engaged in this industry became difficult when they started facing the competition of *zardozi* workers scattered in the outskirts of the city. The stockists, mostly Sindhis and Punjabis who had migrated to the city after Partition, had started hiring cheap labour in the surrounding villages, where most of the work is now done.

The Sindhis and Punjabis entered the *zardozi* business and created new markets for the traditional *zardozi* workers: Delhi, Chandigarh, Ludhiana, etc. Artisans became their labourers and the embroidery techniques became more mechanised while the demand for *zardozi* increased. The stockists would copy the craftsmen's designs and give them to the villagers for reproduction. Consequently, the value of their work diminished.

Sindhis, who also supplied the raw material required for *zardozi* (they had created a supply chain of raw material from Surat and Delhi), were also able to impose their prices and their trade practices. Workers who were earning daily wages started getting paid by the piece and had to follow stricter deadlines. This led to the dwindling of their income and the number of workshops.

Some Shias have today become stockists themselves and have established their own workshops. Many workers complain that they are as exploitative as the other stockists and that it has not led to any economic upliftment of the Mohalla.

Confronted with this ordeal, *zardozi* workers started to organise themselves and created the *Anjuman-e-Zardozan* (Embroiderers' Association) in 1971. They filed complaints against the theft of designs by the stockists, organised 'flying squads' to check the veracity of these claims in the villages. The Association started registering their designs and exerted pressure on shops and showroom owners in the city to improve the prices and guarantee the payments of dues. The association became very popular among the workers, Shias and Sunnis alike.[40]

The organisation, however, started to decline in the early 1990s, for two reasons. Firstly, the organisation had guaranteed yearly wage increases to the workers (wages were distributed once a week) while the price for saris—fixed by the stockists—remained stagnant. The promise could not be kept. Secondly, stockists had installed moles inside the organisation to undermine its influence by generating conflicts over fixing wage levels. The organisation collapsed in early 2000 and the concept of daily or weekly wage was abandoned.

The quasi-exclusive dependence on *zardozi* accounts largely for the economic deprivation of many inhabitants of Kashmiri Mohalla. The economy of this sector of activity also created barriers to upward mobility, requiring skills acquired through practical learning and not formal education. In addition to the exploitative character of the relation between producers and retailers, the irregular demand for *zardozi* saris throughout the year further increases the pressure on the producers. Every year, between March and June, a market slump occurs. In September, the month is called 'Sitamgar' (atrocious) for no orders come from the markets for their products. Many households live through these months of penury using up the savings they have accumulated during the high season.

The 1970s, however, saw a type of change that would deepen the economic imbalance between Shias and Sunnis in Lucknow while generating fresh avenues of prosperity. In 1977, after the Emergency, the Morarji Desai Government decided to relax the regulations pertaining to passports issuance. This enabled thousands of Lukhnavis, mostly Sunnis, to migrate and seek employment in the Gulf Remittances started flowing back and helped the community improve its economic condition. Compared to Shias, Sunnis had a double advantage: firstly, by virtue of belonging to this branch of Islam they could migrate to Sunni-populated countries; secondly, being manual labourers, they were much sought after by employers in the Gulf.[41] Shias lacked the contacts or helpers who could assist them in migrating from India. Some Shias however still manage to migrate and have also started to remit funds to their relatives and community. Clerics also took advantage, later on, of the relaxing of the passport regulation to travel and collect funds from members of the diaspora.

The remittances have enabled many families to invest in their trade—mostly *zardozi*—to hire employees and start workshops. It has also enabled them to build better houses and to obtain better amenities. The former often translates into building additional floors and rooms on former gardens, which are earmarked for tenancy. This has consequently led to increase of real estate value. These additional incomes also helped some families to invest in the education of their children, thus offering them wider career opportunities.

Leaders of the community acknowledge the fact that many Shias are doing well economically. This trend does not counter however the process of spatial marginalisation described earlier. As a result, Kashmiri Mohalla today offers to the visitor a contrasted landscape of large houses of solid bricks and mortar, co-existing with shanty constructions and slums.

(Self-)segregation

'The Mohalla is a way of life. It has many good aspects. When someone falls ill, dozens of people will flock at his place to take care of him and to make sure that his family does not lack anything. In times where Muslims feel insecure, the Mohalla provides them with a sense of security'.[42]

The Mohalla provides a sense of security and familiarity to its inhabitants. The stroller will be struck by the difference in ambience as soon as he/she quits the busy congested noisy arteries linking the different localities of the city for the narrow lanes leading to the inner alleys of the Mohalla. The noise recedes; the streets are quiet and sparsely occupied by dwellers courteously greeting each other. Skirmishes and riots always occur on the fringes of the Mohallas, in the congested area of *Nakhas* and on the major roads dividing the Shia from the Sunni pockets.

Despite its apparent socio-economic diversity, the Mohalla however, does not provide to its inhabitants the economic opportunities that would enable them to ameliorate their standards of living (most of the well-off households still being involved with the *zardozi* trade). Leaving the Mohalla is then the only option for those seeking a better life. A recent trend has started, particularly among the youth, of leaving the Mohalla to pursue their education and then seek employment.

'The representation of Muslims in the police is decreasing.[43] In the civil services, too. The Central Government schemes for minorities don't reach Muslims. They are not even aware of the existence of such programmes. Those who have access to education come to these areas to lead a quiet life or move out elsewhere'.[44]

The lack of private sector jobs, the difficulty of obtaining salaried employment in the city itself and the corruption barring entry to public jobs have pushed many of the educated young members of the community to moving out to seek employment. Many of them are leaving Kashmiri Mohalla to find work in cities like Delhi, Noida, and smaller towns like Meerut, Faridabad or further on in Punjab.

How does this upward social mobility impact on the community at large? As we saw, the incentives to invest into *zardozi* are few and the younger generation is leaving the trade en masse. Irfan[45] belongs to a family of *zardozi* workers established in Kashmiri Mohalla for more than 100 years. The poor situation of the trade pushed him towards education, first as a Science student at the Calvin Taluqdar College, and then as a Math student at the Shia College. He finally opted for an MBA course in Finance and Controls, and currently works as an Assistant Manager in a retail bank in Roorkee.

'The situation of *zardozi* has not been good. I felt naturally inclined to study. But finding a job outside is difficult. Getting the right education is difficult. We have no guidance. We follow rumours to make decisions and decide our careers. There is also a scarcity of jobs in Lucknow. Most people will stay here and then relocate whenever they can'.

All do not necessarily leave Lucknow but settle in other parts of the city that are not associated with minorities, where they can live more anonymous lives.

Conclusion

The late 1960s–70s were a turning point for the Shias of Lucknow. Politically, it marked the end of the Congress domination in the state and the city, a party they had always supported in the past. Economically, it marked the beginning of new opportunities with the increased flow of remittances from the Gulf and other areas. However, their socio-economic status continued to be low over the entire period and remains so even today. Lack of education and jobs, the deliberate neglect of the minority within the minority by public authorities and political parties deprive them of the opportunities offered by a rapidly changing economic context.

This period is marked by the territorial polarisation between Sunnis and Shias in Lucknow and the growing marginalisation—spatial, political, and economic—of the former. If the Shia-Sunni divide is deeply rooted in the colonial days and in the period preceding independence, the process of spatial marginalisation and the subsequent transformations of cultural and religious practices are much more recent phenomena.

Those that have access to education and its promises of upward mobility leave the Mohalla and strive to lead an anonymous and peaceful existence. The story of a community transforms itself slowly into the many narratives of individual trajectories, thus putting into doubt the emergence of a Muslim middle class. This drain of a potentially new Shia elite has the perverse effect of furthering the marginalisation of those who stay, as those who could have contributed to changing the Mohalla's lot abandon it in pursuit of their personal aspirations.

5

ALIGARH

SIR SYED NAGAR AND SHAH JAMAL, CONTRASTED TALES OF A 'MUSLIM' CITY[1]

Juliette Galonnier

A middle-size Class I city of 660,087 inhabitants located in the Central Doab,[2] Aligarh is renowned for its Muslim University, which has made the city an educational hub for Muslims. Making up 41% of the population (2001 Census), the Muslims of Aligarh also constitute a conspicuous minority, whose culture and language (Urdu) are supported by the presence of the university.[3]

Aligarh actually consists of two distinct towns separated by the railway line. The Old City, with its congested lanes, radiates to the west and the south and comprises the main Muslim places of worship such as the Jama Masjid and the *dargah* of Shah Jamal. The Civil Lines, where the Aligarh Muslim University (AMU) was established, is by contrast a much more airy and green area. Civil Lines are characteristic of cities where the British exerted their influence and refer to the civilian urban area where the colonial elites resided, which was demarcated from the military cantonment. In Aligarh, it houses the main offices of the city and the district administration: law courts, post offices and the railway station are to be found in this residential area where wealthy businessmen, AMU staff and servicemen have settled.

Despite the fact that it is not a Muslim majority town, Aligarh has retained a Muslim image because of its university. But are the Muslims more at ease in a town which has been pointed at as a bastion of Muslim separatism in Indian public debates? Are they present among the elite of a town whose university has generated Muslim leaders for decades? How homogenous is the Muslim community in a city which has been described as the symbol of Muslim identity in India? To answer these questions, this chapter focuses on three localities: Upar Fort (or Upar Kot) in the Old City, where the majority of the Muslim population of Aligarh resides; Shah Jamal, a peripheral backward locality which

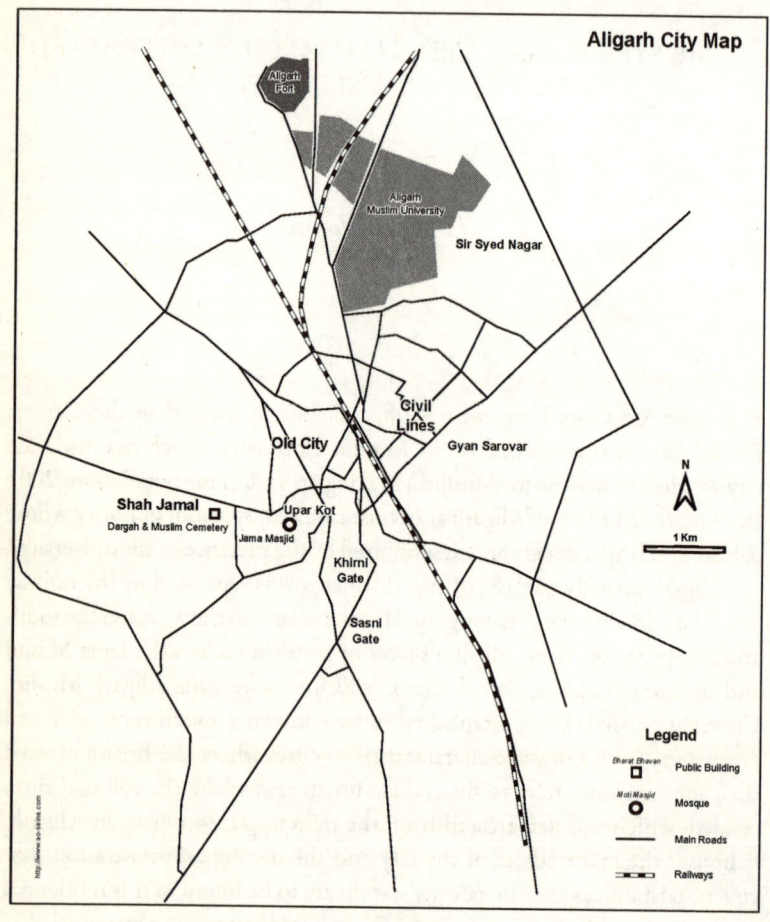

Map of Aligarh

has been pointed at as a 'Muslim ghetto' by many Aligarhians; and Sir Syed Nagar, a so-called 'intelligentsia colony' of the Muslims, situated in the Civil Lines, whose residents are overwhelmingly employed in the university and which has been described as the largest colony of educated Muslims in Asia by many respondents.[4]

Aligarh's Muslism History

A Prominent Qasbah Town

Aligarh got its name from the Prophet Muhammad's cousin and son-in-law, Ali, after the storming of its fort in 1775 by a Shia commander, Mirza Najaf Khan, and his lieutenant, Afrasiyab Khan (Siddiqui, 1981: 26).[5]

The city started gaining importance as a Muslim military garrison in the twelfth century. It was described by historian Hasan Nizami as 'one of the most celebrated fortresses in India' (Singh, 1987: 25). However, its role remained limited as a military and administrative centre. Aligarh was rather sought-after for its value as a *zamindari* territory. Its fertile land and its proximity to Delhi made it a strategic location for *zamindars,* who were mainly 'Muslims from high status group or converts from castes of equal status' (Mann, 1992: 22). This Muslim elite turned Aligarh into a *qasbah* town, that is 'a country town with a population of usually not more than 3,000 people, whose social, legal and economic status were of some importance in relation to the district and national issues' (Bayly, 1983: 11). *Qasbah* towns were to become the seed-beds of Muslim society in North India. A specific Muslim culture which 'ran parallel to, though not yet in opposition to, that of the Hindu commercial towns' developed under the influence of the Muslim service gentry between 1690 and 1830 (Bayly, 1983: 190).

From the nineteenth century onwards, however, as a result of the British intervention against land grantees and following the repression of the 1857 revolt, the *qasbah* culture started to fade. The Muslim elite had to sustain a decline and the Muslim *zamindars* a considerable loss of property, particularly in Aligarh district (Zoya Hasan, 1989: 34–35).

AMU: the Arsenal of Muslim India

The trajectory of Aligarh was considerably altered by the creation of the AMU. In 1875, the Muslim reformist leader, Sir Syed Ahmad Khan (1817–98) founded the Mohammedan Anglo-Oriental College that was later to develop into the Aligarh Muslim University. He was an erudite scholar and jurist who sought to find solutions through modern education to the backwardness of his Muslim fellows after the 'catastrophe' of 1857.

But the AMU was not merely an educational institution. As David Lelyveld has shown, it was also a movement (Lelyveld, 2003: 327). The All Indian Mohammedan Educational Conference was launched in 1886 by Sir Syed Ahmad Khan to promote modern education and political unity among Muslims. This movement was to become a political force after his death and the AMU the 'nerve centre of Muslim separatism in the United Provinces in the 1940s' (Zoya Hasan, 1989: 19). According to Mohammed All Jinnah, AMU became indeed 'the arsenal of Muslim India' (Maheshwari, 2001: 1). The Muslim League was launched in 1906 on the occasion of the annual meeting of the Muslim Educational Conference and was by and large created by AMU graduates. In the 1940s, the AMU Students Union adopted the Muslim League program as its own ideology and supported the two-nation theory. At Partition, around 13,000 to 16,000 Muslims left the city for Pakistan (Brass, 2003: 47).

Table 5.1. Evolution of the Muslim population in Aligarh city

Year	1931	1941	1951	1961	1971	1981	1991	2001
% Muslim population	42.8	45.9	34.5	NA	33.1	34.5	37.4	41.0

Source: for 1931 and 1941, E. A. Mann., *Boundaries and Identities, Muslims, Work and Status in Aligarh,* New Delhi: Sage Publications, 1992, p 27. For 1951, 1971, 1981, 1991, P. Brass, *The Production of Hindu-Muslim Violence in Contemporary India,* Seattle (WA): University of Washington Press, 2003, p 47. For 2001, National Data Bank for Socio-Religious Categories, 2001 Census data.

The Muslims who left were largely drawn from the elite groups. Those who remained (metalworkers, butchers, agricultural labourers, weavers...) had to bear the legacy of the Partition. While Aligarh's Muslims have demonstrated since then their attachment to the Indian nation, the AMU is still, for many *Hindutva* supporters, the bastion of Muslim secessionism and 'a citadel of Pakistani agents'.[6]

The AMU today: Embodying Muslim Culture

The AMU today attracts Muslims from all over India.[7] Aligarh has progressively become the hometown of Muslims looking for education or employment within the university. Irfan Ahmad, in his book *Islamism and Democracy*, recalls what Aligarh meant for the Muslim child he was:

'I first heard of AMU when I was a student in a village *madrasa*. The *madrasa* administration asked us students to get "Aligarhi *pajamas*" and *kurta* to wear at an upcoming function. Later, after moving to a government school I heard more about the university from some rich relatives who studied there. As students of AMU, they felt superior to me. Studying at AMU meant not only getting a degree but also embodying "Muslim culture". Such was AMU's place in the Muslim imagination!'

(Ahmad, 2009: 43)

The etiquette, *adab*, remains a crucial element of the daily life of the students. Aligarhians are proud of this distinction and perpetuate it. Studying at AMU offers both a Muslim environment and a guarantee of security and morality, which, allegedly, could not be found in metropolitan cities. It has become the right option for Indian Muslim educated families, who move to Aligarh in their masses either to get a job in the university or to make sure that their children get a high-level education in a Muslim environment. After retirement, many of them chose not to go back to their native places and stay permanently in Aligarh. They settle in residential areas, which are increasingly distinct from the Hindu localities.

A Fragmented City

'I come from a cosmopolitan city [in Bihar] in which there was no distinction between Hindu and Muslim. We lived together in Hindi culture. There was no discrimination. But here I see a dislike of Hindi language in schools with small children. They made me conscious that "this is Hindu culture, and this is Muslim culture". They made me conscious of this distinction'.

Malika Nawab, Professor at AMU, Dhorrah

Hindu-Muslim Segregation

According to historians C.A. Bayly and Mushirul Hasan, the *qasbah* culture was characterised by a strong syncretism between Hindus and Muslims which was embodied, among other things, in their common veneration for the shrines of Muslim holy men. As Mushirul Hasan suggests, 'if Islam cemented the *qasba* structure, pluralism and syncretism were the bricks with which it was built' (Hasan, 2004: 24).

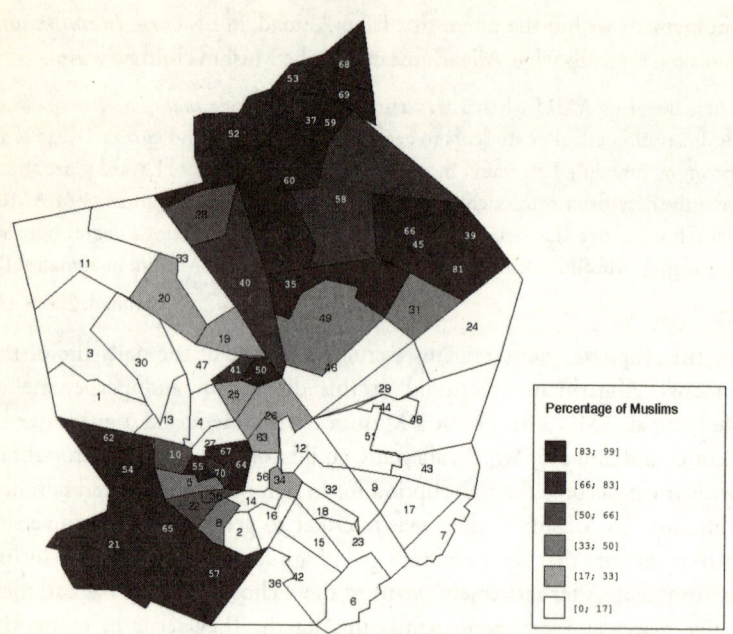

Hindu-Muslim Segregation in Aligarh

NB: the percentage of Hindus and Muslims at the ward level being unavailable in the Census data, we had to use the electoral rolls of the 2006 Municipal Elections and sort the names of the residents to determine the number of Hindu and Muslim voters for each ward. Figures on the map are ward numbers.

Aligarh used to be such a place. But it is no longer the case today. Evidence from fieldwork tends to show that a growing polarisation is taking place between Hindus and Muslims. Mixed areas are becoming rare. Even if Census data on religious affiliation at the *mohalla* level are not available, any inhabitant of Aligarh would tell with certainty which wards are predominantly Muslim and which ones are Hindu.[8]

We find clusters of Muslim settlements scattered around Aligarh (mostly in the Old City and around the AMU in the Civil Lines). The Old City in particular is a mosaic of Hindu-majority and Muslim-majority *mohallas*. We do not observe a clear pattern of 'ghettoisation' of the Muslims in Aligarh city, whose configuration is rather characterised by the juxtaposition of Muslim or Hindu 'pockets'. These clusters are clearly hermetic to each other: Hindus and

ALIGARH

Muslims do not want to live together any more, be it in the traditional Old City or in the highly educated Civil Lines. While many respondents declared they had good relations with members of the other community, the large majority recoiled at the idea of living among them. Below is a sample of what Hindu respondents answered when asked 'Could you live in a Muslim area?'

'Never. Because in every area, communal people live. If Hindus come, illiterate people start thinking that Islam is in danger'.

Ashok Aggarwal, Government employee, Gyan Sarovar.

'I would fear for my life if I resided in Muslim localities. I have fear of communal riots; they would kill me'.

Gopal Shankar, *Mazdoor*, Sasni Gate.

'No. I am not having any relations with Muslims because of their dirty habits. They manufacture garbage. Muslims can live among Hindus but Hindus can't live among Muslims. I don't trust them. They are *Qasais* [butchers]: they are used to slaughtering. Hindus feel pain to kill others but Muslims don't because they are used to it'.

Ritesh Kumar, *Mazdoor*, Sasni Gate.

Now, here is what Muslim respondents had to say when answering the question 'Could you live in a non-Muslim area?'

'No. *Vahan ka mahol accha nahin lagta* [I don't like the atmosphere there]. There is no mosque to offer prayers'.

Salim Qadeer, Retired from lock industry, Upar Fort.

'No. We can visit them but we can't live there. Because the non-Muslim culture is too different. Food, habits, religious practices, lifestyles, everything is different'.

Sima Naseem, Housewife, Upar Fort.

'No. Muslims are kind-hearted. Non-Muslims are not. At the times of communal riots, if a Muslim goes to non-Muslim areas, he faces problems but if a non-Muslim comes in Muslim areas, we are kind to him'.

Mufti of Aligarh City, 8 August 2010, Upar Fort.

'During communal riots, Muslims suffer most, about 80%, so they want to be united and live together'.

Abdul Rahman, Entrepreneur in hardware industry, Upar Fort.

After each round of communal violence, Hindu and Muslim families left the mixed areas of the Old City[9] where they used to live together and joined their coreligionists. Hindu and Muslim newcomers then built their houses in entirely Hindu or Muslim areas (in the Civil Lines for the richest, at the periphery of the town for the poorest). The city got gradually fragmented. One of the paradigmatic examples of this segregation through violence is the *mohalla* of Manik Chowk in the Old City, which, from a large Muslim *mohalla*, was progressively turned into a Hindu area: the Muslim residents, whose crumbling houses deterred the commercial growth of the *mohalla*, were violently evicted by Baniya castes during the riots of the 1970s-80s in order to build a cinema hall (Mann, 1992: 175; Zoya Hasan, 1989:160-161). The segregated urban structure of Aligarh city therefore appears as the product of past communal tensions.

A Riot-Prone City

Varshney has shown that five cities systematically come on top of the classification of India's riot-prone cities: Mumbai, Ahmedabad, Hyderabad, Meerut and Aligarh (Varshney, 2002: 7). Aligarh, a rather small town compared to Mumbai or Hyderabad, notoriously belongs to the 'top five' of violent Indian cities. The riot of 1961, which was one of the first large-scale riots in post-independence India, considerably shook the Indian national leadership. The deadly riots of 1978 were sparked off by the murder of a notorious Hindu criminal and wrestler, Bhure Lal, who had strong connections with the RSS. This killing triggered off retaliations by RSS elements. In 1990-91, tensions rose after the death of *kar sevaks* in Ayodhya. Widespread violence engulfed the town after a conflict between Muslims and the PAC (Provincial Armed Constabulary; the Uttar Pradesh state police).

Table 5.2. Hindu-Muslim riots in Aligarh

Date	Official or newspaper death toll
22 September 1925	6
10-11 April 1927	0
3 November 1946	1
29 March 1946	4
Pre-independence total	**11**
3-4 March 1950	5
6 June 1954	0
14 September 1956	0
1-3 October 1961	15

1966	0
1969	0
2 March 1971	17
June 1971	0
June 1972	1
3-5 October 1974	0
October-December 1978	28
May 1979	5
17 June 1979	0
August-November 1980	11
October 1988	2
10 November 1989	0
November 1990-January 1991	92
December 1992	NA
10 March 1995	8
1 November 2003	0
6 April 2006	4
29 May 2006	3
Post-independence Total	**191**

Sources: from 1925 to 1995, Brass, *The Production of Hindu-Muslim Violence in Contemporary India*. (2003), op. cit., p. 63. For 2003, Asghar Ali Engineer, 'Communal riots, 2003', *Economic and Political Weekly*, 3 January 2004. For 2006, Asghar Ali Engineer, 'Communal riots, 2006' (2007).

Explaining the Communal Divide

Why did Aligarh become such a communally sensitive place? Several explanations have been put forward in the literature, which also shed light on the fate of Muslims in this riot-prone city.

AMU

Aligarh first experienced a growing pre-independence polarisation between a Muslim elite on the wane and fast-rising Hindu merchant classes (Baniyas). This division of society along communal lines stroke the syncretic *qasbah* culture a blow.

The development of the AMU further sharpened communal antagonisms particularly after the creation of the Muslim League in 1906 and during the Partition in 1947. All these events ostensibly backed by some AMU students strengthened the divide between the Muslim institution and the Hindu-majority city.

In the post-independence period, the Hindu-Muslim conflict crystallised over the issue of the affiliation of the Hindu colleges of the town. While Hindu nationalists claim that they should be affiliated to the AMU,[10] Muslim elites argue that doing so would undermine the minority character of the university (Wright, 1966). An increase in the number of Hindu students would indeed lessen the weight of their Muslim counterparts and discredit the claim that Muslims should run the AMU as an institution established by and for them (see note 6).

Issues related to the AMU often sparked off communal riots in the town, such as in 1961 when the crushing defeat of all the Hindu candidates to the AMU Students Union elections led to violence in the city. Similarly in 1978,[11] the campaign to restore the minority character of the institution contributed to foster tensions which culminated into widespread rioting after the murder of Bhure Lal. As Vice-Chancellor Farooqi (1990-94) pointed out, 'this university is a symbol like a *masjid* or a *mandir*,'

Even today, the minority character issue and the enrolment of Hindu students remain a bone of contention between the two communities. While Muslims consider that 'their' institution is being captured by Hindus, Hindu applicants feel that they are discriminated against in the process of admission:

'The admission system in AMU is biased. Non-Muslims qualify for written test but then not for interview. There are lots of complaints. They favour Muslims'.

Rajesh Varshney, Government employee, Gyan Sarowar.

'AMU is very good. But it has started discrimination: non-Muslims are now getting admission more than the Muslims. Because of the Vice-Chancellor, now, there are more Hindus. The VC fired Muslim employees'.

Adeel Mirza, Worker in the steel industry, Upar Fort.

The Failure of the Congress Party

Historically, the communalisation of Aligarh's social life is a direct consequence of the failure of the pre-independence Congress city party to integrate both communities. Stuck in factional divisions, it proved unable to implement a secular policy. Its association with the Arya Samaj and the Hindu Mahasabha during the civil disobedience campaign turned many Muslims away. The pre-independence Congress in Aligarh appeared in the Muslim eyes as a pro-Hindu body[12] (Zoya Hasan, 1989: 85-87). The strength of Hindu nationalism, actively promoted by the economically-dominant Baniya castes, is indeed one of the striking features of the town.

Brass (2003) considers that Aligarh has witnessed the formation of an 'institutionalized riot system' (IRS). Riots generally happen during electoral periods: they contribute to reinforce the antagonism between Hindus and Muslims and polarise the electorate along communal lines, so that the Hindu majority population votes massively in favour of Hindu parties. The role of the late K.K. Navman, a Varshney businessman and former BJP MLA, in the instrumentalisation of the riots has been extensively documented (Graff, 1991). These political calculations come along on top of individual motives: at a micro-level, riots are often a way to gain control over some urban territory, undermine the influence of economic rivals, settle personal scores or evict undesirable neighbours.

Economic Rivalries

The lock industry, for which Aligarh is famous, started in the 1880s. This industry has traditionally been dominated by Muslim artisans, but Hindus have progressively gained ground in the field. A kind of division of labour has taken shape: the *mazdooris* (workers) and the skilled artisans are largely Muslim while the marketers, exporters and suppliers of raw materials are rather Hindus from Baniya castes (Aggarwal and Varshney). This situation has created resentment among the Muslim *mazdooris,*

Muslims in the Local Elite Groups

The Intelligentsia's City

Maybe more than other North Indian cities, Aligarh has been able to retain a prominent Muslim elite thanks to the AMU. According to Mann, 'the AMU has perhaps allowed Aligarh's *qasbah* elite to survive to an extent not found in other *qasbah* towns'. (Mann, 1992: 39). With around 2,000 teachers, mostly Muslim, working in the university, one can imagine the attraction that the town exerts on Muslim graduates.[13]

Scarce Businessmen

But while Muslims are predominant among the intellectuals of the town, they remain relatively rare in the business field. Of course, Muslims are conspicuous in the lock industry of Aligarh. 9,000 units are currently producing locks within the city (Sharma, Sharma, Naqvi, 2005). Besides the lock industry, the two other biggest employers of Muslims are building fittings and brass casting or hardware.

But the local lock industry is experiencing a sharp decline due to the massive arrival of Chinese locks in the Indian market. And Muslims remain small-scale entrepreneurs. The biggest businessmen of Aligarh are largely Baniyas, mostly working as contractors in the building field. Among the Muslims, only one lock manufacturer has risen to a high position: Zafar Alam, owner of the Link Locks factory, the second largest Indian manufacturer of locks (the first one is in Mumbai). With a sales figure of Rs. 50 crores last year, Zafar Alam has managed to carve out a niche for himself. But by his own admission, Zafar Alam is not so prominent among Aligarh's businessmen:

'Top businessmen don't belong to the Muslim community. In the top five of Aligarh, there is not one single Muslim. I am not in the top five. Among the Muslims I am the only one. But if you take the whole of Aligarh, I am nowhere'.

Zafar Alam, 8 August 2010, Civil Lines, Aligarh.

Deserting Lawyers

Muslims are far from numerous among the judiciary elites of the district, as evidenced by the lists collected at the Aligarh Civil and Criminal Bar Associations:

Table 5.3. Judiciary Elites in Aligarh District

	Total	Muslims	% Muslims
Lawyers in the Civil Bar Association	610	30	5%
Lawyers in the Criminal Bar Association	1,778	126	7%
Judicial Officers in Aligarh District	44	11	25%

Source: Lawyers: lists collected at the Aligarh Court in July 2010, Judicial Officers: Allahabad High Court, http://www.allahabadhighcourt.in/District/Aligarh.htm (accessed on April 2011).

This scarcity of Muslim lawyers is all the more surprising as the AMU has one of the best law faculties of the country. But new law graduates generally leave the district in order to achieve better careers.

ALIGARH

Policemen

The presence of Muslims among police men is equally thin. The website of the Uttar Pradesh police provides a record of its gazetted and non-gazetted officers in the district of Aligarh. Although this document is not necessarily up to date, the figures show that Muslims are massively under-represented:

Table 5.4. Police officers in Aligarh posting district

		Total	Muslims	% Muslims
Gazetted Officers	Indian Police Services (IPS)	4	0	0%
	Provincial Police Services (PPS)	17	1	5.9%
Non-Gazetted Officers		1,112	39	3.5%

Source: Gazetted Officers: http://uppolice.up.nic.in/; Non-Gazetted Officers: http://uppolice.lucknowinfo.com/login/hc/searchl.php

Some Muslim respondents pointed at the largely 'Hindu' character of the police:

'The police always give favour to the non-Muslims. They want to control the Muslim areas which are illiterate. They oppress people. Due to the same religion, they give favour to the Hindus. During the riots they even caught children and put them in jail'.

Ali Ziauddin, Doctor, Shah Jamal.

Looking for Political Leaders

'This is our bad luck *(badkismati)* that there is no leader in Aligarh. There are religious leaders, but for political affairs, there is no one'.

Mufti of Aligarh City, 8 August 2010, in his house, Upar Fort, Aligarh.

Aligarh's political life is regulated by three kinds of elections: the Parliamentary elections, the State Assembly elections and the Municipal Corporation elections. The constituency for the Parliamentary elections being district-wise, the issue of the election is largely determined by the four rural *tahsils* of the district (Brass, 2003: 221). They are generally not hotly contested in Aligarh City. Citywide mayoral elections have been held in an erratic way, although

Table 5.5. MPs and MLAs from Aligarh Parliamentary and Assembly constituencies (1951–2009) (names in bold characters are Muslims)

Year	Member of Parliament		Member of Legislative Assembly for Aligarh constituency	
	Winner	Runner-up	Winner	Runner-up
1951	Shri Chand Singhal (INC)	Mewa Ram (SCF)	**Nafizul Hasan (INC)**	Amar Singh (Ind)
1957	**Jamal Khwaja (INC)**	B.P. Maurya (SCF)	Anant Ram Verma (INC)	L.N. Mathur (Ind)
1962	B.P. Maurya (Rep)	Shiv Kumar Shastri (Ind)	**Abdul Basir Khan (Rep)**	Anant Ram Verma (INC)
1967	Shiv Kumar Shastri (Ind)	R.M. Pratap (Ind)	Indra Pal Singh (BJS)	Ravind Y. R. Khwaja (INC)
1969		**Modh. Yunus Saleem (INC)**	**Ahmad Loot Khan Sherwani (INC)**	Shri Chand Singhal (BKD)
1971	Shiv Kumar Shastri (BKD)			
1974			Indra Pal Singh (BJS)	**Khwaja Haleem (INC)**
1977	Nawab Singh Chauhan (BLD)	Gan Shyam Singh (INC)	**Moziz Ali Beg (JNP)**	**Khwaja Haleem (INC)**
1980	Mrs Indra Kumari (JNP-S)	Gan Shyam Singh (INC-I)	**Khwaja Haleem (JNP-S)**	Nem Singh Chauhan (BJP)
1984	Mrs Usha Rani (INC)	B. P. Maurya (LKD)		
1985			Captain Baldev Singh (INC-I)	**Khwaja Haleem (INC)**
1989	**Satya Pal Malik (JD)**	Usha Rani (INC)	Krishna Kumar Navaman (BJP)	**Khwaja Haleem (INC)**
1991	Sheela Gautam (BJP)	Baldev Singh (JD)	Krishna Kumar Navaman (BJP)	**Mohd. Sufiyan (JD)**
1993			Krishna Kumar Navaman (BJP)	**Abdul Khalik (BSP)**
1996	Sheela Gautam (BJP)	**Abdul Khalik (BSP)**	**Abdul Khalik (SP)**	
1998	Sheela Gautam (BJP)	Captain Baldev Singh (SP)		Krishna Kumar Navaman (BJP)

1999	Sheela Gautam (BJP)	Sahab Singh (BSP)	
2002		Vivek Bansal (INC)	Deepak Mitral (BJP)
2004	Bijendra Singh (INC)	Sheela Gautam (BJP)	
2007		Zamir Ullah (SP)	Sanjeev Raja (BJP)
2009	Raj Kumari Chauhan (BSP)	Zafar Alam (SP)	
Total number of Muslim MPs 2 in 58 years (15 elections)		**Total number of Muslim MLAs 7 in 58 years (15 elections)**	

Source: Statistical Reports on Lok Sabha elections and Assembly elections, Electoral Commission of India.

http://eci.nic.in/eci_main/StatisticalReports/ElectionStatistics.asp (accessed on April 2011).

BJP Bharatiya Janata Party; BJS Bharatiya Jan Sangh; BKD Bharatiya Kranti Dal; BLD Bharatiya Lok Dal; BSP Bahujan Samaj Party; INC Indian National Congress; INC-I Indian National Congress (I); Ind Independent; JD Janata Dal; JNP Janata Party; JNP-S Janata Party (Secular); LKD Lok Dal; REP Republican Party; SCF All India Scheduled Castes Federation; SP Samajwadi Party.

the situation has been improving from the 1990s onwards. In contrast, Legislative Assembly elections are the ones that arouse the interest of most Aligarhians. Aligarh City is divided into two constituencies: *mohallas* situated mainly in the Old City fall under the Aligarh constituency while wards of the Civil Lines belong to the Koil constituency.[14]

There have been only two Muslim MPs elected out of fifteen elections. The businessman Zafar Alam who contested the last parliamentary elections of 2009 for the SP lost to the BSP candidate.

Muslim candidates have been more successful for MLA posts: they won seven elections out of fifteen. The current MLA, Zamir Ullah, who is also from the Samajwadi Party, belongs to the Muslim community. He is however heavily criticised for his lack of education. According to Brass, the success of Muslim politicians in the Legislative Assembly elections can be explained by the delimitation of the Aligarh constituency. While Hindu areas have been excluded, the new *mohallas* incorporated in the boundaries of the constituency are predominantly Muslim (Brass, 2003: 155).

The delimitation for the Municipal Corporation elections, which incorporates predominantly Hindu localities, is not as advantageous to Muslims. It is indeed what we find when we analyse the Aligarh Municipal Corporation, whose composition is given in Table 5.6 for the 1995 and 2006 elections.

Table 5.6. Caste/Community members of the Aligarh Municipal Corporation

	1995	2006
Hindus and Others	29 (48%)	45 (64%)
Muslims	19 (32%)	25 (36%)
Scheduled Castes	12 (20%)	NA
Total	60	70

Source: For 1995, P. Brass, *The Production of Hindu-Muslim Violence in Contemporary India* (2003), op. cit., p 57. For 2006, Detailed Lists of Contesting Candidates with their Valid Votes for the post of member, Aligarh district, http://sec.up.nic.in/ (lists in Hindi).

Not a single Muslim ever succeeded in becoming mayor of Aligarh in post-independence India (Shahid, 2007). Mayors of the city have been predominantly Hindus affiliated to the BJP, particularly from the Baniya castes. The current BJP mayor, Ashutosh Varshney, who was elected in 1995 and re-elected in 2006, belongs to this caste, as was his predecessor (O.P. Aggarwal). This can be explained by the historical strength of the Baniyas in the city: among them the subcaste of Barahsenis (Varshneys) have long supported the Arya Samaj, the Jana Sangh and the BJP (Graff, 1991: 145).

'You know 80% of the economy of this town is in the hands of these Baniyas and they are BJP supporters. The mayor elections are money oriented. Muslims can't afford these expenses. So again a Baniya has come as a mayor. He is an exporter. He paid about two million to an actress who came here during two or three hours. She was paid to attract the crowd'.

Zafar Alam, 8 August 2010, in his house, Civil Lines, Aligarh.

The Muslim community of Aligarh seems therefore poorly represented in the political sphere, except maybe in the Legislative Assembly of Uttar Pradesh (Vidhan Sabha), where Muslim candidates have been able to win because their community forms a majority in the delimited constituency. The potential Muslim leaders who could have emerged, Zafar Alam, Zamir Ullah, Abdul Khalik, the Congresswoman Roohi Zuberi and most of all Khwaja Haleem are not particularly trusted by the Muslims of Aligarh who have lost faith in their politicians. Although many of my respondents expressed their preference for Muslim candidates, they also pointed at the inefficiency and corruption of politicians in general. These Muslim personalities were also sometimes presented as corrupt puppet politicians in the hands of political parties. In short, politics was hardly seen as an effective way to empower the Muslim community.[15] And the representativeness of Muslim political leaders is all the more problematic as the Muslim community of Aligarh is not a monolith.

What Muslim Community?

Biraderi vs. Ummah

Elisabeth Mann identifies twenty-four *biraderis* in Aligarh city, among which the largest are the Momin Ansars, the Abbasis, the Saifis, the Qureshis, the Pathans and the Telis, who form a majority in some *mohallas*. Aligarh *biraderi anjumans* (caste associations) seek to improve the conditions of these castes through the mobilisation of resources.[16] They are the institutional expression of *biraderi* divisions. Muslims are as segmented as the majority community: one can find in Aligarh *mohallas* entirely peopled with members of a single *biraderi* (Graff, 1991: 146). It appears that caste-based considerations are often taken into account during elections of Muslim candidates. This is particularly true for the elections of ward corporators in Muslim-dominated localities. One ward corporator confides:

'I will fight the next elections, but not in this ward (62). I will fight for ward 54 because there are larger numbers of people from my own caste (Telis) in this ward'.

Ward corporator, ward 62, 18 August 2010, Shah Jamal.

Civil Lines vs. Old City, Elite vs. Non-elite

The class-based division among Aligarh Muslims is reflected in the already mentioned spatial divide between the Civil Lines and the Old City, the elite Muslims living in the Civil Lines while the non-elite Muslims are stuck in the old and congested city. The *kathpulla* (wooden bridge) which connects the two symbolises the tremendous social gap that separates them. The class division of Aligarh Muslim community is therefore materialised in the physical structure of the town too. This divided spatial structure is a direct legacy of the colonial period. The British urban planning aimed at separating the various urban functions of the city (Dupont & Heuze, 2007: 23): the Civil Lines were the space where the Civilians and the 'Civilized' used to live (segregated from the natives). The establishment of the AMU in the Civil Lines reinforced this legacy, as educated people, largely drawn from the Ashraf castes, agglomerated around the university while labourers remained in the Old City. Residents of the Civil Lines (university professors, businessmen and government employees) hardly go to the City and balk at doing so, as exemplified by this Muslim woman, a professor at AMU, who, while born and brought up in Aligarh, hardly visits the Old City:

'—Do you often go to the Old City?

No... No. I rarely go there. I went just twice or thrice.

Why?

It is not a place of interest. There are types of markets there which do not suit us.

And Shah Jamal?

I have never been.

Even to the *dargah*?

Yes, I have heard of it. Even this Jama Masjid [in Upar Fort], I have heard of it. But I have never seen it'.

Firzana Ali Beg, Professor at AMU, Sir Syed Nagar.

There is a clear disconnect between the two worlds.

ALIGARH

'We are cut off from the city. What we know from the city, it is just hearsay. I just went once to Shah Jamal. Although we are in Aligarh, we are not in Aligarh'.

Mohammed Qutub, Professor at AMU.

'We are not similar people. We are educated. They are not educated. It is not to say that it is good or bad. It is just that we have nothing to say to them'.

Shoaib Shakeel, Professor at AMU.

Muslims living in the Civil Lines insist on their social etiquette, *adab*. They consider the Old City as dangerous, archaic, communal, uncivilised and insalubrious. This is what Irfan Ahmad has coined 'domestic orientalism' (Ahmad, 2009: 39). By contrast, the Civil Lines appear as a dream for many Muslims living in the Old City[17]: moving to the Civil Lines is a sign of upward social mobility and economic success.[18] On the other hand, the disdain of Civil Lines residents is deeply resented by non-elite Muslims, who remain attached to the atmosphere and morality of their *mohallas*. They often describe the Civil Lines Muslims as lazy and individualistic *kothiwallas* (people living in large *kothis,* that is, mansions), who 'consider themselves as superior' and 'have education but don't have humanity'. For many, they have lost their values and Islamic morality.

'One of my relatives who used to live in the City shifted to the Civil Lines. When he died, not a single neighbour noticed his death. But when his body was brought to the City, all the people around came and shopkeepers closed their shops. In the City there is more communication, and people pay more attention to others. In the Civil Lines, they are only concerned about themselves. Many people are shifting to Civil Lines because they become rich and want better education for their children but then they want to come back!'

Amina Qadeer, Student at AMU, Upar Fort.

The elite and non-elite Muslims are therefore separated by a cultural, spatial, social, educational and political gap, which seems insuperable.

The AMU Contribution: Locals vs. Outsiders

Although a Muslim university is located in their town, Aligarh Muslims remain largely uneducated. This is one of the paradoxes of Aligarh which precludes any hasty generalisation about the well-being of its Muslim population. The AMU has generated a tremendous demand for education but also many frustrations, particularly among the Old City's Muslims who failed to get admission and saw their university being 'captured' by Muslims from outside. Surrounded by huge advertising boards for private schools and tuitions, Aligarh local Muslims cannot afford such education and have to content themselves with the (cheap but low-ranked) government schools. While educated Muslims from all over India come to Aligarh with a clear residential strategy linked to the education of their children, who get admission in the best schools of the town (Our Lady of Fatima, Delhi Public School, Al-Barkaat, etc.), local Muslims from the City remain semi-literate. Clearly, AMU has done very little for the Muslim masses of Aligarh. If individual initiatives of social work are being launched by some professors, the institution as such has not contributed to improve the conditions of its community in the Old City or in the poorest localities of the Civil Lines (Jamalpur, Jivangarh, Maulana Azad Nagar...). This situation has created resentment and has sharpened the antagonism between the university and the town. This tension can be exemplified by the competition over the label Aligarhian': in the Old City, it refers to the local inhabitants of the town; in the University, it refers to the *alumni*, students and professors of the AMU, be they from UP or from Kerala.

'The people who get jobs in AMU, the professors, they keep links with their own regional identities. They try to help their own people and give them posts in the AMU. But Aligarhians never get this kind of facilities. AMU must fix some reservations for Aligarhians, for the local people of Aligarh'.

Shahnawaz Hussain, Export businessman, ADA Colony, Shah Jamal.

The riots of the 1970s, which were linked to the minority status of the university are still vivid in the minds of some residents, who feel betrayed by the AMU.[19]

'Those who sacrifice themselves for the AMU, they never benefit from AMU. In 1971, there was agitation. There were some problems against AMU. Aligarhians, local people agitated in favour of AMU, against the government of India's plan. We were kept by the policemen and sent to jail for fifteen days. After this agitation, AMU got its own authority. We sacrificed ourselves for this university but this university has done nothing for us'.

Shahnawaz Hussain, Export businessman, ADA Colony, Shah Jamal.

The Muslim community of Aligarh is clearly not a monolith. It is through-and-through crossed by various lines of divisions, be they ideological, political, caste- and class-based, spatial or educational. This situation creates antagonisms, the Muslim poor of the City resenting the indifference of their AMU-educated coreligionists from the Civil Lines. The high heterogeneity of Aligarh's Muslim population can probably be best grasped by a study of two contrasted localities: Shah Jamal and Sir Syed Nagar.

ALIGARH

Shah Jamal and the 'Truly Disadvantaged'

An Outcast Locality

Shah Jamal is a *mohalla* situated at the southwest periphery of the town (across wards 62 and 54). To the rest of the city, Shah Jamal is a backward and depressing area. The judgments of my respondents on this locality, be they professors at AMU or artisans in the Old City, were sometimes desolate, sometimes very harsh and despising. Shah Jamal was described to me as a 'problem area', a symbol of the failure of the local administration, a *mohalla* where child labour was rampant because people 'didn't want education for their children and preferred to send them to the factory'.

'Shah Jamal is a ghetto, a Muslim ghetto. It is like a slum. If it is raining heavily, it is not approachable. Drainage is not effective, roads are bad'.

Abdul Naqvi, Professor at AMU.

'You are going to Shah Jamal! I had a friend who lived there. I used to go to his home but I was never able to reach there alone, it was too congested and complicated. We used to say that he was the only person getting English newspapers from this locality. And the only one who got post-graduation'.

Ibrahim Siddiqui, student at AMU, Civil Lines.

By-and-large, people in Shah Jamal are labourers, rickshaw-pullers or small-scale entrepreneurs. Residents, including women and children, are mainly involved in *garam kam:* they work in noisy lock factories, brass and hardware manufacturing, etc. They earn between Rs. 3,000 and 5,000 a month. The noise and smoke emanating from these industries is highly polluting. Most of these small-scale factories are located within the houses themselves and therefore belong to the informal sector. The population is largely illiterate. The habitations are mainly *kaccha* houses (made of clay), although we also find some *jhompris* (makeshift houses made with bamboo, grass and tarpaulin) at the outskirts of the locality.

Residents of Shah Jamal are used to surveys. The image of a backward *mohalla* never leaves it and the neighbourhood often becomes the focus of interest of foreign researchers,[20] university students or government employees. Residents appear either as social work clients or as embodying the typical poor Muslim masses. They are either taken as an 'exotic' object of study by foreigners or as a target of 'domestic orientalism' by other residents of Aligarh.

Dargah, Idgah and Waqf

Shah Jamal's name does not depict its reality well (*jamal* is an Arabic word meaning 'beauty'). As put by a resident: 'Shah Jamal is not a Shah Jamal. It is a place of problems'.

Another paradox is that Shah Jamal, while an extremely backward locality is also a site of great religious value for all the inhabitants of Aligarh. A Muslim graveyard is located in the *mohalla*, which hosts the much venerated tomb of Shah Jamal Shams-ul-Arfin. This *dargah* welcomes many visitors from the whole city, both Hindus and Muslims. It is registered by the UP Waqf Board under Waqf 63, 'one of the richest and largest in Aligarh district' (Mann, 1989: 151). Shah Jamal is also known for its two *idgahs;* the old one *(purani idgah)* and the new one *(nai idgah)*. Residents are proud of the latter, which attracts people from all over the district to celebrate Eid.

Shah Jamal used to be a forest land surrounding the *dargah* and the *purani idgah*. In the 1970s, fleeing the congested streets, small houses and financial problems of the Old City, Muslim inhabitants started building their homes around the *dargah*. The settlement progressively grew to its current size, particularly in the 1990s when communal violence periodically engulfed the Old City and scared the Muslims away: they decided to settle in the outskirts of the town, where Hindu and Muslim neighbourhoods are less entangled than in the Old City. The way they acquired their lands and built their houses is rather unclear. Many claim that the land was given to them by the Waqf board, an assertion refuted by the local administrator of the Waqf who said that these people had actually encroached upon the land of the graveyard after the riots.

'To understand Shah Jamal, you have to look at one thing: the riots between Hindus and Muslims. Where should the Muslims go after that? During the riots in Aligarh, Muslims migrated. They illegally possessed the lands after breaking the graveyards, the tombs. They migrated for the safety of their lives. And there was also poverty. It was not possible to buy lands in the city so they occupied Waqf lands. These were the Muslims, the Waqf Board is also Muslim: so how can we dispossess them? There is a moral problem'.

Local senior administrator of Waqf, informal talk, 23 August 2011.

'Kill the Living and Pray for the Dead': Dargah and Riots

While the *dargah* is a place where Hindus and Muslims coexist and share a common veneration, Shah Jamal has also been the field of tensions between the two communities. At the root of this conflict, lie two other places of mourning and worship: the Muslim graveyard itself (where the *dargah* is located) and a Hindu crematorium *(marghat)* located at the very heart of Shah Jamal. Hindu processions coming from the adjacent Hindu localities used to carry their dead bodies through the Muslim graveyard to reach the *marghat* and perform their religious rituals. The macabre parade of dead bodies, accompanied with Hindu religious songs across the graveyard and the smell and smoke of burnt bodies in the *mohalla* created resentment among the Muslim population, which asked the Hindus (mainly Dalits) to go through the main road instead of crossing the Muslim cemetery. However, the Hindus insisted that they were following the ancestral route. It is true indeed that the *marghat* existed long before the Muslim settlement, which extended from the vicinity of the *dargah* and progressively surrounded it. This highly emotional death-cum-mourning-related issue coupled with a clear pattern of segregation on communal lines was to be an explosive one. It was the reason for a serious communal riot in 2006. This paradoxical occurrence of riots in the vicinity of a *dargah* led an old resident of Shah Jamal to say ironically:

> '*Zinda ko mare, murda ko puje!*
> Kill the living and pray for the dead!'

The map on the following page offers a good spatial representation of those disputed sites.[21]

Even if they feel safer than before, when they were living in close proximity to Hindus, the aggregation of Muslims in the peripheral locality of Shah Jamal has not been sufficient to protect them from communal riots. The poverty of Shah Jamal still makes it an easy target.

Waiting for Development

Shah Jamal appears as a neglected locality. Not a single government school, not a single government hospital, not a single bank is to be found in the *mohalla*. To get these services, residents have to go out of the area. The state is virtually absent. Private schools have progressively mushroomed, but a large majority of the residents cannot afford to send their children there. The locality is hardly cleaned by the municipal corporation employees (Hindus from the Dom caste [Dalits]) and the residents have to give bribes or employ private cleaners to clean the drains or collect the garbage. Efforts are made only before Muslim festivals such as Eid-ul-Fitr or Eid-ul-Adha when the surroundings

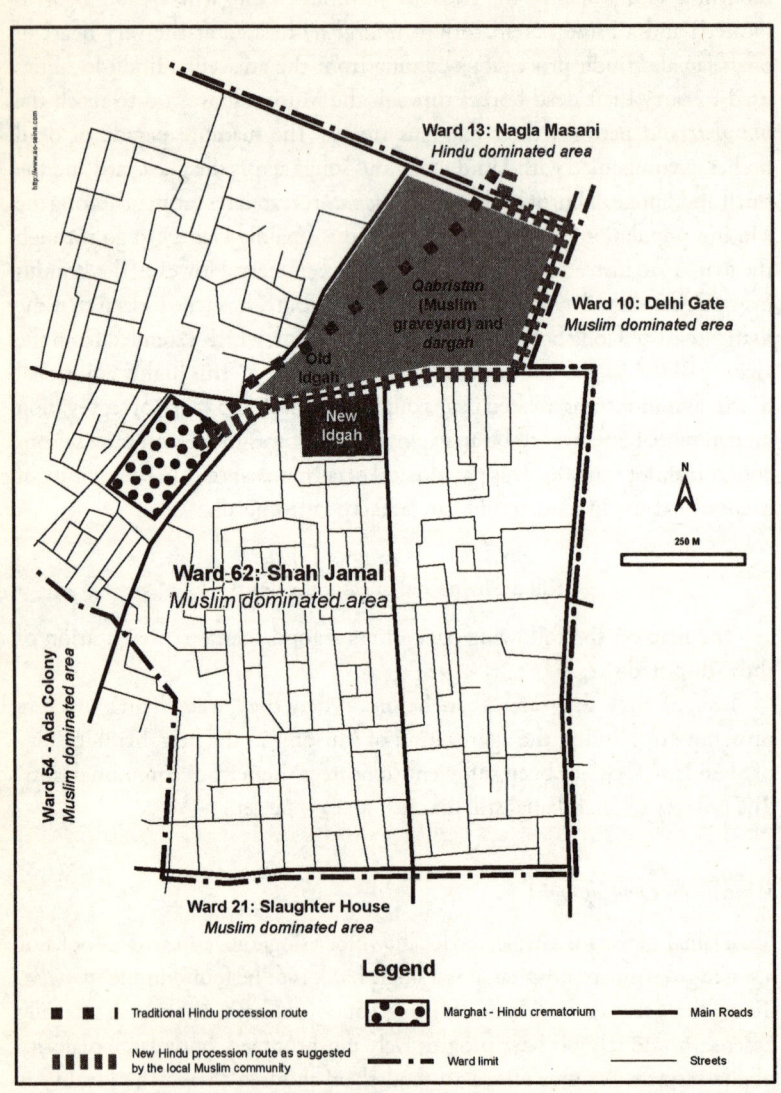

Disputed Sites in Shah Jamal

of the *idgah* are carefully cleaned. There is also the strong perception that Shah Jamal is not getting any developmental facilities because of the corruption of the local administration. The political distrust is particularly strong in Shah Jamal.

'Even the ration system is not working. They distributed rations only after four months. During three months we couldn't get anything. Normally we get 1.9l. of kerosene oil per head. It is fixed by the government. But they gave us only 1l. or 1.10l. Because of corruption'.

Ahmed Ansari, Tea-shop owner, Shah Jamal.

'There is a police *chowki* in Shah Jamal. In Aligarh everyone tries to shift his post to Shah Jamal due to the illiteracy of people, they can ask money to solve the problems, they can ask bribes'.

Ward corporator, ward 62, 18 August 2010, Shah Jamal.

The two ward corporators (wards no. 54 and 62), who belong to the Samajwadi Party, considered that Shah Jamal was victim of anti-Muslim discrimination. Because Shah Jamal is a Muslim-majority locality, there is a strong feeling that the Hindu-dominated administration does not want to develop it. Residents often compared their localities to adjacent Hindu localities or even to posh Hindu areas in the Civil Lines such as Ramghat Road: there, garbage was collected, concrete roads were built, drains were cleaned more regularly, etc.

'The mayor is a BJP man: why should he bother about Muslim areas? If you go to Hindu localities, the condition is much better. These localities are ignored because of their agenda'.

Zafar Alam, 8 August 2010, in his house, Civil Lines, Aligarh.

'Agar koi area mein ap gandagi dekhte hain, iska matlab hai keh woh Muslim area hai. [If you see some garbage in one area, it means that it is a Muslim area]'.

Roohi Zuberi, Congresswoman, 21 August 2010, in her house, Civil Lines, Aligarh.

But unlike the residents of Juhapura in Ahmedabad[22] who organised themselves for their own development after middle-class Muslims joined them in the ghetto (see chapter 2 in this volume), the Muslims of Shah Jamal have not launched any such initiatives yet. Some of them confessed that they could not mobilise the residents to fight for their rights. Poverty, feeling of discrimination and widespread discouragement have warded off citizen mobilisations:

'The non-Muslim people always demand for their development and launch agitation against the authorities but in the Muslim community, people are not ready to agitate. Because Muslims are busy with their daily needs. They have no time, they have no money. If they go for agitation, then who will provide them with food?'

Shahnawaz Hussain, Export businessman, ADA Colony, Shah Jamal.

'There is one saying in Urdu: 'if the child does not cry, the mother never gives milk'. If people complain, Zamir Ullah will have to do something. But people don't go. Some people go there individually but this has no influence'.

Ali Ziauddin, Doctor, Shah Jamal.

Among the Muslim population of Aligarh, Shah Jamal's residents therefore appear as the 'truly disadvantaged'.[23] While the Muslims of the Civil Lines live in rather posh areas and benefit from high educational opportunities and while those of Upar Fort, the historical core of the city, live in a socially mixed environment and experience greater social mobility, residents of Shah Jamal constitute the Muslim underclass of Aligarh. Relegated at the periphery of the town, they fail to access basic services and to benefit from educational opportunities.

The 'Homo Academicus' of Sir Syed Nagar

The Elite Locality

Contrasting with Shah Jamal is another Muslim-dominated locality situated near AMU in the Civil Lines, in which the intellectual elite of the city resides. While Shah Jamal's name did not suit the former, Sir Syed Nagar is an ideal name to designate this locality in which a large majority of the professors of Sir Syed Ahmad Khan's institution have settled. Sir Syed Nagar is an agglomeration of AMU professors, an elite colony of the Muslims. There, the monthly income is rather of Rs. 1 lakh. Coming from different parts of the country (Bihar, Bengal, Orissa, Kerala, etc.), the Muslim graduates of modern India have gathered in the large *pucca* houses surrounding the university. Residents like to recall that their locality was once identified in the Guinness book of records as the most educated colony of Asia. While Sir Syed Nagar does not represent the local Muslim population of Aligarh, this locality cannot be ignored in a volume paying attention to the place of Muslims among India's urban elites.

Why are so many Muslim intellectuals coming to Aligarh? Apart from the fact that AMU provides good opportunities of employment for them and that Aligarh, as an educational hub, offers guarantees of good education for their children, the will of residing and bringing up their children in a Muslim cultural environment is also a decisive factor of their migration. While in Shah Jamal the Muslim identity is often referred to as a stigma leading to spatial relegation, in Sir Syed Nagar the 'Muslimness' of the residents (Kirmani, 2008) is a matter of pride and prestige. The Muslim *mahol* (atmosphere) of the locality is praised by the residents. And contrary to big metropolises, Aligarh is seen as a moral, safe and friendly town.

'Aligarh is supposed to be a place which will keep us in touch with our culture. Well-off Muslims in big cities, their children are not used to Muslim social gatherings'.

Aisha Syed, Professor at AMU.

'Many people buy houses in Aligarh just for their education or the education of their children. Just nearby my house there is a Bengali woman. She came just for that. And then they leave and sell their houses'.

Shahid Akhtar, Professor at AMU.

Sir Syed Nagar is peopled with local avatars of the 'Homo Academicus', an expression borrowed from Pierre Bourdieu's study on French academics.[24] They work for the university, want their children to study in the university, live near the university, have friends in the university and fight for the university. Their world is indeed bounded by the university.

The 'Petro-Dollar' Colony

While they hardly visit other parts of the city, Sir Syed Nagar residents travel a lot to foreign countries. In particular, their links with the Middle East are rather strong. As many middle-class Muslims in India, they find job opportunities there which they cannot get in their native country or in the West. Some of them made a fortune in these countries and came back with large remittances to invest. This is why Sir Syed Nagar is often ironically referred to as 'the petro-dollar colony', as in the speech of these two professors at AMU, one Hindu and one atheist, who criticise the religiosity of their colleagues:

'Up to 1970, there were only three or four houses here. It was even quite frightening to come here at night! It developed after the petrodollar boom. Virtually all the houses have petrodollars. There are employment links and religious links. You can see, when people come back, they say *namaaz* more regularly, they start wearing *burqas*. In the Indian culture, we say *Khuda Hafiz*, it is a term derived from Persian. But after the petrodollar boom, we started saying *Allah Hafiz*. They are more religious after coming back from Saudi Arabia'.

Asghar Abbas, Professor in AMU, Sir Syed Nagar.

'Many big houses in Sir Syed Nagar are empty because most are in jobs elsewhere in Muscat or in Saudi Arabia'.

Satish Aggarwal, Retired Professor at AMU, Gyan Sarovar.

An Enclave Mentality?

Urban segregation is above all a matter of aggregation. And many respondents, referring to Sir Syed Nagar, spoke of an 'elite ghetto', however oxymoronic this statement may be:

'I won't call Sir Syed Nagar the largest Muslim intelligentsia population but the largest Muslim intelligentsia ghetto. It is inward-looking. Muslims here are insular. If you look at Delhi, people live together. In Aligarh there is a ghetto mentality. The government is very happy to get Muslim intelligentsia into this kind of 'base' that is called Sir Syed Nagar. So even in this kind of Muslim-dominated area where Muslim intelligentsia is predominant, communal feelings are very high'.

Sultan Sherwani, Professor at AMU, Zohra Bagh.

While the use of the term 'ghetto' might not be sociologically relevant in the case of this well-developed locality (see the introduction of this volume), one can say that residents of Sir Syed Nagar are withdrawn on themselves on at least two grounds: communal and political.

First of all, Sir Syed Nagar is almost entirely Muslim. Although my respondents claimed that they had many Hindu friends, hardly a single Hindu family is to be found in the area. Friendship and neighbourly relations are two different things, as emphasised by this woman living in the area: 'We can come and visit their houses but permanent residence we don't think of. While this posh and highly educated locality did not experience communal riots massively,[25] the probability that riots might happen in the future has been enough to prevent Muslim intellectuals from residing near their Hindu counterparts. Even in the rich areas of the Civil Lines, one finds entirely Muslim and entirely Hindu localities (such as Vikram Colony). In these places, the need for security is not virtual but rather envisaged and foreseen. The murder of Ahsan Jafri in Gulberg Society in Ahmedabad in 2002 had for instance a considerable impact on the Muslim intelligentsia of Aligarh.

'In Sir Syed Nagar, there were only rumours of riots. But people truly run away. Even old people. In Aligarh, in the Civil Lines, Muslims from all over India purchase their lands because they feel safe. But there was this... what is his name... this Jafri.

ALIGARH

He was killed in Gujarat. In this society. And it was a very good society, with educated people. A mob gathered and killed him. The police did nothing. Here we are surrounded by a sea of majority community. They are not different from us. But during the communal riots, they become changed individuals. That's why we never feel safe to live among them. This ghetto mentality caused by the riots is harmful, it retards our own progress. But what can we do? Even educated people are afraid'.

Safina Rizvi, Professor at AMU, Sir Syed Nagar.

Secondly, while an elite colony, Sir Syed Nagar is poorly handled by the Municipal Corporation. As a result, the roads, too small to welcome the new big cars, are deteriorating; the garbage is not always collected and the new flats that mushroomed recently[26] exert pressure on the ground which is gradually decaying. Eventually, the complaints of Sir Syed Nagar's inhabitants are not so distant from those of Shah Jamal residents. But in such an educated locality as Sir Syed Nagar, one would have expected the residents to demonstrate for their rights or to launch public campaigns. This has not been the case. Some of my respondents severely criticised what they considered to be 'a lack of civic sense':

'University people are not concerned about what is happening in their community. They don't take public stands. Life is comfortable. Most of them enjoy it. We should not always blame others. We should think as a community what we have done. We have not done much. Everyone says: 'there is discrimination, look at Hindu localities'. Even the intelligentsia is blaming the municipality. They all say: *'kya karen? kya kar sakte hain?'* [What to do? What can we do?] Their only task is to prepare their lecture and go back home'.

Malika Nawab, Professor at AMU, Dhorrah.

Conclusion

Aligarh, politically and economically dominated by Hindus yet symbolically associated with Islam and the Indian Muslim community, has become notorious for its communal riots. Mistakenly considered as a bastion of Muslim separatism by Hindu communalists, the AMU has been a bone of contention between the majority and minority communities of the town. This tense atmosphere has left its mark on the Muslim population which has gradually gathered into clusters.

The Old City got fragmented as Hindus living in Muslim-dominated areas and Muslims living in Hindu-majority localities left their houses after each round of communal violence.

Some Muslims also shifted their houses to the outskirts of the town near the *qabristan* of Shah Jamal where they could buy some land at cheap rates and build their houses far from the congested, Hindu-neighboured *mohallas* of the Old City. The Shah Jamal area is still expanding today, welcoming at once Muslims from the city and from the rural areas of the district.

Some Old City Muslims who experienced social mobility also moved to the Civil Lines but again settled in areas where their community formed a majority. Similarly, the newcomers to Aligarh, who came for service jobs or employment and education in AMU, elected their place of residence according to their religious belonging.

The heterogeneity of the Muslim population of Aligarh precludes any hasty conclusion regarding its residential pattern. There are actually several Muslim towns in a single city. Aligarh's Muslim population features at once instances of peripheralisation (in Shah Jamal) as in Ahmedabad; instances of great accomplishment within the AMU in the Civil Lines; and instances of residence in the historical core of the city (Upar Fort) as in Hyderabad or Bhopal. This old centre is not as repulsive as one could think. Many successful small entrepreneurs who could move to the Civil Lines balk at doing so, as the Old City embodies values of solidarity and Islamic morality which are not found elsewhere. As far as the Civil Lines are concerned, it is highly unlikely that the middle-class Muslims living there would join their co-religionists of the periphery if ever a riot was to occur in this residential area, as was partly the case in Ahmedabad. The social and spatial gap that separates elite and non-elite Muslims is too large. The communal segregation of the town is thus coupled with a social one, both of them being equally insuperable.

6

BHOPAL MUSLIMS

BESIEGED IN THE OLD CITY?[1]

Christophe Jaffrelot and Shazia Aziz Wülbers

Before 1947, Bhopal was known as the second largest Muslim state after Hyderabad. Its rulers left an ambivalent legacy as far as Hindu–Muslim relations were concerned. The city was not a riot-prone area and it never became one. But Muslims were at its helm until the Nawab was in office and this balance of power gave this community a special status.

After independence, the local Muslim elite had a hard time reconciling itself with the new rules of the political and social game. The city modernised and expanded without the Muslims of Bhopal, who, at the same time, withdrew in their shell psychologically and physically, the Old City becoming their refuge. The 1992 riot and the rise to power of the BJP only made things worse. This trend is well illustrated by the situation of Ibrahimpura and Jahangirabad, the two localities on which this chapter is focusing.

Yet, a new Muslim middle class is emerging from the traditional elite and, sometimes, from more plebeian groups.

The Princely Rule's Legacy—Neither Communal Nor Neutral

The Bhopal dynasty was created by an Afghan adventurer from the Warkzai tribe, Dost Muhammad Khan, who arrived in India with his father in 1696–97.

He laid the foundations of the city wall of Bhopal on 30 August 1723.[2] His successors held the title of Nawab within the Moghul Empire, after which Bhopal became a princely state in 1818. During the colonial era, Bhopal got the unique distinction of being ruled by four women, Qudsia Begum (1819–37), her daughter Sikandar Begum (1847–68), Shah Jahan Begum (1868–1901) and then her daughter Sultan Jahan Begum who ruled Bhopal state for twenty-five years (1901–26).[3]

The Begums were keen to modernise their state. Not only did Qudsia gave up the *purdah* tradition in order to rule more effectively, but she tried to rationalise the bureaucracy and promote education. Sultan Jahan Begum took up the same tasks, considering her *mansabdars* were men 'who passed their time in indolences [sic] and whose extravagant habits had led them into heavy debts'.[4] In 1903, she started a school for the sons of the Sardars, Alexander School, but 'Jagirdars refused to send their boys in the institution'[5] because the modern subjects which were taught there (English, Mathematics, etc.) 'did not fit their boys to the sort of employments that were open to them',[6] mainly those of landlords and army officers. She decided, therefore, to send her son, the future Nawab, to Aligarh, and Bhopal remained badly equipped in terms of education. Until 1930, Bhopal students had to appear as private candidates in high school examinations held at Aligarh. In 1930, the Bhopal high schools were affiliated to the Osmania University (Hyderabad). But Bhopal still had no college.

While modernising the state, the Begums tended to promote the interests of their Muslim subjects, while keeping a balance with the Hindu majority. Qudsia, who had the Jama Masjid built, 'allocated separate revenues to pay the salaries of Hindu priests'.[7] Similarly, 'in her reign the Muslims enjoyed jagirs of the value of Rs 38,000 while the Hindu grants totalled not less than Rs. 30,000'.[8] Shah Jahan made Bhopal state more Islamic. In 1892, she reformed the army which now consisted of 'six battalions, five composed of Mohammedans and one of Sikhs'.[9] In 1906, it was decided that 'Bhopal state being under a Mahommedan Ruler, whose language is Urdu, the language of the laws should be such as may be an example to others and an authority in expressing legal ideas'.[10] This decision was resented by the Hindu lawyers. In 1917, the Apostasy law was reintroduced, which fostered the opposition of Hindu organisations. 'According to that law, the man who renounced Islam after having embraced it, was subject to imprisonment for a term of three years and also to pay a fine'.[11] This was part of the canon laws for ages, but it had been deleted in 1912 from the Bhopal Penal Code. In 1917, it was reintroduced after a citizen of

BHOPAL MUSLIMS: BESIEGED IN THE OLD CITY?

Bhopal state approached the Court. The extent to which the Begum endorsed that act—which was to be taken back by her successor—is not clear.

In 1926, Sultan Jahan Begum abdicated in favour of her only surviving son, Hamidullah Khan, who became the last Nawab of Bhopal (1926–48) and who followed similar policies. On one hand, he tried to modernise the state. In 1927, he inaugurated a legislative council which introduced some (still very limited) democracy. In 1928, he had the first municipal elections organised. On the other hand, he was accused by the Hindu Mahasabha, whose Bhopal branch had been founded before the Congress in 1932,[12] to favour Muslims in terms of recruitment. When Sardar Patel came to Bhopal in October 1947, he was presented a petition with the following figures:

Table 6.1. Hindus in the power architecture of Bhopal state in 1947

Posts	Total number	Hindus
Ministers	5	0
Secretaries and under secretaries	30	1
High court judges	4	1
Session judges	2	0
Other judges, magistrates, munsifs	18	4
Inspector General of Police	1	0
Deputy Inspectors General of Police	2	0
Superintendents of Police	5	1
Inspectors of Police	12	2
Sub-inspectors of Police	63	3
Head constables	140	5
Constables	1000 at least	Hardly 50
Nazim and Deputy Nazims	4	0
Tehsildars	20	3
Naib Tehsildars	25	2
Military personnel	2000 at least	Hardly 100

Source: Saptahik 'Bhopal-Samachar', 7 October 1947, reproduced in *Kamla Mittal, History of Bhopal State. Development and Constitution, Administration and National Awakening*, 1901–1949, Delhi: Munshiram Manoharlal, 1990, p. 213 (Hindi).

Hindu activists were already arguing for years that such an underrepresentation of their community was all the more unfair as Hindus were five times more numerous than the Muslims: 597,203 (including 187,243 Dalits) against 109,870 Muslims in 1941, when Jains and Sikhs were 69,003.

The Nawab reacted to the Hindu mobilisation in a repressive way. He attacked their newspapers, including *Hindu Outlook* (the Hindu Mahasabha mouthpiece) in justice[13] and became closer to the Muslim League to which he gave money.[14] The communal atmosphere became tense in the 1940s. While a minor Hindu/Muslim riot had taken place in 1937,[15] a major one occurred in 1946 when Hindu shops were looted (the losses were computed by the state at Rs. 8,749).[16]

Yet the communalisation of Bhopal politics and society remained limited. First, the Hindu and Muslim intelligentsia shared one common grievance vis-a-vis the Nawab. If the Hindus were not happy with his recruitment policy which they found biased in favour of the Muslims, the local Muslims were not happy either because the Muslims the Nawab recruited were 'foreigners'. Educated in Aligarh, Hamidullah found that the local applicants were not good enough and he developed a 'systematic habit of importing people in Bhopal from Punjab and Kashmir'.[17] In 1934, local Hindus and Muslims launched together the Mulki movement whose motto was 'Bhopal for Bhopalis'.[18] The organisations behind this agitation were the Hindu Sabha and the Anjuman Khuddam-e-Watan which had been started by Inayatullah Khan Tarzi Mashriqi, a Lahore educated Urdu journalist who had already founded the nationalist Young Men Association in 1930.[19] It is from this agitation that the State People's Conference emerged in 1938. This 'Conference' which, like elsewhere, was to become the local branch of the Congress, gathered together Muslims and Hindus. Among the Muslim leaders, the most noticeable figures were Shakir Ali Khan—a trade unionist—and Saidullah Khan Razmi, who had started an Urdu magazine called *Nadeem* in 1919. On the Hindu side, the main Conference leaders—Pandit Chatur Narayan Malviya, Lal Singh, Vithal Das Bajaj— were all members of the Hindu Mahasabha.[20]

Local Hindus and Muslims continued to join hands against the Nawab when, as Chancellor of the Chamber of Princes, he tried to defend his domination.[21] He tied up with rulers who wanted to 'form an organisation of those states which were scattered from Bhopal to Karachi' with the support of Jinnah.[22] Partition destroyed these plans. But then the Nawab of Bhopal resisted the merger of his state with the rest of the Indian Union. And like in the 1930s with the Mulki movement, Hindus and Muslims rallied around the Congress to mobilise the masses in favour of such a merger. The Nawab conceded defeat in 1948 and Bhopal state became a Part C state in 1949.

Both movements, the Mulki one and the merger one, fostered a new sense of solidarity between Hindu and Muslim leaders. The Congress was the crucible of their unity. The Bhopal Congress Committee that was founded in 1945 had Inayatullah Khan Tarzi Mashriqi as its first president; he and his committee supported the formation of the first government of Bhopal state that was headed by the former Hindu Mahasabha leader, Pandit Chatur Narayan Malviya.[23] Subsequently, in the first democratic government of Bhopal State, headed by Shankar Dayal Sharma, the then youngest Chief Minister of India, who was to become President of the Republic, Inayatullah Khan Tarzi Mashriqi was the Minister for Food and PWD.[24]

This relative communal harmony reflected forms of tolerance and syncretism symbolised by a practice that is today recalled with nostalgia by the elderly people: in Bhopal, Hindu merchants used to provide with prayer carpets the Muslims who could not enter the (so small) Jama Masjid during the Eid celebrations.[25] Certainly, Hindu merchants were interested in communal peace also because their shops were often located in the vicinity of the three mosques of Bhopal, including the Taj-ul-Masjid which became the largest in India at the turn of the twentieth century.

The communal peace which tends to prevail in Bhopal is all the more remarkable as the city welcomes thousands of Muslim pilgrims every year when they come to celebrate Tablighi Ijtema in the Taj-ul-Masjid, the largest mosque in India.

While the Congress was the framework for some Hindu–Muslim collaborative work against the Nawab and while communal peace prevailed at the time of Partition, Muslims were undoubtedly not as much involved in the Mulki movement, in the freedom movement and in the merger movement as the Hindus. In the official list of the 114 freedom fighters of Huzur Tehsil, the tehsil covering Bhopal city and the neighbouring small town of Berasia, one finds only 12 Muslim names.[26] Similarly, there were only Hindus and Jains among those who were arrested for taking part in the merger of Bhopal state in 'the India Union' in 1949,[27] a clear indication of an unprecedented marginalisation.

Towards Marginalisation

Bhopal grew quickly after independence, especially after the city was made the capital of Madhya Pradesh in 1956. It recorded a population increase of more than 80% between 1951 and 1961 and of more than 60% between 1961 and 1971. The population of the city tripled in 20 years, jumping from 102,333 in 1951 to 298,022 in 1971. This was partly due to inflows of thousands of bureaucrats, but it was not just that. In fact, two new cities were gradually added to the old one, known as Shah-i-khas.

Table 6.2. Variation in Bhopal city population, 1901–1971

Year	1901	1911	1921	1931	1941	1951	1961	1971
Numbers	77,023	56,204	45,094	61,037	75,228	102,333	185,374	298,022
	(incl. 54.5% Mus.)				(incl. 63% Mus.)	(incl. 61.5% Mus.)	(incl. 49.6% Mus.)	(incl. 38.5% Mus.)
% of variation		−27.03	−19.77	+35.36	+23.25	+36.03	+81.15	+60.77

Sources: P.N. Shrivastav and S.D. Guru, *Madhya Pradesh District Gazetteers.Sehore and Bhopal*, Bhopal: Directorate of gazetteers—Department of culture, Madhya Pradesh, 1989, p. 95; and, for the number of Muslims in Bhopal, C. Lehri, *Socio-demographic profile of Muslim Study of Bhopal city*, New Delhi and Jaipur: Rawat Publications, 1997, p. 49. In 1981, this source mentioned that Muslims were 187,475 in Bhopal city.

BHOPAL MUSLIMS: BESIEGED IN THE OLD CITY?

Shah-i-khas and Its Mohallas

The urban core of Bhopal, still known as Shah-i-khas, or the 'proper city', took shape under the aegis of the founder of the state himself, Dost Mohammad Khan. This warlord not only constructed his own fort, Fategarh, in 1722, but connected it with the old fort of Raja Bhoj, the Hindu king who had already established a fortress near a dam *(pal)*—hence the name of the place, 'Bhoj pal', which became Bhopal. That was the nucleus of a walled city which the successive rulers improved continuously. Gates were built and named after the days of the week: Pir and Jumerati on the north side, Itwara and Budhawara on the east. Others were added to these four: Imami, Ginnori, Kila Darwaza. Until the rule of Qudsia Begum, 'the population consisted mainly of Afghan adventurers seeking military service and with no intention of settling down permanently'.[28] Things started to change by the mid-nineteenth century. The troops were removed out of the city limits to Jahangirabad on the southern bank of the lake, and *mohallas* were developed within and outside the walled city. While the *mohallas* of the Dalits, butchers, weavers and milkmen were outside—be they Hindus or Muslims—those of the Pathans, Kayasthas, Jains etc. were inside. In fact, the very name of many *mohallas,* Chamarpura, Loharpura, Ahirpura, Kumbarpura, Lakherapura, etc. shows that the city was not organised according to religious criteria, but according to caste and occupation. During the colonial era, the Begums and the Nawab added many new buildings, mostly in the Old City or in the adjacent northern area. Shah Jahan Begum initiated the Taj-ul-Masjid, the largest mosque in India, which started in 1887, being built on the model of Delhi's Jama Masjid and was completed in the 1970s. Her daughter, Sultan Jahan Begum, created the suburb of Ahmedabad.

Bairagarh, the Sindhi Township

After independence, Bhopal started to develop out of the walled city. Immediately after Partition, Sindhi refugees arrived from Karachi and Hyderabad (Sindh) and were resettled in Bairagarh, the military township that the British had built for themselves. Out of 10,609 Sindhi refugees, 6,567 were engaged in 'Commerce' and 5,839 in 'Services', according to the 1951 Census.[29] They attracted more Sindhi refugees in the 1950s, so much so that according to the 1961 Census, the residents of Bhopal born in Pakistan were 17,946,[30] which is about 10% that of Bhopal city. As victims of Partition—and therefore of the Muslim League—Sindhi refugees have traditionally been strong supporters of the Hindu nationalist movement. Unsurprisingly, as soon as Bairagarh

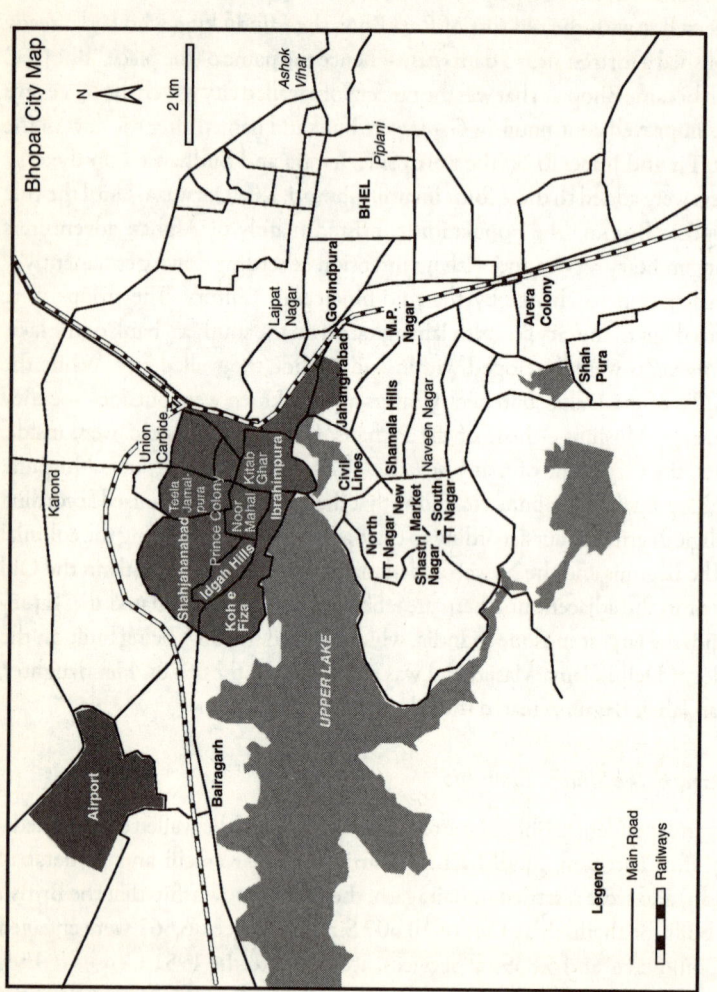

General Map of Bhopal

BHOPAL MUSLIMS: BESIEGED IN THE OLD CITY?

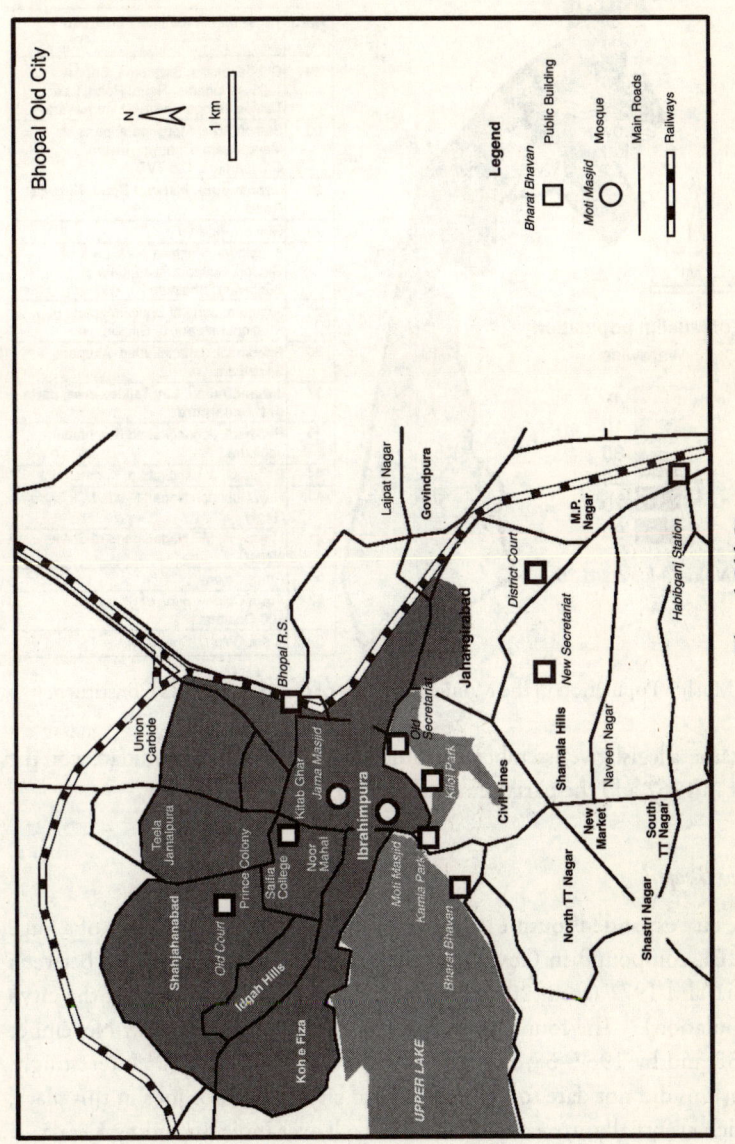

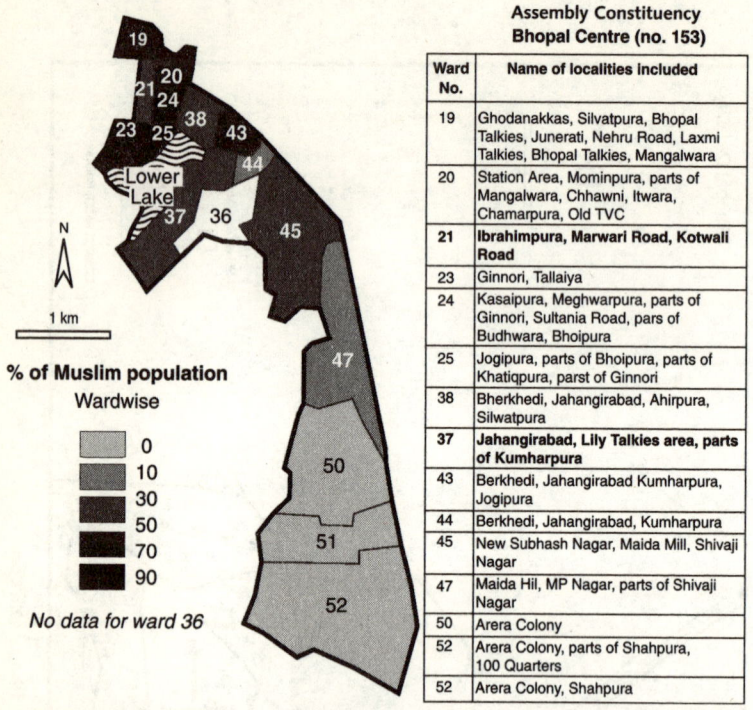

Muslim Population in the Municipal Wards of Central Bhopal's Constituency

became a legislative assembly constituency, the Jana Sangh candidate won the seat in 1967 and the party retained it in 1972.

New Bhopal

The city expanded south-eastward in the 1960s with the creation of a huge BHEL compound in Govindpura, an area which grew by 160% between 1961 and 1971 (from 20,747 people to 53,922—that is 18% of the city's population).[31] The foundation stone of the factory was laid in November 1958 and by 1967–68, the BHEL had 16,000 employees.[32] Interestingly, Muslims did not dare to leave the walled city to look for jobs in this place, which eventually attracted workers from all over India, including Kerala.

The third area of growth was southward. Tatya Tope Nagar (popularly known as T.T. Nagar) grew in phases with the creation of New Market and the transfer of the Secretariat, which used to be in the old town. After New

BHOPAL MUSLIMS: BESIEGED IN THE OLD CITY?

Table 6.3. Religious composition of Bhopal district, 1951–1971

	1951 Pop.	1951 %	1961 Pop.	1961 %	1951–61 Decade variation	1951–61 Decade variation %	1971 Pop.	1971 %	1991 Pop.	1991 %	2001 Pop.	2001 %
Hindus	414,887	79.62	615,510	81.56	+200,623	+48.36	880,135	81.12	975,122	72.2	1,346,829	73.1
Muslims	101,633	19.50	126,364	16.74	+24,731	+24.33	179,200	16.52	323,860	24	421,365	22.9
Others	4,596	0.88	12,810	1.7	+8,214	+178.72	25598	2.36	52,497	3.8	75,316	4
District total	521,116	100	754,684	100	+233,568	+44.82	1,084,933	100	1,351,479	100	1,843,510	100

Source: P.N. Shrivastav and S.P. Guru, Madhya Pradesh District Gazeteers. Seharand Bhopal, op. cit., p. 103; and *Census of India 2001, District Census Handbook. PartXII-A&B. Village and town directory. Primary Census Abstract, Bhopal*, Directorate of Census operations, n.d., p. 392.

Market and T.T. Nagar, Maharana Pratap Nagar and Arera Colony developed further down towards the south. These are the places where most of the banks, offices, companies, media and press houses are now located. In addition, the good schools of Bhopal, like Campion School (Arera Colony) and Carmel Convent (BHEL compound), are also at the periphery of central Bhopal, which gradually lost all its other attributes, including Government press.

Besieged in the Walled City?

Not only has the centre of gravity of the city moved, in terms of development, from the so-called Shah-i-khas, but the Muslims have been submerged by the newcomers to Bhopal at large. Before independence, Muslims tended to represent an increasingly important proportion of the population of Bhopal (a small place at that time): they jumped from 54.5% of the city's population in 1901 to 63% in 1941, whereas the Hindus declined from 43% to 34%. The 1951 Census showed that this trend was discontinued because of the 1947 and 1949 events (Partition, which took some Muslims to Pakistan and brought Sindhis, and then the merger which attracted other Hindus): the proportion of the Hindus grew to 36% and that of the Muslims eroded by 1.5%. The trend continued with the development of the BHEL and the southern neighbourhoods—so much so that Muslims represented only 38.5% of the city's population in 1971.

However, at the district level, the erosion of the proportion of Muslims was even more pronounced. From 19.5% in 1951, their share declined by 3% twenty years later, whereas that of the Hindus increased by 1.5% point.

The comparison between tables 6.2 and 6.3 shows that the proportion of Muslims remained twice as high at the city level than at the district level in 1971. Since then, religion-based data are not available at the local level below the district, but one may take the percentage of Muslim voters in different municipal wards as a proxy. While the city developed out of the historical core, Muslims tended to remain confined to this walled city. According to the voters list of 'Bhopal central' constituency, less than 1,500 Muslim voters live in Arera Colony, less than 1,000 in Shahpura and more than 13,000 Muslim voters live in the Jahangirabad area. The community-based map of the constituency of Bhopal Central shows that the closer the wards are to the Old City, the larger the number of Muslims is (see Map 3).

The Muslims of Bhopal are more and more concentrated in the Old City where no development work has been undertaken—except the airport road that the politicians need to use to reach Bairagarh airport. Shah-i-khas which was at the heart of the market centre, now only houses small and very small businesses with very few schools, public services and government-related jobs.

When the RTO (Regional Transport Office) was transferred from the Old City to MP Nagar, this move cost many Muslims their livelihoods. They were mainly working as 'dalals' agents at the RTO and, since its move, have had to look for another way of earning their living. Similarly, the Municipal Corporation Workshop, which was situated in Fatehgarh, a predominantly Muslim area, was moved to Shajahanabad which is a mixed area. A similar situation arose when the district court moved from Shahjahanabad, to Jail Road. The Muslim *babus* and clerks from this mixed area have then lost their livelihood. According to them, these steps were taken by the BJP government to make the Muslims suffer. None of these Muslims who suggested this government behaviour felt that these particular Muslims who lost their jobs could have travelled to the new part of the city to keep their jobs.

Besides, the Old City's monuments have not been maintained—far from that. The palace of the Nawab is in a derelict condition. In the late 1940s and 50s, most of the gates of Old Bhopal have been demolished—Pir Gate, Ginnauri Gate, Budhwara Gate and Itwara Gate. Imami Gate was razed to the ground in 1962. Since the 1990s, the rise to power of the BJP has resulted in additional assaults. While Madhya Pradesh has briefly been governed by the BJP in 1990–92, since 2003, this party has been ruling the state and before that, it won the municipal elections in Bhopal in 1999.

The Hindu nationalists, who have already tried to occult the Muslim past of Ahmedabad (see chapter 2), want to do the same with Bhopal, which they tend to call Bhojpal, after the name of Raja Bhoj, the 'real' founder of the city in their view.[33] In April 2010, the Urban Development Minister, Babulal Gaur, ordered to demolish three heritage buildings—Jumerati Gate, a portion of Sheesh Mahal (the former residence of the princely family) and the first Post Office building of Bhopal in the Jumerati area—to create parking spaces, because these monuments were 'symbols of the feudal past'.[34] The High Court imposed a stay order on this decision.[35]

While Bhopal Muslims were affected by the declining status of their Old City, they felt no inducement to leave it; on the contrary. In fact the 1992 riot, the only significant one in post-independence history, dissuaded them to do so.

The 1992 Riot

The 1992 communal riot which affected Bhopal was part of a cycle related to the demolition of the Babri Masjid. It was the most devastating in terms of casualties in the whole of the Hindi belt, with 139 dead. The riot was sparked off in the Old City by victory processions celebrating the mosque's demolition, but also and more decisively by the BBC's reports of this destruction. On the morning of 7 December, bands of Muslim youths attacked government buildings and Hindus in Jahangirabad, notably with a view to enforcing a bandh.[36] The sitting MLA, Arif Aqueel (see below), was arrested on the night of 7 December because of his protest against the demolition of the Babri Masjid.[37] Until the afternoon of the 8th, 'it was Muslims in the age group of 15–25 who took over the streets'.[38] Hindus reacted by instigating riots from then onwards. Their actions were sparked off in part by rumours and false or sensational information published in the Hindi press. *Nau Bharat* and *Jan Charcha,* two local newspapers, wrongly announced that girls' hostels had been attacked. *Dainik Bhaskar,* one of the largest Hindi newspapers in Madhya Pradesh, described how people were burnt alive in a locality where Hindus were known to be in a minority; it referred to the gang rape of a woman whose breast was said to be severed; and the newspaper also published reports on how train passengers under attack were protected by *kar sevaks* returning from Ayodhya—which suggests that the target of the rioters were Hindus.[39] These press reports, which turned out to all be wrong, provoked further outbreaks of violence.

Sangh Parivar activists took an active part in the riot, from 8 December onwards. Bajrang Dalis took to arms. One of the young men in charge of the organisation's office in Bhopal—incidentally, the son of a policeman—spontaneously declared that he had played a role in this unprecedented phase of communal violence:

'We received the order from the Sangh Parivar not to go to Ayodhya [on 6 December] because there was the premonition [*purvabhas*] that some fighting might erupt here [in Bhopal]. Therefore, a few people stayed here in alert [...] We took part in the riot. Muslim people killed policemen and looted the people. Therefore we took part [in the riot] and then scared Muslims away'.[40]

As usual, the violent action of the Hindus is presented as purely defensive. But the District Collector himself declared that riots and attempted arson were pre-planned in at least two localities, Govindpura (in the BHEL area) and Piplani.[41] The premeditated nature of the violence was attested by the techniques used by the rioters to create panic and provoke aggression.

BHOPAL MUSLIMS: BESIEGED IN THE OLD CITY?

At night, cars were parked in sensitive localities and played at full blast cassette recordings of slogans and the noise of crowds.[42] This led the residents to prepare themselves for an attack and even be on the offensive mode themselves.

Kar Sevaks returning from Ayodhya by train were not allowed to alight at Bhopal station because of the unstable situation there. They got out at Habibganj station, near the BHEL complex. Violence engulfed the BHEL township, where nearly seventy dwellings belonging to Muslim factory workers were completely looted.[43] The riot also affected Muslims from the slums, which had developed within the BHEL compound. In Acharya Narendra Dev Nagar, located next to the BHEL, on 8 December, a dozen dwellings were put on fire and after a short while a group of men armed with firearms arrived by lorry.[44] After the attack, the survivors were able to identify the assailants, who were all members of the Bajrang Dal. In Indira Nagar, on 8 December, Bajrang Dal activists, accompanied by policemen, raided the colony and 400 huts were razed.[45] In most of the places where Muslims were in a minority, Bajrang Dalis wearing saffron headgear and orange *tikas* to make identification easy, stormed these pockets accompanied by the local police.[46]

The BJP state government showed little urgency in containing the rioting or caring for the victims. In fact, a female BJP member of the Bhopal Municipal Corporation, who had returned from Ayodhya on the night of the 8th, along with other *karsevaks,* was even named by the victims as having participated in the riot.[47] On 9 December, the state unit of the party organised a *bandh* in protest against the arrest of Hindu nationalist leaders. On the same day, Babulal Gaur, the MEA of Govindpura, was deputed by the state cabinet to the railway station to receive *karsevaks* coming back from Ayodhya,[48] a decision which was bound to foster Hindu militancy. Last but not least, soon after the riot ended, Gaur staged a demonstration before a police control room in protest against the arrest of Hindus who were accused of arson, looting and killing in his constituency of Govindpura.[49] Far from moderating communal feelings, the BJP—and even more the Bajrang Dal—tried to exploit them. Eventually, the army was deployed. By and large, the Bhopal rioting lasted a whole week and 16,895 people (one third of them Hindus) were forced to find shelter in thirty-one refugee camps.[50]

The 1992 riot showed Bhopal Muslims that they were more secure in the Old City than in places like the BHEL area or New Bhopal where they were in a minority. Certainly, those who could afford to move out of the most congested part of the walled city continued to do so from the 1990s onwards, but they tended to shift to Koh-e-Fiza and Idgah Hills, which were mixed residential areas north of Old Bhopal.

CHRISTOPHE JAFFRELOT AND SHAZIA AZIZ WÜLBERS

Muslims Among Bhopal's Elite Groups

Muslim elites were adversely affected by several of the decisions the Congress government took in the 1940s and 50s. As early as 1949, Hindi was adopted as the language of the government offices in place of Urdu,[51] which, until then, was the language of the court.[52] The Muslims, by losing Urdu were at a disadvantage for getting clerical jobs, all the more so as Bhopal was still lagging behind in terms of higher education.[53] The merger of Bhopal state into the Indian Union and its implications were therefore responsible for some elite Muslim families leaving the city and sometimes even the country, as is evident from the case of A.Q. Khan, the father of the Pakistani nuclear bomb, whose family migrated in 1952.[54]

The Muslim community was also greatly affected by the abolition of the *jagirdari* and *zamindari* systems in 1953–54 and the granting of occupancy rights to the tenants. The 190 Muslim big landlords were ill-equipped to get alternative jobs since they had never been interested in modern education. Some of them started to run hotels, transport companies or became contractors.[55] Besides, the decline of the Muslim aristocracy had serious consequences for the Muslim artisans—especially those working in the textile sector, like the zari industry—who were deprived of most of their patrons and customers and who reconverted in less prestigious activities. In her book on the Muslims of Bhopal, C. Lehri, who studied 500 households (2,779 persons) from 44 wards located mostly in the Old City, came to the conclusion that 'the fields which are dominated by Muslims are city-bus services, autorickshaws, auto-repairs, vegetable sellers, mechanics, tailoring. Their proportion in government services is lower than their representation in the total population of city'.[56]

The Elusive Muslim Businessmen and Lawyers

Traditionally, in Bhopal like in the rest of the Hindi belt, elite Muslims were better known as a landed aristocracy than as good businessmen. After 1947, things became even more difficult because of the competition, not only of the local banyas (traders and industrialists) but of those who were coming from outside—be it Sindh or other parts of India.

The only Muslim businessmen who resisted their competition were the few Bohras who lived in the Old City, but none of them became big or even medium industrialists. The few Muslim entrepreneurs who did well came from the aristocratic milieu. In 1983, the grandsons of Obeidullah Khan, the

BHOPAL MUSLIMS: BESIEGED IN THE OLD CITY?

second son of Nawab Sultan Jehan Begum, opened the Jehan Numa Palace in one of the mansions of their ancestor, who had built it when he was Commander-in-Chief of the Bhopal state army. Obviously, land and real estate played a key role in this success story—more than management skill, at least in the initial phase. An even bigger Muslim businessman of Bhopal, Sikander Hafiz Khan, had a similar family background. His grandfather, Col. Rehman Ullah Khan Bahadur, was a military officer, a *jagirdar* and the Controller of the Royal Household of the Begum Sultan Jahan and then of the last Nawab. His father, who had completed his studies at Doon (the best school in India) and at Sydenham College (Mumbai), 'breaking with a long tradition of a family of Jagirdars, Landlords and Army Officers',[57] started a firm distributing the cigarettes of International Tobacco in Bhopal in 1945. Sikander Hafiz Khan built on his father's achievements to form the Reliable group in 1976, which has developed tobacco processing and manufacturing activities and made them more export-oriented. But he has added many new divisions: his firm has become the largest transporter in central India and has invested in the real estate sector to establish Special Economic Zones and premium housing projects near Bhopal. The Reliable group also entered the tour and travel business. Last but not least, it has converted a 1920 palace of the former ruling family of Bhopal into a luxurious hotel. This success story is partly due to the connections— mainly in terms of exports—that the Reliable Group has established with Saudi Arabia[58] and Dubai (where Sikandar Hafiz Khan's elder son has become an NRI and where his youngest son has been partly educated before returning to Bhopal). Sikander Hafiz Khan is involved in charitable activities—including the creation of a hospital in Bhopal where patients are treated almost for free—which have Islamic connotations. The Rahmaniya Charitable Trust that he has founded has donated seventy acres for the organisation of the Tablighi Ijtema. He has built a mosque on this place. Sikander Haziz Khan has been associated with the organising committee of the Ijtema for forty years and has been at its helm for ten years.

Except for a couple of gentlemen, most of the Muslim businessmen are small self-employed shop owners in the Old City. Ibrahimpura, a bazar which was the heart of Bhopal city a couple of decades ago has seen the Muslim domination being broken by the increasing Sindhi businesses in the area. Muslims had a monopoly of electrical goods shops, sweets shops and general stores,[59] now most of these shops are owned by Hindus (including Sindhis).

Hakims, who were mostly Muslims, had a monopoly of selling Unani and herbal medicine. Now these medicines are available at the Himalayan Drug

Company and other chemist's shops. Hakim Mohd Rizwan Khan is the last Hakim of a dynasty of Hakims that lived in Ibrahimpura. His ancestors opened their Unani Clinic in 1915; the clinic is bound to disappear, since none of his children wants to continue with the profession.

Bhopal Muslims have inherited huge properties from their aristocratic past. But few of them have converted this asset in a business-oriented meaningful way. A senior member of the local chamber of commerce explains the marginal part they play in the business world of the Madhya Pradesh capital by their lack of the relevant ethos of entrepreneurship.[60]

The number of Muslim lawyers has declined after independence too. That was partly due to the de-recognition of Urdu as the Court language and to the implementation of the Advocates Act of 1961. Before this act there were many Muslim lawyers who were practising law without having studied law. After this Act, a law degree was the basic requirement for becoming a member of the Bar Association, the Bar Association membership giving the right to practise law.

Out of the 4,503 members of the Bhopal Bar Association,[61] 557 are Muslims, that is 12.4%. Besides, out of the present seventeen members of the Bhopal district higher judiciary, only one is Muslim and out of the forty-one subordinate judges of the district of Bhopal, only one is Muslim.[62]

The fact that Muslims lawyers are losing ground is also evident from their marginalisation among the office bearers of the Bhopal Bar Association. Between 1965 and 1992, except in 1977–79 and 1981–86, either the President or the Secretary was a Muslim—in 1975–77, there were Muslims in both positions. Between 1992 and 2010, a Muslim has occupied the post of President only once, for one year, in 2005, and no Muslim has been secretary. In 2005–07, there were only two Muslims among the twenty-eight members of the executive body of the Bhopal Bar Association. This marginalisation is not resulting from an attitude of renunciation. In January 2010, out of 139 candidates, forty-four were locked in competition for posts of responsibility, including six Muslims. But none of them was elected.[63]

The Political Elite: A Problem of Leadership

'From Above' Leaders and Defections to Hindu Nationalism

After independence, the former ruling family did not join politics.[64] The political battlefield was wide open to those who wanted to represent the Muslims of the place. In the 1950s and 60s, Muslim politicians were relatively successful. Until Bhopal was a Part C state, the Muslim community was well

BHOPAL MUSLIMS: BESIEGED IN THE OLD CITY?

represented in the government of Shankar Dayal Sharma by the MLA of Jahangirabad, Inayatullah Khan Tarzi Mashriqi. At that time, the speaker of the Legislative Assembly was also a Muslim. This man, Sultan Mohammad Khan, was elected in Sehore, a locality of Bhopal district, where Muslims were not in large numbers but which often elected two Muslim candidates to the assembly—Inayatullah Khan Tarzi Mashriqi was returned from there in 1957 and 1962 and Aziz Qureshi in 1972 (when Inayatullah Khan Tarzi Mashriqi was elected from Sironj). In 1952–57, out of thirty MLAs, Muslims were five, that is one-sixth of the total.

Bhopal was also able to send an MP to the Lok Sabha in the 1950s. In 1957, Mrs. Maimoona Sultan won the seat. Daughter of Asghar Ansari—the Bhopal Registrar of Societies—she had got her BA from Aligarh and drawn the attention of Shankar Dayal Sharma, who gave her the Vidhan Sabha ticket for Kotri (near Sehore) in 1951—and she had won. In Delhi, she got closer to Jawaharlal Nehru, who provided her international exposure (she led the Indian delegation to the UN in 1958). Subsequently, Indira Gandhi granted her a Rajya Sabha seat in 1974 and again in 1980.[65]

Maimoona Sultan represented a certain category of 'from above' Muslim leaders. These personalities, which were from the traditional elite, have usually been picked up by Congress leaders who were looking for minority figures. But once in office they usually enjoyed the benefits of their situation without doing much for their community. This class of Muslim leaders was also well-illustrated by another Bhopal female politician, Najma Heptullah, PhD from the University of Colorado and the daughter of Mr Yusuf, a distant nephew of Maulana Azad, who made use of this connection when she embarked on a political career. She was working in Bombay for *Femina*, a women's magazine, as a correspondent, when she was spotted by Indira Gandhi who offered her a Rajya Sabha seat in 1980. She was re-elected three times and then shifted to the BJP in 2004, when she got a Rajya Sabha seat once again. While she has been deputy chairman of the upper house on two occasions, she has never contested popular elections.

The political careers of Maimoona Sultan and Najma Heptullah are typical of elite politicians who have been promoted by Congress national leaders to represent their community but who have been relatively cut off from their community—in fact, that was a precondition for their promotion and they left the local scene in a rather irreversible manner. However, in Bhopal, there were politicians of a different quality too, right from the beginning. Shakir Ali Khan, whom we saw at the helm of many agitations in the 1930–40s, was elected MLA of Bhopal in 1957, 1962, 1967 and 1972. A trade unionist and an Urdu journalist—well-versed in Persian—by profession, he had started a Mazdoor Sabha (workers' association) in 1943 and got the labour force involved in the anti-Nawab agitations in the late 1940s. He joined the Communist Party of India in 1952 and became the president of its local unit. He also became the president of the local Kisan Sabha, the communist peasant association, by the end of his career. At the same time, Shakir Ali Khan remained very much immersed in the Muslim milieu. From 1968 to 1970, he was the chairman of Madhya Pradesh Waqf Board.[66]

While he won the Bhopal seat four times in a row, each time, the runner up was from the Hindu Mahasabha or from the Jana Sangh, a clear indication of the communal polarisation of the city and of the marginalisation of the Congress, which even gave up the idea of contesting in 1972. In fact, all the neighbouring constituencies, Berasia, Bairagarh and Govindpura, were gradually won by the Jana Sangh, respectively in 1962, 1967 and 1974 during a by-election. Gradually, the Bhopal Muslims' impression of being under siege in terms of political representation got reinforced.

The 1977 redrawing of the legislative assembly constituencies made this feeling even stronger since there was now only one seat left where Muslims were in large numbers: Bhopal North.

In 1977, the man who won the seat, Hamid Qureshi, was the only one among the successful Janata Party candidates (they were all in Bhopal) who did not come from the Jana Sangh but from the Congress.[67] Yet, he joined the BJP in 1980. The Bhopal MP seat also went to a Janata Party Muslim candidate, Arif Baig who was to join the BJP in 1980 too. Born in Indore and a lawyer by training, Arif Baig had first joined the socialist movement—he had been elected an SSP MLA in Indore in 1967—before shifting to Bhopal as a JP candidate, and then to the BJP, a party which got him an MP seat from Betul in 1989.[68]

In 1982, Hasnat Siddiqui, a brilliant journalist who had been a NSUI—the Congress student union—leader and had left Congress in 1977, joined the BJP. He won the South Bhopal seat in 1985.[69] The Muslim voters, therefore, were increasingly confronted to a new type of Muslim leader who had little hesitation in joining the Hindu nationalist forces which had always been strong locally and which offered tickets and ministerial posts to woo Muslim socialists and congressmen.

Bhopal North: The Besieged Citadel

As mentioned above, after 1977, the only 'safe seat' where the Muslims of Bhopal could get one of them elected was Bhopal North. Bhopal North, in fact,

BHOPAL MUSLIMS: BESIEGED IN THE OLD CITY?

was the only place in Madhya Pradesh—with Burhanpur—where Muslim voters were in a position to decide the fate of the candidates since they represented about 45% of the voters until 2003 (the constituency has been bifurcated before the 2008 elections, some wards remaining in Bhopal North, others being amalgamated with Bhopal Central). A Muslim candidate has always won there, except in 1993 when the polarisation of the voters along religious lines—because of the 1992 communal riots—enabled the BJP to have its (Hindu) candidate elected. Since 1990 (except for the 1993–98 period), the MLA has been Arif Aqeel. A student leader in the early 1970s, he had joined the NSUI and then became president of its state unit in M.P. He then joined the Youth Congress. He became member of the Bar Council (after getting his LLB) and of the Waqf Board the same year. Then he became president of Saifia College, of the Waqf Board of M.P. in 1995 and of the Municipal Cooperative Bank of Bhopal in 1998. To begin with, he contested the elections as an independent in 1990 and won.[70] Then he got the Congress ticket and was elected in 1998, 2003 and 2008. He became minister in Digvijay Singh's government in 1998, in charge of the Welfare of the Backward Classes. Aqeel does not owe his popularity to his commitment to the working class like Shakir Ali Khan, but to his active defence of the Muslim interests and identity. He is known for his emotional style of politics emphasising the vulnerability of the Muslim minority. He was especially keen to defend the interests of the Muslims when the *waqf* properties seemed to be misused or affected by the attitude of the government, including the BJP government's encroachment policy.

None of the other Muslim politicians or opinion makers we met in Bhopal look at him as their leader. Muslim local journalists denounce openly his muscle power and corruption and other Muslim congressmen are locked in factional rivalries with him, including his past protege who contested (unsuccessfully) in the neighbouring constituency of Bhopal Central in 2008,[71] a very senior leader, Ghufar Azam,[72] and a much younger one, Yassir Hasnat, the son of Hasnat Siddiqui, who was appointed as co-spokesman in the Madhya Pradesh State Congress Committee (he is the only one from State Youth Congress to be picked up for the senior committee).[73]

Thus, the presence of Bhopal Muslims within the local political elite has gradually shrunk. There has not been a Muslim MP returned in Bhopal since Arif Beg in 1977 and the only 'Muslim seat' left is Bhopal North whose incumbent relies on self-limiting identity politics in the same way as the MIM in Hyderabad (see chapter 7).

The fact that Muslims are politically confined to Bhopal's Old City is also evident from the municipal elections. The under-representation of the

Muslims in the Municipal council was very pronounced in 1994 because of the post-riot polarisation of the electorate. Things improved from the late 1990s onwards, but Muslims are still under-represented and all their corporators are naturally Congressmen or Independent candidates. In 2009, the Congress nominated thirty-nine Muslim candidates and thirteen were elected, whereas the BJP gave tickets to seven candidates and none of them won.

Table 6.4. Muslim members of Bhopal Municipal Corporation

Year	1994	1999	2004	2009
Muslim members (%)	7 (10.6%)	11 (16.6%)	14 (19.7%)	14 (19.7%)
Total	66	66	71	71

Source: Bhopal Election Commission

Secondly, in spite of being a minority and confined to the Old City, Bhopal Muslim political leaders fail to join hands. They are locked in factional fights. These divisions are amplifying the effect of the forms of leadership we have identified above. Besides genuine, popular leaders 'from below' like Inayatullah Khan Tarzi Mashriqi and Shakir Ali Khan, Congress Muslim leaders 'from above' like Maimoona Sultan and Najma Heptullah have gradually ceased to be recognised as their leaders by the local Muslims. In this typology, a third category is made of Muslim leaders who have shifted to the BJP, Arif Beg and Hasnat Siddiqui. A fourth type needs to be identified, though, that is well-illustrated in Bhopal by Arif Aqueel and Naser Islam (the unsuccessful Congress candidate of Bhopal Central in 2008). These Muslim leaders are entrepreneurs in identity politics, who do not focus on development as much as emotional issues like *waqf* properties in defence of their community constituencies where Muslims are in large numbers.

To sum up, Muslims are clearly under-represented among the elite groups of Bhopal. This is not true of Bhopal only but of the whole of Madhya Pradesh. In 1997, the Deshbandhu Publication Division, a media company, prepared a 'Who's Who' of personalities who had been associated with the public life of the state. Out of 1,980 people, only 53 (that is 2.6%) were Muslims. And even more importantly, among them, a majority (28) were sportsmen and chess players (20) or artists (8)![74] Incidentally, one of the (few) Muslim MPs of Madhya Pradesh, was a hockey player, Aslam Sher Khan, who was elected in Betul in 1984 and 1991 on a Congress ticket.[75]

BHOPAL MUSLIMS: BESIEGED IN THE OLD CITY?

A Micro-perspective: Ibrahimpura and Jahangirabad

Ibrahimpura and Jahangirabad, at the heart of the Old City, have respectively 90% and 70% Muslim population.[76] Both are semi residential/semi commercial localities where the lanes—though they are forming a geometrical grid—are so narrow that cars cannot enter. There are two major differences between both localities. First, unlike Ibrahimpura, Jahangirabad has seen more development because of the transfer of the police headquarters in this area, the Lal Parade ground and the presence of two cinema halls. Nevertheless, the Muslim zones have not benefited from these changes. Second, if one goes by the voters list, Ibrahimpura is an entirely Muslim area, whereas Jahangirabad has pockets of Hindus—hence the contrasting figures mentioned above. However, Ibrahimpura is a mixed area during the daytime because many Muslims who usually own the local buildings have rented some of them to non-Muslim shopkeepers. One of the lanes of the bazar is therefore named after the 'Marwaris', a Hindu trading caste. In the evening, when the shops close and the Hindu traders return home, Ibrahimpura changes its characteristics.

Not only are Ibrahimpura and Jahangirabad not Muslim-dominated, but they are also part of a BJP-ruled city and state, in a place—Old Bhopal—that Hindu nationalists have been putting under pressure for twenty years.

The feeling of insecurity was omnipresent in the interviewees' minds when we made fieldwork in these two localities in 2010. They were worried, though to different degrees, that they would have to face again the 'reality of communal riots'.[77]

This sense of insecurity was either perceived, because they had not been directly affected by the communal violence, or real where they had either suffered during riots in Bhopal or some of their family member or friends had been attacked or looted.

All of them saw 1992, the demolition of the Babri Masjid and the riot that followed as a turning point in Bhopal. For example, we interviewed Munawar Khan, a twenty-nine-year-old employee in a number plate shop in Ibrahimpura, who told us that before 1992 he thought 'there was peace in Bhopal'. Others said that before 1992, police repression was not as common as it has now become. Indeed, the police headquarters have apparently been transferred to Jahangirabad in order to watch the Muslims more closely. Informants said that the police *chowki* had only one Muslim, the rest of the staff is 'Hindu'— an information that we could not cross-check.

This sense of insecurity was also fostered by the fact that the Muslims were constantly taunted and asked if they have four wives or if they would favour

Pakistan during a cricket match. Sheikh Zahoor, butcher, fifty-five, Jahangirabad, said, 'Hindus have asked me if I have more than one wife. Don't they know that it is already expensive to have one wife?', he finishes jokingly. He also said that if he had the choice to move he would move to a place where he would be 'surrounded by Muslims'.

For Shafeeq Ahmed, a fifty-six-year-old butcher from Jahangirabad, the only place Muslims feel like a 'majority' is in the mosque, but then he went on to say that now the mosques aren't safe either. Through this peculiar comment, Ahmed referred to the destruction of the Babri Masjid, and said that just as they demolished that, 'they' could do it to other mosques: 'The other day when I was walking to the mosque, two Bajrang Dal hooligans were staring at me and I thought to myself, I hope they are not up to some tricks (*gundagardi*).

While Muslims of Ibrahimpura and Jahangirabad do not feel safe enough, they are confident that they can frighten Hindus away in Old Bhopal. Zakir Shah, a thirty-six-year-old employee in a shop of Ibrahimpura, and Mehmood Saeed, a thirty-year-old rickshaw driver from Jahangirabad, said that the Hindus are 'afraid' of Muslims and that is why they do not mingle with them. For the latter, 'No Hindus enter in the Muslim areas because they know that if they do, they will be thrown out'. Still, both of them ended their interviews by saying that they do not feel safe where they live and they plan to go 'abroad'.

In addition to feelings of insecurity, Muslims of Ibrahimpura and Jahangirabad consider that they are discriminated against. Most of the shopkeepers declared that they were in this business because they could never get a job in the administration, in the army or even in companies run by Hindus. When asked if they had tried for themselves, the answer was negative. This presumption of being marginalised anyway has led them to get into jobs which have as little to do with the Hindus or the state as possible. The only interaction with the bureaucracy, for most of the shopkeepers, was getting registered as a business. They organised loans on their own[78] and set up shops in their own houses or rented from family or friends. Since these were informal procedures, the government tax reduction scheme or land acquisition for business purposes scheme for small businesses did not apply to them. They did not apply for power or water subsidies, transport subsidy etc. The same can be seen in other professions too, like doctors and lawyers. Their work places are in their homes and they have seen that they do not have to depend on any government help or the help of 'others' to sustain themselves.[79]

There was the case of Farhan Alam, twenty-six, who lived in Jahangirabad, where he had a job in a private company, but has now joined his father's business of buying and selling two-wheelers and four-wheelers. He said that he has worked in a company, faced religious discrimination and now prefers to be in a place without such pressure.

However, all the interviewees across all social levels, doctors, lawyers and shopkeepers alike considered that only education could improve the conditions of Muslims. Even if the parents were not well educated, their children were going to school, to learn 'science and maths and computer science'.[80] It is another question whether they finish their school education or whether this school education gets them any job in the future.

While the children are getting a better education than their parents, they usually study in the schools of the locality, most of them in the government or private schools and a small minority also in *madrasas*. But in most cases the *madrasa* was in addition to the school and was not visited exclusively.

Regarding the marginalisation of their localities within the city, the Muslims interviewed spoke about minor 'cosmetic' development efforts like repairing the streets, changing broken street lamps etc. before elections, but have not seen any sustained long-term programs which address basic civic amenities like cleaning the streets of the dumps of accumulated garbage. They insisted that the government was ignoring them intentionally and that these dumps were nowhere to be seen in the new Bhopal areas. If a digger repairs phone lines or electrical lines in their areas, they remain open and unworked for many months. This will never be the case, they emphasised, if some repair work were to take place at 10 Number or T.T. Nagar. The BDA (Bhopal Development Authority) some said should be renamed as the New Bhopal Development Authority.[81]

Most of the people interviewed expressed a desire to move to a 'better colony', an idea that was less linked to security than economic prosperity. Koh-e-Fiza, a middle-class colony, was the favourite destination, not only because it has large pockets of Muslims but also because it is like the northern suburb of Bhopal Old City and adjacent to it, like Idgah Hills.

This case study confirms that the Muslims of Old Bhopal not only are affected by different forms of discrimination—all the more so since the BJP is in office—but tend also to withdraw in their shell. They have learned to organise themselves, without any governmental help, and prefer to remain confined to the Old City. All Muslim Bhopalis do not suffer from such inhibitions, though.

A New Muslim Middle Class?

Some Bhopal Muslims have started to adjust to the new rules of the educational game that unfolded themselves in the 1950s when Urdu ceased to be an

Table 6.5. Residence of the participants to the 'Way Forward' workshop (Bhopal, 30 August 2008)

Location	Old Bhopal (total = 61)							Govind Pura (7)	New Bhopal (total = 7)	
Sub-units	Kab-e-fiza	Idgab Hill	Jahangirabad	Moti Masjid	Shajanabad	Ibrahimpura	Other		Shamla Hill	Shahpura
Participants	28	2	10	6	4	2	9	7	6	1

official language and when 'degrees from *madrasas* lost their relevance'.[82] They gave up the Urdu-only strategy they had followed until then, though reluctantly, while retaining some knowledge of this language and a clear attachment to it, as evident from their demand of an Urdu Academy that was initiated in 1976.[83] In 2001, while the Muslims represented about 23% of the population of Bhopal district, the Urdu speakers were only 12.3%—96.5% of them living in the urban part of the district.[84]

If some Bhopal Muslims give up their historical language, it is partly because they were interested in learning Hindi and English in order to get better education and better jobs. This is especially the case of the new middle class whose most explicit manifestation took place in August 2008 when about 100 members of this new social category met for one day at Hotel Lake View Ashoka to discuss a document called 'Way Forward'. This document had been prepared and circulated in advance by Farhan Ansari, a young executive from Reliance who wanted to 'give back' to his community.[85] While he paid attention to the politics of numbers and aspired to use the Muslim voters' leverage vis-a-vis the Congress—the MPCC president, Suresh Pachori took part in the meeting—Farhan Ansari emphasised the need to organise the new Muslim middle class in order to be part of the modern India in the making, educationally, economically and socially. Out of 94 participants, 58 were between 24 and 35 years old and 28 between 36 and 45 years old. Thirty-six of them had a diploma in business management, 34 had one in Arts and Mass Communication and 13 in Engineering while 8 got a medical degree and 3 had a diploma in Law and/or finance. Correlatively, 46 of them worked in the corporate sector, 8 had their own business, 8 were doctors, 8 worked in the media, 8 were teachers, 8 were in the public sector, 4 worked in an NGO, 2 were architects and 2 were lawyers.

Their parents, by contrast, were often civil servants (professors, employees, clerks etc.) and were more part of the lower-middle class. Correlatively, most of the participants to the 'Way Forward' workshop—out of the 75 of them whose addresses are known—have moved out of the walled city (where their parents used to live in many cases) but to settle down in neighbouring, more affluent mixed areas of North Bhopal (like Koh-e-Fiza) in general. Few of them went to Govindpura or New Bhopal (see table 6.5).

After the meeting, each of them provided personalised feedback on the complete 'Way Forward' document. The spontaneous comments that Farhan Ansari selected for reproduction in the minutes of the meeting are revealing of a rather managerial political culture.

1. *We don't want to be the prisoners of the past. We want a new beginning, a new deal. Let's look ahead.*
2. *Minority is upset most with its representatives/leaders only. We are willing and ready to be led by one who encourages our participation and makes us inclusive and pull the community out of social exclusion.*
3. *We don't advocate reservation since its win-lose—we would appreciate win-win. Incentivise all those who (corporate/public sectors/educational institutes and govt. offices/builders and colonisers etc) encourages minority participation and Diversity and Inclusiveness.*
4. *Minority girls and women should be educated—they are the ones who can turn around the environment. TEACH MOTHER*
5. *Religious leaders are not necessarily community leaders and community political leadership has only betrayed.*
6. *We want fresh breath fresh leadership—role modelling of minority real achievers.*
7. *Education is the key for minority upliftment—dropouts to be monitored.*
8. *DO IT WE ARE WITH YOU*
9. *PLEASE IMPLEMENT*
10. *IDENTIFY—INDIAN YOUTH—will find in each colony/sector who can shape and contribute to Nation Building.*

We have communicated by e-mail with over a dozen participants of the 'Way Forward' workshop. To the question 'What should be done to improve the condition of your community in Bhopal now?', all the respondents referred to the need for modern education. Some of them added that Muslims should be given 'livelihood opportunities' but none of them mentioned any form of discrimination. They considered, on the contrary, that if Muslims were lagging behind, it was largely their fault, not only because of 'the failed political leadership', but also because of the lack of social reforms. One of the respondents argued on the following lines:

'the community needs reforms from within so that average life of a girl child, woman improves. There is a pressing need to improve hygiene and health among Muslims. The genuine NGOs are mostly missing, so there is a need for social movement at the grass root—*mohalla*, block—level. The Islamic concepts of charity and *waqf* need to be put to some good use so that the spirit of Islam in aiding, assisting the needy is met. Lastly, instead of waiting for something spectacular to happen or blaming fate, the community needs to put its act together at micro level through 'each one, teach one', adult literacy, rational usage of money/resources, environmental awareness and integration with the national mainstream'.

Another respondent suggests, 'Interactions of Muslim youth with Muslim Professionals serving in organisations of good repute and a focused approach to motivate the youth towards career and opportunities (something like career counselling workshops). [...] The best and the easiest way to attain this would be to take the newly appointed Sheher Qazi into confidence and explain him the benefits of such a connect to empower the youth. Next step could be, piloting it in a few masjids (mosques) during Friday prayers and slowly organizing the masses for empowerment'.

The 'Way Forward' workshop suggests that a new middle class is emerging among the Muslims of Bhopal. This social category does not expect much from the state and does not ask for any positive discrimination program either. It believes in self-help and in the private sector to promote the interests of its community—not only because it belongs to this sector but also because its members feel that anti-Muslim discrimination is more pervasive in the public sector. At the same time, the very invitation that had been extended to the President of the Congress MPCC demonstrated that the workshop organisers did not ignore politics. Another caveat needs to be highlighted, though: while the place of work of members of this new Muslim middle class is often located in New Bhopal, they continue to reside in Old Bhopal, an indication of a certain (self-)segregation.

Conclusion

The Muslims of Bhopal have experienced a decline after the abolition of 'their' princely state, which resulted in the marginalisation of Urdu and forced the old aristocratic elite to reconvert itself in new professions—something it was not intellectually equipped for. They have failed to remain well represented in all the elite groups, including the business community where they have always been weak. Their decline was also due to the inflow of Hindu newcomers, especially after Bhopal became state capital, and the rise to power of the Hindu nationalists, which amplified the impact of the traumatic riot in 1992.

While the Muslims of Bhopal suffer from discriminations, especially on the job market, they are also penalised by a feeling of victimisation and self-censorship—something which has prevented them from trying their luck out of the Old City. They seem to withdraw in their shell physically, barricading themselves in the walled city, which is lagging behind in every respect—while Bhopal is expanding southward.

However, a new middle class groomed by the private sector is emerging and fights against this overall attitude. It may be able to reform its community from within if it continues to interact with what it calls 'the bottom of the pyramid'—which remains to be seen.

7

MUSLIMS OF HYDERABAD—LANDLOCKED IN THE WALLED CITY

Neena Ambre Rao and S. Abdul Thaha

Hyderabad distinguishes itself not only by its large number of Muslims (40% of the population), but also by a unique political history—until today. Hindu-Muslim relations have been tense as early as the 1930s, largely because of the attitude of the Nizam, the ruling elite, and groups from the Hindu right such as the Arya Samaj. More importantly perhaps, Hyderabad, the largest Muslim princely state of the colonial era, was the only one to resist the integration into the Indian Union in 1947–48 to such an extent that New Delhi had to order a military operation.

This legacy explains some of the characteristics of post-independence Hyderabad. On one hand, the Muslim elite was decapitated there more than elsewhere, the direct heirs of the old order being either attracted by Pakistan or unable to stay in office. On the other hand, Hyderabad remained a Muslim stronghold in India—a symbol even—as evident from the resilience of a Muslim political party, the MIM, in the city, something that is not to be found anywhere else, except in Kerala.

In spite of their political importance, the local Muslims have retreated in the Old City, which has become more and more homogenous in religious terms after the Hindus left the place in the wake of an increasingly pervasive communal violence in the 1980s and 90s.

If they are their own masters in the Old City, 'their' party has not been able to develop the place. In fact, on the contrary, it is alleged that the local rulers may not even be willing to develop the place in order to retain their influence over masses who are trapped, therefore, in identity politics.

A Legacy of Communal Polarisation

Hyderabad was founded in 1591 during the rule of Bahamani Sultan, Muhammad Quli Qutb Shah (1580–1611) on the Musi River five miles east of Golconda. In the seventeenth century, Golconda's fame, strategic location and legendary wealth attracted the Mughal Emperor, Aurangzeb, who brought it under his control in 1687. The same year, the Golconda sultanate was merged with the Mughal Empire and the city of Hyderabad became a part of the Deccan Subah of the latter. However, the capital was shifted to Aurangabad and Hyderabad declined.

As the Mughal Empire began to disintegrate, during the eighteenth century the viceroy of Deccan, Mir Qamaruddin, who was given the title of Nizam-ul-Mulk Asafjah by the Mughal Emperor, asserted his independence in 1724 and established the Asaf Jahi dynasty.[1] During the rule of Nizam Ali Khan Asaf Jah II, the capital was shifted again from Aurangabad to Hyderabad in 1769, reviving the importance of the city.

The Nizam of Hyderabad was the first native ruler to sign the Subsidiary Alliance with the British,[2] a treaty which curtailed drastically his sovereignty.[3] Throughout the Raj, the Nizams of Hyderabad remained loyal to the British.

In order to cultivate these good relations with the British, the Nizam targeted even more than other princes the Congress party. Like in Bhopal this party recruited among Hindu activists who had been the first to mobilise politically on behalf of their religious rights against the Nizam's pro-Muslim policies.[4] In 1938, Congressmen and Hindu nationalists launched a *satyagraha* on behalf of these rights and against the under-representation of the Hindus in the armed forces and the bureaucracy.[5] The *satyagraha*, which was launched by a Congressman, Swami Ramananda Tirtha, in conjunction with the Arya Samaj and the Hindu Mahasabha, brought no result.[6] To counter the activities of Hindu organisations like the Arya Samaj, the Nizam had already supported the creation of the Majlis Ittehadul-Muslimeen (MIM). This movement was also pitted against the Andhra Mahasabha and the Communists who questioned the feudal order that sustained the Nizam's rule.

In the 1930s, the 'Majlis' President Bahadur Yar Jung launched a programme of conversion in order to remedy the Muslims' minority status in Hyderabad State. Jung was credited with the conversion of 24,000 Hindus. In a speech he made in Lahore in 1940, he proclaimed that 'Muslims had conquered Hyderabad through the sword and it would remain that way'.[7]

In reaction, Hindus, who had already been attracted by a very militant Arya Samaj, mobilised behind the Hindu Mahasabha, which organised a great agitation called *'satyagraha'* in 1938.[8] The first recorded communal riot occurred in April 1938 in this context over a small piece of land between a mosque and temple.

While independence was approaching, the MIM then supported a paramilitary organisation, the Razakars which, in 1947, comprised over 150,000 'volunteers'[9] who unleashed unparalleled violence against Hindu populations, the communists and all those who opposed the Nizam—who, eventually, demanded an independent state. During this agitation, over 30,000 people took shelter in the Secunderabad cantonment alone to protect themselves from these 'volunteers'.[10]

All efforts of moderates were opposed by the Razakar leader Kasim Rizvi.[11] The movement of the Hyderabad State Congress under the leadership of Swami Ramananda Tirtha was supported by the Arya Samajists in 1938 and in 1947 to force Hyderabad to join the Indian Union.[12]

When it became clear that negotiations with the Indian Union for an independent Hyderabad state were stalemated, the Razakars also courted confrontation with Indian forces, at their own cost. On 13 September 1948, the Indian Army began its 'Police Action'.[13] On 19 September 1948, Hyderabad was occupied by the Indian army.[14] As there was no alternative, the Nizam surrendered and the Hyderabad State was merged with the Indian Union.[15]

The Decline of the Muslim Elite Groups

Partition and then the integration of the Nizam's State made a huge impact on the Muslims of Hyderabad city. The creation of Andhra Pradesh[16] was the last blow since, by attracting bureaucrats from outside, it further diluted the role of the local elites, whose members left in larger numbers. This trend is evident from table 7.1 which shows that the decade 1951–1961 witnessed large-scale outmigration of Muslims from the Old City. Those who left were mostly from the elite groups. They went either to Pakistan or to the US and UK in search of security and new sources of prosperity. This class of Muslim outmigrating population had the financial means and the networks to move from the troubled areas of Old City to greener pastures.[17]

The Shias, who had held high positions in the previous administration, are a case in point. They almost disappeared from the Old City. Their proportion decreased from 22% to 6%. In 1981 it came down to as low as 4%.[18] Many migrated to Pakistan while others moved north, especially to Lucknow and other places in UP. Some from the highest level elite groups were absorbed in the Indian Governmental machinery.

Besides the literati, the old aristocracy was severely affected too. During the Nizams' rule most of the Muslim nobility lived on the land revenue as Jagirdars or served in the army and police, where the highest offices and the lower ranks were occupied by the Muslims, leaving some room for Hindus and others in the middle levels; especially those requiring technical skills or specialised applied services.

These Muslims who enjoyed considerable social and economic status in the state lost their power with the end of the Nizam's rule. With the abolition of the Jagirdari system in 1949, both the Jagirdars and their immediate dependent families and employees lost their income and employment. The Nizam and his immediate family received a generous privy purse for his maintenance as Rajpramukh from the new government but the other families of the ruling elite lost most of their resources.

The big business families had different kinds of experiences. Prominent among them were Mir Laiq Ali, Camar Tyabji, Alladin and Babu Khan. Mir Laiq Ali's properties and companies were taken over by the government as he moved to Pakistan. The Tyabjis also went into oblivion due to reasons not known. Out of the prominent businessmen only Alladin and Babu Khan survived in the new dispensation as they were not directly linked to the Nizam government. Alladin's famous factory Allwyn Metal Works used to produce 14,000 refrigerators annually before the government took it over in 1969.[19]

The new administration disbanded the majority of Hyderabad State Force in 1950 which left around 33,000 Muslim individuals and their families jobless and without a source of income. If roughly estimated on an average of five members per family, the affected Muslim population due to this would be around 165,000. Some of the civil servants were asked to step down or removed or demoted or sent to other parts of India, under some pretext by their superiors in the new government just because they were not wanted in Hyderabad anymore.[20] IqbalMasood alleged that '...Indian Income Tax Department had focused on the elite and rich Muslims of Hyderabad' and that 'Income Tax administration had practically declared a war against them....'[21] However, civil servants who had started their career just before 1948 could remain in the new administration because of their non-involvement in the Nizam's rule.

In the late 1940s-early 1950s, lawyers and teachers trained in the Nizam's legal system and with Urdu medium background began to feel the narrowing of the prospects due to change in the language from Urdu to English and Telugu. School teachers and the faculty at Osmania University were also adversely affected due to the change in the language of instruction.

If we look at the Osmania University's changing employment situation, the presence of Muslim faculty members steadily declined since independence. In 1990, of the 215 professors, 23 were Muslims; of the 60 Chairmen of Board of Studies, a mere 5 were Muslims. In 1997, out of the 332 full professors, there were only 27 Muslims, 12 from the familiar subjects of Arabic, Islamic Studies, Persian and Urdu Departments; if these departments are excluded, the Muslim numbers will be reduced further.[22] Today except in the above said traditional subjects, there are hardly half a dozen Muslim faculty members working in different capacities in other subjects.[23]

To sum up, the 1940s and 50s were a turning point for Hyderabad Muslims, even more than in other places—including Bhopal—because after Partition came the integration into the Indian Union in a highly communalised atmosphere. Not only most of the elite groups were decapitated—many of their members going to Pakistan or elsewhere—but those who stayed behind suffered from the opprobrium attached to the Nizam's rule. The only significant exception was the local political elite, as evident from the MIM.

A Resilient Political Elite

Towards the end of the Nizam's rule and at the time of integration of Hyderabad State into the Indian Union, Kasim Rizvi, the Majlis leader, was imprisoned and his organisation was banned in 1948. Rizvi was released in 1957 on the undertaking that he would leave for Pakistan within forty-eight hours. Before he left, though, he met some of the erstwhile activists of the Majlis and passed on the presidentship of the party to Abdul Waned Owaisi, a famous lawyer and an Islamic scholar who had also been jailed—for ten months or so—during the 1947 agitation. However, until the 1960s, the Majlis remained a marginal player in Hyderabad politics. It could not win more than one Assembly seat, although every election saw a rise in its vote share.

In 1969, the Majlis won back its party headquarters in a judicial battle, Dar-us-Salaam—a sprawling 4.5-acre compound in the heart of the New City. In

1976, Salahuddin Owaisi took over the presidentship of the Majlis after his father's demise. The 1970s were also a watershed in the Majlis' history as after a long period of thirty-one years, Hyderabad witnessed large-scale communal rioting in 1979. The Majlis came to the forefront in 'defending' Muslim life and property. Owaisi continued to win Parliamentary elections from 1984 until 2004. His elder son Asaduddin succeeded him in 2004 and won the Hyderabad seat in the 2004 and 2009 elections.

The resilience of the MIM is also clear at the level of the state assembly seats. In the 2009 elections, it continued to hold sway in the Old City. Out of the total fifteen Assembly constituencies in Hyderabad District, the Congress and the MIM won seven seats each with BJP retaining its lone seat.

The municipal scene is very similar. Since the Greater Hyderabad Municipal Corporation (GHMC) is the fifth biggest civic body in the country, to be elected to this Corporation is considered prestigious and a good way of laying a foundation for future political aspirations. Particularly in the Old City area, the MIM has been in strategic position either on its own or with the help of another major party either the Congress or the Telugu Desam Party (TDP).

In the 2009 municipal elections, out of 150 seats, Congress won 52, the TDP 45, the Majlis 43, the BJP 5 and the others also 5. Majlis entered into a post poll understanding with the Congress and agreed that the post of Mayor and Deputy Mayor would be shared by the two parties on a rotation basis.

Although the party's presence is felt mainly in the Old City area it claims to be the voice of the Muslim population of the entire state. In fact Majlis leaders have begun to project themselves as national leaders. Asaduddin Owaisi is a member of the Babri Masjid Action Committee and was also a member of the All Party Delegation that visited Kashmir in September 2010.[24]

So far, the Majlis has come forward to fill the gap of under-representation of Muslims in the legislature. This party alone sent seven Muslim members to the Assembly, while the Congress and TDP together were able to send only four Muslim members in the last elections. When other parties, therefore, give the impression that they are not serious about the political empowerment of Muslims, the members of this minority seek the available Muslim political leadership, in whatever form, to raise their voice in the legislative bodies and can only find the MIM. With an MP representing Hyderabad in the Lok Sabha, seven members in the Andhra Pradesh Assembly, forty-three municipal corporators, the grip of the Majlis on the community remains strong.

The Old City, a Cultural Mix Turned into a Muslim Citadel

In the early days Islam-based orthogenetic cultural forces dominated the city's landscape, although this dominance was amalgamated with native Telugu culture. Much later, during the Asaf Jahi period, the cultural influences of migrant groups from other regions in India, and indeed also from countries outside India, penetrated the Old City of Hyderabad.

The architectural style and building facades of these cultural zones are reflective of their distinctive identity, as are the lifestyles of the people who live in them. The places where these ethnic groups first settled continued to act as a nucleus for further settlement.[25] Prominent among these ethnic groups were the Arabs from Yemen, the Marathas, the Marwaris, the Bohras, the Kayasths and the Khatris, aside from the two major Islamic sects, the Shias and the Sunnis.

Originally, the Old City was spread around the old trade route which connected the fortress of Golconda to the port of Masulipatnam. It had four quadrants of settlements along the four directions of the crosscutting roads, with the groups mentioned above occupying specific areas in each quadrant.[26] Different ethnic communities lived in the same quadrant but in different localities or smaller subsets and not as mixed neighbourhoods.

This pattern changed during the Asaf Jahi rule. The Marwaris and the Bohras settled in the western corner of this quadrant, in Hussaini Alam (old Kabutar Khana), to facilitate their financial transactions with the nobility. In the northeastern quadrant was the Purani Haveli palace of the Nizam and palaces of nobles such as Salar Jung (the Dewan Deodi) who belonged to the Shia community. This area therefore became a nucleus for Shias of all classes.[27]

In the later stages of Asaf Jahi rule, a part of the south-eastern quadrant was occupied by the palaces of the Prime Minister, Sir Kishen Pershad Bahadur who was a Hindu Kayasth. Bordering this quadrant was land given to some of the regiments in the Nizam's army. The Arabs and the Marathas settled here, the former in Barkas (local pronunciation of 'barracks') and the latter in the Shah Ali Banda and Brahmin Wadi (now Gowlipura). These were the heydays of a (partly mythical) *'ganga-jamni tehzib'*, that is a cosmopolitan culture based on communal harmony—and social divisions.

The Dalits and castes categorised as scheduled castes and scheduled tribes today, resided at the edges of the Old City like in most other cities in India. Today, some of these border settlements are well-known slums. Slums with a Muslim preponderance such as the Mecca Masjid, Damika Bagh and Jagdish Huts, are located in the inner core of the Old City.[28]

Table 7.1. Community-wise population: size and growth rates, 1951–1981 (straight numbers)

Sl. No.	Community	1951 No.	1951 %	1961 No.	1961 %	1971 No.	1971 %	1981 No.	1981 %	Growth rate (per cent) 1951–61	1961–71	1971–81
1.0	Muslims	220,613	69.15	89,080	54.66	1 16,266	54.61	147,791	61.33	−8.67	2.70	2.43
1.1	Shia	68,704	21.53	9,078	5.57	12,541	5.89	8,641	3.59	−18.32	3.28	−3.66
1.2	Sunni	151,909	47.62	80,002	49.09	103,725	48.72	139,150	57.74	−6.21	2.63	2.98
2.0	Hindus	81,889	25.67	72,776	44.66	94,117	44.21	91,528	37.98	−1.17	2.60	−0.28
2.1	Kayasth	8,038	2.52	907	0.55	1,676	0.79	381	0.16	−19.60	6.33	−13.77
2.2	Marwari	8,117	2.55	7,374	4.53	9,405	4.42	3,626	1.50	−0.96	2.46	−9.09
2.3	Other Hindus	65,734	20.60	64,495	39.58	83,036	39.00	87,521	36.32	−0.19	2.56	0.53
3.0	Others	16,526	5.18	1,099	0.67	2,526	1.18	1,643	0.69	−23.74	8.68	−4.21
3.1	Jain	6,541	2.05	431	0.26	1,448	0.68	423	0.18	−23.81	12.88	−11.58
3.2	Sikh	3,379	1.06	462	0.28	688	0.32	461	0.19	−18.04	4.06	−3.93
3.3	Buddhist	1,497	0.47	20	0.01	47	0.02	0	0.00	−35.05	8.92	0.00
3.4	Christian	5,109	1.60	166	0.10	320	0.15	722	0.30	−29.01	6.78	8.48
3.5	Misc.	–	–	20	0.01	23	0.01	37	0.02	–	1.41	4.87
	Total	319,028	100	162,955	100	212,909	100	240,962	100.00	−6.50	2.71	1.22

Source: Office of the Directorate of Census Operations, AP, Hyderabad, cited by Ratna Naidu, *Old cities new predicaments: A study of Hyderabad*, New Delhi: Sage Publications, 1990, p. 24.

MUSLIMS OF HYDERABAD

According to the 1881 Census, 123,675 people lived in the Old City area. A century later, as per the 1981 Census, this population had raised to 240,962. As per the 1951 Census, which was conducted immediately after the dismantling of the Nizam's Dominions, when there were 319,028 people living in the Old City area, the Muslims formed the majority community, comprising 69% of the people. The Hindus constituted 25% and the rest (Jains, Christians, Sikhs, Buddhists and others) formed 5% of the total population. In 1961, the population in the same area was reduced to 162,955. This trend of decline reflects the turmoil of the years following the integration of Hyderabad State with India and how it led Muslims from all classes to move in search of security and livelihood. In the 1940s–50s, the outmigration of local Muslims resulted in distress sales and, therefore, in some lowering of the property prices in the Old City. Hindus, attracted by the opportunities that the new capital offered, took advantage of these developments and invested in these properties. Thus the proportion of Hindus into the Old City during the years 1951–61 was 56% of the total immigrants. Their share in the population increased from 21% to 40% during this decade. These immigrants were mainly from the business communities from North India.

However, there was a dramatic reversal of population trends in the 1980s. Not only Hindus, but also Jains, Sikhs, Christians and Buddhists—who were in smaller numbers—started to leave the Old City of Hyderabad. Simultaneously, Muslims from the rural areas started fleeing towards the Old City. While this process looks like a reverse trend, the new comers were not from the same social background as those who had left in the 1940s and 50s. They were mostly plebeians from the periphery in quest of safety because of the multiplication of communal riots.

Table 7.2. Communal riots in Hyderabad

Year	Description
1938	First communal violence in Hyderabad city.
1948	Retaliation on Muslims during and after Police Action.
1978	Riots started after the rape of a Muslim woman, Ramiza bee, by the police. The first large-scale deadly communal riot in Hyderabad since the Police Action. 19 people died.
1983	Desecration of a mosque, followed by the call for a Bandh by MIM. 45 people died.
1984	Politicians started riots during the brief stint of Nadendla Bhaskar Rao as Chief Minister.
1990	Arrest of Bhartiya Janata Party Leader, L.K. Advani, in Bihar, while he was entering UP on his way to Ayodhya. 165 people died.

1990	It is reported that 134 people were killed and over 350 injured following a fight between two gangs of land grabbers belonging to different communities. It is alleged that the violence was instigated by the major political parties for their political mileage.
1992	Post-Babri Masjid demolition violence.
1995	Communal clashes occurred on the occasion of Ganesh procession. Two people died.
1997	Communal tension arose in 1997 following the searching of Muslim women in a jewellery shop.
1998	The trouble began after the circulation of an anonymously produced pamphlet lampooning the religious sentiments of Muslims. Four to eight people died.
2000	A Hyderabadi Jeweller Mahaveer Prasad had sparked off a furore in 1997 when he ordered his staff to search a burqa-clad Muslim woman who he wrongly accused of shoplifting. Later he was killed. It was assumed that the concerned jeweller was killed by the assailants in 2000 as a vengeance to the wrongful allegation of theft.
2003	One person had died in clashes on 5 June night and this further provoked violence. Communal violence in Melapalli and Nampalli areas on 6 June.
2006	A religious place was desecrated in Karwan locality.
2010	Riots over hoisting religious flags. Two people died.

Sources: Vishal Agraharkar, *Political Incentives and Hindu–Muslim Violence: A Study of Hyderabad, India*, BA Thesis, Williams College, Massachusetts, 2005, p. 50; B Rajeshwari, *Communal Riots in India: A Chronology (1947–2003)*, Institute of Peace and Conflict Studies, IPCS Research Papers No. 3, March 2004, pp. 4–33; and *The Hindu* for 2006 and 2010.

To make matters worse terrorist activities have developed in the city since 1992. It began with the killing of G. Krishna Prasad, the additional superintendent of police. Since then the frequency of the attacks has been on the rise. These attacks have reinforced the impact of communal riots, exacerbating feelings of insecurity vis-a-vis 'the other' in mixed areas, impressions the local police have fostered by immediately pointing a finger to this or that Islamist or—much less frequently—this or that Hindu nationalist group (see the last column of table 7.3).

Because of communal riots and terrorist attacks in Muslim-dominated areas, Hindus are increasingly moving out. For instance, in the last 20 years Hindus have completely fled away from the Baraks, a locality of Chandrayangutta dominated by Muslims of Arab descent from Yemen. As a result, this communally very sensitive area does not witness the same kind of violence anymore.

MUSLIMS OF HYDERABAD

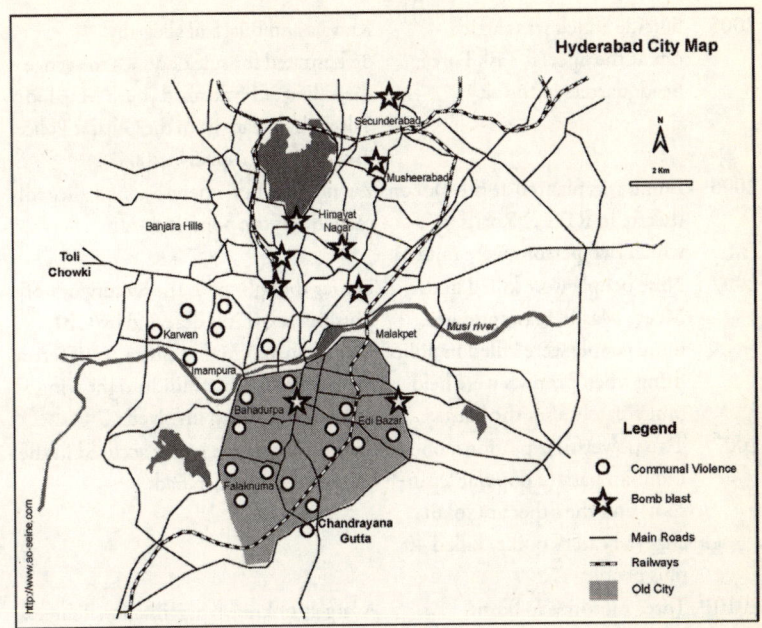

Map of Hyderabad

Table 7.3. Terrorist attacks in Hyderabad

Year	Terror incidents	Accused/suspects pointed at by the police
1992	Killing of Mr G. Krishna Prasad, IPS, the additional superintendent of police, during an encounter in Tolichowki area.	ISI-sponsored terrorist Mujeeb Ahmed, who was the prime suspect and subsequently shot dead by police.
1993	Pappaya Goud, VHP leader, and Nandaraj Goud, BJP leader, were killed.	Allegedly shot dead by four ISI agents/ Lashkar-e-Taiba terrorists for participating in *kar seva* at Ayodhya that led to the demolition of Babri Masjid.
1994	Bombs were planted inside the Madina Education Centre, on the AP Express and Secunderabad Railway Reservation Complex.	Allegedly planted by Jaleel Ansari's gang of Mumbai.
1999	Devender Sharma, an RSS worker was killed.	Allegedly killed by the members of the Lashkar-e-Taiba.

199

2005	Suicide attack was carried out at the Special Task Force headquarters in the city.	Khwaja and Bilal had allegedly orchestrated the suicide attack to avenge the killing of Hyderabad youth Mujahid Saleem by a team from the Gujarat Police in the Andhra capital in 2004.
2006	Bomb was planted at the Odeon theatre in RTC X Roads in which two persons were injured.	Zia ul Haq, LeT operative, had allegedly carried out the bombing.
2007	Nine people were killed in the Mecca Masjid blasts and five more people were killed in police firing when protests were held immediately after the blasts.	Earlier thought of as the handiwork of Muslims, now it is detected by CBI, Rajasthan and Maharashtra Anti-Terror Squads (ATS) that Hindu-right wing activists have been involved.
2007	Two powerful explosions: one at Lumbini park (a popular leisure spot) and the other at Gokul chat (an eatery point) killed 40 plus people.	Shahid Bilal is the prime accused in the blast cases in Hyderabad.
2010	Three motorcycle-borne assailants opened fire on a police picket killing a constable and injuring two others in the Old City.	A largely unknown organisation Tehreek-e-Ghalba-e-Islam (Movement for supremacy of Islam) claimed responsibility for the attack as a revenge for police firing during Mecca Masjid blasts.

Tied to the sentiments and symbols of the Old City, Muslims seem to have rooted themselves even more deeply in that citadel where they have regrouped. This is because of fear, but also because of a zeal to defend the community's way of life.[29] Interestingly, in the Muslim pockets, which are surrounded by Hindu *mohallas,* when families are evacuated before the riots occur, their houses are not left entirely vacant. Often one or two young male members remain behind to defend their spatial rights, lest the entire area may be taken over by Hindus or looted.

A Decaying Old City

The Muslims of Hyderabad are showing a great attachment to a declining place. The Old City of today, once the political and administrative capital of the Nizam's feudal rule, has lost its importance to the northern half of the city.[30] Along with Secunderabad (Hyderabad's twin city), this northern half has grown into a throbbing metropolis while the walled area has lapsed into decay and neglect. Although some pockets within a few localities show modern buildings and although the newly built 'Ring Road' connects the city to the airport, overall the Old City area is in a state of decadence.

Hyderabad's Old City offers a classic case of 'urban deprivation'[31] and more specifically of 'multiple deprivation,'[32] a notion which refers not only to a lack of infrastructure and facilities but also to poor education and training, low income, poor diet and hygienic conditions leading to low efficiency and ability to enhance incomes.[33]

The New City area which is one of the IT hubs of modern India is clearly the beneficiary of not only the booming economy but also of the amenities provided by the Government through the public's tax money at large. In the Old City, 91% of the Government Schools are in rented buildings and the number of playgrounds and Anganwadi centres government sponsored child care and mother care centres is proportionately much lower than in the New City although in terms of population the New City population is only 6% higher.

Table 7.4. Hyderabad comparative information (Old City and New City)

Sl.No.	Particulars	Old City	%	New City	%	Total District
1	Population (2001)	1,799,030	47	2,030,723	53	3,829,753
2	Literacy	66%		71.29		68.80
3	Government schools	471	57	351	43	822
4	Government schools in rented buildings	178	91	16	9	194
5	Government junior colleges	5	26	14	74	19
6	Government degree colleges	1	14	6	86	7
7	Parks	34	5	650.00	95	684
8	Parks Total Area (acres)	23.80	6	367.04	94	390.84
9	Playgrounds	210.00	43	279.00	57	489
10	Playgrounds Total Area (acres)	32.99	37	55.99	63	88.78
11	Anganwadi centres	259.00	40	380	60	639

Source: M. Srinivas, 'Hyderabad Old City: A Saga of Discrimination', *People's Democracy*, Vol. XXXIV, No. 15, 11 April 2010; statistics tabulated by COVA organisation, under the PUCAR Program, Hyderabad, 2010. Here the Old City area comprises of area south of the Musi River.

A major study conducted in 1984–86 by Ratna Naidu concluded that 50% of the working population in the Old City was in the informal sector and was regularly in debt.[34] Corroborating the findings of these studies, the AP Minorities Commissions 1989 survey reported acute illiteracy and educational poverty among Muslims in all parts of the state, including Hyderabad. When Muslims are lagging behind educationally, it is natural that they cannot compete with others for government jobs.[35] Muslims represented barely 3% of the successful candidates in the AP State Public Service Commission examination held at all levels of jobs.[36]

The Backward Class Commission also reported a low level of recruitment of Muslims in various government positions. Out of 4,899 positions allocated through competitive examinations, Muslims were appointed to 171 positions, i.e. a meagre 3.49% only.[37] Since Muslims do not have access to stable jobs or government employment entitling them to housing loans, home ownership and such other benefits are lacking in the community. Indebtedness is the natural outcome of poverty. Omar Khalidi stated that about 55% of the Muslim households were found to be in debt, as against the state average of about 32%.[38]

Unemployment is found to be higher among Old City Muslims, with an unemployment rate of 21% as against 10% at all-India level. The higher rate of unemployment among the Muslims may be attributed to their past association with the Nizam's administration. About 30% of Muslim households in the Old City have at least one member or ancestor who has been associated with the Nizam's administration or family in the past.[39] The lower level echelons from the Old City, in particular, lost their livelihood after the Police Action and declined for two reasons. First, the nature of their previous occupations was such that it required no particular qualifications. Employment was granted mostly out of patronage and on the basis of the employee's proficiency in Urdu, the language of the now defunct administration. Second, families that experienced a sudden fall in status, such as those of *jagirdars* and the middle-level officials, continued to maintain a false sense of dignity, preferring to subsist on a meagre pension rather than work in the new administration, which was considered below their dignity.[40]

Muslims with an aristocratic background were not the only ones who abstained from taking 'despicable' jobs. In a study on women and child labour conducted in the Old City of Hyderabad it is observed that, '...Almost all the women interviewed preferred to be housewives taking in work at home because they felt they had no other skill. They did not want to go out and work as wage labourers or domestic helpers since they considered both occupations to be below their dignity. Neither did they feel capable enough to establish their own small businesses while salaried jobs were beyond them. Hence most of the women saw themselves as housewives doing extra paid work because of lack of any other opportunities. The husbands and fathers of these women had no salaried jobs and no other major source of income'.[41]

Most of the Muslims living in the Old City are artisans and semi-skilled or even unskilled workers. One of the important semi-skilled works is bangle making,[42] a trade which has given the Old City of Hyderabad worldwide recognition. Other important works are conducted particularly by girls and women, including *zari* (embroidery done on saris and other textiles with golden, *zari*, threads), *agarbatti* (making of incense sticks), tie and dye work (printing of designs with dyed colours on textiles), *pandan* (making of small boxes of silver and brass, with intricately designed tops, for keeping betel leaves and nuts), leather and rexene work (making purses, bags, travel bags, scooter-and car-seat covers from leather and rexene, a type of scrap plastic), and a number of other handicrafts.[43]

The condition of these workers is deplorable. In addition to poor working conditions and low wages, child labour is rampant, with both boys and girls assisting their parents in the various trades. Due to the poverty of families many children are deprived of the opportunity to continue their studies or even to attend school at all. As a result, although some do receive education, there are also large numbers of illiterate children and school dropouts. This is in spite of the fact that many NGOs work for the welfare of the weaker sections of the population in the Old City.

According to an article in *Siyasat* (one of the leading Urdu newspapers of Hyderabad) out of the total 113,737 government school-going children in Hyderabad City, 72,251 belong to the Old City, 31,944 are from the New City and 9,542 from the Cantonment area. This is indicative of the higher proportion of poor people in the Old City as it is the poor who mostly depend on government schools.[44] According to the same article, there are 315 Urdu Medium Schools in Hyderabad. The majority of them are located in the Old City and their average number of students is 188—incidentally, the average of all the government schools put together is only 136. While there is an increasing trend to send children to non-government, English-medium schools for better education, the poorest of the lot living in the Old City cannot afford to send their children to such schools.

Compared to those of the New City, government schools of the Old City often lack basic facilities such as toilets (in the case of eighty-three of them, compared to thirty-seven in the New City) and the supply of water (172 against fifty respectively).[45] Moreover, textbooks translated for the Urdu medium of education are not only full of errors but even their publication are often delayed by six months and they are not adequate in numbers to meet the requirement of students. In over 50% of government schools, even the basic minimum amenities are not available and the plight of Urdu medium schools is even worse. While 86,062 children were studying in Old City government schools in 2006–07, 20% of them, i.e. 27,031, dropped out. In the New City, the number of dropouts is 3,762 out of a total strength of 53,080, i.e. 4.5%. In the cantonment area, out of 11,624 students, 1,691 (10%) dropped out.[46] A majority among these dropouts in the Old City are girls.[47] As a result, the percentage of Muslims who passed the SSC is low compared to other groups, except the Dalits (see table below).

Table 7.5. Community pass percentage of SSC (Secondary School Certificate = X class), 2006–07 results

S.No.	Community	Appeared	Passed	Pass %
1.	Hindus*	159,701	131,359	82.25
2.	Scheduled castes	172,954	109,376	63.24
3.	Backward classes	417,113	298,580	71.57
4.	Scheduled tribes	52,346	35,984	68.74
5.	Muslims	70,900	45,472	64.14
6.	Christians	2,758	2,242	81.29
7.	Others	463	331	71.49

Source: District Education Office (DEO), Hyderabad.
*Non SC and non OBC

As per the interviews with a few academicians of Maulana Azad University hailing from the Old City and the staff of the Confederation of Voluntary Associations (COVA) one of the most important reasons for the deterioration of education standards in the Old City is due to deprivation from government schools of permanent buildings and moving them to private buildings. Out of the total rented government school buildings, 91% are from the Old City.[48]

Chandrayangutta

The general trends observed in Hyderabad's Old City are well illustrated by the Muslim localities we have selected for fieldwork, namely Chandrayangutta,[49]

which is located on the southern side of the Old City of Hyderabad. It is considered to be the most communally sensitive area in the Old City and a stronghold of the Majlis party. It has a total population of 34,191 and comes under Ward No. 32, Circle No. 4 in the South Zone of Greater Hyderabad Municipal Corporation with the recent boundary process. More than 85% of the population of this neighbourhood is Muslim.

Within Chandrayangutta we focused mainly on two localities, Hafeezbaba Nagar and Barkas. Hafeezbaba Nagar is one of the poorest slum areas of the Old City. Residents here are involved in occupations such as tailoring, embroidery, provision stores, pan shops, meat shops, rickshaw pulling, auto rickshaw driving, brick-making, making plaster-of-paris (gypsum cements used for making moulds and sculptures) items for house construction, helpers in function halls, assistants to cooks, supply attendants in functions and carpentry.[50]

Barkas is an important locality in Chandrayangutta that used to serve as the military barracks of the Nizam of Hyderabad. It is inhabited mainly by the Arab-Chaush community who are descendants of Arab military servicemen hailing mostly from the Hadramaut region of Yemen. Once their jobs died out with the end of the Nizam's rule, they became unemployed and started small business outlets (leather works, auto repairs) in that locality. Today, they are mainly employed in the fruit business and some of them have recently begun to export fruits to Middle East countries.

This area being communally sensitive, it has a police station and the police is always on high alert. However, all the Hindus have left the locality, which is, therefore, quieter. The people of the Barkas area in Chandrayangutta are better off economically and did not complain about the civic amenities.

The MIM has repeatedly won the Chandrayangutta Legislative Assembly segment and the seats it contested during the municipal elections. Current member of the Legislative Assembly Akbaruddin Owaisi is the brother of the MIM president and Lok Sabha Member of Parliament for Hyderabad, Asaduddin Owaisi. When we interviewed him he informed us that he owns six schools in this area. As the national highway and road connecting to the airport passes through this area the real estate prices have risen here and people are generally well off in this area. In the recent municipal elections held in 2009, MIM candidate Qavi Ansari was elected as Corporator from Chandrayangutta ward.

In Chandrayangutta prominent problems are contaminated water due to the mixing of sewerage pipes and water pipes and lack of waste disposal facilities. But the condition of roads and the lack of social infrastructural facilities such as schools, colleges, hospitals, parks and playgrounds are also very problematic.

Identity Politics

Why do the Muslims of the Old City continue to support local politicians who have not delivered in terms of development and resign themselves to being ruled by them when, they know, resources are not that limited? For instance, the *waqf* properties of Andhra Pradesh—dominated by Hyderabad-based institutions—are richer than that of most of the other states.[51]

Interviews and group discussions with Old City inhabitants indicated a kind of mistrust on their part for their own local leaders. Allegations were made against them: 'There is a conspiracy in shifting government schools into private buildings. On one hand by encroaching land allotted for government schools, leaders seal the possibility of construction of permanent buildings for government schools. On the other hand, they prevent or stop private building owners from getting their premises vacated. The vexed owners eventually sell their property to the leaders at the rates decided by these leaders...'[52]

The reason for underdevelopment of the Old City is generally attributed to the MIM's neglect of socio-economic issues. Several respondents representing different constituencies alleged that this party not only neglected the real issues but also has a vested interest in maintaining the status quo. Zahed Ali Khan, the editor of *Siyasat*, who contested parliamentary elections on a TDP platform and lost to Majlis chief Asaduddin Owaisi in 2009, said that he is 'fighting a corrupt and communal party that has not brought any change to the lives of even ordinary Muslims for which it claims to speak'.[53]

Siyasat is one of the most respected newspapers among educated middle-class Muslims. Its trust is involved in a wide range of developmental activities such as midday meal programmes for school children, education programmes and vocational training for the Old City and other Muslim populations in the Deccan region. However, these attempts by some progressive Muslims to bring in change have not translated into votes.

Despite charges of hooliganism, communal violence, corruption, family-based nepotism and embezzlement, the Majlis party continues to remain popular among Old City Muslims because it is seen as one fighting for Muslim pride and identity. Muslims from the Old City consider that when all other parties are trying to promote particular caste groups, it is only logical that the Muslims support the Majlis. M.A. Khan, a resident of the Old City, while reacting to the question of political representation of Muslims, opined that, 'The major political parties want the Muslims to vote for them and treat them as vote banks. But they don't want the largest minority group to become a political power. Six per cent Reddys or the five per cent Kammas are continuously sending more than fifty candidates to the state assembly for the last several decades, but these parties could not send fifteen Muslims to the Assembly... Muslims have the right to get adequate representation in the legislative bodies'.[54] Such a view bears testimony to the power of identity politics for a besieged minority entrenched in the old part of the city, currently a symbol of Muslim decline rather than a reminder of this population's past glory.

The latest episode illustrating the resilience of identity politics in Hyderabad occurred in 2010 when the MIM insisted on transforming Eid Milad-un-Nabi (the birthday of Prophet Muhammad), into a massive celebration. The Old City was covered with green flags in February. One month later, Hindu nationalists seized the occasion of Hanuman Jayanthi to replace the green flags with saffron flags, the battle for space taking the form of a competition between the custodians of flags of different colours. This was precisely what the MIM wanted, communal polarisation—with the blessing of its Congress allies—comforting its position in the traditional stronghold of the party that is the Old City.[55]

Escaping the Old City

Out of the Old City, life is easier with better infrastructural facilities and security for the Muslims of Hyderabad, as suggested by the case of Tolichowki and the rise of a new Muslim middle class more and more connected to the Middle East.

Tolichowki or the Muslim Quest for Anonymity

This locality is situated on the old Bombay highway. It has a total population of 39,467 and comes under Ward No. 70, Circle No. 7 in the Central Zone of Greater Hyderabad Municipal Corporation.[56] More than 90% of the population of this neighbourhood is Muslim. During the last Greater Hyderabad Municipal Corporation elections, the Majlis party's candidate Jaffar Hussain Meraj was elected as Corporator of Tolichowki and was chosen as Deputy Mayor of Hyderabad in alliance with the Congress party.

The majority of Muslim residents of Tolichowki have come from the Old City of Hyderabad. They have migrated to this locality in search of peace and better living conditions to escape from the congested or riot-prone areas of the Old City. One correlative, interesting aspect of this locality is that the majority of the latest colonies developed have been given Hindu names: Aruna Colony, Brindawan Colony, Janaki Nagar colony and Surya Nagar, although they are predominantly Muslim. On being asked about this anomaly, an educated Muslim resident, Mohammad Moid replied that it was because '... this area is an upcoming one and we don't want it to be recognised as a Muslim alone area. We want to attract non-Muslims also, so developers named them after Hindu names. Moreover, when this locality was laid with layouts, nobody expected that this area would attract large numbers of Muslims; real-estate developers kept both the Hindu and Muslim names to project it as a cosmopolitan locality'.

As this locality is near Jubilee Hills (one of the most affluent localities of Hyderabad) and the Hi-tech city area, the rental value has shot up and the house owners are happy about the sudden rise in their incomes. However, many layouts do not have municipal sanctions, which is a big issue for housing loan providers.

Tolichowki is not as communally sensitive as the Old Hyderabad and offers more opportunities as it is situated in an upcoming suburban area exposed to modern industry. It is also closer to the institutions of higher education. The majority of the population here is educated and upwardly mobile. Most of the inhabitants are employed either in the nearby Hi-tech city area or in the Middle East. They emphasise that they do not suffer from the same kind of discrimination as those who live in the Old City.

Razi Anwar, an MBA graduate who has worked for an MNC Bank, opined that, 'In Hyderabad City, most areas which are blacklisted by the banks are Muslim-dominated areas'. He added that 'it is not entirely the fault of the bankers, because most of these Muslim clients do not have pan cards, IT returns, permanent address proofs and other such necessary documents etc., to avail bank loans. However, other than Muslims even Police and journalists don't get credit cards easily...' M.A. Basit, a twenty-eight-year-old Muslim journalist working for a TV news channel who is living in Tolichowki said that he has never faced any discrimination although his family is residing in the Mehraz colony of Tolichowki.

Things are not so simple so far as the housing market is concerned. Some of the interviewees mentioned instances where the sale or renting of a house was denied to them only because they were Muslims. While the Tolichowki Muslims migrated in their quest for anonymity, they have been rather quickly identified as forming a new pocket of 'otherness'.[57]

MUSLIMS OF HYDERABAD

The Gulf Connection

The employment opportunities in the Gulf have been a ray of hope for the otherwise dismal picture of employment among the Muslims of Hyderabad. The impact of remittances sent by migrant workers from the Middle East countries since the 1970s is visible through a number of tangible signs. For instance, new branches of banks have been opened in the Old City, in locations where there were none earlier: they are transacting foreign currencies. There is also an increase in land prices and in rates of construction and housing repair, as well as in the opening of deluxe taxi services from the Old City to the airport.[58]

While Indians of all religions and regional groups migrate to the Middle East, Muslims have migrated in larger proportions than others.[59] In Hyderabad, the impact of the 'Gulf connection' is so widespread that a journalist, M.A. Siraj, has described the phenomenon as 'Hyderabad Muslim economy from penury to opulence'![60] However, this assessment of the Gulf boom needs to be qualified because of the short-term nature of the job visas, the lack of protection against unscrupulous employers in foreign countries and above all, the fact that most Gulf workers are unskilled labourers rather than skilled professionals.[61] East but not least, only a few were able to divert money into productive investment.

A New Muslim Middle Class

Remittances-related or not, some improvement is also seen among Muslims in private business in Hyderabad. Muslims' representation as owners of small firms has increased from 11.97% in 1983 to 15–48% in 1994, which is a clear improvement.[62] The Hadramawti Arabs, long known as small-scale fruit growers, have become exporters to the Middle East.[63] Al-Kabir meat plant, equipped with modern technology in the Medak district, 50 km away from Hyderabad, has been successful in the export business too. However, it has invited the wrath of anti-Muslim groups wanting to ban animal slaughter.[64]

A new generation of men has entered the banking sector. For instance, Sayyid Abid Hasan Rizvi founded the Charminar Cooperative Urban Bank (CCUB) in 1985. The CCUB had a spectacular rise and fall. It increased its deposits from a mere 17 crores in 1996 to a staggering 8,000 crores in 2002, before irregularities began. Matters came to an end when its chairman committed suicide in 2002 due to involvement in questionable practices.[65] Two smaller, less spectacular, examples are the Toor Baitulmal and Dasussalam Cooperative Bank that have been in operation since the 1960s and 1980s respectively but have become more prosperous recently.

Besides Gulf-related sources of prosperity, new economic activities are on the rise among Hyderabad Muslims. Zaheer Ali Khan, the Managing Editor of *Siyasat*, cited several areas in which the Muslim youth is forging ahead. According to him 60–70% of medical transcription professionals are Muslims. He said, today, we can find nearly 2,000 cars plying 24 hours between the Old City and the Hi-tech City areas.[66] Nearly 50,000 professionals are working in the city of Hyderabad and the Old City contains a large proportion of them. Today, Muslim girls have also started working in the BPO sector. Hence, it seems that even the most underdeveloped areas of the Old City of Hyderabad are not immune to the wind of change blowing over the city at large.

Conclusion

The Hyderabad state ruler's suppression of Hindu parties and various cultural organisations, his patronage to parties like the MIM and their offshoots like the Razakar Movement before 1947, the Partition-related migration of Muslim elite groups to Pakistan, the Nizam's refusal to integrate with independent India and—once this integration took place—the subsequent additional migrations and inflows of Hindus in the late 1940s to 1950s—all these historical factors put the Muslims of Hyderabad at a disadvantage after independence. All the more so as, with the disappearance of the Nizam's state, the Jagirdari system and an Urdu-speaking administration disappeared too. More than elsewhere, the Muslim community was decapitated and victim of the majoritarian as well as official opprobrium.

While the economic and intellectual elite groups almost vanished, the political one showed some resilience. Indeed, the Old City became a stronghold of the MIM, which acquired an increasingly greater influence at the municipal level in the 1980s–90s in the context of communal polarisation.

Indeed, communal violence developed in the 1980s–90s in Hyderabad as in so many other Indian cities and resulted in the usual unmaking of the Hindu-Muslim mixed areas. Hindus left the Old City where violence occurred recurrently, and Muslims came to this urban centre when the isolated pockets where they lived among Hindus were under attack.

Today, these migrants and the traditional inhabitants have to confine themselves to the decaying areas of the Old City in search of security. They have taken refuge in a place affected by poor infrastructure facilities such as inadequate and unsafe water supply, pollution, congestion, irregular electricity supply and poor or lack of health and education facilities.

The irony of this situation is that it concerns a place where a Muslim party, the MIM, is in office. On the one hand, the local Muslims vote for its candidates in spite of the fact that the party does not deliver in terms of development, because it represents the Muslims as an ethnic group: they transfer their emotional attachment to an Islamic space to the political arena. On the other hand, the MIM leaders cash in on this identity politics and neglect education and other facilities in order to retain their influence over a group they maintain in their dependence that way. The moment the poor Muslims of the Old City feel safe and acquire some education as well as socio-economic means, they may well free themselves from their traditional spokesperson.

This moment may come since some changes are taking place. First, those who can afford to leave the Old City migrate to places like Tolichowki where they try to downplay their Muslim identity. Second, many Muslim families have benefited from the Gulf boom in terms of remittances or export-oriented activities. Third, Hyderabad has a growing number of Muslim middle-class members, partly because of the Gulf boom, partly because of the economic rise of one of the most dynamic economic centres in India.

Consequently, there is also a growing awareness of the importance of education among the Muslim community. The desire to regain the confidence and rebuild the past strength among the newly educated middle class of the Muslim community is striking. The rising, educated middle class of Hyderabad city is free from the guilt of issues such as the rejection of the Indian Union and the Razakar Movement that their forefathers grappled with.

Whether these new developments will radically alter the fate of the Muslims of Hyderabad remains to be seen. On the one hand, the MIM continues to dominate the community's political elite. On the other, out of the Old City, Muslims are also suffering from discrimination. This is true not only of those Muslims who are seeking rented housing, but also of those who are doing well financially and willing to purchase houses and properties in more affluent areas. The recent study conducted by a National TV Channel, CNN–IBN, was a good eye-opener on this aspect.[67] Some of those who are willing to venture out and mingle with the rest of the Hindus are therefore led to retreat back into Muslim pockets.

8

SAFE AND SOUND

SEARCHING FOR A 'GOOD ENVIRONMENT' IN ABUL FAZL ENCLAVE, DELHI[1]

Laurent Gayer

'By the grace of God, local Muslims are prosperous [*khushhal*] and to a large extent unity prevails among them. But despite the fact that large and beautiful mosques have been erected here and that large numbers of devout Muslims attend them, the number of religiously inclined [*dini mizaj*] and moral individuals [*sha'ur rakhne wale*] is declining'.[2] This is how Mohammad Abul Fazl Farooqi, the real estate developer who gave his name to the Muslim locality of Southeast Delhi known as Abul Fazl Enclave (AFE), describes in his autobiography the moral landscape of his extended neighbourhood. This harsh statement comes from a pious bourgeois who developed through the years a business relationship and some ideological affinities with India's prime Islamist organisation, the Jama'at-i-Islami Hind (JI-H). In any other context, this would suffice to make Abul Fazl an original, if not a marginal figure since the Jama'at has always been a lightweight presence in Indian Muslim politics.[3] But AFE houses the headquarters of the Jama'at, and such a moral critique is far from being an oddity in this Jama'ati stronghold. As such it points to the 'wars of morality'[4] which have been brewing in the neighbourhood, particularly after its population

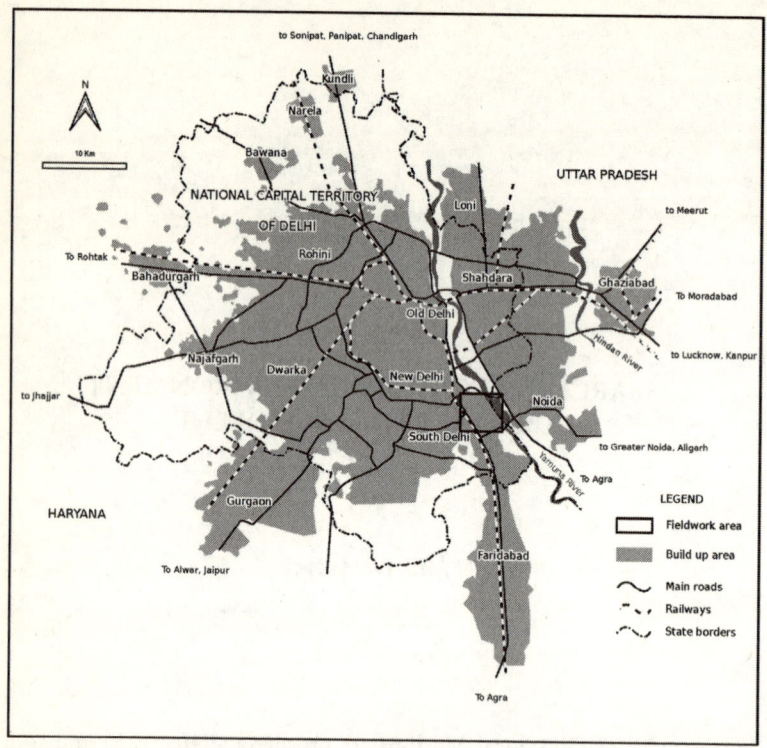

General Map of Delhi

became more heterogeneous, socially as well as politically, in the course of the 1990s.

This social and political diversity is the result of successive waves of Muslim settlement in the neighbourhood. The first batch of residents, who settled in the early 1980s, was primarily composed of the teaching staff and students of the adjacent Jamia Millia Islamia. They were followed by merchants and retailers escaping the congested Old City, by migrant workers from Uttar Pradesh and Bihar, and later on by cadres and activists of the JI-H in the early 1990s, after the organisation moved its headquarters to the neighbourhood. The rise in Hindu-Muslim violence across North India, after the destruction of the Babri Masjid, also led a number of wealthy Muslim industrialists to relocate here. Although the neighbourhood is undergoing a fast process of gentrification, it retains some elements of social pluralism—at least as far as

SAFE AND SOUND

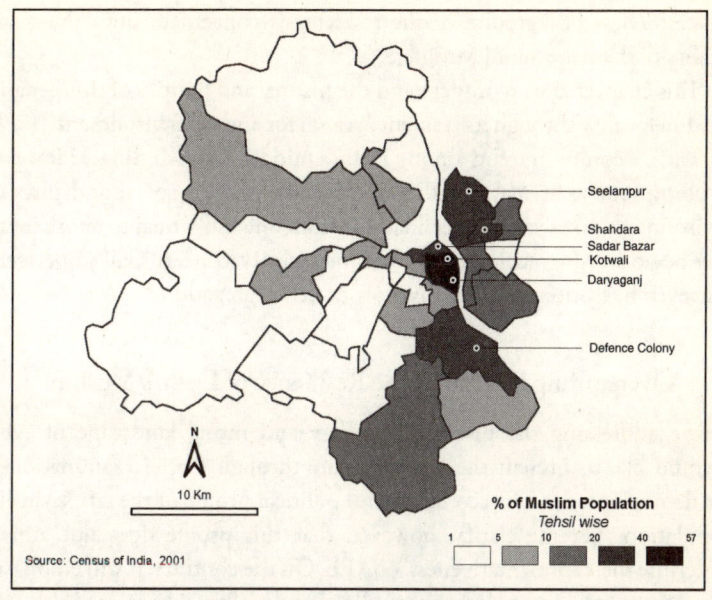

Muslim Population in Delhi's Tehsil

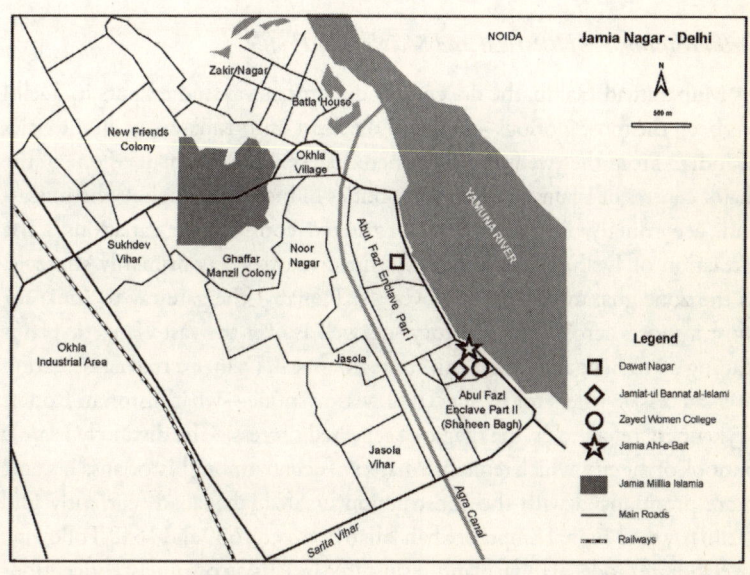

Map of Jamia Nagar in Delhi

the caste/class background of the residents is concerned, since the quasi-totality of them are Sunni Muslims.

This chapter aims to understand the history and politics of this peculiar Muslim locality through its residents' search for a 'good environment' (*achha mahaul*), a common trend among Delhi's middle-class Muslims.[5] However, as ubiquitous as it may be, this quest for a 'proper' social and physical environment takes various declinations from one individual to another and may be addressing ecological, moral, or security concerns, all imperfectly conveyed by notions of 'ghettoisation' or 'self-segregation'.

Overcoming Partition: The Resilience of Delhi's Muslims

Before addressing the history, sociology and moral landscape of AFE, I would like to present the larger picture through a brief examination of the demographic, socio-economic and political profile of the city's Muslim population. Let me clarify, however, that this profile does not aim to underline the 'representativeness' of AFE. On the contrary, it will emphasise the singularity of this largely middle-class locality, whose scholarly and political significance is inversely proportional to its statistical relevance.

Delhi Muslims: A Historical and Sociological Profile

As Muhammad Habib, the doyen of Indian medieval studies, puts it, 'Delhi has been the most glorious—and also the most unfortunate—of all the cities of India.'[6] From the twelfth to the nineteenth century, it remained one of the major centres of Islamic culture and politics in India, although its fortunes—and, accordingly, its population—registered considerable variations.[7] The attraction of Delhi to successive Muslim dynasties was primarily strategic, as the zone guaranteed control over the Punjab—the gateway to India for most invaders across India's history—as well as over the vast Gangetic plains leading up to Bengal. Beyond this strategic appeal, Delhi exerted a fascination over successive rulers for its special power mystique—what historian Robert Frykenberg refers to as 'the magic of repeated success'.[8] The distinctly Islamic outlook of the city, which remains a matter of debate among historians,[9] became more pronounced with the construction of Shahjahanabad (currently Old Delhi) by the Mughal Emperor Shah Jahan between 1639 and 1648. Following an elaborate model of town planning inspired by Persian organicist conceptions of urban space as well as by Hindu Shastric texts, Shahjahanabad revolved around the *axis mundi* of the 'auspicious fortress' (*Qila Mubarak*).¹⁰ Within the walled city, which in 1650 housed 65–75% of the city's total population, this model was reproduced at the microscopic level of the *mohalla*, whose social and economic life revolved around the *havelis* (mansions) of the nobility. Other *mohallas*, however, were organised along caste/occupational lines, particularly when these activities were considered polluting by Hindu as well as Muslim 'upper castes', such as in the case of Qasabpura, the butchers' *mohalla*.

This partially Islamic city, where Muslims constituted almost a third of the population until Partition, did not survive the repression of the 1857 uprising. After reasserting their authority over the city, the British occupied the imperial palace and set out on a major programme of urban 'renewal' akin to Haussmann's in Paris at the same time. The construction of a new capital city south of Shahjahanabad in the first decades of the twentieth century, which displaced the centre of political power, completed 'the near destruction of the city as might be understood by the Mughals'.¹¹ If the repression of the 1857 uprising dealt such a severe blow to Delhi Muslims, it is also because the entire Muslim population of the city was evicted by the British. And if those facing expulsion gradually returned in the years following the revolt,¹² they had to pay a fine that amounted to 25% of the value of their real estate in the case of Muslims (against 10% for Hindus).¹³

However, it is truly with the transfers of population induced by the Partition of 1947 that Delhi lost its 'reputation as an Indo-Islamic city', following the exodus of two-thirds of its Muslim population.¹⁴ Between 1941 and 1951, the proportion of Muslims in the city's total population declined from 33.22% to 5.71% (see Table 8.1). Fifty years later, according to the 2001 Census, Delhi had a Muslim population of 1.62 million, which amounted to 11.72% of its total population and placed this union territory a little below the national average. The bulk of this population traces its roots to Delhi itself, or to other provinces of North India (Uttar Pradesh and Bihar in particular, with a smaller presence of Kashmiris). Out of Delhi's nine districts, four have a substantial Muslim population (higher than 10% of the total population): district North-East (including the slums and lower middle-class localities of Seelampur and Mustafabad); district South (including the middle-class localities of Nizamuddin West and Okhla, among which is AFE); district Central (including the Old City of Shahjahanabad); and district North. District North-East and district South have, in absolute terms, the largest Muslim populations (481,607 and 314,015 persons respectively) but the share of Muslims in the total population is highest in district Central (29.88%, against 27.24% in district North-East and 13.85 in district South).¹⁵

Table 8.1. Delhi's Muslim population, 1941–2001

Year	Muslim population of Delhi	% of the total population of Delhi
1941	304,971	33.22
1951	99,501	5.71
1961	155,543	5.85
1971	263,019	6.47
1981	461,802	7.75
1991	889,641	9.40
2001	1,623,520	11.70

Source: Adapted from Omar Khalidi, *Muslims in Indian Economy*, Delhi: Three Essays Collective, 2006, table I, p. 62.

Overall, Delhi Muslims are more educated than the average Indian Muslim, but less than their coreligionists in other states like Maharashtra and Tamil Nadu, that have a Muslim population of more than 70%. Their literacy rate reaches 72.3% for males and 59.1% for females, which also makes them less educated than local Hindus (whose literacy rate reaches 88.8% for men and 75.4% for women) and 51.3% of them are professionally active (against 50% in Maharashtra and 52% in Tamil Nadu), for a rate of work participation of 52.1% among local Hindu men. This local Muslim workforce is primarily male: only 4.8% of local Muslim women have a professional activity other than domestic (against 12.7% in Maharashtra and 11.9% in Tamil Nadu).[16]

Delhi's History of Communal Violence

Until the 1920s, Delhi remained largely unaffected by communal violence. Although Muslims could rely on the Qasais (butchers) and Hindus on the Jats to ensure their protection or resort to punitive actions, communal riots were extremely rare.[17] The first modern episode of Hindu-Muslim violence witnessed by the city occurred in 1924, when fifteen Hindus and one Muslim were killed in Sadar Bazar, which remained the city's communal hot spot even after independence.[18] The worst episode of mass communal violence ever witnessed by the city occurred in September 1947, when 10,000 to 20,000 Muslims were killed by Hindu mobs with the support of the Rashtriya Swayamsevak Sangh (RSS),[19] and sometimes with the complicity of the police and army.[20] Historical accounts also suggest that approximately 44,000 Muslim houses were occupied by non-Muslims in the aftermath of Partition,[21] while scores of Muslim shrines and graveyards across the city were demolished by angry mobs and later on by unscrupulous entrepreneurs and officials of the Public Works Department.[22] Claiming that Muslims no longer felt safe in 'mixed areas', the Indian government decided to rehabilitate those Muslims who did not want to migrate to Pakistan into so-called 'Muslim zones'.[23] The Indian government was actually unable to enforce this plan of relocation, due to the pressure exerted by non-Muslim refugees but also in the face of the complicity of the police with the refugees, which facilitated their infiltration into localities earmarked for Muslims.

The regrouping of Delhi's Muslims into religiously 'homogeneous' colonies was in fact a much later phenomenon, which was the result of two cumulating trends: the overcrowding of the Old City and the state of fear induced by communal riots. The deconcentration of the Old City started in the 1980s: whereas its density was 740 inhabitants per hectare in 1961, it had declined to 616 in 1991.[24] Those Muslims leaving the walled city for the less congested periphery (and in particular Jamia Nagar) generally belonged to wealthy bazar families, who retained their shops in the Old City while moving their place of residence. From a trickle, this movement of Muslims within the city turned into a stream after a state of fear engulfed the whole country in the 1990s. This is despite the fact that, unlike other cities of North India, Delhi was not a major site of Hindu-Muslim violence. Over the period 1950–95, 'only' ninety-three people lost their lives in episodes of Hindu-Muslim violence in the city (against 1137 in Bombay, 1119 in Ahmedabad, 312 in Hyderabad and 265 in Meerut).[25]

This could suggest that there was no objective threat against Muslim lives and properties, at least not on the scale justifying the gathering of the city's Muslims into religiously 'homogeneous' enclaves for their security. But such aggregate figures cannot account for the deterioration in Hindu-Muslims relations in certain areas of the city in the wake of the Ram Janmabhoomi movement, a fact emphasised in the report by PUDR activists on the Old Delhi riots of May 1987, which left eighty-eight injured and nine dead.[26] Moreover, as shown by Nida Kirmani in her doctoral dissertation on Muslim women in Zakir Nagar,[27] this line of reasoning only pays attention to episodes of violence involving Hindus and Muslims, to the detriment of other forms of communal violence—such as the anti-Sikh pogrom of November 1984, which left a deep imprint on the Muslims of Delhi. Finally, the mere counting of fatalities neglects the psychological impact of episodes of communal violence that took place elsewhere in the country, such as the 1992–93 Bombay riots or, more recently, the 2002 Gujarat pogrom. In Delhi as elsewhere in India, Muslims' social trajectories in the city have been informed by a memory of violence that extends through time and space, and which lingers on well after the violence has receded.[28]

The Place of Muslims in Delhi's Political and Economic Elites

Muslims constitute a substantial part of Delhi's electorate and their votes prove decisive, both in regional and general elections, in a number of constituencies. As far as Lok Sabha elections are concerned, this is particularly true of Chandni Chowk, Delhi East and Delhi South. As far as Vidhan Sabha elections are concerned, this is true of Matia Mahal (with a staggering 75% of Muslim voters), Seelampur (67%), Ballimaran (50%), Okhla (40%), Paharganj (33%), Babarpur (26%) and Qarawal Nagar (25%).[29] It is estimated that there are 400,000 Muslim voters in the capital, including 100,000 in district South and 115,000 in Chandni Chowk, with smaller concentrations in New Delhi and Karol Bagh (approaching 45,000).[30]

This electoral weight and their concentration in some constituencies has enabled Muslims to remain fairly well represented in the city's political scene: although only one Muslim MP (Sikander Bakht)[31] has been elected from Delhi since 1952, the share of Muslim representatives among local MLAs has shown a remarkable continuity, around 7% of the total number of MLAs (see Table 8.2).

Table 8.2. Muslim MLAs from Delhi, 1952–2010

Number of MLAs	1952–1956	1993–1998	1998–2003	2003–2008	2008–
Grand total	48	70	70	70	70
Number of Muslim MLAs	3	5	5	5	5
% of the total number of MLAs	6.25	7	7	7	7

Source: http://delhi.gov.in for 1952–1956; Sanjay Kumar, 'Changing Face of Delhi's Politics', art. quoted for 1993–2008; and press reports on announced results for 2008.

Delhi's Muslim politicians have high incumbency rates: the four most preeminent Muslim MLAs of the capital have never been beaten in any election after meeting with their first electoral success. Three of them have exerted four consecutive mandates (Parvez Hashmi in Okhla, Mateen Ahmed in Seelampur and Shoaib Iqbal in Matia Mahal), whereas the last one (Harun Yusuf in Balli Maran) was elected three times consecutively. Such resilience explains the long-lasting influence of these Muslim politicians over their party and beyond. As a result, some of them have become ministers in the Delhi government, such as Parvez Hashmi (who was Transport Minister between 1998 and 2003) and Haroon Yusuf (who has been Development, Revenue, Food and Civil Supplies, Flood and Irrigation Minister between 1998 and 2003, Transport and Power Minister between 2003 and 2008, and Industries Minister since then). A newcomer, among these Muslim MLAs, is Asif Mohammad Khan, who was elected in Okhla in 2009 on a Rashtriya Janata Dal (RJD) ticket after the seat was left vacant by Parvez Hashmi (who had recently been elected to the Rajya Sabha). This humiliating defeat[32] of the Congress in one of its bastions was probably a sanction for the Batla House incident of September 2008, when two young Muslim residents of this locality were killed in a police raid. The Delhi police claimed that these youths, who hailed from Azamgarh (Uttar Pradesh), were militants of the Indian Mujahideen—a shadowy terrorist group suspected of being responsible for the bombings that had taken place a few days earlier in the capital. However, the vast majority of Muslim residents of Jamia Nagar (of which Batla House is a part) remain convinced that this was a 'fake encounter' which targeted innocent students. The reluctance of the Congress provincial government to order an enquiry into the incident deeply alienated the Muslim population of Jamia Nagar/Okhla. Khan capitalised on this discontent and put the incident at the centre of his campaign. His first public gesture after his victory was to visit the Panj Piran graveyard in Nizamuddin and offer prayers for the souls of Atif and Sajid, the two youths killed in the 2008 'encounter'. It remains to be seen if this highly atypical Muslim politician, who served time in jail for supporting the Student Islamic Movement of India (SIMI) after its ban in 2001, will have the same longevity as his predecessor. It is therefore too early to talk of a revival of Muslim identity politics in Jamia Nagar, although some signs do point in this direction.

If the political 'peripherisation' of Muslims is not as blatant in Delhi as in other cities covered by this volume, what of their socio-economic marginalisation? As we have seen, about two-thirds of Delhi's Muslim population left for Pakistan in the months that followed Partition. Among these *muhajirin* figured most of the city's Muslim elites. Ten years later, the city police force had no Muslim officer at all and only four Muslims served in the civil service.[33] The remaining Muslim population of Delhi was mainly composed of lower castes.[34] The situation has not changed in any major way during the following decades. A survey conducted between 1992 and 1994 by the Institute of Objective Studies (a Zakir Nagar-based think tank close to the JI-H) among 6,220 Muslim households across Delhi found that 87.57% of them had a monthly income of less than Rs 7000, with a majority of household heads being manual workers (90.40%), often self-employed (58.71%).[35]

Local and national politics has taken its toll on this small Muslim economy. Shopkeepers of the Saudagaran and Piracha castes have been severely affected by state policies, particularly during the Emergency (1975–77), when Indira Gandhi and Jagmohan Malhotra (the rabidly anti-Muslim vice-chairman of the DDA)[36] sent bulldozers and trigger-happy policemen to 'cleanse' Muslim-dominated localities of the Old City. The local Muslim economy has also, occasionally, been disrupted by Hindu mobs, such as in the Sadar area of Old Delhi in May 1974 (at the time the worst riot witnessed in Delhi since independence, during which eleven people were killed and property worth 1.2 million rupees was destroyed)[37] and in Seelampur in December 1992 (where twenty-three were left dead).

Despite the overall precarious economic situation of this population, success stories do exist. This is the case, for instance, of some meat merchants and exporters (although they have also been suffering from public policies such as the displacement of the great Old Delhi abattoirs),[38] real estate developers and pharmaceutical companies trading in traditional Yunani or Ayurvedic medicine, such as the Hamdard Laboratories and Himalaya Drugs companies. A new generation of Muslim entrepreneurs has emerged around individuals such as Taab Siddiqi and Adil Hassan of Harvest Gold Bread, or Arif Sheikh of the grocery chain Sabka Bazar.[39] Muslims have also made their presence felt at the Delhi Bar but their share in the most prestigious bar associations remains well below their share of the population. In 2005, there were only 136 Muslims among the 5,164 members of the Delhi High Court Bar Association (2.6% of the total number of its members),[40] and very few Muslims have made it to the position of High Court judge through the years (out of 124 judges appointed at the DHC since 1966, only seven were Muslims).[41] The share of Muslims in the local police force (2.3% in 1991), for its part, is one of the lowest in the country.[42]

However useful this data may be to draw the demographic, socio-economic and political profile of Delhi Muslims, it overlooks the diversity of this population and tends to depersonalise individual experiences. The following section, which presents the results of prolonged ethnographic fieldwork in a middle-class Muslim locality of South Delhi, aims to give greater texture to Delhi Muslims' lives. The Muslims of Jamia Nagar are in no way representative of Delhi Muslims at large, as they are, on average, better educated and they have had easier access to government jobs, while being less confined to manual work.[43] Nevertheless, the development of AFE deserves academic and political attention, as it sheds light on the moral and territorial formation of a burgeoning Muslim middle class, which remains virtually off the scholarly radar in comparison to its Hindu counterpart.

Tales of a Locality: The Conflictive Narratives of AFE

AFE is a Muslim-dominated residential colony of South Delhi. It is located along the west embankment of the Yamuna River and constitutes a part of a larger conglomerate of Muslim localities, such as Zakir Nagar, Batla House, Ghaffar Manzil, Noor Nagar... known as Jamia Nagar (university town), which developed around the university of Jamia Millia Islamia (National Islamic University) (see Map).[44] With approximately 375,000 residents, 90% of whom are thought to be Muslims[45] (the small non-Muslim population is mostly composed of OBCs and Dalits), Jamia Nagar constitutes one of the largest concentrations of Muslim populations in Delhi, along with Seelampur and Old Delhi. This Muslim population is almost entirely Sunni, although a small Shia population[46] harmoniously coexists with fellow Muslims of Barelwi, Deobandi, Tablighi or Ahl-e-Hadith persuasion.

Unlike other localities of Jamia Nagar, AFE is well defined, bounded as it is by the old Agra Canal (presently a *nallah*) in the west, by the west bank of the Yamuna in the east and by two roads (that from the junction of Okhla Head in the north and that from Kalindi Kunj to Sarita Vihar in the south). The population of this locality is almost exclusively Muslim, with the exception of a small Hindu-dominated pocket known as Nai Basti (new settlement), at the northwest extremity of the neighbourhood, of which AFE was originally an extension. This locality is divided into two parts: Abul Fazl I, the abode of middle-class and upper-class Muslims, and Abul Fazl II (also known as Shaheen Bagh), which has a higher density of population and a larger concentration of lower-middle-class Muslims, although it is undergoing a rapid process of gentrification.

The history of this Muslim locality, which expanded from 1978 onwards on what were formerly agricultural lands, can be accessed through various narratives. One of these tales of the locality[47] is that of the local Resident Welfare Association (RWA) activists, who have been undermining the religious composition and identity of AFE in their attempts to obtain the regularisation of their colony. A different tale of the neighbourhood is told by its promoters, who do not hesitate, in their oral and written testimonies, to emphasise their Islamic credentials and their ambition to design a Muslim locality. Finally, the residents of AFE have their own stories to tell, which convey ecological, moral and security concerns sometimes echoing those of the RWA or of the promoters but with an idiosyncratic twist.

Downplaying the Muslim Identity of the Neighbourhood: The Tale of the RWA

In the sometimes oxymoronic jargon of Delhi town planners, AFE is categorised since 1994 as a 'legally recognized unauthorized colony', i.e. an illegal colony approved for regularisation. The first settlers and developers breached the law by building on agricultural lands from 1978 onwards. Initially, the owners of these agricultural lands (*bhumidar*), most of whom where Hindus, had obtained, through their attorneys, No Objection Certificates from the Delhi Development Authority (DDA) and all these land acquisitions were duly registered. However, in the face of rapid expansion of the colony, the DDA started issuing notices to stop construction. The residents then exerted pressure on local and federal authorities to prevent demolition of the existing structures. This mobilisation paid off as assurances were given by the country's highest authorities (from Indira Gandhi to I.K. Gujral) that the colony would not be demolished. With the help of the MLA from the Okhla constituency, Parvez Hashmi (Janata Dal and later on Congress),[48] roads and drains were constructed, the electrification of the colony was completed and an underground reservoir was built by the Delhi Jal Board before Sintex tanks were set up across the colony. A primary school was also opened by the Delhi government in 1984, and all this development work conferred a quasi-official status to the colony.

The local RWA was formed in 1981 and registered in 1983,[49] at the initiative of wealthy local residents and cadres of the JI-H. One of the first initiatives of the association was to obtain power connections for the colony by lobbying the DESU authorities. The second major task of the RWA consisted in lobbying the authorities in favour of the regularisation of the colony. In 1989, it filed a civil writ petition in the Delhi High Court against the Acquisition and Demolition programme of the colony. The case remained pending for thirteen years, before the High Court dismissed the case of the petitioners. However, the validity of this judgment was subsequently challenged by the Supreme Court, which passed 'status quo' order in this case on 16 January 2006. In 2008, the Delhi government issued a provisional certificate guaranteeing regularisation of the colony, which had been earmarked for regularisation as early as 1994. However, according to the legal adviser of the JI-H, this was nothing else than a 'political gimmick' on the eve of local elections, as such a certificate could not be valid until the government decided to de-notify the acquisition programme dating back to 1989.[50]

The most striking, in the efforts of the RWA to plead its case in front of Delhi's political class and legal fraternity, has been its undermining of the religious identity of the neighbourhood, at least in its lobbying of local and federal authorities.[51] This is exemplified by the booklet *Abul Fazl Enclave at a Glance*,[52] which was prepared by a local journalist on behalf of the RWA and circulated around 2008. In the first twenty-two pages of this document (out of thirty-three), not a single mention is made of the religious affiliation of the majority of the residents. The presentation of the neighbourhood's population is particularly eloquent in this regard:

'Abul Fazl Enclave is situated in the vicinity of Jamia Milia Islamia, a central university. Majority of the residents are well educated, cultured and enlightened. Naturally, the inhabitants are most peace loving and law abiding people. The crime rate is very low. This is the reason that in spite of poor civil amenities, hundreds of educated families chose to live here. Among the reputed residents of AFE, are many high-ranking government officers, engineers, doctors, lawyers, educationalists, teachers and journalists of repute. A large number of political and social activists also live here. Headquarters of over a dozen well-known NGOs, socio-religious organisations, newspapers, periodicals and publishing houses are also located in AFE. The colony emits no pollution in the River Yamuna. It is also free from all sources which pollute the atmosphere. The entire colony is well-planned and most of the houses are built according to the building laws. Every house has built its own septic tank. Drainage system is in good shape. Roads and lanes are wide and cemented. The residents have employed private operators to clean the roads and lanes and to remove the garbage. Greenery in and around is abundant. Therefore it is an ideal place to live [...]'[53]

This idealistic, almost Utopian, depiction of the neighbourhood conveys the image of a high-profile colony whose residents are not only respectful of the law but also work towards the common good through their economic, social and intellectual activities. Rather than projecting AFE as a victimised Muslim locality, its members chose to secularise their discourse and project AFE as one unauthorised colonies among others, although of a special socio-economic quality. Rather than relying upon identity politics, they preferred to mobilise the social capital of the most affluent residents. Class, not religion, was made the principal marker of the neighbourhood.

Building a Muslim Locality: The Promoters' Tale

The RWA's tale of AFE has been coexisting with distinct and dissonant discourses of the locality. One of them is that by Abul Fazl Farooqi and his entourage, which clearly departs from the secular discourse of the RWA by emphasising the religious identity of the neighbourhood.

Abul Fazl Farooqi was born around 1940 in a small village of Uttar Pradesh (Tehsil Rasra of district Ballia). After completing his primary education in Gorakhpur, he went to Delhi, where he obtained a degree in engineering from Jamia Millia Islamia. After graduating, he joined the Delhi Transport Corporation, before taking charge of a small company established in 1970 by his mother, Friends and Co. In the meantime, he familiarised himself with the real estate business through his involvement in the Chandra Lok Housing Society of Ghaziabad, of which he was made the general secretary in 1975.[54]

Unlike members of the RWA, Abul Fazl Farooqi does not hesitate in putting forward the Muslim identity of AFE, such as in this extract of his autobiography, where he introduces the reader to the locality:

'The Muslim population of this area presents a pleasing scene. While the sun at the end of its day-long journey dips below the western horizon, the echo of Allaho-Akbar rising from the mosques of Abul Fazl Enclave adds to the grandeur of the colony'.[33]

In this autobiographical text, Farooqi claims that from the beginning of his development activities in the area, he aimed to construct a Muslim locality. Apparently, this idea came to him after a seminar organised at Jamia Millia around 1978:

'A unanimous proposal was mooted in the seminar which said that there should be a colony where Muslims could establish their social and family life according to their own culture. That proposal got stuck in my heart'.[36]

With the help of the local *pradhan* and *patwari*, Farooqi started acquiring these agricultural lands directly from their owners. In 1979, he formally began selling the land and some of his 'friends from Old Delhi' booked several plots for themselves. Members of the Jamia Millia academic staff also showed their interest in acquiring land in the area. However, the most important contribution came from the JI-H, which booked ninety-nine plots and paid for them in advance. This initial deal was followed by others, after more plots were sold to JI-H cadres (around a hundred in total)[57] including the Secretary of the JI-H, Maulana Shaft Moonis, who was one of the first to build a house in the neighbourhood. Some of these JI-H members later on sold their plots for a comfortable sum of money, after the price of the land started to rise.[58] However, a large part of these plots was earmarked for the JI-H Markaz, which was eventually shifted to AFE (from Chitli Qabr, in Old Delhi) in 1991.

The development of AFE appears related to the geographical trajectory of India's prime Islamist organisation, but also to the new urban dynamics of Delhi Muslims at large. The re-localisation of the JI-H in AFE, whose ground was laid in the early 1980s and which started effectively a decade later, cannot be seen in isolation from developments in other Muslim localities, particularly Old Delhi. Abul Fazl Farooqi had made a good guess: with the Old City reaching a point of saturation, its residents were increasingly attracted to residential areas with less density. The JI-H was not immune to that trend and the delocalisation of the Markaz took place in the larger context of deconcentration of Old Delhi, although the pressure of law enforcement agencies on the land market should also be taken into account. Thus, according to the former Secretary General of the JI-H, Maulana Shafi Moonis, the decision of the Jama'at to construct on the land it had acquired ten years earlier in AFE was precipitated by a police raid during which law enforcement personnel occupied the land, allegedly to obtain a bribe,[59] although some other long-term residents claim that the rationale of the operation was to construct a police academy on the same site.[60]

In the process of this delocalisation, the JI-H built its own enclave in AFE in the 1990s. The complex of Dawat Nagar (i.e. the City of Preaching) developed gradually. Until the late 1980s, the majority of plots acquired by the JI-H remained devoted to agriculture. Here, India's oldest Islamist organisation cultivated wheat and roses.[61] Around 1989–1990, the JI-H started constructing a mosque on the land demarcated for its Markaz. The Gumbad Wali Masjid was built under the supervision of one of the trusts of the JI-H, the Ishat-e-Islam Trust, and its construction was followed by that of several other buildings, housing the offices of the JI-H's major publications (*Radiance Weekly*, bi-weekly *Dawat*, monthly *Zindagi-e-No*, weekly *Kanti*) as well as that of the publishing house of the Markazi Maktaba Islami, which presently has a catalogue of more than 1,200 titles.[62] Today, the campus of Dawat Nagar also houses a primary school and a library, as well as the offices of the JI-H cadres. A new building of huge proportions is under construction and is intended to provide housing to the JI-H staff. Presently, the JI-H retains a strong moral and social standing in the neighbourhood. Most residents of AFE may find themselves at odds with the political agenda of the JI-H (at least in its original, Maududi-shaped, form), but the organisation retains some sympathies for its philanthropic activities, although these have remained limited in the neighbourhood (the JI-H does not pursue much social work in AFE and its vicinity, but for the ongoing construction of a 'super specialty hospital' in Dawat Nagar).[63] The campus of Dawat Nagar is well integrated into the social life of AFE. Although the main access point to the complex is restricted—by an iron gate guarded by a *chowkidar*—there are two other points of entry which are not, and which allow local residents to cross through the campus as a short cut between Hari Koti and Yamuna Road or between the Bilal Masjid and other parts of the neighbourhood. Moreover, the Markazi Library is open to the general public and attracts local students with no particular affinity with the JI-H, but simply preparing for their examinations to local colleges and universities. Finally, the social integration of Dawat Nagar into the neighbourhood is made complete by its involvement in the social and religious life of the residents. During the *shaadi* season (November-March), it organises wedding receptions for local residents on the campus, the benefits of which go to the JI-H school.[64] And at the time of Eid-ul-Fitr and Eid-ul-Adha, congregational prayers are offered on the lawns of the campus.

To sum up, the promoters' tale of the locality is that of a separatist dream come true with the auspicious support of India's prime Islamist organisation. 'They [Hindus] call it "Next to Pakistan" here. And yes, it is really a "mini-Pakistan" here', proudly states Faznullah, Abul Fazl Farooqi's younger brother and business partner.[65] With utter disregard for political correctness, Abul Fazl and his brother have been making the apology for Muslim separatism in the city. Their isolationism sounds somehow disenchanted, though. They may have fulfilled their dream of constructing a Muslim enclave within Delhi, but to their eyes this has not been sufficient to protect local Muslims from the moral 'pollution' of the larger (read 'Hindu' and 'Westernised') society. Unlike the RWA's, the Farooqis' tale has no happy ending.

The Discreet Charm of Self-Segregation: Residents' Tales

The narratives of AFE produced by the RWA's leadership and the Farooqis may be diverging but they share their elitism. In both cases, the history of AFE is essentially that of its economic elites and their grand projects. As such, these narratives shed no light on the residential trajectories of successive waves of settlers, and the way they fitted—or not—in the development schemes of the neighbourhood's elites. In order to access these other narratives of AFE, I will principally rely upon my ethnographic fieldwork in the neighbourhood, which started with tri-weekly visits to my Urdu teacher (2007–08), followed by a two-month stay with his family (October–November 2009) and a series of formal interviews with a wide range of residents, from *madrasa* teaching staff to RWA activists (October 2010). Despite my occasional interactions with other sections of residents, this fieldwork essentially brought me into contact with AFE's pious petty bourgeoisie: self-conscious Muslims studded with some cultural and economic capital, engaged in worldly activities but committed to lead their private and public lives in accordance with their religion (*din*).[66] This self-conscious and outwardly expressed religious commitment does not preclude sectarian or political differences within this 'Muslim middle class', a category that would deserve further historical and sociological elaboration but which can be broadly defined as those Muslims who neither belong to the old Mughal/Nawabi elite nor to the plebeians. In the case of Delhi, these Muslim professionals, traders, entrepreneurs or bureaucrats seem to have emerged as a separate class, both in terms of economic position and habitus, in the aftermath of the 1857 rebellion, 'which deprived the traditional culture of its centre and patronage, and discredited the leadership of the nobility'. In Delhi at least, the binding force of this Muslim middle class has been reformist Islam, which set its members apart from the nobility and the lower classes, 'both of which continued their reliance on traditional Sufi practices'.[67] Most of my friends and respondents in AFE were indeed followers of reformist Islam, and more specifically of the Deobandi *maslak*. They were, in their majority, Deobandi *madrasa alumni* as well as cadres, activists or sympathisers of the JI-H and its controversial offspring, the SIMI.[68] The strict *parda* environment maintained in the homes or the public places where these interactions unfolded prevented me from getting access to women. This has induced a gender bias in my study, which I deplore, but which is also revealing of the socio-religious milieu where this ethnography is located.

My Friend the Maulana

Echoing Mukulika Banerjee's call to 'put some flesh on the bones of this rather two dimensional category of "the Muslim"',[69] I would like to open this section on AFE residents' tales with a portrait of my friend, teacher and lodger in AFE, Maulana Wali Sheikh.[70] In his late thirties, Wali-ji was born in the remote village of Rampur (Bihar) in an Ashraf family of landowners. He lost his parents at an early age, possibly in a case of looting and arson perpetrated by a gang of local *goondas*. He was subsequently brought up by his elder sister and brother-in-law, who encouraged him to pursue a religious education at Deoband, the largest and most prestigious of all South Asian *madrasas*. After completing his religious education in 1994, he moved to Delhi, where his sister was already settled. For a few years, he lived with his sister's family in the mixed locality of Rohini, in northwest Delhi, before shifting to Zakir Nagar (a locality of Jamia Nagar) in 1999. The motive behind this relocation was primarily professional, as Wali-ji was at the time involved in the editing of an Urdu-Arabic dictionary, whose publisher was based in Zakir Nagar. Soon after the completion of this project, the same publisher offered Wali-ji the post of an editor in a local Urdu journal, which led him to settle permanently in Jamia Nagar. In 2003, he got married to a fellow Bihari and the following year, his wife gave birth to a son, Nasir.[71] The expanding family shifted to a two-room rented flat in AFE and lived there for a few years. However, after the birth of his second child, Wali-ji felt that the place was becoming too small to bring up two children and he sent Nasir to stay with his aunt in Rohini. There, Nasir attended an English-medium school whose pupils were mostly Hindu. This cultural milieu exerted a strong influence over the young boy and Wali-ji resented the fact that Nasir was gradually adopting Hindu manners in his everyday life. Thus, instead of greeting people in a traditional Muslim idiom, the boy folded his hands to salute them with a 'Namaste!' This worried his father, who feared that Nasir would soon detach himself from his religious and cultural community under the influence of his immediate environment. By then, Wali-ji's daughter had grown up and it seemed easier to regroup the family, which was all the more imperative since Nasir's physical estrangement from his parents was taking its toll on the boy's morale. Wali-ji then sold some land he still owned in Bihar and bought a three-room apartment in Shaheen Bagh, where the reunited family relocated in 2008.

Himself a Deobandi Sunni, Wali-ji does not feel uncomfortable with the sectarian diversity that prevails in AFE. Sectarian tensions are unheard of in the locality, where Deobandi, Ahle-Hadith, Tablighi, Jama'ati and Shia mosques and *madrasas* coexist peacefully.[72] Thus, the principal of the largest Shia *madrasa* in AFE, the Jamia Ahl-e-Bait, spoke to me of his 'friendship' (*dosti*) with the Tablighis running the adjacent Zayed Women College. To prove his point, he told me how, during a power-cut, the Tablighis once offered a Shia congregation the use of their generator so that they could complete their *majlis* in better conditions.[73] In this context, if Wali-ji occasionally denigrates Muslims of a different persuasion, it is always in an ironical and benign kind of way. One day, during a breakfast-time conversation with the imam of the local Deobandi mosque he attends, Wali-ji exchanged words against some local activists of the Tablighi Jama'at, whose presence is increasingly felt in AFE.[74] He burst out laughing when the imam started questioning the morality of their wives, suggesting that whenever their men left for *chillah* (40 days' *da'wa* assignments), they opened their doors and beds to strangers. Interestingly, most of the sectarian humour and gossiping I heard at Wali-ji's place involved Tablighis, Jama'atis or activists of the SIMI. This sectarian gossip was therefore a 'narcissism of small differences', an 'idiom of intimacy'[75] which helped to maintain not so obvious boundaries with Deobandis of different persuasions.

Wali-ji's decision to move from Rohini to Jamia Nagar was primarily informed by professional motives. However, his decision to stay in the neighbourhood was reinforced by cultural and moral concerns, after Nasir's experience in Rohini convinced him that his children needed to be brought up in a 'proper' environment. These fatherly concerns should not be read as an endorsement of a separatist agenda similar to that advocated by the Farooqi brothers. Thus, if he was previously concerned about his son's Muslim identity being altered by his Hindu-dominated environment, he is presently concerned about the boy's social integration into the larger Indian society. In order to help the boy retain relations with non-Muslims, he sends him to a mixed private school (English medium) in Nizamuddin, another locality of South Delhi with a substantial number of Muslims but with a larger Hindu population.

Wali-ji's professional and pedagogical concerns also coexisted with an acute longing for greater security. This is a point he not only consistently put forward in our discussions, but also confirmed in his behaviour, such as in the aftermath of terrorist attacks in Delhi and elsewhere in India. I remember meeting him two days after a series of bomb blasts in Ahmedabad in July 2008, and he told me that he had been afraid to move out of his home after the news of these blasts came out, for fear of reprisals by Hindu mobs. Yet, by his own admission, the concentration of the Muslim population in AFE and the quasi-absence of Hindu localities in the vicinity (the Hindu population of Nai Basti is too small to present a credible threat) made AFE perfectly safe.

Ecology, Security, Morality: The Concerns of AFE Residents

This concern for safety seems to be particularly acute among older residents of the neighbourhood, whose memories of the communal violence of the 1990s are still vivid. Thus, all my interlocutors aged thirty-five to seventy-five emphasised their security concerns in the course of our discussions, even if the first wave of settlers (those who constructed houses in the early 1980s, before the Ram Janmabhoomi movement) sometimes ranked these after their ecological preoccupations in the list of factors which informed their decision to relocate in AFE. Thus, Syed Mansoor Agha, a former journalist at the Jama'ati bi-weekly *Dawat* (and later on editor of the Urdu daily *Qaumi Awaz*), who wrote the booklet *Abul Fazl at a Glance* discussed above, decided to settle in AFE in 1983, 'because it was pollution-free and close to the office of the Jama'at [*i.e.* of *Dawat*].' The older buildings of AFE I bordering the Yamuna are a testimony to the ecological appeal of the locality over its first settlers. Although most of these 'historic' buildings are currently in an advanced stage of decay and are being demolished one after the other, to be replaced by glass-tiled apartments or shopping complexes, the inscription 'Riverview Complex' could still be seen on one of these doomed buildings in early 2011. This typically middle-class longing for silence and solitude[76] was sometimes shared by later settlers, such as Syed Muhammad Askari, the principal of the Shia *madrasa* Jamia Ahl-e-Bait, in Shaheen Bagh. If the latter chose to open a school (in 1996) on the side of the Kalindi Kunj Road, facing the Yamuna River, it is because the land was cheap (*sasti*) and he found the location serene ('*koi nahin tha, bhir nahin thi, shor nahin tha*' [there was no one, there was no crowd, there was no noise]) and conducive to studies ('*Education ke liye yeh jagah hamein bahut bhai. Ek kone mein baithkar ap shehr ki bhir se dur parne parhane ka kam achha ho sakta hai*' [We really found this place suitable for educational activities. By withdrawing from the city crowd you can study and teach better]).[77]

If it did not systematically overcome ecological or economic concerns, security became a major issue with the rise of Hindu-Muslim violence in the early 1990s, as the editor of the Jama'ati *Radiance Weekly*, Ejaz Ahmed Aslam, emphasises:

'In 1992–93, my younger brother, a journalist, lived in a Hindu *mohalla* in Sukhdev Vihar [about one kilometre southwest of Jamia Millia]. At that time the BJP started saying 'Lakhs of Bangladeshis have come [to Delhi]. We will chase them out'. Madan Lal Khurana, who would later on become the Chief Minister of Delhi, led Hindu mobs which threatened Zakir Bagh. Everyone felt insecure. My brother and his family then decided to shift to Noor Nagar [a Muslim-dominated locality of Jamia Nagar], while others took refuge here [in AFE]. Now, nobody feels threatened any longer'.[78]

SAFE AND SOUND

The same sentiment is echoed by Zafarul Islam Khan, editor of the *Milli Gazette* and former head of the Muslim Majlis-e-Mushawarat:

'The first reason for the growth of AFE is insecurity. For the moment, there is no insecurity but only a few years ago it was different: there was curfew, riots... Muslims who lived in mixed areas have had bad experiences. Some apprehension has remained among the people and they feel they are safer in homogeneous neighbourhoods. Even millionaires, at least three/four of them have come from posh localities such as New Friends Colony, Greater Kailash, Moti Bagh... It's a fact we are safer. They [Hindu mobs] cannot enter this area. They are apprehensive to come'.[79]

This narrative is not limited to local intellectuals and political activists. It can also be heard from other sections of residents, such as petty shopkeepers. Thus, the owner of a small *chai khanah* once told me that 'Because of the riots, Muslims started gathering in the same place for their security [*hifazat ke liye*]'. However, one has to emphasise that the notion of 'security' takes different significations from one resident to another. If, for the majority of my respondents, it was understood in physical terms, I also encountered some dissenting voices. Thus, for a street vendor selling *paan* on the side of the Kalindi Kunj road, security was primarily understood as protection from eviction. The fact that the colony remained unauthorised meant that land prices remained at a relatively low level, whereas the listing of AFE for regularisation in 1994 infused a sense of tenure security in this petty shopkeeper, who sold his boutique to buy an apartment in AFE I. His precarious economic situation was therefore only apparent and hid a rational calculus through which he traded a higher socio-professional status for propriety rights, making the best of the apparent contradiction in the official status of AFE as a 'legally recognized unauthorized colony'.[80]

If this emphasis on (in)security was quasi-systematic among the older generation, it was less frequent—although not unheard of—among the youths I encountered. Thus, Zafar,[81] a young journalist who has been one of the most vocal critiques of SIMI's ban in the local press, denied any role to communal riots in the growth of Muslim localities in Delhi since the 1990s. According to him, Delhi has not seen as intense episodes of communal violence as the small towns of Uttar Pradesh, and insecurity cannot offer a proper explanation for changes in the residential patterns of local Muslims. The explanation he gave me to his own relocation in the neighbourhood was two-fold: he had been offered a good job (at a local Urdu monthly) and lodging (in Shaheen Bagh) by another Azamgarhi. At a time when it was becoming difficult for young men hailing from Azamgarh to find lodging, even in Muslim-dominated areas, due to the projection of this Uttar Pradesh district as a 'terrorist den' in the national media, Zafar had jumped at the chance. His insertion into the neighbourhood was thus facilitated by a migrants' network, which happened to intersect with politico-religious networks. Thus, Zafar felt a great sympathy towards the owner of the aforementioned *chai khanah* (which he referred to as '*buzurg*' or 'old/wise man') and regularly visited the shop not only because the latter was a fellow Azamgarhi, but also because both of them were *alumni* of the Jamiat-ul-Islah, one of the two most important *madrasas* of the JI-H.[82]

For other youths I encountered at this local *chaikhanah*, where I spent a great deal of my time during my 2009 fieldwork, the memory of the riots of the 1990s was fading away and the primary asset of AFE was that it offered a '*dini* [religious] environment', to quote a young interior decorator who used to live in a mixed neighbourhood and resented walking several kilometres to offer *namaz*. If these upwardly mobile young Muslims emphasised that they could practise their religion more freely in AFE, this is not to say that they were insulated from the rest of the city. On the contrary, the younger sections of the local Muslim middle class seem to have greater interactions with non-Muslims, in the professional sphere at least, than their elders. And it is precisely this higher degree of interaction that seems to nurture the desire of upwardly mobile Muslim professionals to protect their 'culture' (*tehzib*) within their residential environment. As a relative of Wali-ji, currently completing a degree in dentistry, once told me: 'At work, I mostly interact with non-Muslims. At least, here [in AFE] I can protect and practice my culture freely'.[83] In the midst of Eid-ul-Adha celebrations, another relative of Wali-ji also suggested to me that in AFE, Muslims were free to perform rituals and to indulge in socio-religious activities—such as the preparation, consumption and distribution of sacrificial meat—which the Hindus found abhorrent.[84] A similar assertion was made by the grandson of a former central leader of the JI-H, presently a computer engineer at IBM India, who suggested that 'It is easier to practice our religion and transmit values to our children [when living in a Muslim-dominated locality]', although he also regretted that this regrouping induced a lack of knowledge of non-Muslims and the formation of a 'closed society'.[85] In other words, the younger sections of the local Muslim middle class are not arguing for separation from the larger society, but simply for moral and cultural autonomy in their place of residence.[86]

This concern for morality among AFE middle-class youths is not specific to the Muslim community and should be related to larger trends among India's new middle classes, whose struggle for material success and social status is accompanied by 'claims of high moral value'.[87] As an ideology of achievement,[88] these middle-class moralities should be distinguished from the moralistic discourses coming from the clergy or from Islamist activists and sympathisers. Unlike the former, these conventional discourses on morality are systematically pitted against a threatening Other ('Western' and 'Hindu' culture, often thought to act in tandem) as well as an enemy from within ('secular', 'Westernised' Muslims). In AFE, this internal enemy often takes the shape of the bachelor, flat-renting student from the nearby Jamia Millia Islamia, an institution described by one of my respondents, a teacher at a local Deobandi *madrasa*, as the 'gate of sin' (*gunah ka darvaza*).[89] Upwardly mobile middle-class Muslims seem less preoccupied with the alleged immorality of some of their neighbours and coreligionists. Their concern for morality appears more related to personal development than to the regulation of public behaviour. Nevertheless, the opposition between 'older' and 'newer' forms of morality among AFE's middle-class residents should not be pushed too far. Islamist youths, such as the activists of the student branch of the JI-H, the Student Islamic Organisation (SIO), have been critical of this reduction in ethics to 'the development of personal life and the promotion of managerial skills' (*shakhsi zindagi ka erteqa aur intezami maharat ka farogh*).[90] Rather than a generational effect, these contrasted conceptions of morality seem to be the product of different socialisations. Nowhere is this more apparent than in the different interpretations of the notion of *akhlaq* (ethic/good manners), which is primarily understood by *madrasa*-educated, Arabic-speaking and/or Islamist residents as Islam's ethical norms, whereas lay Muslims tend to associate it with a disposition of character—namely, that of civility[91]—which along with the notion of *adab* has been integral to the ethos of ashraf Muslims since the medieval period. Where matters become more complex is when parents send their children to *madrasas* or *maktabs* with the view of strengthening this civility, so that their siblings can better navigate the secular world.[92]

Conclusion

The element of choice that seems to inform the housing careers of AFE's middle-class Muslims suggests a phenomenon of self-segregation rather than ghettoisation. However, this notion of 'self-segregation' needs to be qualified. The difficulties encountered by Delhi Muslims to rent accommodation from non-Muslims—a trend already pointed to by a group of pre-eminent Indian social scientists in the early 1990s[93]—tend to limit their residential options, whatever income group they belong to. Moreover, the feelings of insecurity conveyed by most of my interviewees suggest that their decision to move to AFE was often seen as a 'choiceless' one,[94] or at least as a trade-off (*len-den*) made under duress, through which these middle-class Muslims renounced some of the advantages of their former residential milieu (religious and cultural mixing, better civic amenities) for greater physical and residential security. As a young computer engineer at IBM India puts it, 'The basic issue is security. If I could live in a [mixed] posh locality I would, but it is too risky. [...] There is a trade off: security vs. good facilities'.[95] Finally, some residents—particularly migrant workers with a limited knowledge of the city—did not consciously choose to live in AFE but simply followed their relatives or took a job opportunity here.[96]

If the characterisation of these residential trajectories as self-segregation is so problematic, it is also because AFE's residents do not live an insular existence. AFE is well connected to the rest of the city by public transport, its residents are not immune to the influence of national and global media[97] and a large part, possibly the majority of them, work elsewhere in Delhi.[98] Although difficult to quantify, the emergence of a new middle class is perceptible in the neighbourhood, around highly educated youths searching for economic opportunities beyond the traditional Muslim economy. The private sector is more appealing to these upwardly-mobile youths than the public, if only for their comparative disadvantage with Hindu SCs and OBCs in this job market. These professional evolutions, as well as the educational careers that made them possible in the first place, imply frequent interactions with non-Muslims, nurturing new anxieties but also offering new opportunities. Ethnographic evidence also suggests that residents animated by a spirit of cultural protectionism may try to compensate for their geographical estrangement from non-Muslims—and that of their children—through counter-segregative strategies (such as sending their children to English-medium schools in mixed localities). Even *madrasas*, all too often projected by Indian and Western media as retrograde, if not subversive institutions, are attentive in providing their students with a window to the outside world, through modern subjects such as English or computer sciences.[99] All this evidence suggests we need to adopt a nuanced, multifaceted interpretation of the dynamics of 'enclavement' in this locality, as they have as much to do with class as with religion.

9

MARGINALISED IN A SYNCRETIC CITY

MUSLIMS IN CUTTACK

Pralay Kanungo

While Muslims feel unsafe and insecure in some communally sensitive Indian cities, the syncretic city of Cuttack in Orissa[1] presents a different story. Muslims of all hues in this thousand-year-old city nostalgically and proudly talk of Cuttacks age-old tradition of *bhaichara* (brotherhood). Despite occasional occurrences of communal clashes in the recent past, they do not perceive any threat to their life and property, and continue to live with their Hindu neighbours in the traditional *sahis/mohallas* (mixed neighbourhoods) rather than contemplating to move out to live in an exclusive Muslim enclave. However, notwithstanding these feelings of security and stability, a large number of Muslims of Cuttack are economically, educationally, politically and socially marginalised.

The first section of this chapter traces the evolution of this historic city, its Muslim connection and the emergence of syncretic cultural traditions at the popular level showing how Hindu-Muslim relations hinged on the trajectory of assimilation and integration rather than conflict and collision; even the gale of communal wind in the post-independence period could not blow off the tradition of Hindu-Muslim 'brotherhood' and thereby failed to shake the security, confidence and belongingness of the Muslims of Cuttack. The second section maps out the backwardness, marginalisation and under-representation of the Muslims in various spheres, demonstrating how the post-colonial state has failed to address the needs of the community. Focussing on Muslim educational institutions it shows how the Muslim elites, who demonstrated great insight, initiative and enterprise by launching vibrant educational institutions back in the early twentieth century, handed them over to the state, thereby letting these institutions languish under utter neglect. However, experiments such as the Anjuman of Dewan Bazar shows the revival of community initiatives. The final section, while undertaking a survey in a locality of Muslim butchers (*qasais*), not only demonstrates their economic backwardness and failure of the state but also reveals that the Muslim upper strata/castes exclude them socially as Untouchables: thus, this 'minority within the minority' protests both against the apathy of the state as well as the caste hierarchy of the community.

The Resilience of a *Bhaichara* Culture

Cuttack, popularly called 'Kataka' in the Oriya language, etymologically refers to a military camp or a city. One of the oldest cities of India, Cuttack was founded in 989 AD and remained the capital of Orissa for many centuries and in the course of time became synonymous with Orissa.[2] Muslim expeditions to Orissa began in 1205 when Bengal's ruler Bakhtiyar Khalaji made an unsuccessful attempt to conquer it. In 1243, another attempt made by Tughan Khan of Bengal was also thwarted. The Delhi Sultan Firuz Tughluq invaded Orissa in 1361 and reportedly destroyed many temples. However, the final onslaught was yet to come. Mukunda Deva, the king of Orissa, was emerging as a rival to Sulaiman Kararani, the Afghan Sultan of Bengal. Mughal emperor Akbar entered into an alliance with Mukunda Deva to checkmate Kararani. But while Akbar was busy in the siege of Chitore, Sulaiman attacked Orissa and occupied Cuttack. Mukundadeva was the last independent Hindu ruler of Orissa but with the fall of the Barabati fort, Orissa was passed on to the hands of the Afghans in 1568. Afghan rule was short-lived, however. In 1590, Orissa was annexed to the empire of Akbar, became a province of Bengal and Cuttack continued to be the capital of Orissa. After the death of Aurangzeb in 1707, Orissa was ruled from Bengal by Muhmamad Taqi Khan, followed by Suja Uddin and Alivardi Khan. Frequent Maratha incursions compelled Alivardi to hand over Cuttack to the Bhonsla of Nagpur in lieu of twelve lakhs of rupees (one-fourth of the revenue). Cuttack became an important trading centre. Maratha rule came to an end with the occupation of Barabati fort by the British in 1803.

Muslim Influence: Landscape and Socio-cultural Space

Monuments and Bazars

Under Muslim rule (1568–1751) many impressive monuments like Lal Bagh Palace (1633), Diwan Bazar Mosque (1666), Jama Masjid (1690), Quadam Rasul (1715), adorned Cuttack's landscape (Hussain, 1990). Moreover, the city was a conglomeration of bazars and lanes. Even today people frequently cite an old proverb: *kataka sahara—boun bazar tepan gali,* which suggests that Cuttack consisted of fifty-two bazars and fifty-three lanes. In 1814 the then acting magistrate M. Ainsle divided Cuttack into six units (*mohallas*) and listed fifty-three areas of the city (Dhar, 1990). The six *mohallas* were: Baloo Bazar, Telingah Bazar, Kafeelah Bazar, Gunga Manzil, Jallaupoor or Kuddumrasool, and Bukshee Bazar; three of them had Muslim names.

The very naming of Cuttack's bazars sends some interesting signals. First, the city has a rich composite culture and every bazar and lane represented a heritage of its own. Second, the naming of these bazars represented different linguistic, regional/ethnic, religious, cultural and professional categories. Besides Oriya names they have tribal names (Meria Bazar), Sanskrit names (Ganga Mandir), regional names (Telenga Bazar, Bangali Sahi), Muslim names (Mohammadia Bazar, Azam Khan Bazar, Bakharabad, Buxi Bazar, Alisha Bazar, Chandni Chowk, Kazi Bazar, Dargha Bazar) and European names (Firangi Bazar, Gora Kabar). Thus, the preponderance of Muslim names of the bazars and localities suggest a deep Muslim engagement with the city.

Persian-Oriya Interface

In Orissa, some Persian and Arabic words were found in the inscriptions of the pre-Muslim period. But the impact of Persian and Arabic on Oriya language and literature became more pronounced during Muslim rule. As Persian became the court language and continued to remain so even after Muslim rule, interest in learning Persian grew. Distinguished Oriya writers like Upendra Bhanja, Brajanath Badajena, Fakir Mohan Senapati and Radhanath Ray used a large number of Arabic, Persian and Urdu words: more than 2,000 Persian and Arabic words were found in Oriya language and literature. Abdul Majid, an Oriya Muslim writer, translated the *Pandnama.* written by a thirteenth-century Persian poet Shaikh Sadi into Oriya as *Prabodh Kabya* in 1868, which became popular in Orissa (Khan, 2004). Many Oriya and Sanskrit words also made their way into the Urdu lexicon as well. Such interactions and exchanges influenced the dialect, intonation and pronunciation of the respective languages in Orissa. As a result, Cuttack's Muslims today speak a kind of hybrid/creolised Urdu. An Urdu-Oriya bilingual periodical, called *Sada-e-Odisa*, published in Cuttack, demonstrates this coexistence, by dividing each issue into two sections—Urdu and Oriya.

Popular Islam and Popular Hinduism

Lord Jagannath of Puri, the most popular Hindu deity of the Oriyas, has a hegemonic influence on Oriya culture, which is often referred to as Jagannath culture. Traditionally, this culture has shown syncretic manifestations. Sal Beg, a seventeenth-century Muslim poet, composed thousands of devotional songs in Oriya dedicated to Lord Jagannath. He has become a household name and his songs have become an indispensable part of the temple routine as they are sung before the Lord every morning. Hindu-Muslim socio-cultural integration endured beyond Muslim rule. The two communities continued to actively participate in each other's religious festivals. For instance, the Muslim Dalabehera (military/administrative head, a designation bestowed by the king) of Manikagada village has been acting as the hereditary *Marfatdar* (custodian) of the village Durga Puja for centuries. On Dusshera day, dressed as a Brahmin, he is brought to the Puja Pandal in a procession. Sitting on the Pandal he authorises the Brahmin to perform the worship of Durga on his behalf (Khan, 2004).

Cuttack, which celebrates Dussehra with great gaiety, has Puja committees in each *sahi/mohalla*. Muslims are not only the members of these committees, some of them are also active office-bearers. Even the famous Chandi (silver) Medha (background motif behind the idol) of Choudhury bazar has been donated by Mumtaz Ali, the former chief engineer of Orissa. During festival days, popular Muslim singers, musicians and artists perform in these Puja Pandals. A large number of Muslims take part in the immersion procession, which is in contrast to many other cities where Hindu-Muslim clashes invariably take place during festivals. Similarly, Hindus also take part in Eid celebrations and Muharram processions.

Worship of *Satya Pir* has been a shared tradition between Hindus and Muslims. *Satya* (Sanskrit-Hindu) and *Pir* (Persian-Muslim) signify both religious as well as linguistic confluence, and many literary and vernacular tracts have been published in this tradition and are enacted as *Palas* (a form of balladry), showing Hindu-Muslim syncretism. Cuttack's tradition of *Jatra/ Tamasha* (opera) also illustrates cultural borrowings and assimilation. As Hindus have deep faith in the Sufi and Pir tradition, they flock to many Muslim shrines in the city such as the Qadam-i-Rasul, the shrine of Malang Shah Wali in Dhobi Lane, the Bibi Alam in Alamchand Bazar and Mastan Dargha (Khan, 2004). There has been a strong intermingling of Sufi and Hindu folk traditions in Orissa and some conversion to Islam might have followed the Sufi route. A fusion of faith and culture is witnessed at the shrine of Hazrat Bokhari Baba in Kaipadar at Khurda. Here *Shirni/Prasad*, flowers and sandalwood paste, are sold only by Hindu shopkeepers who have been allotted *Sanands* (records) for the same through the ages.

Cuttack has been a unique example of Hindu-Muslim social, cultural and religious harmony and unity. In customs, manner, dress and food the borrowing from each other is quite evident. Some Muslims even believe in Hindu astrology and make horoscopes for the newborn child. Aminul Islam[3] of Cuttack published thousands of booklets of songs in Oriya (*bhajans, kirtans* like the *Koilli*) which became popular in Orissa. His greatest contribution to Hindu-Muslim relations lies in his publication of an authentic Oriya almanac in 1935 known as Orissa Kohinoor Press *Panjika* (almanac). For Hindus, this *Panjika* has been an indispensable guide to their religious rituals and is even found in many Hindu homes. This almanac, published by a Muslim, has found acceptance in the Jagannath temple for its authenticity and the temple rituals are conducted according to its calculation.

Sectarian Division among Muslims: Deobandis and Barelwis

In Orissa in general and in Cuttack in particular, Muslims are overwhelmingly Sunnis. While there is hardly any Shia presence in the city, there are a few prosperous Ahmadias (Qadianis). As elsewhere in India, Sunnis are divided between Deobandis and Barelwis. Deobandi reformers, who emerged in North India during the post-Mutiny period, were inward looking and worked on grassroots reforms, insisting on purity and devotion (Metcalf, 2002). Barelwis, the followers of Ahmad Raza Khan, who call themselves the *Ahle Sunnat wa Jama'at,* are more conventional in their acceptance of customary practices associated with veneration of Syeds, holy men, saints, and the Prophet (Sanyal, 1996). Orissa Muslims perhaps were amenable to the Barelwis due to the variety of Sufism that prevailed here. However, of late, the Deobandis have grown substantially, perhaps outnumbering the Barelwis. Tablighi Jama'at, a Deobandi group preaching a missionary brand of Islam, has been able to attract Muslim youths. Moreover, Deobandi elites like doctors, engineers and professors make regular tours motivating the Muslims to offer regular *Namaz* and observe religious purity and piety, thereby helping the sect to grow. Barelwis mobilise the Muslims focussing on Dawat-e-Islami. This competitive mobilisation has split Muslim institutions and even mosques are identified on sectarian lines.[4]

Communal Politics in a Syncretic City

Cuttack witnessed some communal tension in the 1940s when both Muslim and Hindu leaders from Bengal visited the city to mobilise their respective communities. But Orissa did not witness any communal riots in the pre-Partition or post-Partition years (Kanungo, 2003). The first communal riot occurred in March 1964 in the industrial town of Rourkela, where trains carrying Hindu refugees from East Pakistan were stopping for food supplies. The RSS allegedly provoked Hindus against Muslims, which culminated in a communal riot killing seventy-two people.

Cuttack experienced its first communal riot in 1968 after a judgment passed by the Supreme Court. Hindus of two villages of Cuttack district filed a writ demanding the right to play music before a mosque and pleaded that they should not be bound by the agreement between the two communities reached in 1931, which denied them this right. The Supreme Court in its verdict allowed the Hindus to carry out processions before a mosque. This judgment came when Cuttack was celebrating *Kartikeswar Puja*. and Hindu leaders wanted to enjoy this newly bestowed right. Muslim leaders opposed this, arguing that there was no such tradition in the city. However, after negotiations, they allowed the immersion procession to pass in front of their Masjids. After a week, on 25 November 1968, some footballers from Christ College were allegedly stoned and beaten up by Muslims near the Sutahat Masjid. Then the riots spread throughout the city, but unlike the Rourkela riots, there was no killing. A different trend was noticed here: the rioters mainly looted and set on fire the shops and houses of Muslims. Thus, this riot primarily targeted Muslim businesses. While many political parties thought this riot to be the handiwork of anti-social elements, the Communist Party of India blamed the RSS. However, the Swatantra-Jana Congress government exonerated the Sangh Parivar. Communal riots undoubtedly rejuvenated the RSS in Cuttack.

Shakhas multiplied, enrolling Hindu boys. The central RSS leadership declared Orissa as a separate *prant* (province) in 1970 and appointed Bhupendra Kumar Basu, a lawyer of Cuttack, as the first *prant sanghchalak* of Orissa. Thus Cuttack became an important centre of Hindutva politics.

In 1992, Cuttack was threatened by another bout of riots during the Ramjanmabhoomi agitation. The Biju Patnaik government did not allow any riot to take place in the city. However, one Muslim was stabbed to death at Alisha Bazar. Muslim leaders strictly instructed their youth not to get provoked and indulge in any kind of violence. Hindu leaders of their *sahis/mohallas* also assured them security. Leaders of both communities also effectively countered rumours. In Oriya Bazar, where Muslims live in a sizeable number, some Hindutva activists were reportedly planning to attack Muslims. Mahima Mishra, a powerful Hindu businessman of the locality, took a tough public posture by stating that the rioters had to confront him first before attacking the Muslims of Oriya Bazar (*Mahima Mishra aga, Muslim pachha*). Mishra's popularity and clout acted as a deterrent and nothing happened. Muslim youths of Oriya Bazar greatly appreciate Mishra's courageous stand as well as the measured reaction of the local Hindu population.[5]

Muslim leaders of Cuttack observe that the communal events of 1968 and 1992 could not be classified as full-fledged riots as there was hardly any loss of life and the citizens of *sahis/mohallas* successfully prevented a communal flare-up. Moreover, in 1992, the state government acted firmly. The logic is that while only a small section of supporters of the Sangh Parivar harbour communalism, the overwhelming majority of the city still follows the age-old tradition of Hindu-Muslim *bhaichara*. Thus, there is no danger of majoritarian communalism in Cuttack. Even the tremor of anti-Christian violence in Kandhamal in 2008 has not shaken their confidence; they argue rather that as Muslims have no agenda of conversion they do not invite majoritarian antagonism and Cuttack is a different case.

Thus, despite the emergence of Hindutva forces, Cuttack Muslims do not perceive any threat to their security. They have been living in peace with Hindus in the *sahis/mohallas* for centuries. Minor skirmishes have occurred once in a while. But the local leadership has usually treated them as normal conflicts between individuals and among local groups and resolved them amicably, and these conflicts have rarely taken a communal turn. For instance, inter-religious marriage has created tension between families, but it has rarely involved communities.[6] Muslims in the city by and large feel secure and would like to live in their traditional mixed neighbourhood rather than moving out to a new locality and creating a ghetto. The bonding that arises out of the everyday forms of engagement between the two communities in the *sahis/mohallas* has always proved to be a bulwark against communal riots.[7] Living in an exclusive Muslim enclave would not ensure safety and security and given the negligible number of Muslims, such forms of enclosure would probably be unsustainable economically anyway. Socio-economic transactions between the two communities have always remained complementary. Even the visiting Tablighi Jama'at leaders from North India, who come to Cuttack to preach 'pure' Islam, acknowledge that this unique tradition is quite different from their own region and any programme to mobilise Muslims on radical lines does not attract enough potential converts.

The Sangh Parivar also faces similar constraints vis-a-vis mobilisation of Hindus in a syncretic milieu. Samir Dey of the BJP, who represented Cuttack Assembly constituency thrice (1995, 2000, 2004), knew well that communal polarisation would not work with Cuttacks citizens. Hence, he preferred to court the Muslims by providing financial support and patronage to *madrasas, darghas,* clubs and other Muslim institutions.[8] Besides, the BJP was prevented from playing the communal card even when it was a junior partner in the coalition government led by the secular Biju Janata Dal (BJD) in which Dey was a minister.

Credit for championing secular politics goes to Syeed Mustafiz Ahmed, a Muslim who was elected from the Cuttack Assembly seat twice (1985 and 1990) from the Janata Party/Janata Dal and was a minister in the Biju Patnaik government. Ahmed was known for his secular and pro-poor politics. Some Muslim activists criticise him for paying more attention to the poor slum dwellers of other communities rather than promoting the interests of his own community.

Thus, in the past twenty-five years, Cuttack has been largely free of communal politics, due to its syncretic nature. The state also acted tough and did not allow communal forces to disturb the peace. While the city legislator from the BJP was constrained by the compulsion of coalition politics and preferred to 'appease' the Muslims in this non-communal city, the Muslim legislator displayed deep secular conviction and prioritised class over religion and community. All these factors further strengthened the tradition of Cuttack's *bhaichara* culture.

Cuttack Muslims on the Margins

In spite of the *Bhaichara* culture, Cuttack Muslims are on the margins. Physical security has not ensured economic security. According to the 2001 Census, the total urban population of Cuttack district is 641,130: 579,461 Hindus (90.38%); 49,463 Muslims (7.71%); 9,329 Christians (1.46%); and 432 others (0.45%). Though the Muslim population of the state is only 2.07%, urban pockets such as Cuttack, Bhadrakh, Kendrapada, Salepur have higher concentrations of Muslims. In Cuttack, Muslims live in the heart of the city, having a sizeable presence in Wards 7, 9, 10, 11, 12, 14, 15, 16, 19, 20, 21 and 29 (see map).

Table 9.1. Growth rate of population in Cuttack (in %)

Year	1971	1981	1991	2001
Total	36	52	37	32
Hindus	23.35	19.13	19.11	15.86
Muslims	51.64	29.33	36.83	31.88
Christians	88.49	26.80	38.67	34.77

Source: Census of India, 2001.

The decadal growth rate of the Muslim population shows that since 1981 it has remained below the average growth rate of the city. Thus, the city has failed to attract Muslims from rural areas and perhaps it lost out to the adjacent sprawling capital city of Bhubaneswar, which has seen rapid urbanisation. Muslim migrants might have opted for the latter for better economic prospects.

The literacy rate in urban areas of Cuttack according to religion is as follows: Hindus, 76.02%; Muslims, 66.40%; and Christians, 83.38%. Thus, with regard to literacy, Muslims are roughly 10 percentage points behind the Hindus and about 20 percentage points behind the Christians. As some Muslim youth activists mentioned, Muslim literates will be much less than the Census figure as, during the Census count, anybody who can read the Quran is counted as literate by officials.

Table 9.2. Classification of Workers in Cuttack (in %)

Religious Groups	Total	Male	Female
Hindus	31.89	86.52	13.48
Muslims	29.37	93.52	6.48
Christians	30.91	75.21	24.79

Source: Census of India, 2001.

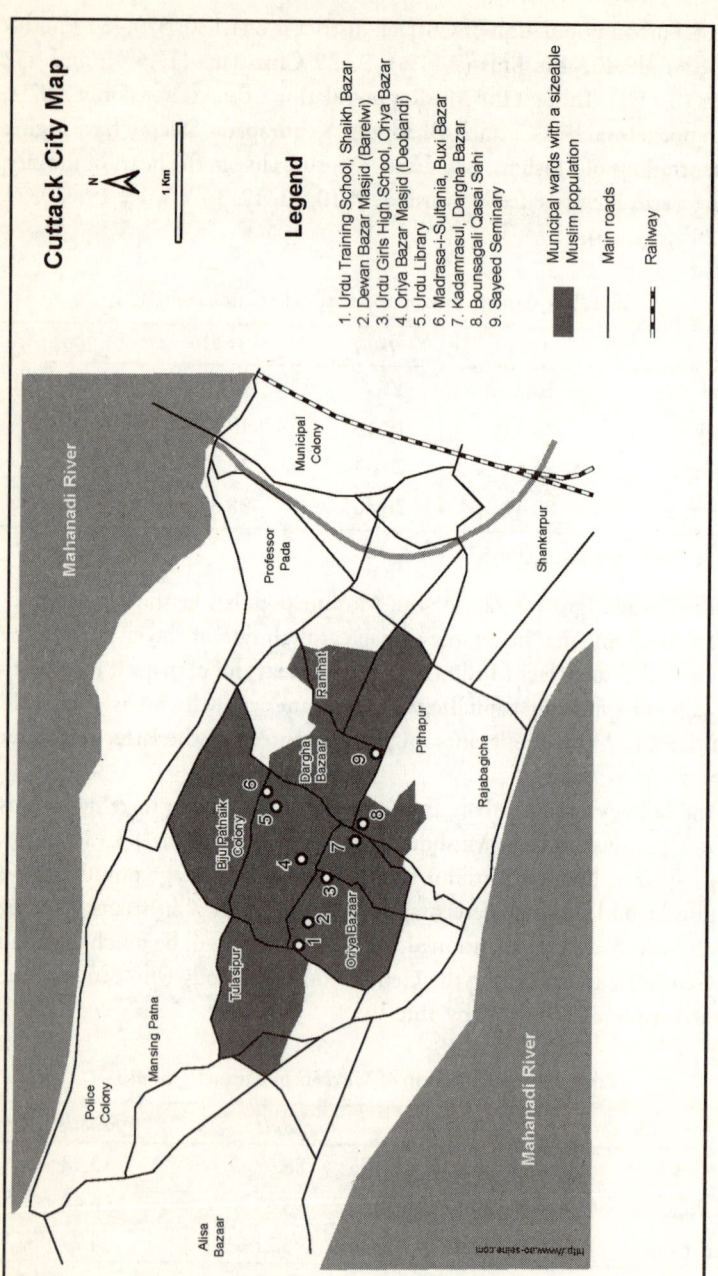

Map of Cuttack

MARGINALISED IN A SYNCRETIC CITY

Data on the religious distribution of main and marginal workers shows that the percentage of the Muslim non-working population is higher in comparison with the Hindus and Christians. More strikingly, Muslim women workers are 7 percentage points below their Hindu counterparts and more than 18 percentage points less than Christian women workers. This suggests that while poor Hindu women go out to work as daily wage-earners and other menial jobs, poor Muslim women for their part rarely work outside their homes.

Political Representation

No Muslim has ever been elected to the Lok Sabha from Orissa. Only one Muslim politician, Mohamad Hanif, was elected to the Rajya Sabha in 1966. Orissa Legislative Assembly has 147 seats and the maximum number of Muslims elected to any assembly has been three. On occasions there has been a complete rout as well. For instance, the present Assembly does not have a single Muslim member. Representation of Muslims in Orissa Assembly indicates some peculiar trends. Bhadrak town, which has a large Muslim population (close to 50%), has elected a Muslim just once; Cuttack and Mahanga constituencies, with a much smaller Muslim population, have elected Muslim candidates twice and four times respectively. Even a constituency like Nawrangpur with a marginal Muslim population has elected one Muslim candidate, Habibulkh Khan, eight consecutive times, twice from the Swatantra party and six times as a Congress candidate. Interestingly, one Muslim candidate was elected on a BJP ticket in 2004 from Melchhamunda constituency. This trend suggests that Muslims vote on party lines rather than community lines. Political parties do not feel constrained to field a Muslim candidate from a constituency with a large Muslim population and a Hindu candidate from a constituency with a large Muslim population. Thus, the elections in Orissa have been more or less a secular exercise.

Despite this erratic nature of representation some Muslim leaders have found a place in the state government. Maulavi Latifur Rahman became a minister in 1937 and Maulavi Abdus Sobhan Khan was in the Council of Ministers in the 1941 coalition ministry. Both Rahman and Khan were prominent lawyers. In the post-independence period, Orissa has had four Muslim ministers: Habibullah Khan, Sheikh Matlub Ali, Muzzafar Hussain Khan and Syed Mus-tafiz Ahmed, the first three from the Congress and the fourth one from the Janata Dal. Habibulla Khan, whose forefathers came from the North-West Frontier province, is a big landowner and has been a very popular grassroots political worker. Ali, a postgraduate, is a well-known writer and has acted as the President of the Orissa Sahitya Academy. Mustafiz, who comes from a business family, has been a grassroots activist.

Cuttack used to have one parliamentary and one Assembly segment. After the boundaries were redrawn, the city got three assembly constituencies. However, as discussed earlier, Cuttack Assembly constituency has elected Mustafiz Ahmed, a Muslim representative, for two consecutive terms from 1985 to 1995. Cuttack Municipality had some prominent Muslim councillors: M.A. Amin was a councillor continuously (1952–80) and was Vice-Chairman for many years and another councillor, Mohammad Yusuf, was also Vice-Chairman. The Municipality became Cuttack Municipal Corporation (CMC) with effect from 1994 onwards, and at present the CMC has 54 wards. In 1997, one Muslim corporator was elected from Ward 7, in 2003, two Muslim corporators were elected from Ward 12 and Ward 14, and in 2007, two Muslim corporators were elected from Ward 16 and Ward 29. Both the young corporators belong to the ruling BJD. While one corporator, Muhammad Ayub, has a doctorate in Oriya literature, the other, also well educated, worked in the private sector before contesting the elections. Ayub is secular and is a champion of the syncretic traditions of Cuttack: his doctoral thesis is full of such examples.

The number of Muslim bureaucrats working in Orissa under different all-India services is almost nil. Out of a total of 370 posts in the Indian Administrative Service, Indian Police Service and Indian Forest Service, there is just one Muslim officer. Only seventeen Muslim officers are working in the Orissa Administrative Service out of 1,680, constituting barely 1%.[9] Similarly, among the city lawyers the number of Muslims is again quite low: in the High Court Bar Council there are only forty-nine Muslim members out of 3,884. There is no Muslim judge in Cuttack High Court. As far as doctors are concerned, there are about forty Muslim doctors out of 400 practising doctors in the city.[10] Some of the Muslim doctors are also working in the Gulf countries. The entertainment industry has many Muslim film directors, actors, musicians and singers.

Business and Enterprise

As discussed earlier, Cuttack's Muslim business elite sponsored community educational institutions a century ago. In the post-independence period, the city has had some successful Muslim businessmen, particularly in the tobacco-related industry. Brand products like Akbari Khan *Gudakhu* (tobacco paste) and Towntara *Bidi* (a type of cigarette with tobacco flakes wrapped in *tendu* leaf) were not only well known all over Orissa, they also had a strong presence in the neighbouring states. Some Muslims also owned hotels, theatres and shops and did well in manufacturing and retail businesses. The absence of a general business environment in Orissa, the incapability of the state to extend financial and infrastructural support, and domination and control of trade and commerce by the Marwaris and outsiders, did not encourage Oriya businessmen in general and Muslim entrepreneurs in particular to prosper.

The changing business environment in the state in the 1990s and the availability of capital have encouraged some Muslim entrepreneurs like the Metro Builders to emerge as key players in Cuttack's construction sector. But there remains a huge untapped Muslim enterprise in the small informal sectors, which does not find outlets for its business potential. Neither the state nor the banking sector comes forward to offer credit to small entrepreneurs. The Prime Minister's 15-points programme for the welfare of the minorities has hardly made any headway. While most of the states have set up independent subsidiaries of the National Minorities Development & Finance Corporation (NMDFC), the Orissa government made the Orissa Backward Classes Finance and Development Cooperative Corporation as the Channelising Agency to NFDMC. Surprisingly, not a single group/section of Muslims has been listed under the state list of Backward Castes.

As Muslims have a negligible presence in formal sector jobs and are largely self-employed in the city, it would be worthwhile to examine this aspect. The data on Swarna Jayanti Sahari Rojgar Yojna[11] under the Urban Self Employment Programme shows that out of the total 921 beneficiaries, the number of Muslim beneficiaries is 87 (9%). The vocation for which they have applied for loans shows the kind of occupations the poor Muslims are engaged in: petty shopkeeping (grocery/betel/stationery/garments/electric goods/butchery), mobile vending, tailoring, cycle repairing, trunk making, book binding, electronic repairing and supplying home-made food products. Besides these occupations, a large chunk of the Muslim population either remains unemployed or earns a paltry income by working as mechanics, waiters, vendors, artisans, band players, labourers and rickshaw-pullers.

Muslim Educational Institutions in Cuttack: Rise, Decline and Revival

The blending of boundaries in the *Ehaichara* culture does not imply that the Muslim identity has been blurred. Rather, this culture gave Cuttack Muslims enough leverage, freedom and confidence to maintain a distinct identity, to pursue their ways of living and value systems, and to create their religious, cultural and educational spaces and institutions. In the early twentieth century, the Muslim elites of Cuttack consisted of a few zamindars, some businessmen and traders, government servants, teachers and lawyers. Some of them took initiatives in setting up a number of educational institutions in the Muslim localities of the city (see the map) to provide religious as well as modern secular education to Muslim boys and girls and to promote Urdu.

Madrasa Education: Madrasa-i-Sultania

In 1910, a city merchant, Mohammad Sultan, started the first Muslim educational institution called Madrasa-i-Sultania in a rented house. The present premises at Buxi Bazar were purchased in 1919 and education was provided up to the middle standard (*Wastania*). Subsequently it was upgraded to a high school (*Moulvi*) in 1936 and graduation (*Alim*) was introduced in 1970. Initially, the *madrasa* was affiliated to the Bihar Madrasa Board but after the Orissa Madrasa Education Board (OMEB) was constituted in 1971 it was affiliated to the latter in 1972. At present there are about 200 students enrolled in Madrasa-i-Sultania. These students come from poor backgrounds; rich and middle-class Muslims prefer to send their children to English-medium schools.

Cuttack has twenty-two *madrasas* affiliated to the OMEB: seven fully aided, eleven recognised and likely to receive aid soon, and four non-recognised. There are about forty private *madrasas/maktabs* in the city. *Madrasa* education faces a serious crisis. First, although the language of instruction is supposed to be Urdu, there are no teachers who can teach subjects such as mathematics and science in Urdu. Second, books on various other subjects are not available in Urdu. The Orissa Board did not translate any Oriya-language books into Urdu. Hence, the students have no choice but to study the books written in the Oriya language. In the examinations the questions are asked in Oriya although the answers are written in Urdu.[12] This creates some confusion and penalises Urdu-educated students.

Moreover, the government aid to the *madrasas* only meets the salary of the teachers and the staff without taking into account other expenses. Government-aided *madrasas* like the Madrasa-i-Sultania therefore face a serious financial crunch. Dilapidated buildings, unkempt classrooms, broken furniture and unhygienic kitchens are symptoms of this situation. Hostel inmates, consisting of thirty poor Muslim students, just manage to get food twice a day.

The Madrasa-i-Sultania has limited sources of income. It receives meagre rent from a few shops located on the campus, which has not been revised for decades. To meet routine expenses the *madrasa* occasionally rents out its premises/classrooms for marriage functions, thereby adversely affecting the sanctity and environment of an educational institution. The major source of income on which the *madrasa* depends is *zakat* (religious donations) collected during Ramzan. However, the community prefers to donate to the un-aided private *madrasas* rather than contributing to the government-aided ones. Thus, Madrasa-i-Sultania languishes because of the government tag whereas community/private *madrasas* receive generous donations. If the community could channel *zakat* donations by prioritising the areas and ensuring equitable distribution of the 'spiritual capital' (Shariff, 2010), then it could benefit many ailing community institutions such as Madrasa-i-Sultania.

While the community response is lukewarm, the state response is quite apathetic. The Orissa government, unlike the government of West Bengal, does not take an interest in *madrasa* education,[13] complain some teachers. For instance, six out of seventeen teaching positions have remained unfilled since 2003. Though the government has appointed teachers to vacant positions on a contract basis in other schools, it has not done so in this case. While criticising the state government's insensitivity, the teachers appreciate the central government's Scheme for Providing Quality Education in Madrasas (SPQEM).[14] *Madrasas* across the city, including Madrasa-i-Sultania, demand modernisation, realising their increasing irrelevance as only those who cannot afford the cost of private education send their children to *madrasas*. The *madrasa* teachers think that by giving priority to subjects like English, Science, Mathematics and Information Technology they can stop their decline; but neither the government nor the community shows any interest.

Modern Education: The Sayeed Seminary

Four teachers, namely Mohammad Sayeed, Akshoy Kumar Roy, Allah Bux and Qumruddin, who were expelled by the Victoria school for demanding a salary raise, founded a 'Muslim Seminary' in 1913, collecting donations from the citizens of Cuttack. One of the major donors was Qasim Ahmad Oraji, a Muslim merchant of the city. Akshoy Kumar Roy, a Hindu, was the first headmaster of the Muslim Seminary, thereby showing the secular character of Cuttack Muslims. Later the school was named 'Sayeed Seminary' recognising the contribution of one of the founder-teachers, Mohammad Sayeed. Initially, the school started from a rented building with 500 students on its roll. As the government paid only Rs 500 per month the school was largely dependent on donations. The enterprising community leaders even managed to persuade a generous merchant of Madras, C. Abdul Hakeem, to donate the present land and building. Even the Nizam of Hyderabad made a monthly grant of Rs 50 (Hussain, 1990).

The Sayeed Seminary became a reputed high school in the city that offered education both to Muslim and Hindu students in Urdu and Oriya. The school has produced many distinguished *alumni* like Sushil Kumar Sinha (scientist-administrator), Abdul Majid (popularly known as Bachhan) who represented the Indian football team in the 1951 Asian Games, M.Q. Khan (Vice-Chancellor), Dr. Saifullah (paediatric surgeon), Md. Fakhruddin (educationalist), S.M. Osatullah (Indian Administrative Service), S.A. Huda (Indian Police Service) and S. Mustafiz Ahmed (Minister). The school had also produced some outstanding sportsmen both at state and national levels.

The Sayeed Seminary gradually declined from its old glory. As the community elites became economically weak and politically marginalised, they lost interest in community projects and it became hard to generate resources. Thus, they conveniently passed on the responsibility to the government to run the school, keeping only a token presence in the management. On its part, the government did not address the specific needs of a minority institution. Reductions in grants, abolition of posts and a refusal to fill vacancies adversely affected the image and performance of this school. More interestingly, the government asked the management to surrender the surplus land of the school and threatened to stop aid if it did not comply. Thus, the school became a site of legal contestation and in this process it remained accountable neither to the state nor to the community, thereby ensuring its erosion. A huge school building with a big playground in the heart of the city assumed a ghostly and deserted look. It became the last resort for those students who had no other school to fall back upon.

Educating Muslim Girls: Urdu Girls High School

A Muslim merchant, Moulvi Sayeed Mukkaram Ali, founded the Urdu Girls High School at Oriya Bazar in 1926 to provide education to Muslim girls in Urdu. Initially started as a lower primary school it soon became a primary school. Later, the Cuttack Municipality brought it under its management and introduced class VI. A two-storey building was constructed with public donations and the High School started in 1960.

At present the high school has 300 students, all of whom are Muslim girls, mostly coming from the poor families of rickshaw-pullers, daily labourers, mechanics and small shopkeepers. The poor students are primarily attracted to it because of the nominal tuition fees. Wealthy Muslim parents do not send their children to this school as it is a dying institution in every respect—from teaching to infrastructure. Absenteeism is very high and results are below average. Poor Muslim households do not provide a congenial atmosphere for study. Although the parents have an urge to educate the girls they fear that it may be a constraint in marriage. Hence, they do not take enough interest.[15] The school employs eight trained teachers, five Muslims and three Hindus. Like in the case of the Madrasa-i-Sultania, the government does not fill the vacancies, not even on a contract basis. The school follows the syllabus prescribed by the Orissa Board. Ironically, although the objective of the school is to impart education in Urdu, most of the teachers cannot deliver in Urdu and subject books are not available in the language. Hence, most of the students write in Oriya and very few of them have any interest in Urdu. Thus, the very purpose of the promotion of Urdu has been defeated. Similar disadvantages are seen in West Bengal as well (Hasan and Menon, 2005: 154).

Promoting Urdu: The Urdu Secondary Training School

The Mohammadan Teachers' Elementary Training School started at Dargha Bazar in 1912. Later it was moved to Sheikh Bazar in 1915 with an intake capacity of eight students, and was renamed the Urdu Teachers' Elementary Training School in 1963, expunging the religious label. The school became coeducational in 1962 and was upgraded to the Urdu Secondary Training School in 1969. Its present intake capacity is fifty and this is the only Urdu training institution in the state. Despite having a huge campus, this training school again shows the symptoms of a declining institution as Urdu training does not ensure employment. The government's lackadaisical attitude towards Urdu could be gauged from the pitiable condition of the State Urdu Academy, which has been languishing without funds and leadership initiative. Muslim scholars refuse to head this institution as they do not have much hope in aid from the state government. Some Urdu scholars allege that the state government, rather than promoting Urdu, is conspiring to abolish the language from government colleges by not filling existing vacancies.

A Community Initiative: The Anjuman Islamia Ahle Sunnat-o-Jama'at, Dewan Bazar

In the midst of these once dynamic but currently declining institutions, there have been initiatives by some community organisations to create new institutions and attempt to resurrect the old ones. One such initiative, the Anjuman, was founded in 1953 at the holy shrine of Hazrat Bukhari, Barabati Fort, Cuttack. Soon it started Madrasa Madinatul Ilm and Islamia Yateem Khana in the premises of Jama Masjid, Balu Bazar, to provide free education to poor and orphan Muslim boys. The Anjuman then raised resources from the community and constructed a two-storey building at Dewan Bazar on the land donated by Haji Samiruddin. The *madrasa* was moved to these premises in 1996.

The Anjuman introduced a modern syllabus in 1998 in order 'to cope with the ever-developing present day world' (Anjuman, 2003). This dispels the myth that community *madrasas* resist modernisation. In Orissa, the community elites are ready to walk the extra mile as they realise that only education can bring a turn around in Muslim fortunes. The new syllabus included subjects such as Oriya, English, Mathematics, Science and Social Studies. Apart from preparing the students for the Moulvi (High School) certificate, it also provides classes on Hafiz, Querat and Alia. There is also an emphasis on computers and tailoring. However, those who want to study the Quran and do Hifz (to become a Hafiz) do not have any equivalent certificate/degree. After becoming a Hafiz only a few become Imams and the rest land up with low-paid jobs, observes one teacher.

The Anjuman has six affiliated *madrasas* in the city in which 300 boys and girls are enrolled. It also runs two *madrasas* outside the city. An annual budget of Rs 1 million is earmarked for the maintenance of the Anjuman and its *madrasas*. Providing free education, accommodation, food, uniforms, toiletries and medicines to 150 students and paying salaries to twenty-nine teachers is a tough job, observes one office-bearer. Furthermore, as the Anjuman does not have adequate infrastructure, it uses the hostel rooms as classrooms during the day. But unlike the Madrasa-i-Sultania, they are clean and well maintained.

The Anjuman is a Barelwi institution. Close to the *madrasa* stands the 350-year-old Tatar Khan Mosque, which is the headquarters of the Barelwis in the city.[16] The Anjuman/Mosque Committee contracted a bank loan to build a housing complex and rented it out to generate a steady income for the mosque. Thus, the mosque has become self-sufficient. The mosque committee also runs a dispensary called the Lok Sevak Hospital on a public-private partnership basis.[17] The Anjuman's social concerns were appreciated when it extended help to the victims of the 1999 super cyclone.

Quest for Modern Education: Revival of the Syeed Seminary?

The legal battle between the state and the Muslim community to control the prime land of the Sayeed Seminary School took a new turn in 2006, when the Orissa High Court declared that the school 'is purely a minority institution founded, funded and managed by the minority'. This judgment rejuvenated the community elites and the Sayeed Seminary Welfare and Educational Trust was thus formed to provide vocational, professional, job-oriented and skilled-based training to Muslim youth. The trust has prepared a blueprint to build a modern educational complex on the surplus land of the school and has been exploring the possibility of raising 10 crore rupees for this project.[18]

Meanwhile, the Al-Siddiquia Trust has adopted the Sayeed Seminary for its overall development.[19] By providing four months of intensive coaching to students before the high-school examination it has raised the pass rate from 55% in 2007 to 77% in 2008. The Trust has installed fans in the classrooms, provided clean toilets, supplied pure drinking water, distributed books to poor students and facilitated the process of computerisation.

Both the Anjuman experiment and the recent effort to modernise the Sayeed Seminary show that the community, despite its decline, does not lack in commitment, social capital and enterprise. When a vibrant Anjuman Madrasa is compared with a lacklustre state-aided Madrasa-i-Sultania, it shows how the right kind of community initiative could make a difference to Muslims. Similarly, the Sayeed Seminary project has the potential to bring a turnaround in this declining public institution. But the community is still sceptical about these endeavours. The Muslim Youth Cultural Association, once a leading community organisation of the city, has become completely defunct due to nepotism and factionalism. Moreover, sectarian division acts as a big deterrent in developing a common perspective in resurrecting the old ailing institutions and creating new relevant ones like the Industrial Training Institutes for the Muslim youth.

Margins within Margins: The Muslim *Panchams* of Bounsagali

Muslim elites are evasive when asked questions about caste hierarchy and practices among the Muslims of Cuttack. Indeed, these internal divisions challenge

Islam's egalitarian principle. Muslim elites do not seem to be concerned with the categorization of *Ashraf, Ajla* and *Arzal*; for them, it has no relevance in Orissa. They also observe that categories like '*Bade Bhaiya*' and '*Chhote Bhaiya*' may be prevalent in Bihar, but not here. They refer to four classifications among Muslims—Syed, Sheikh, Mughal and Pathan—but these divisions, as they rightly mention, have been made on ethnic lines rather than on the basis of caste. Unlike in North India, they observe, there are no service castes like *Dhobis* (washermen), *Nais* (barbers), *Mochis* (cobblers) and *Julahas* (weavers) among Oriya Muslims, thereby suggesting that all Muslims in Orissa belong only to the upper crust/higher castes. Though they agree that some kind of subtle hierarchical relations exist among the four sections of Muslims, the rigid social divisions are fast disappearing with inter-group marriages and due to the emergence of new kinds of social and economic interactions. However, most Muslim elites feel uncomfortable when asked about the *Qasais* or *Qussabs* (butchers). Where are they placed within this four-fold division? The uniform response is: 'they are different: unclean, filthy, uneducated and uncultured'.

Livelihood of the Qasais

To explore the conditions of livelihood, education and social status of the Qasai community, who remains at the bottom of the socio-economic hierarchy of the Muslims in the city, a survey was conducted in the 83 households at *Bounsagali* (literally Bamboo Lane), in Oriya Bazar, one of the slums of the city where the Muslim butchers live. The lane is so named perhaps because it is long and narrow like bamboo. As the data on Muslim slum clusters indicate, out of 49,463 Muslims of the city, 13,584 living in 2,594 households are slum-dwellers. Thus, 27.46% of Cuttack's Muslim population live in slums.

Data was collected from eighty-three households of Bounsagali, the slum of Muslim butchers. These households contain a total number of 426 persons, with an average family size of five, which is exactly the same for the city. In this locality, not a single Muslim has more than one wife, which demolishes the myth of an oft-repeated slogan of the Sangh Parivar—'*Hum Paanch, Hamare Pachhish*' (We are five and have twenty-five children).

While 44% of the adult male population is working and has an income, 56% reported that they do not have any income and are dependent on their working family members. There are some variations in the income: an overwhelming 89% of the working population fall within the income range of Rs 1,500–3,000 per month, 7% within Rs 3,000–5,000 and only 4% earn above Rs 5,000 per month.

Most of the working population of these households make a living by following their traditional occupation—butchery (cow: 55% and goat: 16%). Though professionally they butcher two different kinds of animals, they are all referred to as Qasais: different nomenclatures are not used to identify each of them as observed in Delhi (Ahmad, 2011). While 6% run small shops, 23% have all kinds of odd occupations. Those who have an income of more than Rs 5,000 per month are small contractors and shopkeepers. The difference in income among the butchers occurs as they are divided into two groups: shop owners and labourers. The shop owners employ labourers for killing, chopping, cleaning and transporting animals. While the shopkeepers make little profit, each labourer earns only Rs 60 to 80 per day despite hard work.[20] Moreover, work is not guaranteed every day. The business is good only for three days a week (Monday, Wednesday and Friday) and during the rest of the week it is dull.

In the colonial period, Cuttack Municipality issued 16 licenses to butchers to open shops. With the promulgation of the Orissa Prevention of Cow Slaughter Act in 1960, the killing of cows became illegal.[21] The licenses were not renewed and Cuttack's butchery (*Kilkhana*) was closed down. Meanwhile, the number of shops multiplied with the expansion and division in the families of the original licence holders. At present there are about a hundred outlets in the city and the demand for beef is growing as it is cheap and, besides poor Muslims, it is consumed by poor Christians, Telugus and Dalits.[22] The High Court has passed an order to move the butchery business to the outskirts of the city. While shopkeepers fear that the volume of sales would decrease affecting their profit margins, the labourers are worried that it would be hard for them to travel long distance every day for a paltry wage. The butchers have been requesting the government time and again to allot them a site within the city where Muslims are residing. But the government does not respond positively perhaps fearing the communalisation of the issue by the Sangh Parivar.

While the butchers are facing a crisis in their livelihoods, the Orissa Prevention of Cow Slaughter Act has given free licence to the police to harass the butchers and extract money from traders and shopkeepers quite regularly. Sangh Parivar elements also occasionally threaten and beat up the transporters and shopkeepers and even local musclemen (*dadas*) demand their share. This makes the butchers' struggle for livelihood even more difficult. The butchers are left with no other option but to convert their homes to slaughter houses, which has a detrimental impact on the health and hygiene of their family members. Besides, flushing and draining out the blood becomes a huge problem and they have to make an outlet from their house to the main drain located in their backyard. In order to avoid public anger, they have to clean up everything and finish the entire slaughtering work by early morning.

Literacy and Education

The children of the butchers of Bounsagali go to government schools and only a few attend *madrasas* in childhood. While every child is enrolled in a school, many drop out eventually. Only two students of this locality have completed school education and joined college. The school drop-out rate for boys is higher than girls. Most of the boys drop out between middle school and high school primarily to support their families, as about 50% of them mentioned economic hardship as the reason for discontinuing education. In the case of girls, though, this trend can be related to their patriarchal family environment. Parents discourage them to pursue their studies as it would make it more difficult to find them suitable husbands. However, the attitude of the community has been changing favourably towards women. The community runs one *Khabatin* (for education of adult Muslim women). In one Ali Anwar-donated space, about fifteen women and adult girls attend classes regularly. The community has hired two teachers and pays them every month an amount of Rs 750 each.

Stigma of Being a Qasai

While the way Hindus treat Qasais, the butchers of cows by profession, as pariahs, is expected, it is more surprising that the upper sections of the Muslims also attach social stigma to the Qasais. The butchers were asked if they considered themselves as backward, and if so, then how do they qualify their backwardness—as economic, social, or educational? Surprisingly, despite struggling for their daily livelihood, an overwhelming 92% of the respondents consider themselves as *socially* backward. It became apparent from the interviews with the residents of Bounsagali that upper-caste Muslims of Cuttack attach stigma to the Qasais and would not enter into a marriage alliance with them. Hence, the Qasai community is compelled to be endogamous and has emerged as a cohesive *biradree* without social divisions and stratifications within the community despite variations in income level. Thus, the butchers seem to be more concerned with their low social position rather than their economic and educational backwardness.

This becomes more evident when 89% say that upper-caste/class Muslims do not treat them equally. Only 4% think otherwise and 7% have not responded. Why does the Muslim upper caste/class treat them unequally? None of the respondents attributed this unequal treatment to their poverty: 87% say that the unequal treatment is only due to their low-caste status. One youth revealed during the interview that once a Qasai from Bounsagali went to the house of an upper-caste Muslim and sat on a sofa. Soon after he left, the sofa was cleaned and the room was washed.[23] Thus, the butchers perceive that they are treated as Untouchables by upper-caste Muslims. This is in clear contrast to the elite perception that caste does not exist among the city Muslims.

On the other hand, the butchers have good neighbourly relations with Hindus from the lower and backward castes. No respondent has had any unpleasant relationship with his Hindu neighbours, while 63% describe their relationship as very good, 31% find it good and 6% have not responded. As one BSP activist puts it succinctly, 'The upper-caste Muslims like Syeds and Mughals treat them as untouchables. They would never enter into a marriage relationship with the Qasais. On the other hand, Qasais and Hindu Dalits have similar life experiences; both are poor, uneducated and are exploited by a hierarchical order. Hence, a fraternal relationship exists between the Qasais and the Hadis (sweepers)'.[24]

While earlier the Qasais of Bounsagali prefixed Mohammad and Sheikh to their names following a pattern towards Ashrafization (the Muslim variant of 'Sanskritization'), now they have started asserting their identity as Qureshi.[25] In this age of networking some young leaders of this community have affiliated themselves to the All India Jamiat-ul-Quresh (AIJQ). They are becoming aware of their entitlements and demand backward caste status and reservation in education and employment rather than remaining under the illusion of a casteless Muslim society in Orissa. The butchers of Bounsgali would not like to suffer under a so-called seamless Muslim identity, which does not even treat them with equality and dignity. They want to carve out an identity for themselves and claim from the state their legitimate entitlements at least to enhance their economic and educational status. Strangely, unlike other states, Orissa has not included a single Muslim group in the list of socially and educationally backward castes despite the widespread deprivation, marginalisation and under-representation of a large number of Muslims. Besides the butchers, many other Muslim groups, who remain marginalised in every sense, deserve to be included in this list.

The state has not even bothered to provide some minimum civic amenities to the Bounsagali residents. The Municipal Corporation has not found it necessary to maintain the approach road to this colony though the adjacent roads are fairly well maintained. Open drains overflow and filth is all around. The residents blame the BJP councillor/corporator who represented this area for nearly two decades for deliberately denying infrastructural facilities to punish them as they did not vote for him. When this municipality ward was reserved for a woman in the last Municipal Corporation election, a Muslim woman candidate from Bounsagali's butchers' community contested for the corporator's seat on a BJD ticket but lost by a few votes to a Hindu candidate of the Congress. The loss of a Muslim woman candidate in this ward despite the presence of a sizeable Muslim population and a strong BJD wave surprised the residents of Bounsagali. Many believe that the upper-caste/class Muslims did not want a lower-caste Qasai woman to win and hence voted for the Hindu candidate. As some secular Muslim activists observe, conservative Muslims did not vote for the candidate as they did not want the presence of a Muslim woman in the public sphere.[26] These views may not necessarily explain the complex story of an electoral victory or defeat. But both the dimensions of caste as well as gender could certainly not be wished away.

Conclusion

Though Cuttack Muslims, living in a syncretic city and sharing a *bhaichara* culture, consider themselves secure, physically as well as psychologically, they remain on the margins—economically, educationally, politically and socially. The state has not cared to make any sincere effort to uplift the community from its marginal status and the political class has somehow taken the community for granted as Muslims constitute a miniscule minority and they do not vote on community lines even where they have a sizeable presence. The Orissa government has neither included a single group/section of Muslims in the state list of Backward Castes nor even constituted the State Minority Commission despite persistent demands. The implementation of measures such as the Prime Minister's 15-points Programme and the working of the NMDFC has been partial and half-hearted. Muslim leaders of Cuttack are becoming increasingly conscious of their marginal status and are expressing resentment against the apathy of the state government.

But if the state has a major role in the marginalisation of the city Muslims, the community is also responsible for this state of affairs. Cuttack's Muslim elite, who once built up a credible community education network, conveniently passed it over to the custody of the state for economic reasons, thereby allowing these institutions to deteriorate and adversely affect the empowerment of the community. However, some recent innovative experiments have raised new signs of hope. Sectarian divisions have also been detrimental to the unity and solidarity of the community and weakened its capacity to negotiate with the state and develop a common welfare agenda. More importantly, caste prejudices against poor lower-caste Muslims such as the Qasais by upper-caste Muslims have created 'margins within the margins' by pushing a section of Muslims to face further marginalisation and vulnerability. Thus, voices of protest have emerged among the Muslim *Panchams* ('Untouchables'), seeking equality within the community, demanding legitimate entitlements from the state and searching for new social and political alliances.

10

KOZHIKODE (CALICUT)'S KUTTICHIRA

EXCLUSIVITY MAINTAINED PROUDLY

Radhika Kanchana

Kozhikode (formerly Calicut) is a potential exception from the larger evidence of marginalised Muslim localities in urban India. Multiple factors explain its relative uniqueness—namely the historical origin and evolution of local Muslim communities and the socio-cultural and political developments in Kerala. Urban ghettoisation, or 'slum-like' economic and social deprivation is ruled out in the locality studied, Kuttichira. It continues today as an enclave of the Muslim community, a legacy from the city's foundational design and the medieval practice of spatial groupings of different communities on the basis of occupation and social status that could be a common feature with other historical Indian cities. Kuttichira remains a Muslim cluster without the negative tag of decline or marginalisation that has usually been the fate of such historical localities in other cities. It is upheld as a mark of pride for a socially (and often economically) elite Muslim group in Kozhikode. Two lines of focus defined the research. First, can we talk of segregation in the residential patterns of the community in the city? Second, is the nature of inter-community relations in the city responsible for a process of segregation?

RADHIKA KANCHANA

Kozhikode Muslims in the Broader Canvas of Kerala

Kozhikode is situated on the southern coast of India on the Indian Ocean and is among the Tier-II cities of India (less than one million in population, ranking after the metro cities). It is the third-largest city in Kerala. In medieval times, it was the capital of the Zamorin kingdom and renowned for its spice trade. Under British rule, it was made the headquarters of the Malabar district. Here, a note should be added on the singularity of urbanisation in Kerala. First, there is usually no clear demarcation between the urban and the rural,[1] which are rather extensions of each other with no large empty stretches between them.[2] Second, the state has a high density of population[3] as compared to other states.

Table 10.1. Regional comparative figures in area and population

Kozhikode city		Kozhikode district		Kerala state	
Area	Population	Area	Population	Area	Population
84.232 sq. km	436,556	2,344 sq. km	2,878,498	38,863 sq. km	31,841,374

Kozhikode is therefore a medium-sized city, under a Municipal Corporation (it has twelve Assembly and two Parliamentary constituencies and fifty-five electoral/thirty-nine revenue wards).[4] It is considered the headquarters of print journalism[5] and the political headquarters of the Muslims in Kerala (IUML party headquarters). A commercial city,[6] it is also emerging as the higher educational hub of Northern Kerala, with prominent institutions such as the Indian Institute of Management (IIM-Kozhikode), National Institute of Technology, University of Calicut and Farook College.

Muslim Population

Kerala has a relative balance in the religious composition of its population, compared to other Indian states: Hindus at 56%, Muslims and Christians together at 43%, with the Muslim and Christian populations at 24% and 19% respectively (Hindus 17,883,449; Muslims 7,863,842; and Christians 6,057,427 [Census 2001]). Keralite Muslims—locally known as *Mappilas*[7]—are concentrated in the four northern districts: Kasargod, Kannur, Kozhikode and Malappuram. The region (minus Kasargod but adding Palakkad) was included in the 'Malabar district' of the Madras Presidency under British administration. The state was reorganised in 1956 on the basis of language (Malayalam).

KOZHIKODE (CALICUT)'S KUTTICHIRA

Christians generally have a marginal presence in the northern region (1–3%) and tend to be located in the interior plantation areas. The majority of local Muslims follow the Sunni Shafi school while a small but influential minority is affiliated with reformist currents such as the Mujahids of the Kerala Naduvathul Mujahideen (KNM).[8] Mappilas are also divided on caste lines, with Thangals and Arabis corresponding to the Ashraf (nobles) of North India, claiming foreign ancestry. Malbaris, for their part, 'correspond more closely to the Pathans and Mughals [North Indian Muslim upper castes]'. They claim origins similar to the Arabs but have forgotten their patrilineal Arab lineage and have adopted the local system of matrilineal descent (see below).[9] Finally, Pusalars and Ossans correspond to North Indian Ajlaf castes, being descendants of local Hindu converts and, in the case of Ossan barbers, being traditionally associated with lowly occupations. These Muslim castes practise strict rules of endogamy and commensality, and have separate mosques, organisations and burial grounds.[10] Other Muslim groups exist. Kozhikode, for instance, has a small population of Dawoodi Bohra (Shia) and Kutchi Memons.

Divergent historical developments have induced significant variations within the northern districts and their Muslim populations in terms of class, origin, occupation and socio-cultural practices. In Kasargod, Muslims are allegedly closer to their Mangalore neighbours in Karnataka. Kannur Muslims show a different profile from the Kozhikodans in terms of education and occupation and in interior districts like Malappuram and Palakkad, Muslims mainly represent the population of local converts and are employed in agricultural activities. Similarly, the current profile of Muslim populations found in Trivandrum and Cochin regions (said to have migrated from the northern region) could be a reflection of their access to better socio-economic opportunities under earlier regimes. While Malabar was initially part of Mysore and then of the Madras Presidency during the British and the early post-independence periods (1766–1792–1956), Travancore (1729–1947) and Cochin (circa the twelfth century until 1947) were princely states that merged as Thiru-Kochi after independence (1949–1956). The three regions combined in 1956 to form the modern Kerala state. Therefore, Kerala Muslims or even North/Malabar/*Mappila* Muslims are not a homogeneous group and support certain differences.

In total, around 60% of Kerala's Muslim population is from the four northern districts. With Palakkad, the number is 70% from the former Malabar region. The religious composition of Kozhikode district's population is relatively balanced (Hindus: 1,669,161; Muslims: 1,078,750; Christians: 127,468 [2001 Census]). Although figures for the share of Muslims in the population of Kozhikode city are not available, the current estimate suggested was between 40 to 45%. The addition of three Muslim-dominated *panchyats* (Beypore, Cheruvannur and Elathur and two more on the cards) should raise the city's population to nearly 600,000 and area to 118.2 sq km, and should also raise the Muslim share in the total population.

Table 10.2. District Muslim population (DMP) as a percentage of district (DP) and state population (SP)

District	DMP	% DP	% SMP	% SP	Muslims in Urban areas	% Muslims in Urban areas
Malappuram	2,484,576	68.5%	31.6%	7.8%	241,710	67.9%
Kozhikode	1,078,750	37.5%	13.7%	3.4%	422,485	38.4%
Kasargod	413,063	34.3%	5.3%	1.3%	86,108	36.8%
Kannur	665,648	27.6%	8.5%	2%	379,913	31.3%
Palakkad	703,596	26.9%	8.9%	2.2%	79,824	22.4%

Source: *Census of India, 2001.*
Note: 1. Total Muslim population of the State (SMP) is 7,863,842; total population of the State (SP) is 31,841,374. 2. The figures for the last two columns (Urban Muslim population based on Census 2001) were drawn from the website of All India Council of Muslim Economic Upliftment (AICMEU).

The Place of Kozhikode Muslims in Politics and the Local Economy

Business, trade or related sectors are traditionally identified with local Muslims in Kozhikode and are still their most preferred economic activity. The majority is today divided between local business and work engagements in the Arab Gulf region that has emerged as a dominant employment option—a Kerala-wide practice, this migration is most noted in the northern districts (highest Malappuram) and among Muslims.[11] Gulf migration is also significant in states like Uttar Pradesh and Andhra Pradesh, specially among the Muslim population. However, Kerala leads in India as the earliest and largest sending state.[12]

Muslims occupy important positions at different levels of the local and state administration/government and across the other sectors. However, proportionally the community is under-represented. Marginal in the professional category, Muslims have a strong presence in business, which has been reinforced during the past decades by the monetary flow induced by migration to the Gulf (see below). Pre-eminent Keralite Muslim entrepreneurs are Non Resident

KOZHIKODE (CALICUT)'S KUTTICHIRA

Table 10.3. Kerala/Kozhikode Muslims in important local posts (as of January 2010)

	Kozhikode	State-wide Muslim representation
Judiciary	District Judge	4/29 District Judges in the High Court
Assembly	1 Minister, 4 MLAs (One Chief Minister briefly [1979, IUML])	2/19 Ministers, 32/140 Members of Legislative Assembly (15 CPM, 7 IUML, 6 INC, 4 other parties)
National Parliament		3/20 Kerala Members of Parliament in the Lok Sabha (2 IUML (one is Minister of State for Railways) and 1 INC). 2/9 MPs in the Rajya Sabha
In local administration	District Collector, District Panchayat President, Deputy Mayor and 15/55 Councilors in the Municipal Corporation and lady Vice Chancellor of Calicut University (6/9 since 1968)	
Literary and public circles	(from Kuttichira) Popular writers like Vaikom Mohammed Basheer and N.P. Mohammed. Mamukoya won Best Comedian in Malayalam cinema 2009	

Indians (NRIs). M.A. Yusufali, of the UAE-based Emke group, heads a retail conglomerate with branches across the Middle East, garment factories in Kenya and Indonesia as well as meat-processing units in several parts of India. P. Mohammed Ali, for his part, presides over the Galfar Engineering and Contracting EEC, a construction multinational company based in Oman. P.V. Abdul Wahab of the Peevees group is the third leading figure among these 'NRI tycoons', who have been major investors in Cochin's airport, 'India's first non-government airport venture'.[13] Beyond these well-known figures, Kerala has seen the emergence of mid-range Muslim entrepreneurs in sectors as diverse as jewellery retailing (M.P. Ahammed's Malabar Gold), edible oil refining (N.K. Mohammed Ali's Parisons group), cargo transport (V.K. Moidu Hajee's Kerala Roadways), spices and condiments

(M.E. Meeran's Eastern group), real estate (Rafi Mather's Mather Projects and Constructions), hotels (Ahmed Usman Salt's Abad group), travel and ticketing services (K.V. Abdul Nazar's Akbar Travels of India) or IT (Javad K. Hassan's NeST group). Most of these entrepreneurs hail from the districts of Malappuram and Kozhikode, a 'historically backward region of the state that has undergone remarkable transformation due to the Gulf bonanza and resurgent Muslim capital'.[14]

Kerala's persistent 'two-party system' (the United Democratic Front, UDF, led by the Congress or the Left Democratic Front, EDF, led by the Communist Party of India-Marxist) is in truth a coalition political system that prevents the emergence of a single group. There is evidence of tough inter-community competition to be in government (CPI (M) is known to be dominated by the Ezhavas[15] and the Kerala Congress by the Christians). The Indian Union Muslim League (IUML, reconstituted in Kerala from the All-India Muslim League after 1947), played a key role in the political mobilisation of Kerala Muslims.[16]

Among only two Muslim parties to do so, the IUML has maintained a consistent presence in the national Parliament since 1952.[17] In Kerala, the IUML today plays the role of a 'king-maker' in the government, partnering with either the LDF or UDF camp. In government, it successively held the education portfolio and took encouraging initiatives like the establishment of the University of Calicut (1968) for the higher education needs of the northern districts. It also lobbied successfully for the creation of a new Muslim-majority Malappuram district (1969). As a platform, it effectively connects Muslim entrepreneurs and provincial political circles, whereas some Muslim entrepreneurs have even joined the party, such as P.V. Abdul Wahab, elected to the Rajya Sabha in 2004 on an IUML ticket.

The Singularity of Kuttichira and the Koyas

The previous section attempted to set Kozhikode and its Muslim population in the broader canvas nationally and at the state and district levels. The following section focuses on the attributes of the local community and the selected locality.

Unlike in the rest of India, Islam did not arrive in Kerala via invasion and conflict. Arab migration to Kerala, mostly for trade, might have begun as early as the seventh century, although some historians suggest that the earliest Muslim presence only dates back to the eighth or even ninth century.[18] Historically, Mappila Muslims had settlements along the Kerala coast, especially its northern part. This was mainly because of their descent and occupation linked with the oceanic trade. The inland Muslim population developed later with propagation, local conversions and possible inward movement when the trade declined. The port city of Kozhikode (lit. 'fortified city') and its prosperous Muslim traders are referred to by travellers such as Ibn Batuta (travel period, 1342–47), Abdur Razaak (1442), Ma Huan (1413–31) and Barbosa (sixteenth century).[19]

Kuttichira represented the residential district of the merchants handling sea trade under the patronage of the Hindu dynasty of the Zamorins (also known as Samudri Rajas, or 'Oceanic kings') during the medieval period. It predominantly comprised the Muslim traders and their support groups, who exerted a near monopoly over the Zamorins' overseas trade in goods like pepper, spices and timber and who benefited from the protection of local Hindu rulers in return. Indeed, 'the Samudri's reputation depended crucially on the security he was able to afford merchants'.[20] Merchant families from other regions such as the Gujaratis and the Jains resided at the margins of the colony. The poorer sections of the population, who were often involved in fishing or other shipping-related service occupations, had residential settlements more immediately on the coastline. Thus, Kuttichira originally symbolised an elite social class of prosperous 'foreign' merchants and their descendent families including the Muslim, Gujarati and Jain communities. Muslims today constitute almost 95% of its population. A medieval city, Kozhikode is believed to have been built on the traditional *vaastu*-architectural principles, where the rest of the royal city extended around the centrally-located temple/palace compound.[21] Other communities generally had settlements around their own places of worship or according to their occupations. The Namboothiri Brahmin priests lived around the royal Tali temple, the Nair soldiers/administrators either lived within the extended palace quarters or in other areas within the city, the artisans and other professions like the weavers and the shopkeepers had their own localities and Dalits generally lived outside the city.

As I was about to begin my fieldwork in Kuttichira, a Hindu hotel owner warned me: 'you will almost feel you are in Pakistan'. This somewhat negative initial observation and the subsequent positive references to the city's 'heritage', 'oldest area' and 'special place of the Muslims', both by Hindus and Muslims, increased my curiosity for this specific locality. Being a non-Keralite and a non-Muslim, it took multiple visits to the locality and interactions to note its acclaimed specificity. The *tharavad* or large joint family houses in traditional architectural style were one visible feature. Kuttichira derives its name from a large, 400-year-old pond or *'chira'* located in its midst. Around it are at least three ancient mosques, including the 700-year-old Miskal mosque. For the residents, the *chira* is equivalent to a European 'central square', as a social meeting point, and there is almost a festive air in the evenings.

Thekkepuram (derived from its location 'south' from the erstwhile palace-complex) is the term used for the wider area inhabited by a majority of Muslims, of which Kuttichira is the central locality and which also includes Mugadhar, Pallikandi, Parappil, Idiyangara, Kundungal, Vattampil and Valiyangadi. It is located at the north of the Kallai River (down which products like timber were transported from inland areas to the coast), almost bordering the sea to its west, with the trading hub of Valiyangadi (Grand Bazar) at its north. For a merchant community involved in the sea trade, this strategic position granted them proximity to their occupation and the retainment of a fairly independent self-jurisdiction: barring the more serious ones, crimes/conflicts were allowed resolutions within the community without interference from the king.

The inhabitants, known as Koyas, claim descent from the Arab traders[22] who contracted marriage alliances with local women. They uphold their exclusive identity in the local population. Moreover, the 'local' side of the descent is also generally claimed to be of aristocratic lineage. Women from Hindu upper castes such as Nairs or Namboothiris are claimed to have been given in marriage to prosperous Arab merchants who also enjoyed local prestige (Shabandar Koyas were Kozhikode port officers, members of the court, and so on). This alleged high lineage is manifested in local social and cultural life. However, it is to be noted that there exists an internal hierarchy within the Koyas (for example, some families trace their lineage to women of the lower Thiyya caste).

Occupation in trade is a strong identity marker of the Koyas, pointing to their Arab roots. It sets them apart from other local Muslims of mainly local converts' descent, broadly positioning them in the middle/upper class. A Koya resident commented that although reduced in stature, 'the pier and the sea trade existed almost until the 1990s' (gold smuggling was also a lucrative activity for some time). Wholesale/bazar commerce is also dominant. However, at the moment, employment in the Gulf is the predominant activity.

Identification with Arab descent seems to have a great psychological and cultural impact on the Koyas' daily life and their level of religiosity. A Kuttichiran is supposedly a more diligent Muslim. For the Muslim residents, the presence of some of the oldest mosques in Kerala[23] seems to attach an additional air of reverence to Kuttichira. A further source of authority, two local religious leaders, the *Valid Qazi* and *Cheria Qazi*, reside within the locality.

KOZHIKODE (CALICUT)'S KUTTICHIRA

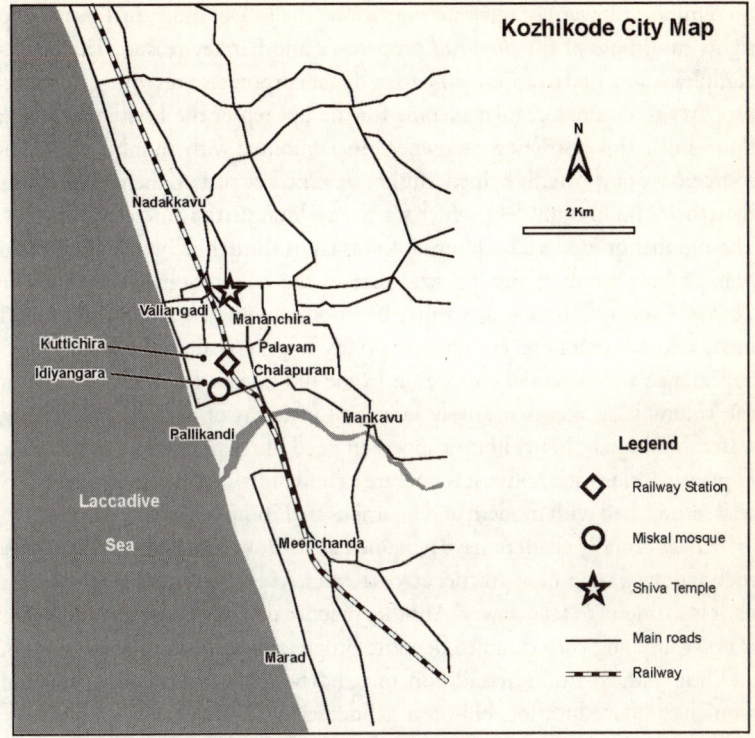

Map of Kozhikode

The Koyas adhere to a matrilineal system of kinship, a rare occurrence in Muslim societies (although a common practice in neighbouring areas of Thalassery, Ponnani, Kannur, Mahe, as well as in the Lakshadweep islands). A sanction from the Caliph in Istanbul obtained by Arakkal Ali Rajas and Beevi rulers of Kannur is claimed to legitimise the practice, which was probably inspired by local Hindu customs.[24] The Koyas' custom, more aptly termed 'main-local' residence, has implications for their settlement patterns. As per custom, there is no change in terms of residence after the wedding except that the new husband would visit his wife living within her *tharavad* (joint family house). At marriage, each girl gets a new bedroom added to the house and customarily the husband has dinner at his wife's house and returns to his own house for breakfast.[25] Continued practice of the matrilocal custom partly explains why the locality remains mainly unchanged: proximity of the residences of the groom and the bride is practical. Kuttichira has witnessed no significant inward or outward migration. The lack of individual ownership rights to dispose of the *tharavad* property is another key reason. The house-complex is attached to a joint-*waqf* trust that incorporates a revenue-generating property to ensure a regular income for the upkeep of the household (e.g. a flour mill). This restriction on ownership, combined with an inbuilt revenue source, have purportedly helped Muslim *tharavads* to sustain themselves better than their Hindu equivalent, which started declining in the nineteenth century. The number of modern buildings is minimal in Kuttichira, where traditional *tharavad* mansions of varying sizes remain the norm. Some mansions like *Thoppil tharavad*[26] have nearly thirty bedrooms and house around a hundred members and sometimes even private ponds. In general, despite the run-down appearance and potential congestion in the old houses, the infrastructure in the colony itself seems relatively satisfying in terms of drainage, electricity, water[27] and roads. Many houses appear in need of repair or modern facilities. However, inside each house, it is not rare to find individual bedrooms/quarters well refurbished with modern and luxurious bathrooms or separate kitchens.

Koyas proudly claim to have remained aloof from prevalent 'evil' customs, such as dowry, a common practice across Kerala. As a Koya resident explains, 'for us, it is shameful to take dowry'. Another practice denounced by Koya Muslims is polygamy, and they claim to be more progressive towards their women: in addition to the matrilineal tradition, there has been a recent encouragement of women's higher education. However, gender segregation remains in force in the socio-economic life of the community. Very few women living in the *tharavads* have much interaction with other communities, for lack of opportunities. This tends to change among women of the younger generation, who are increasingly involved in higher education although they still go mainly to the community-run institutions. In their practice of Islam as well, Koyas claim to be progressive. The Koyas' limited social relations with non-Koya Muslims following the patriliny custom is criticised as entertaining 'false-prestige' (says a Koya academic) and as exclusive: 'they want to keep to their superior culture' (a bitter account from a non-Koya Muslim professional). However, there are increasing instances of marriage alliances with families practising matriliny outside Kuttichira and Kozhikode, such as in Thalassery (Kannur).

The Marginalisation Question

New Relocations Inward and Outward from Kuttichira

Even if this trend has not assumed a dramatic character yet, it is no longer uncommon for families to buy properties in and around the central city and move out of Kuttichira and the *tharavad* houses. Moving out depends on the financial means of individual family members (and particularly the husband) and their capacity to afford the maintenance of a nuclear family and to purchase or construct a new house, giving up their stake in the *tharavad*. Another emerging trend consists in dismantling the traditional houses to build new constructions. Generally, somewhat resembling a sub-colony, several independent houses are built within a single compound and continue to be referred to under the *tharavad* name and the *waqf* 'trust' (individual property rights still do not exist). In rarer cases, a family (generally within Kuttichira) buys other traditional houses for renovation not only for additional housing needs but also for the higher sentimental and cost-premium value attached to property ownership in Kuttichira. In spite of this—still limited—inward and outward migration, today Kuttichira is almost exclusively Muslim, apart from the Gujarati/ Jain areas. This might point to a certain trend of closure: while a Thiyya Hindu service caste community apparently had some presence in Kuttichira until the 1960s, for instance managing its own school, this presence is no longer visible.[28]

Influential Residents and Associational Life in the Locality

Kuttichirans stand out with their dynamic associational life: schools, charity and educational institutions found within the locality indicate self-help initiatives. As an example, the Citizens' Intellectual Educational Social and Cultural Organization (CIESCO) is a socio-cultural organisation located next to the Kuttichira pond with the objective of offering library, community centre and park facilities to the residents of Kuttichira. Residential associations and other entities engage in a range of activities such as mobilising support on local issues: e.g. lobbying for an approach road to Kothi bridge, connecting with localities on the south bank of the Kallai River. Kuttichira also has a support pool of Gulf-NRIs for some initiatives (such as supporting the website *www. thekkepuram.org;* the Kuwait chapter of CIESCO, for its part, helps with the upkeep of the Medical Aid Centre in Kuttichira).

Thekkepuram's residents also take pride in prominent personalities of the past and present. These include two former ministers in the state government, MPs in Parliament, MLAs in the local Assembly, four Assembly members in the erstwhile Madras Presidency, two Mayors and deputy Mayors of Kozhikode, a Chairman of the Kerala Waqf Board and presidents of social clubs such as the Rotary. Select achievers include doctors, a number of academics, a footballer who represented India in the Melbourne Olympics,[29] and others involved in politics, literature and the arts.[30] On the whole, the number of professionals has so far been very small. However, the Kuttichirans' presence in the current business sector of Kozhikode seems to have expanded recently, especially over the past decade or so.

The Gulf link: A Mixed Blessing?

Migration to the Gulf remains a popular option for Keralite youths and the remittances from these migrants (whose numbers are estimated at 2.5 million) have transformed the local economy, growing from 74.7 million rupees in 1972–73 to 136 billion rupees in 1999–2000, with Muslims making up half of the migrants and 47% of the transfers.[31] These remittances have continued to grow in recent years, reaching 3.8 billion dollars in 2003 and 90 billion in 2008, with the sums transferred through the *hawala* system possibly being three times higher.[32] In Kuttichira, each household has at least one member working or doing business in 'Dubai' (a generic term referring to any Gulf country, with UAE and Saudi Arabia being popular destinations). Nearly 60–70% of the male working-age population between twenty and fifty years does not reside in Kuttichira. Poorer Muslims from Malappuram are said to be the forerunners in migration to the Gulf back in the 1950s, and they still provide the largest contingent of migrants. However, Koyas and similar groups with prior descent and trading links with the Gulf (sometimes family links and a relative familiarity with Arabic through the Arabic-Malayalam tradition)[33] seem to have benefited more from the Gulf migration by accessing better placement/opportunities in the host country. Until recently, 'Arab marriages' were another link to the Gulf. Arabs visited India to marry local Muslim girls. Also prevalent in Hyderabad and Mumbai, in Kerala it is currently a minor practice after it became a political and media issue over the large number of malpractice and abandonment cases. The long relationship between the Arab-Gulf region and Kerala, from medieval trade to the latest labour migration, today finds consolidation in an ever-maturing Gulf diaspora.

The 'Gulf migrant story' is not all rosy, though. Earliest accounts (in popular Malayalam novels like *Arabiponnu*) of going to the Gulf were tales of adventure and loss (many travelled on cargo boats from India and some lost their lives while swimming to reach the host shores). Today, harsh living conditions in the host countries, loan burdens at home—mainly among the unskilled and semi-skilled migrants—as well as disrupted family lives are among the lesser-known problems. Moreover, lack of naturalisation options and insufficient migrant rights in the Gulf Cooperation Council countries leave the Gulf expatriates vulnerable but it also potentially contributes to their maintaining closer links with their homeland, in addition to the proximity factor (compared with the Malayalee diaspora in Europe or the USA).

The larger proportion of Koya migrants is engaged in semi-skilled or service professions and the number of entrepreneurs and skilled workers is currently growing. Of the signs of consolidation achieved in the host countries from a migration now spanning at least four decades, one could mention the increased frequency of migrants taking their families along with them and the rising instances of expatriates living into their second or third generations in the host country. The extent of support systems like the expatriates' social associations within the host country and the homeland is also illustrative. One could mention the Kozhikode District Committee of Kerala Muslim Cultural Centre[34] as well as CIESCO Kuwait. The Gulf diaspora also played a critical role in the establishment of Kozhikode international airport, which started operating in 2006 and claims to be the twelfth busiest in passenger traffic in India, with nearly all its international flights serving or connecting destinations within or via the Gulf region.

The positive aspects of migration for the community take the shape of the Gulf remittances and investments. Expenditure (household expenses, buying or building houses and education of children) used to take up the largest chunk but in recent decades, investment patterns in real estate and business ventures have been rising. Philanthropy is also a common practice, with Muslim entrepreneurs investing in education in particular, in a mix of piety and economic calculation: 'By promoting modern education among Muslims, entrepreneurs seek to promote economic development while also embedding economic practices within a framework of ethics and moral responsibilities deemed to be "Islamic"'.[35]

The Koyas' skills-set, trading backgrounds and socio-economic standing provide them with some leverage as far as entrepreneurship is concerned. For example, a similar scale of entrepreneurial activity is not seen in Malappuram. A Kozhikodan who landed in Qatar in the 1970s now runs a chain of supermarkets called Grand Shopping Mall after a long career with the local host government—one illustration among others of Keralite Muslims' entrepreneurial ventures in the host-Gulf countries. Such businesses are often linked with Kerala for sourcing supplies or, through their local branches, involving regular inter-commuting. Changes observed today in Kozhikode's local market away from the traditional bazar business to new businesses like shopping malls involving modern management practices and catering to an increasingly consumerist society point to the Gulf-induced liquidity and investment factor in the society. Many local and new entrepreneurs concede to having investment partners or support from their Gulf-NRI family/friends or are themselves returnees. Earlier, such local investment was not an attractive option or involved many failed ventures largely due to lack of growth prospects and facilitative infrastructure in the local market. In fact, in many instances the investments instead moved to neighbouring states such as Tamil Nadu or Karnataka. However, Muslim entrepreneurship in Kozhikode also includes a lot of participation by non-local Muslims from Kannur or Malappuram, for example. Also, a newer trend in Kozhikode is the mushrooming of private/community-funded higher educational institutions[36] and new 'international-standard' English-language schools with the premium on CBSE/other syllabus. These are indicative of the community's increased willingness and capacity to fill the perceived institutional gaps compared to the advancement of other regions/communities in Kerala, but they are also a reaction to the increasing competition in the Gulf, especially for the white-collar jobs demanding higher skills/educational levels. Another demand source for the booming education industry are the children raised in the Gulf but who are sent to India (or abroad) because of the dearth of higher educational institutions in the host countries, something attested to by the numerous institutions with residential facilities.

It should be noted that in the case of Kerala Muslims, migration to the Gulf is mainly limited to males, constrained by local rules and harsh living conditions in host countries, often implying decades of separated marital lives with only short, periodic visits over the years (the well-known migration trend of nurses from Kerala is absent among Muslim females). A trope of 'sacrifice' informs the discourse and practices of both spouses. The 'sacrifices' made by expatriate husbands translate into heightened pressure on their wives, who are expected to show full dedication to the family and to display an exemplary morality, thus inviting greater vigilance and restrictions. Prolonged estrangement (ranging from several years to often the entire working life, thirty to forty years) has individual and societal repercussions. These include acute psychological distress in the case of spouses. Prolonged absence of the fathers also has negative repercussions on children's upbringing. On a more positive note, Gulf migration seems to have relatively empowered at least a section of those women left behind, with comparatively more financial freedom and greater opportunities to acquire life-skills (such as two-wheeler driving, handling certain routine works outside their home...). These are born out of the new necessity of managing a household alone in a context where the nuclear subdivision of families is becoming increasingly common. Moreover, female education has been encouraged by the community during the past decade, so that lone mothers can better steer their children's careers and cope with their husbands' prolonged absence. Until recently, pursuit of higher education was notably lower among men, mainly because they are constrained to work at an early age. There may also have been fewer incentives for higher education for them as Gulf jobs were a popular option, available with minimum education. An alumnus of Madrasatul Mohammadiya High School, one of the two prominent Muslim schools in Kuttichira, and currently a successful engineer and forty year resident in Oman, laments a noticeable decline in professional education among the Kuttichirans with the advent of the Gulf factor: his generation in the late 1960s was allegedly among the last to have produced significant alumni with successful careers as engineers, doctors and advocates. In fact, migration has become a central element in the constructions of masculinity of Keralite youths—both Hindus and Muslims—by marking the transition to maturity and by making the accumulation and display of cash a powerful demonstration of virility[37]

In a state where remittances amount to 20% of the Net State Domestic Product, the larger public verdict is that migration is a necessary evil (Zachariah and Rajan, 2007). In Kuttichira itself, the most productive members are often residing abroad, leaving mainly older males, women and children as residents. For most families, direct or indirect Gulf income is the major revenue source, a trend also visible in the wider economy of Kozhikode.[38] But the monetary inflows from remittances have not been channelled into long-term infrastructural and productive investment. Only in the past decade have business investments significantly risen and they are still limited to the retail industry, hospitality and real estate. Thus, the community and the region would be vulnerable if Gulf opportunities came to burst.

The Myth of Kozhikode's Amity and Its Current Contradictions

There is a relative under-representation of Muslims in government jobs and in professional occupations. Also, the disadvantaged sections of the Muslim community do not have similar access to mobility (either through migration or higher education). The converts from fishermen communities and other backward classes are usually poorer than the Kuttichirans and are concentrated in Mughadar, Pallikandi, Kampuram and Kappakkal, other Muslim-dominated areas adjacent to Kuttichira. In addition, despite a separate quota for Muslims in Kerala—coming under OBC reservations (10% in Class I and 12% in Class IV)—gaps in the actual recruitment in government is a recurrent issue. Explanations from respondents on both sides point at discrimination, but also at the fact that 'there is a shortage in applications' (a Hindu government official). Other responses were: 'They [Hindus/Christians] have an advantage because their women are in greater numbers among job candidates' or '[We] generally miss out [for the higher posts] on the educational/eligibility criteria' (a Muslim journalist). In the past, the attraction of Gulf jobs discouraged local Muslim men from pursuing higher education and professional qualifications. As a Muslim youth shares, 'Most of us don't want to study further like you—IAS, IIM, engineering, etc. What is the need when I can get a job with a +2 in the Gulf?' The increasing number of Muslim female students in local higher educational institutions was commonly cited as a promising trend however, although most are discouraged from eventually entering the job market unless it is to become doctors and engineers or to work in the government sector. Kutumbini is a recent pilot initiative (Domestic BPO) specific to the Malabar region, targeting these educated women.

Marad, 'Love-Jihad', Terrorism Expose Cleavages

Located in Kozhikode district, Marad is 10 km away from Kozhikode city. On 3 and 4 January 2002, clashes erupted between Hindu and Muslim fishermen after a trivial scuffle at a public tap. Three Hindus and two Muslims were killed in this violent outburst. On 2 May 2003, eight Hindu fishermen were killed by Muslim extremists (who were affiliated to the National Development Front, NDF) on the local beach. Muslim families in the locality fled en masse, fearing attacks. However, unlike in the rest of India, the guilty were rapidly prosecuted and punished: in 2009, a special court sentenced sixty-two members of the NDF to life imprisonment for their implication in these attacks.

The Love-Jihad episode of 2009 primarily concerned the region between Kasargod and Mangalore but was widely publicised by the local media. It consisted of rumours alleging that local Muslim youths—and in particular activists of the youth wing of a Muslim party, the Popular Front of India

(PFI)—were encouraged to seduce and convert local Hindu women, so as to recruit them for Jihadist activities.

In March 2006, bombs exploded in two bus shelters in Kozhikode (without causing any deaths). Supposedly to protest against the detention of People's Democratic Party leader Abdul Naser Madhani in connection with the 1998 serial blasts in Coimbatore (forty-six killed), a Lashkar-e-Tayyeba operative from Kannur was suspected of being involved in the incident. These terrorist incidents incite mixed responses, either being branded as the effect of national and international developments, or of the increasing visibility of right-wing factions, or as a result of local youths being misguided by extremists on both sides.

The Prosperity of Muslims, an Object of Jealousy

In the northern districts of Kerala, the migration of Hindus to the Gulf countries is not as significant as in other regions such as Trivandrum. However, the newly acquired wealth of Muslim expatriates has benefited the larger economy. The real estate landscape is particularly revealing in this regard. A visibly content Hindu architect commented that the volume and scale of projects in construction and related sectors are currently high, creating vast employment potential in the industry: 'The prices in Kozhikode and the region have sky-rocketed with NRI spending. Much of the current development activity in construction/leasing of houses, apartments or commercial complexes is by the Muslims'. Naturally, Muslims are favoured clients for being ready to shell out higher prices. On the housing market, Hindus selling ancestral *tharavad* properties in the city generally come from families that have migrated to other Indian metro cities or to the West and who are disposing of their houses in Kerala after the death of parents, or from families contemplating socio-economic mobility (by making a profit on the sale or opting for a cheaper property in the countryside, for instance). Therefore, the larger trend observed is that of Muslim residents moving to other localities in the city, outside their traditional areas along the coast including Kuttichira. Traditional 'posh' localities such as Mankavu are the most preferred ones, while other localities on the moderate budget scale include Nadakkavu and Meenchanda.

As early as the 1970s, there were numerous instances of Kuttichira residents choosing the nuclear option to venture to other city colonies. The large-scale buying-up of property, however, is a recent trend and, as a relatively small city, the changing demographics are fast becoming visible in Kozhikode. As an elderly Hindu residing outside Kuttichira suggests, 'We mix comfortably and there are no problems, but the neighbourhood gets fast-transformed into a Muslim colony: first he would come; then his brother, aunt, neighbour ... would start buying the other houses'. The demonstrated preference of many Muslim families to congregate together was attributed by Muslims to convenience—'Having my brother there, sister there...'—or to the comfort of community solidarity, such as 'having a mosque nearby and celebrating together for our festivals like Ramzan'. Some responses also pointed at a greater sense of 'security'.

Perceptions of the Muslim community 'taking over' are primarily an expression of economic envy. In a fairly short time, there was an impressive mushrooming in the business sector and local property ownership. Currently, in Kozhikode, Muslims seem to have the greater spending power. As a Hindu resident stated, 'Frankly, we're jealous!' The rapid advancement of the local Muslim community seemingly at the 'loss' of other communities in the city thus seems liable to cause resentment.

Infra-Muslim Competition in Kozhikode

At present, various politico-religious forces compete for the support of local Muslims. Although Kerala's Muslims are almost all Sunni, they are theologically divided between 'unreformed' Shafts and reformist currents (the Jama'at-i-Islami and the Mujahid reformists). Despite their affinities with Salafism, in their quest for an 'authentic' Islam purified from illegitimate innovations (*bidah*), the Mujahids profess a self-conscious 'Muslim modernity' and promote secular education (including for girls) as well as communal harmony, while discouraging 'social evils' such as the practice of dowry. One of the explanations for the success of Mujahid reformism among local Sunnis was its ability to 'join forces with the wider modernising middle class on a platform of socio-religious reforms, producing a confluence of orientations towards 'community progress' which coalesce around a perceived fundamental need for 'modern education'. And although only 10% of Kerala's Muslims are formerly affiliated to the reformist camp, 'they—especially the KNM—have set the wider agenda'.[39] However, these reformists have faced the opposition of socially more conservative Muslim groups, be it on gender issues, education or relations with the larger society. The orthodox Sunni factions are further divided on political lines (since two decades), with the AP Aboobaker Moulvi/Kanthapuram faction taking a pro-CPM stance and the EK Aboobaker Musaliyar faction being more supportive of the Muslim League. Finally, the recent emergence of a new blend of Muslim political parties or movements with a tilt to the right currently challenges the dominance of IUML and its largely secularist agenda. The most notorious of these challengers have been the National Development Front (NDF), the Indian Muslim League (IML, a splinter from IUML), and the Popular Front of India (PFI).

The spectacular rise of the PFI in local Muslim politics in recent years is a testimony to the changes currently taking place among Kerala Muslims at large. This new party was formed in 2006 through the merger of three radicalised Muslim groups of South India: the NDF, the Manitha Neethi Pasarai of Tamil Nadu (possibly a reincarnation of the terrorist group Al Umma)[40] and the Karnataka Forum for Dignity. It held its first public gathering in Kozhikode in 2009, which was well attended and where several Muslim 'leaders' from North India made an appearance (such as Zafaryab Jilani, the convenor of the Babri Masjid Action Committee). This success is in large part the result of numerous educational initiatives and a very active strategy of mediatisation: the PFI owns its own media company—Inter Media Private Limited, held by the Thejas Publishing Charitable Trust—which oversees the publication of a local daily (*Thejas*) that will soon have a Saudi Arabia edition. The PFI has also been in the headlines for its 'Freedom Parades': on 15 August of each year, the party organises a paramilitary parade of its cadres clad in military uniforms. In Kozhikode, Muslims 'thronged the roads and packed into the city stadium to watch the march.'[41] However, this show of strength was banned in 2010, in a context of growing communal tensions in Kerala, partly nurtured by the efforts of the PFI at enforcing morality and punishing deviant behaviour within the Muslim community and beyond—as exemplified by the attack of PFI cadres on a Christian college teacher in July 2010 (Ernakulam district), whose hand was chopped off after he allegedly disrespected Prophet Muhammad in the questions put at a school test.

The new thrust towards demonstrating religiosity in the public sphere—through the construction of new mosques or the adoption of the *burqa* by an increasing number of women, for instance—as well as the emphasis on religious education are alleged to have inspired similar behaviour in the Hindu community. As a Hindu respondent notes, 'there is more activity in the temples now and more people participating in public religious events than there used to be even five or six years ago'. Moreover, locals note the progression of elements of exclusionary 'purification' in the wider discourse on Islam, with 'Saudi Islam' being increasingly projected as the only 'true Islam'. This marginalises other practices in the region, such as Sufi traditions, which are increasingly branded as Hindu-influenced 'pollutions'.

The Case for Kozhikode

There is great public will in Kozhikode to assert an ethic of co-existence between communities, an ethic that was once demonstrated in the past. There is also a proclivity for competetive engagement, facilitated by balanced demographic strength, between the communities.

Past Crises Have Shaken but Not Succeeded in Marring Inter-community Relations

The Marad incidents of 2002–03 seem to have made a strong impression on the local memory, affecting trust between religious communities. Two Hindu youths express bitterness: 'Yes, I have Muslim friends but they're not my 'good' friends...In Marad, they were all together and merely a few hours later, they [Muslims] attacked and killed their fellow-fishermen in a pre-planned manner. How can I trust them now?' Despite this local undercurrent, a frequent assertion heard was that Marad was an aberration: 'it would not have happened without involvement of extremist organisations or being politically instigated'. Additionally, it was frequently mentioned that 'the police is not communalised here'. It is the fairly firm and quick action and vigilance by the government and by the communities to contain the incidents that needs to be noted. Public pressure in the case of the 'love-Jihad' episode also instigated the police, community groups and judicial courts to get involved fairly quickly in clarifying that evidence did not bear out the said allegations. *Sparsham* is a local initiative that seeks to relocate displaced families in Marad by rebuilding community relations through the encouragement of mutual-help spirit via livelihood-creating projects involving 'mixed-community women groups'. Individual expressions of intolerant opinion are not rare in Kozhikode. Compared to my hometown of Hyderabad or a few other metro cities, though, there was relatively little blanket stereotyping or mistrust heard during personal interactions in Kozhikode. There was rather a more frank articulation on the perceived faults of both sides. Some Muslim respondents, in reference to the gaps in government jobs, denied deliberate discrimination and, rather, pointed out that the current arrears-based reservation implementation is faulty and should instead take place as a unit of reservation seats at any recruiting point. Some Hindu respondents, while expressing envy at ongoing economic transformation also conceded the role of Muslims in the city as wealth-creators and the fact that the local Hindu community was less risk-taking.

Premium on Participative Politics and Self-propelled Progress by Local Muslims

Kerala Muslims have a greater leverage than in the rest of India due to the specific political culture of the state. Current coalition politics in the state also demand more mutual accountability and cooperation from religious communities and political parties, thus reducing the possibility of excesses. Kozhikode Muslims exhibit vigorous participation not only in Muslim parties like the IUML but also in other parties like the Congress and the Communist parties. A Muslim resident eagerly suggests, 'we elected a Gujarati and there have never been tensions although we lived in the same locality for so many years. So, there is no communal problem here' (a Gujarati Hindu woman from the National Congress Party is currently the Municipal Councillor of Kuttichira ward). The lively debate discussed earlier, in the multi-level socio-religious and political organisations of the Muslim community, also applies to engagement with the wider society on common issues through local civic and socio-cultural entities ranging from literary clubs to local trading associations. The strong media presence in Kozhikode, from newspapers such as *Chandrika*. (representing the IUML) to *Malayala Manorama* (considered pro-Congress), also dynamises the local public debate.

The local environment is probably also a reason why the more right-wing parties have found less of a foothold in Kozhikode district. For instance, the BJP is more popular in Kasargod or Trivandrum districts and similarly, the NDF has more strength in Kollam. In the local Islamic reformist discourse, there is higher stress on a 'rationalised Muslim life' allowing moral as well as socio-economic advancement. As Osella and Osella observe, Kozhikode's new breed of entrepreneurs and traders 'seek ways of embedding their business practices within an Islamic framework of ethics and moral responsibilities', while at the same time being 'committed towards reorienting local Muslim subjectivities and practices towards the requirements of neo-liberal capitalism'. As a result, 'an orientation towards self-transformation through education, adoption of a "systematic" lifestyle and a generalized rationalization—which has acquired wider currency amongst Kerala Muslims following reformist influence—is mobilized to sustain novel forms of capital accumulation' (2010: 19, 23). The aspiration of the local Muslim community to progress and compete—especially with local Hindu and Christian communities—is attested to by a series of local initiatives, such as a novel impulse to promote religious-cultural education while not missing out on scientific education. Thus, local Arabic schools operate between six and eight in the morning, so that their students can also attend mainstream schools afterwards. The Feroke College, which mainly caters to Muslim students, has a new wing dedicated to training for the Civil Services Examinations as a proactive strategy to make up for the lack of Muslim representation in the bureaucracy. Parallel to Quran reading groups organised by the community in Kozhikode, there are also spoken English courses, as well as personality development and leadership courses to face local and global competition (Osella, 2010: 16). In the twentieth century too Muslim reformist movements paralleled the social movements by other communities like the Ezhavas under the SNDP and the Nairs under the Nair Service Society to achieve the goals of education and social progress. As an illustration of this trend, one could mention the leadership of Wakkom Maulavi and the activities conducted by organisations such as the Kerala Muslim Aikya Sangham (founded in 1922) and the Muslim Educational Society (MES, active from 1964 onward). Thus, institutions under Muslim management increased from 472 in 1962 to 1301 in 1993/4.[42]

Muslims Are Not Urban Outcasts

Kuttichira, or wider Thekkepuram, is not a case of ghettoisation or urban segregation in the marginalisation sense that is evident in certain other Indian cities. Its Muslim inhabitants are not urban outcasts or seriously deprived social groups. As we have noted, the history of oceanic trade helps to explain the dominant role of Kuttichira and the Koyas in Kozhikode. Origin, economic activity and cultural practices continue to define the positive exclusivity of the locality's Muslim inhabitants. Deprivation in facilities or infrastructure was not noted. On the other hand, several development plans (Kuttichira Square project, Thekkepuram Development Sketch project) suggest that Kuttichira is not a 'neglected' urban locality. Moreover, local Muslims have set on the path of upward mobility by capitalising on opportunity (for example, migration), by conscious initiatives (reform and education) and by asserting themselves locally (social organisation and political voice). Influential Muslim personalities are represented in the local administration, among popular literary and public figures as well as in the political sphere. Muslim entrepreneurs lead in the city's business activity. Hindus and Christians sometimes express their unease at the rapid changes but they simultaneously talk of Muslims as job creators, for example in such niche areas as health care and education, and as the preferred clients in sectors such as real estate and consumer services, and as the providers of modern and cosmopolitan goods and facilities now accessible in the city such as bakeries, restaurants, international franchises and malls.

Kozhikode has withstood past crises.[43] Without popular or state will, scars might have festered to malign the goodwill between Hindu and Muslim communities. The partnership for larger prosperity was upheld in the Zamorins' era in such instances as the order given to coastal communities to make a Muslim of each child born on a Friday[44] because there was benefit in raising the local numbers in fishing and naval activity and thus promoting the sea trade. Some of Kerala's older mosques resemble the Hindu temple architecture of medieval Kerala. However, this is due to the fact that local Hindu architects and artisans were engaged in mosque construction at the time, rather than to older temples forcefully being converted into mosques. By refusing attractive Gulf-funding offers in the past for the much-needed renovation of the Miskal mosque (a rare five-storeyed construction) but involving 'remodelling' in the more typical minaret-style mosque (which was done with few other mosques in the region), Kuttichirans also upheld the city's common history by not giving in to more narrow identifications. Kozhikode's medieval past, boasting resident traders and travelers from other parts of the world and India, informs claims of a broader cosmopolitan identity. Gujarati-Bohra Muslims have their own mosques and different ritual practices. District Collector P.B. Salim articulates this: 'The voice of the wider public is being allowed to be taken over by a minority seeking to disturb the harmony, who claims to represent all the community. [We] the 'majority' want(s) to be more vocal and not allow them to do so'.

Conclusion

The objective of this paper was to investigate whether a process of urban marginalisation could be observed among the Muslims of Kozhikode. A dominant Muslim locality, Kuttichira was chosen for the study and it is argued that Kozhikode is potentially an exception among other Indian cities, regarding the relative status of the Muslim population, its residential patterns and living conditions. The resident community is not an 'outcast' group in the sense of economic or social marginalisation. On the other hand, the locality and its residents continue to retain an exclusive identity with deep historical roots.

Current challenges to these largely non-conflictual communal relations must be acknowledged, including existing gaps, recent events hinting at radical undercurrents or resentment against the rapid advancement of the Muslim community in the light of dissimilar access to migration. Yet, it could be argued that there seems to be sufficient room for mutual adjustment and progress, inherent in the community's and the city's strengths. Mappila Muslims show an inclination for participative political competition within the wider society as well as self-initiative, boding well for the community. Past actions witnessed on sensitive occasions seem to indicate the determination of the public and the local government to not let spoilers seriously disturb the goodwill between communities.

In Kozhikode, Muslims are not relegated to the peripheral areas but are rather choosing to extend into the city's mixed localities. As the chapter's title indicates, the findings of the research show Kozhikode's Kuttichira locality as continuing to uphold and maintain an exclusive cultural and geographical identity.

11

MUSLIMS IN BANGALORE

A MINORITY AT EASE?[1]

Aminah Mohammad-Arif

In August 2008, after completing an interview on Bangalore's Tannery Road, I took an autorickshaw. Since the neighbourhood had a large Muslim population and the driver was sporting a beard, I assumed that he was a Muslim.

I said: 'There are a lot of Muslims in this area, huh?'

He answered: 'Ya, they are everywhere'. Then he stopped and asked: 'What are you?'

I had a sudden doubt about his religion, and quickly looked around to check whether his name was written on a board (as in most autorickshaws in Bangalore), or whether I could have any clue about his religion like a '786'[2] or a Ganesh sticker. But I could not see anything of the sort and thought safer to answer:

'I am Parsi. What about you?'

'I am Hindu'.

'So, you were saying, Muslims are everywhere?'

'Yes, they are hopeless people, you know, the way they kill animals. And they take everything here, our lands, properties, and all that'.

'Oh, really?'

'And, you know, men can have seven wives![3] And women, when their husbands die, they can marry seven men, can you believe it?! Hopeless people!'

'Ooh, really! How strange, indeed. [...] And the terrorist attacks in Bangalore [a couple of days ago], Muslims must have done it, huh?'

'Nooo, not at all! Politicians did it, there is no terrorism. Politicians do it for their own benefit. [...]'.

'Now that the BJP is in power, do you think things will change for the better?'

'No, they are all the same, hopeless people'.

This dialogue has of course no general value, but it does give several interesting insights. While it is above all fairly coherent with the image of politicians across religions in urban India, which supersedes in its negativity any other representation, it is also in keeping with the envy and fear that minorities can generate, especially when they are in competition with other less privileged groups. Besides, although the negative image of Muslim 'traditions' expressed here reveals the 'typical' stereotypes attached to Muslims across India—and beyond—this dialogue 'un-typically' suggests that Muslims in Bangalore are not mechanically associated with terrorism, and hence with violence. Does this imply that Muslims might be more at ease in Bangalore than in other cities of India?

Feelings of safety, as subjective as they might be, are indeed important because of their influence on the way people position themselves in a society, sentiments of insecurity potentially leading to self-relegation. In order to assess this feeling of ease, I have chosen a neighbourhood, Shivaji Nagar, with a significant Muslim population. After situating its residents in the city at large, I will examine their 'reasons' for living/working in this particular locality, drawing from observations and interviews conducted in 2009 (a preliminary research) and during July and August 2010. Is it a sign of their growing stigmatisation-cum-marginalisation in Bangalore, despite the cosmopolitism-cum-(tremendous)-development of the city that has benefited some sections of the community? If so, is it a self-conscious choice to live with one's coreligionists, or is it imposed by others? Could there be other reasons for living/working in this locality, reasons that are not linked to 'Muslimness'? In other words, is there a correlation, driven by feelings of (in)security or enhanced identity (choice of being with one's coreligionists), between one's religious affiliation (and minority condition) and the localisation in a given place? Or do other reasons (practicality, business) supersede religious/ethnic belonging? Ultimately, what does spatial distribution tell us about communal relationships in the city?

MUSLIMS IN BANGALORE: A MINORITY AT EASE?

Muslims in Bangalore: A Historical and Demographic Overview

Most historians consider 1537 as the founding date of Bangalore[4] and Gowda I as its founding father. As a chieftain warrior, he owed allegiance to the Vijayanagar Empire (1336–1646) but later developed a quasi-autonomous state. Initially shaped as a fortified settlement, Bangalore was one of the fortresses that served as a defence for the entire area. The fall of the Vijayanagar Empire in 1565, subsequent to a Muslim sultanate alliance from the middle Deccan Plateau, reinforced the power of local rulers. The old settlement, or the 'City' as it is called today, was then conquered by successive military powers, the army of Bijapur and the armies of Aurangzeb (with a brief Mughal interregnum in 1687–90), until it was sold to the local ally of the Mughals, Chikka Deva Raja Wodeyar of Mysore in 1690. Political changes and instability compelled trading routes to move further south, gradually transforming Bangalore from a crossroad into an urban centre. Traders and artisans from neighbouring states (Tamil Nadu and Maharashtra) and from other states, like Rajasthan and Gujarat, were also attracted to the city. These migrants included Muslim communities. Although the Sufi presence in the region dates back to at least the fourteenth century,[5] itinerant Sufis were also part of these waves of migration.

It is in this context that two of the most prominent Muslim figures of Mysore state emerged: Haider Ali (1722–82) and his son Tipu Sultan (1753–99).[6] The weakening of the Wodeyar dynasty propelled Haider Ali, chief general of the Rajah of Mysore, to power, and he became the *de facto* ruler of the kingdom. He received Bangalore as his personal endowment from the king in 1759. This coincided with the growing expansion of the British East India Company in the region. In 1799, Tipu Sultan, the last ruler of the region to resist the British, was finally defeated at Srirangapattanam and the Wodeyar dynasty was restored to power. The leadership of Haider Ali and Tipu Sultan was marked by a large development of trade, and contributed to attracting a large number of Muslims to the city.

Bangalore became a British enclave after the colonial power decided in 1809 to move an important regiment from Srirangapattanam to a location a few miles from the city. Henceforth known as the Cantonment, this location symbolised both the subsequent role of the city as the main military pole of South India as well as its expansion as a twin township. While Bangalore originally referred to the fort settlement built by Kempe Gowda, it developed in the nineteenth century as two separate cities with a dual political and legal n ature recognised by separate municipal boards: Bangalore Town, administered by the kingdom of Mysore, and Bangalore Cantonment, placed under British rule. The dual political nature of Bangalore was reflected in the composition of the population. The city had a fairly homogenous population comprising mainly Kannada-speakers (including some local Muslims), while the Cantonment attracted a larger diversity of people from neighbouring regions. After independence, the city and the Cantonment were unified and formed the Bangalore City Corporation (1949).[7]

Since 1947, the population of Bangalore has witnessed a tremendous boom, increasing from 786,343 inhabitants in 1951 to 5,686,844 in 2001. This demographic growth, which has propelled Bangalore to the rank of the fifth-largest city in India, is mainly the result of an important and continuous migration process of different linguistic and religious groups that has largely contributed to the cosmopolitism[8] of the city (at least 40% of the population include migrants arriving from other states).[9]

Bangalore's cosmopolitism is reflected in language: according to the 1991 Census, only 35% of the people stated Kannada as their mother tongue. Others were speakers of Tamil (25%), Telugu (17%)[10] and Urdu (12.7%).[11] However, if the language issue is symptomatic of Bangalore's cosmopolitism, it can become a serious hurdle in terms of job opportunities in the public sector since the Karnataka government made the passing of a Kannada language test a prerequisite for entry into government services in the 1980s. It also generates a strong linguistic nationalism from Kannadigas.

The percentage of Muslims in Bangalore is approximately the same as the national average: 13.3% in 2001. As elsewhere in India, Muslims form a very diverse population, comprising different linguistic and sectarian groups: local Dakkini Muslims and other Urdu-speaking communities coming from various parts of North and South India, Gujarati-speaking Kutchi Memons, as well as Tamil-speaking Labbais and Malayalam-speaking Mappilas. The vast majority of Muslims is Sunni, but they also include a small Shia community, whose numbers are unknown. Caste divisions do not seem to be particularly salient in a cosmopolitan context (and less so in South India than in the north), but they can be pervasive in some instances (lodging and especially marriage). The diversity of Muslims is also reflected in their 'ideological' affiliations: although, as in most other parts of India, a majority of Muslims profess a shrine-based kind of Islam, all major Islamic organisations have established branches in Bangalore: the Barelwis, the Deobandis, the Tablighi Jama'at, the Jama'at-i-Islami, the Ahl-i Hadith, and so on.

MUSLIMS IN BANGALORE: A MINORITY AT EASE?

Muslims in Bangalore's Economic and Political Landscape

The city of Bangalore is usually associated with the image of a high-tech city. However, although Bangalore has indeed become a high-technology hub, other industries have played an important role in the growth of the city with repercussions on the type of populations it has attracted and the subsequent social mapping of the city. Before independence, Bangalore was a fairly prosperous town, with a strong and flourishing textile industry, attracting Muslim tailors and leather workers as well as wealthier retailers (like the Memons).

Several educational and scientific institutions were also established as part of state-sponsored projects. The early emphasis on education, along with a policy of development, contributed to the rise of Mysore as one of the most modern states in pre-independence India. In the decades following independence, new educational institutions were established as part of a large-scale policy: the literacy rate increased from 43.1% in 1951 (as against 29.8% in Karnataka and 18.33% in India) to 84.4% in 2001 (as against 67% in Karnataka and 65.4% in India). Karnataka also adopted a 'progressive' policy in terms of reservations: in order to counter the dominance of the Lingayats and Vokkaligas (beside the Brahmins'), Congress Chief Minister Dev Raj Urs (1972–80) appointed the Havanur Backward Classes Commission in 1972 and added Muslims to the category of Backward Classes: Muslims were given 18% reservation in government jobs and 20% in educational institutions.[12] In 1986, during the tenure of Ramakrishna Hegde, low-caste Muslims were declared as Other Backward Classes (OBCs) through a Government Order. Under Veerappa Moily, all Muslims were subsequently placed under IIB Category of reservation of 4% in educational institutions (1994), and state government services (1995). Karnataka was also the first state of the Indian Union to appoint a Minorities Commission, and to establish the first ministry in India for minority welfare (2002).

Although there are no available studies on the direct benefits of these policies on Muslims (other than the fact that the very principle of reservations enables the people who benefit from it to avoid competition from other groups), their literacy rate did increase (see Table 11.1).

These figures show a fairly high literacy rate of Muslims in Bangalore (including women), albeit lower than the city average and lower than that of other religious groups (see Table 11.2). However, a sheer literacy rate does not necessarily imply enough education and qualifications to get a job in the formal sector of the economy. According to a 1994 survey on the socio-economic and

Table 11.1. Literacy rate of Muslims in 2001 (in %)—Bangalore, Karnataka, India

	Bangalore	Karnataka	India
Males	81.3	76.9	67.6
Females	77.2	63.0	50.1
Total Muslim population	79.3	70.1	59.1

Source: *Census of India 2001*.

Table 11.2. Literacy rate of four major religious groups in Bangalore in 2001 (in %)

	All religions	Hindus	Muslims	Christians	Buddhists
Males	89.1	90	81.3	93.7	91.7
Females	79.7	79.2	77.2	88.0	82.7
Total	84.4	84.6	79.3	90.8	87.2

Source: *Census of India 2001*.

educational status of religious minorities in Karnataka, established by K. Rahman Khan[13] (the first of its kind in the country), 43.2% of Muslims in Bangalore were educated up to the 7th standard, while only 12.8% were educated above the 7th standard. While Bangalore was ranked as the second most affluent city in India (after Delhi) in 2009,[14] another finding of the report was that only 47.2% of Muslims had an income per annum above 10,000 rupees (the lowest percentage of all the religious minorities in Bangalore, including Buddhists). Similarly, Muslims had the highest rate of households living below the poverty line (36.3%) (see Table 11.3).

Equally worrying is the evolution of Muslims' positions in government jobs: liberal policies of the Wodeyar dynasty had secured them a fairly high representation in government positions, including the police and the army. The situation continued to be favourable to the Muslims in the first decades following independence. Hence, in 1950, while Muslims accounted for only 6.3% of the state population, they occupied 10.6% of the open government positions. In 1981, they represented 7.7% of the state judiciary.[15] However, since the late 1980s, the situation has dramatically changed, with a growing under-representation in most departments of government services. Besides, there has been a growing inverse relationship between higher posts and Muslims: today, there are, for instance, only two Muslim judges in the Karnataka High Court and one Muslim in the Karnataka State Bar Council. As for the police, except Nisar

Table 11.3. Annual income of religious minorities in Bangalore in % (1994)

	Below Rs 10,000 per annum	Above Rs 10,000 per annum	Below poverty rate (less than Rs 6,000 per annum)
All minorities	49.02	50.98	33.76
Muslims	52.85	47.15	36.33
SC converted Christians	46.99	53.01	31.91
Other Christians	38.46	61.54	26.39
Buddhists	40.00	60.00	27.27
Digambar Jains	37.07	62.93	26.88
Swetambar Jains	26.57	73.43	21.14
Parsees	25.68	74.32	17.57
Sikhs	27.67	72.33	21.33

Source: *Report of High Power Committee on Socio-Economic and Educational Survey—1994 of Religious Minorities in Karnataka.*

Ahmed, Additional Commissioner of Police, and a fairly prominent figure in the city, there are very few Muslims at the top levels. The Bowring Institute, the largest and most sought after club among Bangalorean elites, includes only 2.5% of Muslims among its life members and 3.8% among its permanent members.[16]

At the other end of the social scale, large numbers of Muslims work in the informal sector, as weavers, tailors, auto-drivers, mechanics, street vendors, and so on. Among them, tailors are particularly affected and economically marginalised by the development of the garment industry that has made their profession partly redundant.

That said, Muslims have benefited from the educational policies and the economic growth of the city, albeit not as much as other communities. They have established a number of colleges throughout Karnataka, affiliated with Bangalore University. Most of the institutions are run under the Al-Ameen movement (1966),[17] which also provides schools for children in underprivileged areas, like Shivaji Nagar. The establishment of these schools and colleges reflects, and has, in turn, brought about the rise of a sizeable (although no figures are available) dynamic and 'modern' educated middle class which has established several other institutions (hospitals, social work organisations, interest-free banks, publishing houses, and so on).

This development is not exclusively community-oriented and has allowed Muslims to gain greater visibility and economic success in some sectors like real estate: the most prominent Muslim builder is probably Irfan Razzaq, a Memon businessman, whose company, Prestige Group, has been involved in large-scale projects. Memons, who comprise several other successful entrepreneurs, have also been fairly dynamic and involved in community affairs through social work and philanthropy. The fact that they are Sunni has in turn helped their full acceptance by other Muslims, although they tend to remain a close-knit community with a fairly strict practice of endogamous marriages.

As far as their political representation is concerned, Muslims are largely under-represented at all levels (not a single MP elected in the 2009 Lok Sabha elections and only thirteen Muslims in the 198-seat municipal corporation). However, Bangalore is home to a few major political figures whose reputation crosses the boundaries of Karnataka, like K. Rahman Khan, the deputy chairman of the Rajya Sabha, and Jaffer Sharieff, former Union Railways Minister (1980–84 and 1991–95). The Muslim political leadership of Bangalore also includes local figures, such as Roshan Baig who has held different portfolios as State Minister (including Home) and Mumtaz Begum, the first Muslim mayor of Bangalore. Since 2009, a Professor of sociology and social work, Mumtaz Ali Khan, has been propelled onto Bangalore's political scene as minister in the first ever BJP government of a South Indian state. His nomination as Minister for Haj, Waqf and Minority Welfare is in keeping with a tradition in Karnataka where, unlike other states, Muslims have often held ministry portfolios, including important ones.

The political representation of Muslims in Bangalore thus offers a mixed picture: while under-representation in sheer numbers is blatant, it is partly compensated by the local and national prominence of a handful of politicians and their presence in local government. However, historically, Muslims have not been a focus of polarisation between parties in the political landscape of the city as caste affiliations (Lingayats vs. Vokkaligas) are the major bases of political cleavages.

As for the history of political violence in the city, while the first major incident of communalism was reported in 1928, rather peaceful relations prevailed in the subsequent decades, until the beginning of the 1980s when tensions rose again, evolving mainly around two issues: linguistic nationalism (riots in 1994 in reaction to the telecast of a ten minute Urdu news bulletin at prime time, which claimed twenty-five lives, making them to this day the deadliest riots in Bangalore against Muslims) and moral outrage (for example, violent reactions of Muslims after the publication in 1986 of an article in the *Deccan Herald* perceived as offensive to the Prophet; police firing claimed eleven lives in Bangalore and five others in Mysore). However, except for these two cases, communal incidents rarely led to deadly violence (at least never on such a large scale) and the polarisation between Hindus and Muslims is not as palpable in Bangalore as in other cities of India or even of Karnataka, where Muslims are, for instance, engaged in confrontations over contested sites, like in Chikmagalur (competitive claim over the Datta Peeta-Baba Budangiri shrine). Moreover, events taking place beyond the borders of Karnataka, like the destruction of the Babri Masjid or the Gujarat pogroms, have not so far had any violent spillover effects on the city.

Shivaji Nagar: A Muslim Enclave?

During the colonial period, the layout of the city was divided by planning authorities in such ways so as to accommodate different communities in separate blocks (Brahmins, Muslims, native Christians, Lingayats, and so on).[18] While there are persisting signs of the colonial past in the spatial distribution of the population, Muslims seem to be nonetheless scattered throughout the whole city in contemporary Bangalore. The wealthiest segment lives in wealthy residential areas like Koramangla, Jaynagar and Indiranagar; average-income groups live in fairly large numbers in localities like Frazer Town, Benson Town and Cole's Park; and underprivileged populations tend to live in enclaves such as Tannery Road (D.J. Halli in particular), Mysore Road, Shivaji Nagar, and so on.

The area I have chosen for my fieldwork is a neighbourhood in Shivaji Nagar, commonly perceived by both 'residents' (meaning here not only the inhabitants but also shopkeepers) and non-residents as a Muslim-dominated area. This locality is also a highly symbolic place that has witnessed most of the major mobilisations of Muslims in the city. Russell Market (built in the 1920s and pronounced by many Muslims as 'Rasul[19] Market') square is indeed the emblematic locus of the city where 'community' feelings over local, national as well as international issues are expressed, staged and performed (through prayers in the public space, burning of effigies and newspapers, and so on): demonstrations against the *Deccan Herald* and the *Indian Express* after the publications of 'offensive' articles, protests against the Danish cartoons and the execution of Saddam Hussein and so on. The easy availability of Muslims at any time of the day and night makes the area particularly attractive for potential mobilisers. Whenever the situation is tense in Bangalore (after bombings or after a pig is thrown in a distant mosque), the neighbourhood, perceived as particularly

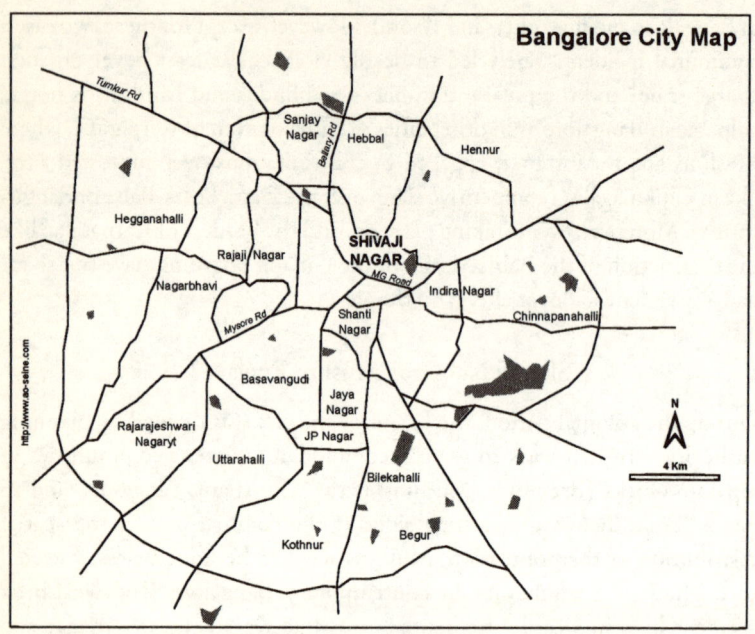

General Map of Bangalore

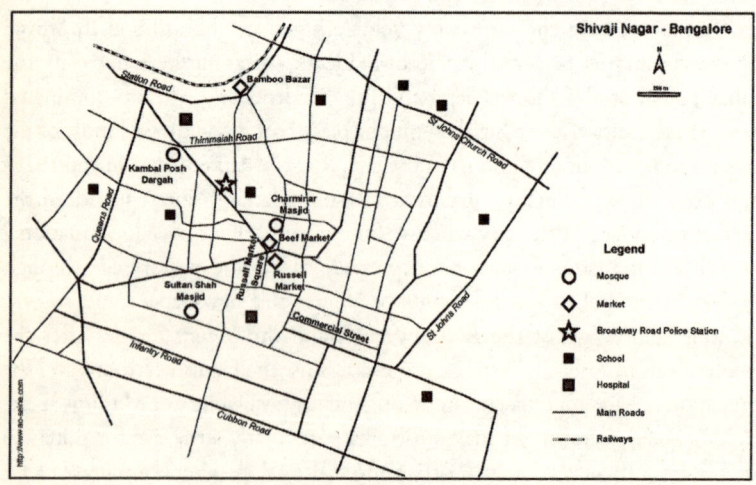

Map of Shivaji Nagar in Bangalore

sensitive, is usually among the first ones to be sealed off by the police. The perceived Muslimness of the area also owes much to Roshan Baig, a Muslim himself and a well-known figure in the city across religions, who has been elected five times as MLA from this constituency.

The constituency of Shivaji Nagar, located in Central Bangalore, officially includes a wide range of areas (Shivaji Nagar, Bharatinagar, Jaymahal, Ulsoor but also Vidhan Soudha, the local Parliament, and so on), and is not Muslim dominated. But there is one particular part of the neighbourhood with an important presence and visibility of Muslims: referred to as Shivaji Nagar as such, it runs west to east from Queens Road to Kamaraj Road and north to south from Station Road, prolonged by Saint Johns Road to Infantry Road. Major Muslim landmarks and concentration pockets include Bamboo Bazar, the *dargah* of Hazrat Sayyid Shah Mohiuddin (known as Kambal Posh), Russell Market Square and the Sultan Shah Masjid, while long rows of furniture shops owned by Muslims can also be seen on the east side of Infantry Road. As for Commercial Street, one of the major shopping centres of Bangalore, although it has attracted an increasing number of various communities and major pan-Indian (Fabindia, Mochi) and international (Nike, Levi's) brands over the years, a significant number of shops still belong to Muslims, and to the Memons in particular (Kashmiris are also to be seen in handicraft shops). In some areas, like Russell Market Square and the adjacent streets and roads, Broadway, Shivaji (which may have given its name to the neighbourhood), Noah or Mir Obaidullah, while people from all origins can be seen on the streets, the dominance of Muslims, both men and women, old and young, is fairly obvious: indeed, the passer-by cannot fail to see the large numbers of women in black burqas doing their shopping, (non-)bearded men in white topis (on Fridays in particular), Muslim names on shops and restaurants (Bilal or Hamza) and Urdu inscriptions on walls. Nor can one fail to hear the speaking of a typical Daccani Urdu or the *azan* coming from nearby mosques. The aroma emanating from roadside stalls of *biryani, paya* and *kabab* cannot be missed either. The decrepitude of the buildings, along with the uncleanness of most parts of this neighbourhood, particularly the segment stretching from the *dargah* of Kambal Posh to Russell Market Square, and the adjacent lanes and by-lanes with slums and more or less decaying houses, are fairly in keeping with the usual stereotypes associated with Muslim areas. The word 'ghetto' was even used by some of the people interviewed (mostly by those who do not live there) to describe the neighbourhood: 'ghetto' in the sense here of a small place with large numbers of lower-middle-class and underprivileged Muslims. But up on the north side of Russell Market, from Thimaiah Road onwards, there are residential areas where populations are socially and religiously mixed (Muslims, Marwaris, Tamils). Beside the religious origin of the residents, the reason why Shivaji Nagar is known as Muslim dominated is also due to the large number of mosques, and to the religious origin of shop- and restaurant-owners.

The important concentration of Muslims has not failed to draw the attention of the major Islamic organisations: while the Tablighi Jama'at (TJ) has taken control of the Sultan Shah Masjid (one of the largest mosques in Bangalore), and the Ahl-i Hadith of the Charminar Masjid, a branch of the Jama'at -i-Islami is located close by, on Queens Road. However, shrine-based Islam remains a dominant trend in the neighbourhood. Some people of the locality may be influenced by the (active) *dawa* of the TJ in their everyday religiosity (by becoming more practising), but most do not formally depart from popular Islam. Hence, Salman, a car mechanic, started saying that he appreciated the Tablighis for the 'good' work they were doing among Muslims, but when I asked him whether the TJ had told them to stop going to *dargahs,* he started laughing and said: 'they would not dare to say it, they know people will beat them up ('*mar khaenge*') if they do. And even if they 'do, people don't care'. Interviews and observations of the types of 'traditional'[20] burqas worn by women also suggest that the 'physical' keeping of *purdah* primarily stems from a 'habit' inherited from generations more than from a recent potential re-Islamisation under the direct influence of any Islamic organisation (as observed in other localities of Bangalore). In terms of sectarian differences, the neighbourhood is (almost) exclusively composed of Sunnis, as Shias, who tend to be more affluent, live either in neighbouring wealthy areas, like Richmond Town, or are scattered throughout the city.

Living in Shivaji Nagar: 'Muslimness',[21] the (Over)-determining Criterion?

As stated before, Shivaji Nagar is 'home' to a large number of Muslims as the result of a process which started long before independence when people tended to live in socially-exclusive areas (Brahmins in Malleshwaram, Lingayats in Rajajinagar, Vokkaligas in Jaynagar, and so on). During the colonial era, Shivaji Nagar, known as Blackpally, was part of the Old Cantonment area, which also used to be divided along 'communities' (religion, region and/or caste).

Although all the people who work in Shivaji Nagar may not be living there, I have included them in my study as their working hours are such that most spend more time in this neighbourhood than in their locality of residence. Moreover, the very fact that they work in Shivaji Nagar (whether out of choice or not) may be related to the very Muslimness of the area.

In terms of the patterns of (non)-residence in the locality the people whom I interviewed can be divided into four main categories. Although the cases presented here are by no means an exhaustive typology they may help to illustrate the diversity of situations and pinpoint the (non)-importance of Muslimness as a criterion for living/working in Shivaji Nagar.

1) The first group includes people who live in the area and have no (stated) aspirations of leaving it. Butchers, largely present in the neighbourhood, are fairly representative of this group. Among the butchers I interviewed, including those with high standards of living (as observed through their homes, for instance, well-furnished and equipped with the latest electronic devices), the reasons put forward to explain their attachment to this area were varied and were mainly, in the discourses at least, endogenous: historical (they had been living in the area for generations); relational (their close acquaintances also live in the area); economic (most of their customers hail from there); and emotional (the pleasure and feeling of security provided by being with 'one's people'). More exogenous reasons can also be suggested. Given the poor image of the Qureshi caste (the Qureshis, also known as Qasais, are traditionally involved in butchering), whose profession is perceived as particularly 'impure' by non-Muslims but also, to a large extent, by fellow Muslims, its members may not easily find a place of residence in a 'non-Qasai dominated area' (which Shivaji Nagar largely is) and even less so in a non-Muslim area, even when they enjoy a high economic status. They may thus self-censor any aspiration of coming out of the neighbourhood. Beyond professions and self-censorship, other people fit in the same group, like Aftab, an auto-mechanic who was born and raised in Shivaji Nagar, who works there, and whose whole family, including in-laws, lives in the area. Hence, Aftab does not see any reason of living outside Shivaji Nagar.

2) The second group comprises people who live in Shivaji Nagar but yearn to live elsewhere. Nazir, a *rickshaw-wala,* once dropped a woman off in Koramangla, and since then has been dreaming of living in a similar wealthy neighbourhood. As opposed to the butchers who may not have many opportunities to leave their locality (and when they do, they usually go to other cities either on business trips or on holiday) and are not therefore in their everyday lives necessarily exposed to other neighbourhoods, Nazir

travels throughout the city daily. Through his customers, he becomes, though not intentionally, the observer of different lifestyles. The almost daily exposure to people with high(er) standards of living has in turn influenced his life projects. A few other people interviewed also said that they would have preferred to live in other areas had they been more affluent.

3) The third group includes people who do not live in the area but simply work there, either out of choice or out of constraint. Among people of this category, there is a pharmacist, Ilyas, and the owner of a bookshop, Riaz. In both cases, the decision stems from family or business reasons. Ilyas said that he opened his pharmacy in Shivaji Nagar because he knew the doctor in the adjacent clinic[22] and because Shivaji Nagar was located in a central and busy area. With a minimum of a hundred patients a day, business is good because the area being unhygienic, lots of people suffer from infections. However, he lives in BTM Layout[23] because 'residentially, Shivaji Nagar is not so good'. As for Riaz, a Gulf-returnee, he owns a hundred-year-old bookshop that used to belong to his grandfather. His mother called him back to India to perpetuate his grandfather's legacy by taking it over. During the interview, Riaz kept complaining about the area and its squalor, saying that he had been working in Shivaji Nagar out of necessity (*majburan*), and added proudly that he lived in a nice house in neighbouring Frazer town.

4) The fourth group comprises people who used to live in Shivaji Nagar, but who were 'expelled' from the neighbourhood and wish to come back. Forty poor Muslim families, along with the same number of Hindu families, were indeed living in small rented or owned *jhopar patti* on the pavement of a street near a hospital (and they were hence 'obstructing' the way of the people who wanted to go to the hospital). They had settled on this footpath hoping that they would get—and they did—some financial support from the *dargah* of Kambal Posh located on the opposite side. They also benefited from the zakat given by affluent sections of the community who tend to see in Shivaji Nagar a privileged (although not exclusive in any ways) place to combine piety and generosity through compulsory alms. These families were promised by the Slum Development Board *pukka,* houses in Sadaramangla, near Whitefields. But after moving to the new place in June 2010, the disillusion was tremendous as they were given houses that were much smaller than what was initially promised, completely isolated and deprived of any kind of facilities (no access to water and electricity, no private toilets and bathrooms and so on). All the people I talked to wanted to go back to Shivaji Nagar and missed their one square feet *kaccha* house on

the footpath, all the more so as most of them still worked in the locality. Whether they were Hindu or Muslim did not matter. Among Muslims, the centrality of Shivaji Nagar and its practical aspects were given as primary reasons because, in addition to the very location, the neighbourhood and its vicinity are provided with all major facilities: (more or less legal) water and electric connections, affordable schools and hospitals in walking distance, public transportation, and so on.

Beyond these examples, Shivaji Nagar witnesses a constant turnover of populations. As per a mobility process, some people move out, as soon as their economic situation improves, while new ones, from rural areas in particular, move in, looking for cheaper rents and job opportunities. Some may be attracted by the locality because Hindu landlords refused them apartments (usually belonging to communities with strict food habits, like Brahmins, Vaishyas and Lingayats). Moreover, Shivaji Nagar is a 'typical Muslim' neighbourhood insofar as food and other products of their taste (dress, perfumes, and so on) are easily available. So are the places where they can publicly express and live their religiosity, namely mosques and *dargahs*, Abid, a social worker, explains: 'Even though it may be inconvenient to live in a place where properties are divided and divided and reduced to pigeon-holes, people would like to live here because of the communal security and the satisfaction of living among their own people. The fear of communal tension is not so much [see below] than the satisfaction of living with one's own community. The relations between Hindus and Muslims are not bad but cultural differences are too many in terms of food, dress, perfumes'. Roshan Baig, the local MLA, said: 'Some people have left but they like to come back in the evening, have tea, gossip and go'.

Living in Shivaji Nagar: Interactions and Inter-community Relations

The interviews showed a striking sense of 'ease' among Muslims living or working in the neighbourhood, including among the most underprivileged ones. By 'ease', I mean feeling ease as Muslims, because the insecurity allied to poverty as such unsurprisingly remains a dominant feature in discourses. For instance, none of the people I interviewed, be they housewives in slums, unemployed young mechanics, autorickshaw drivers or timber workers, established a correlation between their deprivation (of varying levels) and their being Muslim. Nafisa, a cook and slum-dweller, said: '*Ham aisa nahin samajhte ke ham Musalman hain, is liye ham gharib hain, yeh hamari taqdir hai. Kabhi ehsas nahin hua ke Hindu log hamko pasand nahin karte* [We do not believe that it is because we are Muslim that we are poor, it's our fate. We never felt that Hindus did not like us]'.

Similarly, Ilyas, the pharmacist, complained that banks often refused loans to people living or working in Shivaji Nagar because of the bad reputation of the neighbourhood, but he did not link it to the fact that Shivaji Nagar was Muslim-dominated but rather to its lower-middle-class status. He added that similar problems were encountered in non-Muslim-dominated localities. He even said: '*Jitna Musalman Hindustan main safe hain, kahin bhi nahin hain. Jab jhagre hote hain, Musalman* dominate *karte hain. Pakistan, jo 90% Muslim hai, vahan jitna Musalman larte hain* (*Shia aur Sunni*), *itna Hindu aur Musalman nahin larte. Us hisab se, Hindustan safe hai* [There are no other places where Muslims are as safe as in India. Whenever there are clashes, Muslims dominate. Pakistan is 90% Muslim, but Hindus and Muslims do not fight in India as much as Muslims (Shias and Sunnis) do in Pakistan; in that sense, India is safe]'.

While the policies of the BJP government did raise negative comments, they were surprisingly not related to communal issues but mainly to economic ones: all the people complained about the rise in the prices of rice, meat, sugar and gas since the BJP had come to power: '*bare logon ka chalta hai, gharib ko puchnewala koi nahin hai*' [as opposed to the Congress and the Janata Dal] [only rich people have a say, nobody bothers about the poor], said Aftab, the unemployed auto-mechanic. And when I asked them whether they had been affected by the BJP policies as Muslims, hardly anyone said yes. One exception is the butchers of the beef market who, at the time of the interviews, were extremely concerned about the project of the government to ban cow slaughter, as it would mean the end of their trade. They felt directly targeted: '*Humko nahin marte, sidha hamare pet ko marte hain* [They do not hit us directly, they hit the source of our daily bread (lit. our stomachs)]'. This project was also criticised by other inhabitants of the area as it would affect poor people in general, since beef is cheaper than mutton.

How can we then explain this relative sense of ease? Some hypotheses can be put forward:

1) The physical presence of the state in the neighbourhood, through schools, hospitals, police stations and the access to basic services (water, electricity) may nurture this sense of ease. However, state-provided resources happen to be in the area because of its very location in the centre of the city

and the historical proximity to government offices. They were not created or set up to fulfil the needs of local populations (the underprivileged in particular) as such. The sense of abandonment across social classes is fairly prevalent and the state is held responsible for the underdevelopment and squalor of the area (lack of proper roads, underground drainage and so on). Abdullah, a glass worker, said: *'Bahar ki gandagi ke liye, koi kuch nahin karta. Jab MP, MLA ate hain, to saf karte hain, nahin to kuch nahin karte* [Nobody—meaning here the representatives of the state—bothers about the filth of the area. When MPs or MLAs come here, then it's cleaned, otherwise it is just left like that]'. However, once again, the feeling of abandonment by the state did not lead to a subjective linkage with the dominance of Muslims in the locality but rather to inertia or the corruption of state representatives.

As for the symptomatic figures of the potential hostility of the state against Muslims, namely the police, their attitude towards Muslims raised mixed feelings. While Nadeem, a butcher, thought that the police had always a bad attitude with the Muslims (*'police hamesha ghalat karti hai* [the police is always mistaken]'), Akbar, a timber worker, said: *'police ghalat admi ke sath, ghalat karti hai, acche admi ke sath, accha karti hai* [the police is bad with bad people and good with good people]'. In any case, while, according to the local MLA, Roshan Baig, police harassment has increased since the BJP came to power, it remains proportionately low as compared to other cities in India. Abid, a social worker, said: 'there is not much help from the administration but there is no witch-hunting either'.

2) The presence of Muslim politicians in the area, and more particularly the representation of the constituency by Roshan Baig could be another reason for the sense of ease. However, interviews showed mixed perceptions. For instance, Nazir, the autorickshaw driver, appreciated the fact that Baig helped Muslims in admission to schools and colleges, and supported them during police interrogations in the wake of riots. Likewise, Ahmad, a fruit vendor said: *'Accha admi hai, hamare liye sab karta hai, jab bhi taklif hoti, larayi hoti, jhagra hota, unko bulate hain* [He is a nice man, he does everything for us, whenever there is a problem, a dispute, a clash, we call him]'. The butchers also had a positive image of him as he helped in renovating the beef market and went to Delhi to protest against the Anti-Cow Slaughter Bill. But others were more sceptical. Karim, another auto-mechanic, thought that Baig could hardly do anything as his party [the Congress] was not in power. As for Ilyas, the pharmacist and a member of the TJ, he was

very critical of Baig himself and of coreligionists who vote for him on the basis of religion ('people vote for him because he is a Muslim but he does not do anything; *musulman khara to de diya* vote, *dekhte nahin ke admi kaisa hai*' [He is a Muslim, so they vote for him, they do not see how good he is]). The same varied feelings were expressed about Mumtaz Begum, former Mayor of the city, seen as helpful by some and only preoccupied by the interests of the rich by others, and about Mumtaz Ali Khan, the Minister in the BJP government: Nazir, the rickshaw-driver, had expectations that he would do something as a Muslim, while Zaid, a timber worker, was more sarcastic: '*Ek dam* danger *admi. Kuch bhi faida nahin, yahan ki taraf jhankte tak nahin* [He is a very dangerous man, he is of no use for us, he does not even come and look this side]'. Beyond this difference in perceptions, the overall bad image of politicians, observed throughout the city and across social classes, was fairly predominant in discourses, and contrary to the statement of the pharmacist, not everybody thought that it was important to be represented by a Muslim candidate, and many valued instead the quality of the candidates.

3) This sense of ease seems to be in fact primarily stemming from the kind of interactions prevalent in the neighbourhood. First, Shivaji Nagar is a place of interaction for Muslims beyond localities and social classes, as coreligionists from other areas come to the neighbourhood to buy beef or camel meat, a Muslim calendar or novels in Urdu, a piece of cloth for a *shalwar kamiz* or a *ghagra choli*. Admittedly, most come in their cars or in a rickshaw, and, as soon as their purchase is over, rush back to their locality of residence. Thus the interaction does not extend much beyond the exchange of a few words, usually for bargaining purposes. Similarly, on Fridays, men from neighbouring areas come to the Sultan Shah Masjid in huge numbers but as soon as the prayer is over most of them return to work by motorcycle or autorickshaw, although a few of them can be seen taking their time and chatting on the stairs of the mosque. However, as limited as the interaction may be, the neighbourhood is largely open to the outside world, even beyond religious affiliation, as non-Muslims also like to come to the neighbourhood for purchasing purposes, enjoying the famous samosas of Shivaji Nagar sold by their thousands during Ramazan, not to mention Commercial Street and its hundreds of shops and boutiques. Even in the heart of the Muslim area of Shivaji Nagar, shopkeepers have customers from all religious backgrounds (albeit Muslim in the majority). Amir, a butcher, said laughingly that even Brahmins came and bought beef in his stall.

Second, the level of interaction between different groups is important. Muslims themselves come from different parts of India (mainly from the four southern states) and live and work side by side with people from other religions, Hindus, Dalits, or Christians, even though the demographic equation is reversed in Shivaji Nagar (dominance of Muslims) as compared to the larger city. These interactions within the neighbourhood show a relatively peaceful coexistence, (best) symbolised by the 'please do not urinate' handwritten sign on several walls of the area with a Muslim crescent and star, a Christian cross and a Hindu swastika as signatures.

In daily lives, occasions of interaction across religions can go beyond sheer business dealings or shopkeepers/customers relations. On a question about leisure time, Abdullah, the glass worker, said that people from all communities played cricket and carrom board together. In terms of commensality, people from all religions are seen in the major Muslim restaurants of the neighbourhood, Taj, Hilal or Imperial. More significantly, the traditional practice of food exchange, during the major festivals (Eid, Diwali and Christmas), between neighbours from different religions is still observed by several families.

On the issue of the common celebration of festivals by Hindus, Muslims and Christians, opinions varied. According to Roshan Baig, the MLA, Hindus and Muslims celebrate Eid and Diwali together but others disagreed, saying that festivals were celebrated separately (*alag alag*). For Ilyas, the pharmacist, festivals across religions are celebrated only in 'hi-fi (posh) areas'. However, they all agreed (and I could see it myself) that the Kambal Posh *dargah* attracted devotees across religions. Beyond Shivaji Nagar, several *dargahs* in Bangalore continue to fulfil their roles as symbolic public spaces of 'peaceful coexistence'. Hence the famous Karaga festival (the annual performance dedicated to Draupadi), which attracts two hundred thousand people in March and April across religions,[24] stops at the tomb of Hazrat Tawakkul Mastan in Cottonpet.[25] In addition to mosques and *dargahs,* Shivaji Nagar is also home to one of the largest churches in Bangalore, the Saint-Mary's Basilica. The annual nine-day celebration of the Saint-Mary festival attracts thousands of devotees in the neighbourhood. Muslims also join the gathering, although not out of religious fervour, but they take their children to watch because it is very 'entertaining' or to 'admire the nice clothes' worn by people on the occasion. Interestingly, social work can also be an opportunity of interaction across religions as an ashram in Hebbal (a neighbourhood located in the north of Bangalore) and the Hira Welfare association (a Muslim charitable trust mainly supported by the Jama'at-i-Islami) used to run together a school in the slum area until the *jhopar pattis* were removed by the Slum Development Board (see above).

4) In keeping with a peaceful coexistence, low levels of violence in the neighbourhood are probably a key factor in understanding the feelings of security. In normal times, violence at large, usually associated with 'ghettos',[26] is not particularly palpable in the locality. Although the major mafia dons of Bangalore, Koli Fayaz (killed by the police) and Tanveer (regularly put behind bars, particularly so when there are communal incidents) are from Shivaji Nagar, their level of activity does not bear comparison with their counterparts in Bombay, especially in violence terms, except that they enjoy a similar Robin Hood image (*'hafta usuli'* from the rich to help the poor). As for communalism as such, Shivaji Nagar does have the image of a riot-prone area, symbolised by its immediate sealing off by the police whenever incidents take place in any area of the city. But reality is somewhat different. As can be inferred by the above description of communal relations, violent outbursts are fairly rare. From the Muslims' point of view, their sheer dominance in numbers makes it difficult for other religious groups to act violently. Besides, customers from all communities come to the neighbourhood, and clashes or a curfew would mean a major loss for all communities. Kamal, a butcher, said: *'Danga fasad yahan pe hamesha nahin hote, kabhi kabar hote hain. Kachra jagah main zyada hota hai* [There are usually no riots here, or only occasionally. They rather take place in 'rubbish' areas]'. If this statement shows, through the denigrating of other areas, a positive perception of one's locality, outside perceptions tell a different story. According to Nisar Ahmad, the Additional Police Commissioner, the perceived sensitivity of the area points to its image as a neighbourhood 'full of illiterate people', and who hence are supposedly quick to react, but this perception does not seem to be due to the high concentration of Muslims per se. When violence does take place (often in reaction to an outside incident), it usually does not exceed stone throwing, and is rapidly brought under control. Zaid, the timber worker, said: *'jab koi jhagra hota hai, to ham bat ko barhne nahin dete* [whenever there are clashes, we do not let the situation worsen]'. As for the rare cases of widespread violence, it was met with disapproval. Commenting on the riots ignited in Shivaji Nagar after the execution of Saddam Hussein, Abdullah, the glass worker, condemned the riots initiated by politicians and 'causing damage (*noqsan*) to the public'.

MUSLIMS IN BANGALORE: A MINORITY AT EASE?

Conclusion

Muslims in Bangalore seem to be enjoying a relatively privileged situation as a result of a combination of endogenous and exogenous factors. State policies have been fairly favourable. As compared to their coreligionists in other Indian cities, they are more educated and have partly benefited from the economic boom of the city. They have also been spared from being major targets in political debates.

The study of Shivaji Nagar shows that Muslimness, largely defined, plays a fairly significant role in the reasons why people live and work in a Muslim-dominated area. They hope to find (primarily financial) support from coreligionists; escape from 'religion-based'[27] discrimination that leaves no other choice, feelings of security, emotional considerations, and so on. But the above examples also show that religion has hardly been an exclusive if not a dominant, criterion, as other unrelated reasons are not to be neglected: history, caste, acquaintances, family pressure, economic benefits, practicality, and so on. Besides, there is a blurring of borderlines, with economic benefits being sometimes concealed under the garb of religious solidarity, while the boundaries between 'choice' and 'constraint' for living and working in the neighbourhood become unclear. Although there is both objectively (numbers, visibility) and subjectively (inner and outer perceptions) a concentration of Muslims in Shivaji Nagar, it owes more to a complex combination of a historical heritage and economic deprivation than to religious affiliation. Moreover, the variety of patterns in Shivaji Nagar is such that the notion of a 'ghetto',[28] in the sense here of an area with an exclusive Muslim population across class affiliations for whatever reasons,[29] would be fairly questionable. While residence and business may coincide in some cases (butchers and underprivileged groups), it may not in others (non-Qureshi wealthy businessmen tend to live in more affluent areas). Poor populations themselves may live in Shivaji Nagar and work elsewhere or, on the contrary, work in the locality and live in even poorer areas. Even 'enclave' may not be a relevant term insofar as the concentration in a given place does not exclusively result from a self-conscious choice.

Besides, despite the sense of abandonment of the underprivileged populations and whatever the reasons for the presence of the state, their very access to the main resources spares them from the 'typical' isolation of 'ghetto-ised' communities. As for the gap created by the relative absence of the state, it is partly filled by community organisations, like the Hira Welfare Organization, which help out people deprived from basic needs.[30] As such, the role they fulfil partakes in the logic of 'self-sustained' communities that have to rely, more out of constraint than out of choice, on their own resources. In any case, discourses show that the sense of deprivation and exclusion are not expressed through a close correlation between religion and economic marginalisation, thus implying that unequal citizenship is, above all, felt and lived in socio-economic terms and not in religious ones.

Moreover, although Bombay's example shows that cosmopolitism as such is not enough to guarantee the protection of minorities and ensure peaceful relations between communities, Shivaji Nagar's religious diversity (in spite of the dominance of Muslims) permits some forms of interaction: from leisure to social work and from commensality to worship, the occasions are fairly numerous and the areas of socialisation seem to be more extensive than in other parts of India. Describing the 'feelings' between communities, Abid, the social worker, said: 'Otherness does not create hate in Karnataka, or as a whole in South India'. That said, the peaceful coexistence in Shivaji Nagar does not stem from a positive moral attitude of tolerance but rather from a pragmatic one expressed in terms of benefits (*faida*) and disadvantages (*noqsan*). Beyond interests as such, and as elsewhere in India, tolerance is defined here more as a passive non-interference than as an active recognition and respect for the other.[31] There are no attempts at erasing differences, neither in discourses nor in practices. Rather they are essentialised (assumed as 'natural') but they do not translate into overt hostility.

As for the low levels of violence, these are in keeping with the history and larger context of the city, all the more so as Bangalore, with its important middle class across religions and a relatively invisible working class, tends to be increasingly a city of 'teenies' and 'nouveaux riches' with a low political awareness (historically testified by the weak and late emergence of nationalist politics and the quasi-absence of the left). Any disruption of daily life in the form of communal violence or any other form could be unacceptable and perceived as a potential hindrance to further development and enrichment. As a result, instances of violence have remained fairly limited, and they have never reached such a scale so as to (re)define Muslims' occupation of space. In other words, violence has not been a determining criterion for spatial distribution.

That said, finding a house in Bangalore is not always an easy task for Muslims, as they can be flatly refused houses in Hindu-dominated colonies (issue of vegetarianism, perceptions that Muslims are dirty no matter how affluent they might be, and so on). Successful Muslims who move out of

MUSLIMS IN BANGALORE: A MINORITY AT EASE?

Shivaji Nagar usually go to nearby localities, like Frazer Town, Benson Town and Cole's Park, which may be more mixed socially and religiously but which nonetheless do have a fairly important concentration of Muslims. The idea of an imposed or chosen segregation of Muslims in the city, whether blatant or more subtle, should not be therefore completely discarded.

In addition, the two moral shocks[32] induced by the demolition of the Babri Masjid and the Gujarat pogrom did have serious political consequences as Muslims have increasingly perceived themselves as a distinct minority in the state since 1992.[33] Nisar Ahmad, the Additional Police Commissioner, said: 'The dynamics of culture and politics has changed. It's not just because of the BJP. [Previously] the attitude of people towards culture and religion was different. There was tolerance, respect, homogeneity was prevalent. [Now] everybody is moving towards retro. It's beyond culture and community. That is going to lead to various changes. As of today, Bangalore is not a communally sensitive city at all. But there are so many dynamics that at any moment anything can change'. Ilyas, the pharmacist, went further, saying that whenever there were communal clashes, Muslims were usually on one side, and all the other communities on the other side, the Christians included. '*Sabhi log Musalman ke dushman hain. Musalman ko pasand nahin karte. Dost bhi ho, uske dil main rahta hai ke yeh admi musalman hai*. Mumbai blasts *ke bad se differences aa gaye hain logon main, us se pehle thik tha. Mere bachpan main, sab milte the, ab nahin*. BTM Layout main *bhi badal gaya hai* [...] *kab kya ho jae, malum nahin hota* [Everybody is against Muslims, nobody likes them. Even with friends, they consider us as Muslims. Since the Mumbai blasts, differences have come up. Before it was OK. In my childhood [Ilyas is in his forties], people used to mingle freely. Even in BTM layout it has changed. Anything can happen, one never knows]'.

Moreover, the 'city's claim on tolerance'[34] has been called into question since at least the 1980s: not only has a violent linguistic nationalism developed in the city but the most violent episode of communalism witnessed a conflation between linguistic nationalism and religious nationalism. During the 1994 agitation against the Urdu news telecast, the language was portrayed not only as a minority language but as the language of the Muslims. Kannada nationalists hence chose to ignore the historical encounter of Karnataka with Islam as well as statistics that showed that the number of Urdu speakers in Karnataka is higher than the number of Muslims.[35] This deliberate identification of Urdu with Muslims also obliterates the fact that the latter have contributed to the development of Kannada literature and poetry (cf. the poet Nisar Ahmed for instance).

Besides, although Bangalore seems to have been so far spared from blatant attempts to polarise the relations between communities, since the BJP came to power some incidents in other parts of the state show signs of communalisation in ways that have been so far fairly unusual in Karnataka (attacks against a pub in Mangalore, issue over a *hijab* in a college in Bantwal).[36] Hence, the likelihood of a more or less rapid mainstreaming of hardcore Hindutva politics in the state is not to be completely ruled out.

Last but not least, the repeated cases of terror/jihadi attacks in Bangalore could weaken and compromise the efforts of the Muslims to be part of the city's mainstream. Although jihadi attacks have never been so far followed by communal riots in India, this violence might create in the middle-term sentiments of resentment that could be exploited by Hindu nationalists, if need be, while brutal investigations and profiling by the police might further alienate and/or marginalise young Muslims.

CONCLUSION

'IN THEIR PLACE'? THE TRAJECTORIES OF
MARGINALISATION OF INDIA'S URBAN MUSLIMS

Laurent Gayer and Christophe Jaffrelot

'It is easy to think of the prospects of the Indian Muslims in gloomy terms. Long ago denied the sceptre, which many thought essential to their existence, and now suspected by many for their religion and regarded as second-class citizens, is there any future for them other than eventual absorption in the Hindu mass?'
Percival Spear, 'The Position of the Muslims, Before and After Partition', in P. Mason (ed.), *India, and Ceylon: Unity and Diversity,* London: Oxford University Press, 1967, pp. 48–49.

The empirical research encapsulated in the case studies of this volume provides us with some elements of response to the question raised by Percival Spear some forty-five years ago: urban Muslims of India have experienced a significant decline since independence and this evolution has been accompanied by substantial changes in their patterns of localisation in Indian cities, which have been transforming the social geography of the latter.

However, this conclusion needs to be formulated in a nuanced way. First of all, the decline is more pronounced in some regions than in others. Unsurprisingly, Muslims have been more resilient out of the Hindi Belt (also known as the Cow Belt) and Western India (where Ahmedabad and Mumbai top the list of the riot-prone cities of India). In the south (be it in Bangalore or in Kozhikode) and in the east (see the case of Cuttack), Muslims are still well integrated into the local society and some of their leaders still belong to local elite groups.

Second, Muslims are not evenly marginalised. Territorially, the ghettoisation process is far from being systematic, more complex dynamics being at stake. Socially, Muslims are still playing a role in political and/or economic terms in some places. More importantly, a new Muslim middle class is emerging here and there, around economic niches long occupied by Muslims (meat export, leather goods, Unani medicine) but also beyond the traditional Muslim economy (agribusiness, IT, pharmaceuticals, real estate).[1] Moreover, this burgeoning middle class is no longer composed exclusively of traditional mercantile communities but, increasingly, includes successful entrepreneurs hailing from the lowest sections of the Muslim community, such as the Ansaris (a lower caste traditionally associated with weaving) and Qureshis (an 'impure' caste traditionally involved in butchering),[2] as well as Silawats (masons) and Malis (fruit and vegetable sellers).[3] Whether such middle-class Muslims have the capacity, or even the will, to contribute to the alleviation of their poorer coreligionists remains to be seen, however. Moreover, the mechanisation and increasingly competitive nature of sectors such as meat, leather or textile export, in the context of neo-liberal and export-oriented economic policies in India and beyond, have had a cost for small entrepreneurs hailing from traditionally marginal communities. These changes have condemned the least capital-intensive producing units to disappear, as exemplified by the crisis of the handloom industry in Varanasi, which affected around 500,000 weavers in and around the city.[4] And as far as the most competitive sectors are concerned, new entrants (both caste Hindus and Ashraf Muslims) have been making their presence felt in the upper levels, where profits are the most consequential. It is significant, for instance, that India's first meat-exporting firm, Al Kabeer, developed as a joint venture between Ashraf (Sheikh) and Khatri (Subberwal) families.[5]

A major contribution to upward social mobility among Indian Muslims has been their extraversion. Besides the exit strategy of those who left for Pakistan or the UK in the late 1940s to early 1950s, the establishment of some foreign connection has benefited them. On the one hand, economic relations have been developed with Gulf countries where new markets emerged after the oil boom (gem workers of Jaipur could now sell their products there, for instance). On the other hand—and more importantly—Muslims could migrate to this region to get jobs and send remittances (while Kozhikode Muslims are

CONCLUSION

exemplary in this regard, Muslims of all the cities under review in this volume have had access to this kind of—relative—prosperity through expatriation: even Sir Syed Nagar, in Aligarh, came to be known as the 'Petro-Dollar' Colony). The diversity of these migrants' experiences should be accounted for, however. Far from constituting a homogenous group, they have encountered different situations from one country to another (and sometimes from one city to another, in the case of the UAE) or according to their regional origin (with Keralites occupying a dominant position in the service classes and being credited with a greater enterprising spirit than Hyderabadis, for instance).[6] Moreover, unlike the stereotypes about the 'Gulf migrant' as an unskilled bonded labourer suggest, a new type of expatriate entrepreneur has been emerging in recent years among these migrants, with Keralite NRI tycoons M.A. Yusufalli, P. Mohammed Ali or P.V. Abdul Wahab being good examples. The diversity of these experiences is reflected in the representations of these migrants by their home society, which are characterised by a deep ambivalence.[7]

Before offering a more nuanced view of these forms of social and territorial marginalisation through typologies, this concluding essay provides an overview of the reasons why Muslims are losing ground in more general terms than in the previous case studies.

Why Are Muslims Losing Ground?

The decline of the Muslims of India in socio-economic and, to a certain extent, in political terms may be explained in many different ways. In North India as well as in former Muslim princely states, one could argue that Muslim elites never recovered from the loss of power they experienced in the eighteenth and nineteenth centuries. As Satish Saberwal points out, 'Their principal ancestral skill was in a certain kind of governing—a function being pre-empted by the British'.[8] Not only did Muslims retain (some) political power in a few places only—the Nawab or Nizam-ruled princely states and the *zamindaris/jagirdaris* they often managed from the *qasbas* in the Doab and Lucknow area—but in British India they were cornered by Hindus, especially in the United Provinces after Persian lost its monopoly as the language of government in 1837 and even more so after the adoption of the Nagri resolution of 1900, which stipulated that each candidate for government jobs should be fluent in the Nagri and Persian scripts—a measure which worked against Muslims' interests as the latter were less familiar with the Nagri script than Hindu elites with *nastaliq*? An additional blow came from Partition when the literati, landowners and other elite groups, including Gujarati businessmen, left the plebeians, mostly peasants and artisans who had lost their patrons and protectors.[10]

Another interpretation, closely related to the above narrative, emphasises the absence of business-oriented traditions among the Muslims of India. Bohras, Khojas and Memons have produced successful entrepreneurs[11] and Indian Muslim intellectuals have sometimes projected them as role models for the less privileged sections of the Muslim population of India.[12] However, these trading castes (*tijarati biraderi*), most of which descend from Hindu mercantile communities,[13] are not as well integrated to their coreligionists of other castes and sects as their Hindus equivalent, the Banyas, on the majority side. Bohras, for instance, who were formed as an Ismaili sectarian group in Gujarat in the twelfth century, have never been fully accepted by Sunnis and often do not look at themselves as primarily Muslim.[14] Indeed, historians have not found many Muslim traders who moved to industry the way the Marwaris did—even in Western India where the groups mentioned above controlled many commercial houses in Surat. In the 1880s, all the Bombay textile mills belonged to Hindus and Parsis—except one, which was 'projected' by a Muslim.[15] In the following decade, the spectacular rise of the Currimbhoy Mills, established by the Khoja entrepreneur Currimbhoy Ebrahim in 1888, was the proverbial exception.[16] Elsewhere, monographs mention a couple of Muslim traders (like Baker's history of the CP and Berar in the 1920s-30s[17] and Narayani Gupta's history of Delhi)[18] or a contractor (like Syed Maratib Ali who 'became the largest contractor of military canteens in the Punjab' at the turn of the twentieth century).[19] Politically marginalised after Partition, Muslims could not put up with the loss of power in the economic field.

A third interpretation highlights the deliberate marginalisation of the Muslims by the state. While Nehru tried to endow them with all the attributes of fully-fledged citizenship, the Hindu traditionalists who ruled over North India—the Chief Ministers of Uttar Pradesh and Madhya Pradesh especially—never implemented the policies that had been designed by the government, such as the promotion of Urdu. The impact of discrimination by the state is well reflected in the minimal presence of Muslims among the salary earners of the public sector and within the civil service. Since the early 1980s, the percentage of Muslims among the successful candidates in the civil service examinations has oscillated between 1.2 and 1.7%. And in 2000, the percentage of Muslims among central government employees varied from 5.12% in the least qualified positions (Group D) to only 1.61% in the highest posts (Group A).[20]

This alleged discrimination is deeply resented by Indian Muslims at large, to such an extent that some Muslim authors have not hesitated to claim that

CONCLUSION

'there is no future for Muslims in this country'.[21] The immediate impact of this feeling of discrimination has been amplified by a form of self-censorship. In a way, Muslims have withdrawn into their shell. Some sociologists have explained the way Muslims lagged behind in terms of education from this viewpoint, suggesting that 'Muslim parents are less ambitious about educating their children'.[22] This is a highly debatable claim, however. Historically, Muslims were often the first to pursue modern education. Between 1881 and 1901, Muslim males gradually bridged the gap with their Hindu counterparts in terms of literacy, before getting ahead—a trend that persisted at least until 1931 (the last year for which census figures disaggregated on the basis of religion are available). Moreover, for the whole period 1891-1931, Muslims were well ahead of Hindus in terms of literacy in English[23] and it is therefore doubtful that 'Muslims found the process of adjustment to Western education particularly hard'.[24] Rather than in cultural attitudes, the first explanation for the lower representation of Muslims in education, and particularly in higher education, should be looked for in the social stratification of this community, and more specifically in 'the small size of the social strata whose members can be expected to seek educational opportunities'[25]—a pattern that was reinforced by the migration of elite Muslims to Pakistan after Partition. The claim that Muslims would show less concern for education than other religious communities is itself dubious. The example of southern states such as Karnataka and Kerala, where Muslims have massively invested in education and where, as a result, there is a greater number of Muslim-managed schools, is a case in point. The ethnographic evidence gathered here and elsewhere also attests to the growing number of Muslim initiatives in the field of education across India, targeting young men but also, increasingly, women.[26] As we already mentioned in our introduction, only a small minority of Muslim students are enrolled in *madrasas*. But there as well, rapid change is perceptible,[27] with the introduction of modern subjects in the curriculum or the opening of girls' *madrasas,* and more generally with the development of a lively debate among Indian *ulama* on the scope of the reforms necessary to adjust *madrasas* to their times without depriving them of their identity.[28] The fact that the degrees delivered by *madrasas* are increasingly recognised by Indian universities also helps their graduates to complete their education in regular universities, offering them wider option of professional orientation.[29] In any case, the thesis of an estrangement of *madrasas* from the mainstream system of education does not resist empirical evidence: *madrasas* and regular schools often share their teaching staff and administrators, and their pedagogical philosophies are similar, with their emphasis on 'discipline' and 'moral education'.[30] Indeed, for the teaching staff of *madrasas* as well as for the families of their *tuleba*, the pedagogical project of these institutions is not limited to imparting religious education but also rules of civility (*akhlaq o adab*). This emphasis on proper behaviour and etiquette can be supplemented by 'technical' training aiming to transmit practical skills to students so that they can have access to a wider array of job opportunities in India or abroad (especially in the Gulf). As Arshad Alam shows in his recent ethnography of a Barelwi *madrasa* of Eastern UP, Quranic schools can therefore become vectors of extraversion for poor Muslim students, while doting them with some social and cultural capital, 'which in effect give them some degree of mobility'.[32]

However, education is one thing and employment another. Even more so than their Hindu counterparts, educated Muslims are often condemned to 'timepass'—whiling away until they are able to enter the job market. And those educated unemployed Muslims who do not have the luxury to wait are prone to take artisanal work or manual jobs that do not correspond to their level of education, a compromise with high personal costs in terms of self-esteem.[33] Indeed, the fact that Muslims cannot get jobs requiring education because of discriminations is another factor put forward by some scholars to explain the lower literacy and the higher drop-out rates of Muslims.[34] Discrimination in the job market is evident from most of the studies available. Recently, scholars have demonstrated that Muslim applicants to jobs in the private sector were even more affected by selective bias than Dalits. The methodology of testing[35] that they applied made this conclusion perfectly clear.[36] But discriminations are even more marked in the public sector where Muslims are largely under-represented (see Table 3 of the introduction to this volume). Dalits and Adivasis may be victims of similar discrimination, but reservations have a massive compensatory effect and, because of job reservations, 'there is a strong incentive for parents to educate their children'.[37] As a result, Vani K. Borooah argues that, 'if the object of job reservation is to correct for discriminatory bias in the job market, and if reservation is to be extended beyond Dalits, then Muslims have a more compelling case than the Hindu OBCs'.[38]

The manner in which Muslims have felt besieged and have withdrawn into their shell can also be attributed to the increasingly large number of communal riots that affected Muslims in Indian cities—as evident from the number of casualties from this community.[39] Whatever the sources we use (see Annex 1), the available data show an unprecedented wave of communal violence in the late 1980s and early 1990s. Most of these riots have taken place in the

CONCLUSION

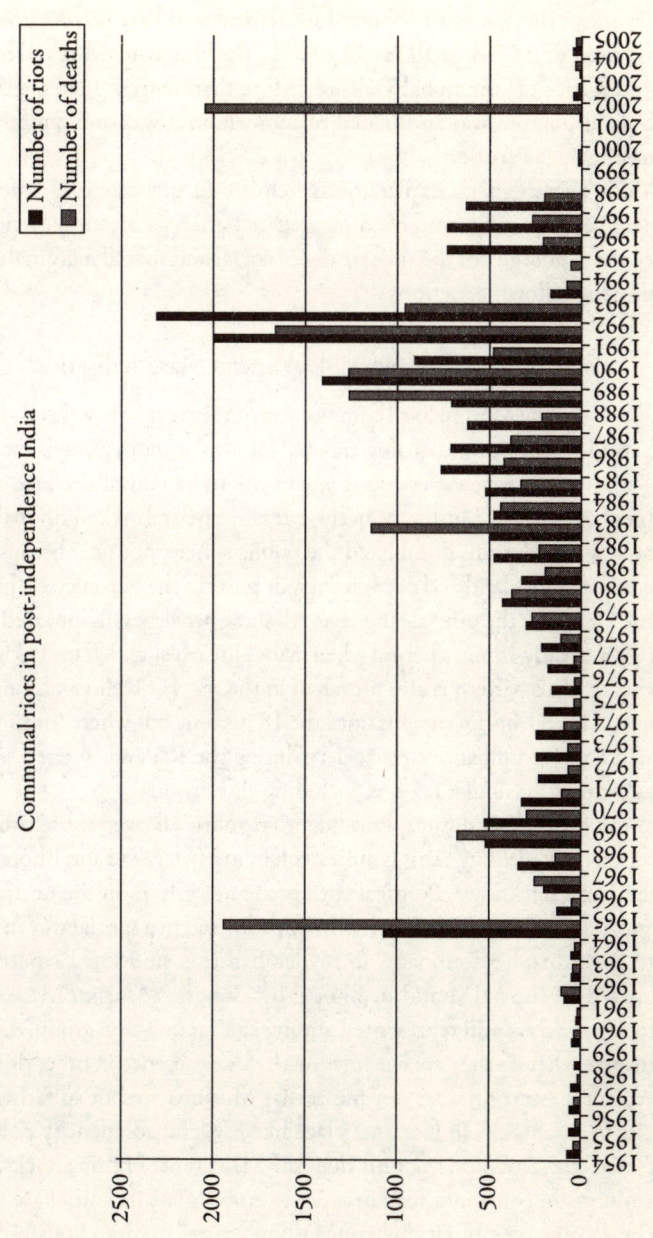

Communal riots in post-independence India

framework of the Ramjanmabhoomi movement and have accompanied the rise to power of the BJP in 1998–99, two election years preceded and marked by a resurgence of communal violence. 'More than ten years later, although the Gujarat pogrom was an isolated phenomenon, it was of unprecedented magnitude since Partition.

While these general explanations help us to put our case studies in perspective, we need to offer a disaggregated analysis of our eleven cities. Hence the typologies of the trajectories of social and spatial marginalisation forming the following sections.

Trajectories of (Irreversible?) Social Marginalisation

While most of the Muslim local communities under review have been affected by Partition—the second major trauma for this minority, after the 1857 one— those who have experienced one of the most radical declines are the inhabitants of former Muslim princely states. In Hyderabad and Bhopal, until the late 1940s, Muslims dominated the public sphere, not only because they owned most of the land and occupied major posts in the bureaucracy, but also because Urdu was the official language. All these privileges disappeared in the late 1940s to early 1950s, a period when many elite Muslims left for Pakistan or elsewhere.[40] This pattern is also prevalent in the cases of Delhi and Lucknow, which had been Muslim capitals until the 1850s only but where Muslims had retained a major influence over society during the Raj and suffered severely from Partition for similar reasons, including elite exodus.

In the former Muslim capitals, identity politics is even more prevalent than elsewhere (although this is more evident in Hyderabad and Bhopal than in Delhi and Lucknow). Political entrepreneurs cash in on the nostalgia of past glories, claiming that Islam has to be protected in a special way in places where it used to be dominant. In Hyderabad this emotional repertoire is articulated by the MIM and in Bhopal by Congress Muslim MLAs. As a result, Muslims are still represented among at least one elite group, the local politicians, whereas they are conspicuous by their absence in other domains. This cultural assertion does not mean that Muslims are not suffering from assaults from outside. In fact, in a place like Hyderabad, identity politics is associated with riots and not only does the MIM resist Hindu attacks, but it also indulges in confrontations in order to consolidate its vote share.

The second type of city where Muslims experienced an equally radical decline combines higher levels of violence with political—and even sometimes

CONCLUSION

cultural—obliteration. The cities in question, both of them in the west, Ahmedabad and Mumbai, are the most riot-prone areas of India. In these traditionally economically dynamic cities, Muslims had never depended upon the landed aristocracy and the bureaucracy-employed literati like in the cities of the first type: their elite was part of the dominant group—the traders and capitalists. Incidentally, while Muslims there are suffering more from violence than elsewhere, they remain richer than almost anywhere else in India. However, Muslims have been sidelined among all elite groups, including the economic ones—except at the medium-size industry level—and have lost their political voice. Not only are Muslim politicians very few (there is no Muslim MP in the whole of Maharashtra and a record under-representation of Muslims among the MLAs of Gujarat), but those who remain in office—mostly on the Congress side—do not articulate any identity politics. This obliteration of the local Muslim identity is imposed from outside where it finds its expression in the (re)naming of Muslim neighbourhoods[41] with Hindu names (like Shivaji Nagar in Mumbai). But it also reflects a form of self-censorship when it results in the erasing of references to anything Islamic (including the Muslim heroes of the past) at the school level. This is evident from some of the new 'Muslim' educational initiatives in Juhapura. These extreme cases of riot-prone areas suggest that 'absorption in the Hindu mass', to use Spear's words, may be the fate awaiting Muslims in these Indian cities. Such trends of cultural occultation seem to be at work even in less riot-prone cities like Delhi—as exemplified by the 'de-Islamised' narrative of their locality produced by the members of Abul Fazl Enclave's Residents Welfare Association. However, these forms of cultural occultation may be tactical[42] and the dynamics of re-Islamisation also at work in Muslim-dominated areas may counter this tendency, with an increasing number of men (and women) turning to religion to redefine their identity and gain social acceptance in their neighbourhood.[43] The future will tell how this tension between re-Islamisation and cultural (self-)occultation will evolve.

The third type, however, comprises cities like Bangalore, Kozhikode and Cuttack, where the resilience of local forms of cosmopolitanism not only enables Muslims to manifest their culture publicly, but also allows them to mix more systematically with non-Muslims. In such contexts, the main cleavages pertain not to religion but to class and caste, as evident from the discrimination affecting the Dalit Muslims of Cuttack within their own community. If the evidence gathered here suggests that this configuration is specific to southern and eastern cities that were least affected by Partition—both in terms of violence and displacements of population—the case of Malerkotla, studied elsewhere by

Anna Bigelow,[44] suggests otherwise. Despite the violence that tore Punjab apart at the time of Partition, this Muslim-majority small town (population 106,802) has preserved the same spirit of 'brotherhood' *(bhaichara)* as the one making the pride of Cuttack Hindu and Muslim residents. Muslims, who constitute 70% of the population, are economically dominant but this does not seem to be resented by the local Hindu minority in any significant way. In other words, pluralistic urban living may prove to be more resilient and widespread than the case studies gathered here tend to suggest. But the case of Malerkotla suggests that the major geographical divide in Muslim trajectories of marginalisation is not so much a north/south phenomenon as one between the Hindi Belt and the west versus the rest. It also confirms the critical role (or the absence thereof) of Partition-related and subsequent communal violence in the resilience of urban cosmopolitism. As in Cuttack or Bangalore, Malerkotla was spared Partition-induced violence and later communal conflicts—a truly remarkable feat in a province that bore the brunt of Partition violence and which was the theatre of a religiously tainted insurgency between 1984 and 1995.

To sum up, we can identify three types of trajectories that qualify the decline of Muslims in the cities of India. The first combines the post-Partition fall and identity politics; the second is over-determined by communal violence and political (sometimes cultural) obliteration; and the third by some resilient cosmopolitism. These are ideal-types which, to paraphrase Weber, nobody meets in reality. First, some 'real' cases fit in two types. Hyderabad, for instance, is also a riot-prone area—somewhat similar to Ahmedabad—and Mumbai Muslims ignore identity politics the Hyderabadi way. But the most influential factors lead us to classify them in two different categories. Second, some case studies do not fit into any of these types. In Aligarh, riots have incited the local Muslims to adopt a low profile, but the AMU has continued to endow the city with a Muslim identity. Third, inner divisions among Muslims do not prevail only in the third type—in Jaipur, Ramganj is identified with low-caste Muslims and in Lucknow sectarian cleavages play a major role. Fourth, these types are dynamic—we are dealing with *trajectories*—and none of them are univocal and linear. The most significant development, in this respect, concerns the growth of Muslim middle classes feeding on strategies of extraversion (including the Gulf connection), the general growth of the Indian economy and a new emphasis on education, even in ghettos like Juhapura where the gathering together of poor and rich Muslims benefits the former—ghetto being a notion to which we need to return to eventually.

CONCLUSION

Patterns of Segregation: Mixed Areas, Enclaves, Slums and Ghettos

As mentioned in the introduction, the expression 'Muslim ghetto' has become part of the common parlance in India today, where it is often synonymous with poverty, parochialism, crime, and even terrorism. Even the critics of these preconceptions tend to sustain the analytical opaqueness of the expression by failing to distinguish between slums and ghettos and by extrapolating from evidence collected in the former definitive assertions on the condition of India's urban Muslims.[45] In fact, fully-fledged 'Muslim ghettos' only developed in cities where communal violence reached an exceptional level, like in Ahmedabad and Mumbai. Instead of ghettos, the most common type of Muslim localities are ethnic enclaves that draw from past (self)segregation of space, some of them being quasi-residential areas while others share more affinities with slums. This distinction between ghettos and ethnic enclaves, recently introduced in urban sociology,[46] can be particularly heuristic in the case of the Muslim localities considered here. It will help us to distinguish, at least theoretically, between 'voluntary' and 'enforced' forms of segregation—although in practice both factors reinforce each other. For instance, the decision of middle-class Muslims to relocate in ethnic enclaves in order to preserve one's culture is often experienced—or at least presented—as a 'choiceless'[47] one, in the face of insecurity or discrimination in the housing market. At the other end of the social ladder, the dynamics of the 'Muslim slum' may vary from one city to another, some being the product of communally tainted state policies and/or of the fear of communal violence (such as Shivaji Nagar, in Mumbai), while others (such as the Muslim slums of Calcutta)[48] are over-determined by economic factors, although—even in a supposedly Muslim-friendly state such as West Bengal[49]— the anti-Muslim bias displayed by government and private recruitment agencies must be accounted for in these processes of social marginalisation translating into spatial segregation.

What 'Mixed Areas'?—The Mosaic Pattern

In most of the cities included in this volume, elderly people expressed the nostalgia of the syncretic culture and of the mixed areas of yesterday, when and where Hindus and Muslims lived together. However, this is partly a myth. As mentioned in the introduction to this volume, Indian cities have always observed some spatial segregation based on caste and religion. This arrangement was not only due to the imprint of the 'Islamic city', where different ethnic groups were separated to avoid clashes, or to the legacy of the 'Hindu city', where castes had to be separated for more ritual reasons. But it also had something to do with contrasting (even antagonistic) customs like rituals and food habits: Hindus—especially from the upper castes—were indisposed by animal sacrifices and the non-vegetarian diet of the Muslims and resented sharing the same space for this reason. Today, vegetarianism is the major argument invoked by Hindu tenants to deny lodging to foul smells-emitting Muslims. In its social implications, this olfactory conflict can be compared to the efforts deployed by the French bourgeoisie of the nineteenth century to insulate itself from the stench of the poor: 'The absence of unpleasant odours permits to distinguish oneself from the foul commoners, stinking like death, like sin, and to justify implicitly the way one handles them'.[50]

Until recently, the response of Indian town-dwellers to the problem of the cosmopolitism inherent in city life generally took the shape of a mosaic in which one could find residents from different creeds, and often of different class, in every alternate street. If the service population often lived side-by-side with wealthy residents in the pre-bourgeois world of urban India,[51] caste-based occupation tended to prevail as an overarching criterion. Thus, Hindu and Muslim businessmen as well as Hindu and Muslim bureaucrats lived together in the same neighbourhoods. In fact, the walled cities encompassed Hindu and Muslim elites—and their dependents—in order to offer them an equally effective protection. While the notion of separation structured space at the micro level, religious communities did cohabit.

This pattern, among the cities we have explored, resisted in the south and in the east only—in Kozhikode, Bangalore and Cuttack. Unsurprisingly, this state of affairs corresponds to cities of our third type, retaining a form of mixity inherited from the past. Elsewhere, processes of local homogenisation (often non-linear) resulted in the formation of enclaves and, more exceptionally, of ghettos.

Enclaves: (Self-)segregation and the Quest for Security

The making of Muslim enclaves often resulted from two cumulative effects. On one hand, it reflected the old desire—mentioned above about the mosaic pattern—to share a common space with members of the same community for cultural reasons. For a long time, some Muslims, particularly the most affluent, have been regrouping in order to protect their religion-based culture—or their distinct caste and sectarian identity in the case of Lucknow Shias, as well as Bohras, Khojas and Memons in the cities of Gujarat and Maharashtra. Today,

CONCLUSION

some parents attempt to keep their children from being exposed to Hindu influences, which would 'corrupt' them. This motivation is especially strong in the cities where militant Hinduism makes the observance of Islam more difficult in mixed areas.[52] On the other hand, the urge to regroup within enclaves is fostered by the problems Muslims face in the mixed areas where they are in a minority. Not only has it become difficult for Muslims to rent or buy a property in these areas, but safety is no longer guaranteed—including in middle-class residential areas, as exemplified by the massacres of the Muslim residents of Rishi Galav Nagar in Jaipur in 1990 and of Gulberg Society in Ahmedabad in 2002. Discrimination and security imperatives are mutually reinforcing factors in the making of Muslim enclaves. Self-segregation, which was already present in the mosaic pattern, is therefore amplified by unequal access to the housing market and by insecurity (or feelings of insecurity)[53] to create Muslims enclaves.

The response of the state, and in particular of the judiciary, to the burgeoning of such ethnic enclaves (a phenomenon that is not restricted to Muslims, although the element of constraint may be stronger in their case) must also be taken into account. The Cooperative Societies Act, which regulates housing societies across India, explicitly prohibits the formation of housing societies where membership would be 'confined to persons of a particular persuasion, religion, belief or region'.[54] However, the commitment of the judiciary to promote pluralistic urban living has been receding in recent years, making way for a more accommodating position towards such 'colonies', as suggested by the 2005 judgment of the Supreme Court on this matter.[55] For its critics, this judgment could reinforce dynamics of ghettoisation already at work in states such as Gujarat, by encouraging the formation of Hindu enclaves *de jure* inaccessible to Muslims and in the other direction by legalising the creation of Muslim 'Bantustans'.

Muslim enclaves did not spring up suddenly. In most cases, those who were pushed to 'safe' areas by communal violence settled in localities that already had a substantial Muslim population.[56] For this reason, these enclaves are not always homogenous in terms of caste and class. Some of them, such as Sir Syed Nagar in Aligarh, are truly residential areas restricted to the most affluent local Muslims. Others, such as Abul Fazl Enclave in Delhi, have a socially more diverse population, with lower middle-class Muslims coexisting with successful but insecure professionals and entrepreneurs. This social diversity may be only temporary, though, as the continuous rise in land prices in these Muslim enclaves and their subsequent gentrification risks pushing the poorer residents to slums and ghettos.

LAURENT GAYER AND CHRISTOPHE JAFFRELOT

The Elusive Ghetto

The urban Muslim poor increasingly regroup in backward Muslim-dominated neighbourhoods or even 'Muslim slums' in cities where they are segregated within their own community (like the Qasais of Cuttack) or/and where they are victims of communal violence like in Mumbai. Shivaji Nagar, in this megalopolis, epitomises the notion of a 'Muslim slum', although it also presents several characteristics of a ghetto, with its relative class diversity and the stigmatisation and sense of alienation of its residents.

In fact, few localities examined in this book conform to the whole set of criteria of a ghetto presented in our introduction. The most emblematic, in this regard, is Juhapura in Ahmedabad. This is certainly not the only locality of India where affluent Muslims have resigned themselves to living alongside their poorer coreligionists, nor is it the most dilapidated. But in addition to these two criteria, in Juhapura, as in some other localities of Gujarat,[57] boundary walls have been erected to defend the locality, a rather extreme form of 'border' between Hindu- and Muslim-dominated localities.[58] Like many other Muslims of Gujarat, the residents of Juhapura cannot easily leave the ghetto, not only because of the absence of public transportation, but also because Juhapura residents are not welcome elsewhere, as exemplified by one of them, interviewed by anthropologist Rowena Robinson:

'Yes, we are safe here. But how is this? They [Hindus] close off all our options to move out from here. We are confined here, but within two or three months of the riots they started coming here. They bring their carts and park them here, and bring their goods into our area to sell. But our people are not allowed to go out and cannot venture into their areas.'[39]

Rather than at a dynamic of self-segregation, what this resident of Juhapura points at here is the unequal right to the city of Hindus and Muslims in BJP-ruled Gujarat. Juhapura residents did not choose to relocate there but were constrained to do so by the security situation, a product of the state-sanctioned discrimination and persecution of the Muslim population. The fact that Juhapura is the only locality covered in this book that fully conforms to our intentionally restrictive definition of the 'Muslim ghetto' singles out the role of extreme communal violence in the formation of the most paradigmatic 'neighbourhoods of exile' of India. It should be recalled here that the 2002 pogrom was accompanied by mass killings but also by systematic episodes of ethnic cleansing, during which Muslims were forcefully evicted from 'mixed areas'.

CONCLUSION

If the Muslim ghettos of Ahmedabad and other cities of Gujarat constitute the most blatant illustration of the relegation of Muslims in Indian cities, it would be misleading to reduce the problem of Muslim ghettoisation to a regional exception. Although a city like Jaipur was far less intensely affected by communal violence than Ahmedabad, the return of insecure middle-class Muslims to the dilapidated walled city they had deserted for more residential and mixed areas, reveals another ghetto in the making. In the case of Mumbai, Sameera Khan suggests that the ghettoisation of Muslims can take different shapes, from 'ruthless' to more 'subtle' forms of segregation.[60] The case studies presented here also tell us of other routes towards ghettoisation, less directly related to Hindu-Muslim violence. This is the case, for instance, of Kashmiri Mohalla in Lucknow, a 'royal slum' where the destitute nobility and the lower sections of the Shia community coexist in a dilapidated environment, largely insulated from an otherwise bustling city. Here as well, violence played a crucial role in the regrouping of the residents around a common religious (or more specifically, here, sectarian) affiliation. However, unlike the residents of Shivaji Nagar and even more so of Juhapura, the Shias of Kashmiri Mohalla did not regroup in a context of Hindu-Muslim violence but of intra-Muslim conflict, following a series of sectarian riots between Sunnis and Shias. This tends to confirm that the ongoing ghettoisation of Indian Muslims in Indian cities, at least in its most blatant form, is primarily the outcome of organised violence—be it communal or, more rarely, sectarian—and only secondly of economic marginalisation or discrimination in the housing market.

The case studies presented here also bring to our attention the irreducibility of individual trajectories to linear and unequivocal collective trends. As Rowena Robinson points out in her study of Muslim survivors of communal violence, the displacement of Muslim families in the aftermath of the Mumbai riots or the Gujarat pogrom often happened gradually and, more often than not, was 'the result of a combination of circumstances'.[61] The ethnographic evidence presented in several contributions to this volume confirms this and extends the argument to the regrouping of Muslims who were not directly affected by communal violence. Entering into the 'mini-Pakistans' of contemporary Indian cities—often to the great dismay of Hindu residents of adjacent localities—the contributors help us visualise the micro-dynamics at work in the new social geography of Indian cities. And it is this ethnographic evidence, which, ultimately, offers a glimpse of hope, by pointing at the idiosyncratic but relentless efforts of many urban Muslims to counter the segregation imposed on them, as well as their own inclination towards cultural protectionism.

In the cities affected by such processes of ghettoisation, the 'easy idiom of shared lives'[62] will be insufficient to bridge the increasing gap between Hindus and Muslims. Preserving, let alone promoting pluralistic urban living—the 'enhancement of diversity' advocated by the authors of the Sachar Committee Report[63]—will require more work from the political society but also from the state, which all too often has renounced providing security to all its citizens irrespective of their caste or religion. The *mohalla* committees set up in Mumbai and Jaipur, among other cities, to prevent further communal flare-ups, could be a move in the right direction.[64]

ANNEX

HINDU/MUSLIM RIOTS IN POST-INDEPENDENCE INDIA

Year	Number of riots		Number of deaths	
	Various sources (see below)	Varshney/Wilkinson dataset[1]	Various sources	Varshney/Wilkinson dataset
1950	–	50	–	167
1951	–	7	–	10
1952	–	13	–	7
1953	–	23	–	27
1954	83	17	34	10
1955	72	13	24	12
1956	74	12	35	29
1957	55	11	12	8
1958	41	2	7	0
1959	42	1	41	0
1960	26	10	14	13
1961	92	32	108	112
1962	60	16	43	27
1963	61	4	26	8
1964	1070	34	1919*	146
1965	NA	6	NA	6
1966	133	8	45	33
1967	209	14	251	56
1968	346	10	133	55
1969	519	38	674	718
1970	521	33	298	216
1971	321	10	103	28
1972	240	11	70	33

327

ANNEX

Year				
1973	242	14	72	35
1974	248	14	87	21
1975	205	10	33	15
1976	169	3	39	0
1977	188	10	36	17
1978	219	27	108	76
1979	304	6	261	124
1980	427	38	375	203
1981	319	22	196	105
1982	474	44	238	98
1983	500	26	1 143**	84
1984	476	44	445	342
1985	525	42	328	158
1986	764	108	418	243
1987	711	75	383	230
1988	611	14	223	88
1989	706	48	1155	521
1990	1404	107	1248	596
1991	905	41	474	161
1992	1991	76	1640	1337
1993	2292	32	952	750
1994	179	9	78	35
1995	40	7	62	11
1996	728	–	209	–
1997	725	–	264	–
1998	626	–	207	–
1999	NA	–	NA	–
2000	26	–	23	–
2001	34	–	52	–
2002	21*	–	2032**	–
2003	52	–	21	–
2004	11	–	34	–
2005	45	–	31	–
2006	28	–	31	–
2007	27	–	17***	–
2008	28	–	152****	–
2009	28	–	23	–

* The Gujarat violence is considered here as one riot only.
** Including 2000 Gujarat casualties.
*** Anti-Christian riots that occurred in Kandhamal district and which claimed 12 lives are not counted here.
**** Anti-Christian riots that occurred in Kandhamal district and that claimed more than 50 lives are not counted here.

ANNEX

Sources: For 1954-85, P. Brass, *The Politics of India since Independence,* Cambridge: Cambridge University Press, 1990, p. 168;

For 1986-88, figures released by the government in parliament and published in *India Today,* 15 October 1990, p. 24 and 15 January 1991, p. 26;

For 1989 and 1990, Communication from the Minister of State for Home before the Rajya Sabha and published in *National Mail (Bhopal),* 18 July 1991;

For 1991 and 1992, *Muslim India,* no. 134, February 1994;

For 1993 and 1994, 'Ministry of Home Affairs. Note for Consultative Committee Meeting on Communal Situation', *Muslim India,* no. 156, December 1995, p. 558;

For 1995, A.A. Engineer, 'Communalism and communal violence in 1995', *Economic and Political Weekly,* 23 December 1995, pp. 3267–3269;

For 1996, 1997 and 1998, Lok Sabha questions, no. 110, 23 February 1999, reproduced in *Muslim India,* no. 196, April 1999, p. 161;

For 2000, A.A. Engineer, 'Communal riots, 2000', *Economic and Political Weekly,* 27 January 2001;

For 2001, A.A. Engineer, 'Communal riots, 2001', (http://www.indianmuslims.info);

For 2002, A.A. Engineer, 'Communal riots in 2002—A survey', *Economic and Political Weekly,* 25 January 2003, pp. 280-282;

For 2003, A.A. Engineer, 'Communal riots 2003', *Muslim India,* 22 (2), January 2004, pp. 15-18;

For 2004, A.A. Engineer, 'Communal riots 2004', *Muslim India,* 22 (11/12), November-December 2004, pp. 1241-1243;

For 2005, 'Communal riots 2005', Indian Social Institute (http://www.isidelhi.com);

For 2006, A.A. Engineer, 'Communal riots 2006, A Review', PUCL (People's Union for Civil Liberties) Bulletin (http://www.pucl.org/Topics/Religion-communalism/2007/review.html);

For 2007, A.A. Engineer, 'Communal riots 2007', (http://indianmuslims.in/communal-riots-report-2007/);

For 2008, A.A. Engineer, 'Communal riots 2008', Centre for the Study of Society and Secularism, Mumbai (http://indianmuslims.in/communal-riots-2008/);

For 2009, A.A. Engineer, 'Communal riots 2009', Centre for the Study of Society and Secularism, Mumbai (http://www.sacw.net/articlel315.html)

Nota Bene: Other sources give similar results. See, for instance, Ashutosh Varshney, *Ethnic Conflict and Civic Life. Hindus and Muslims in India,* New Heaven: Yale University Press, 2002, p. 95; Steven Wilkinson, *Votes and Violence. Electoral Competition and Ethnic Riots in India,* Cambridge: Cambridge University Press, 2004, p. 12; Gopal Krishna, 'Communal violence in India', *Economic and Political Weekly,* 12 January 1985, p. 71; N.S. Saksena, *Communal Violence in India,* Noida: Trishul, 1990; P.R. Rajagopal, *Communal Violence in India,* New Delhi: Uppal Publishing House, 1987.

NOTES

INTRODUCTION: MUSLIMS OF THE INDIAN CITY. FROM CENTRALITY TO MARGINALITY

1. Projection based on the data collected for the 2001 Census and the current rate of growth of this population. The Sachar Committee Report suggested that there were 150 million Muslims living in India in 2006 (*Social, Economic and Educational Status of the Muslim Community of India—A Report* (hereafter Sachar Committee Report), Prime Minister's High Level Committee Cabinet Secretariat, Government of India, November 2006, p. 27).
2. On the socio-political trajectory of this minority, see Mushirul Hasan, *Legacy of a Divided Nation. India's Muslims since Independence*, London: Hurst, 1996.
3. For another perspective on the Partition of India, emphasising the role of the Congress in the creation of Pakistan, see Ayesha Jalal, *The Sole Spokesman. Jinnah, the Muslim League and the Demand for Pakistan*, Cambridge: Cambridge University Press, 1985.
4. Jammu and Kashmir is the only state with a Muslim majority. Out of the 593 districts in the country, only twenty have a Muslim majority.
5. Rowena Robinson, *Tremors of Violence. Muslim Survivors of Ethnic Strife in Western India*, Delhi: Sage, 2005, p. 78.
6. In 1980, the Congress government had appointed a 'high powered panel' which came to be known as the 'Gopal Singh Committee' after the name of its head. This committee submitted a 118-page-long report (with 205 annexures describing the situation of the Muslims of India in every respect) on 14 June 1983. Its release was delayed several times and none of its recommendations implemented.
7. So far, only castes, Other Backward Classes (which turned out to be castes too) and tribes had been surveyed that way.
8. Sachar Committee Report, Prime Minister's High Level Committee Cabinet Secretariat, Government of India, November 2006, pp. 91–96.

NOTES

9. The Sachar Committee has generated research work which could not always be used in the final report but whose findings have been made available recently by two key figures of the Committee, Rakesh Basant and Abusaleh Shariff, who, on the basis of these working papers, have edited a remarkable handbook: Basant Rakesh and Shariff Abusaleh (eds), *Handbook of 'Muslims in India, Empirical and Policy Perspectives*, Delhi: Oxford University Press, 2010.
10. 'NSS, Employment and Unemployment Survey, 2004–05' cited in Jeemol Unni, 'Informality and Gender in the Labour Market for Muslims', in Basant Rakesh and Shariff Abusaleh (eds), *Handbook of Muslims in India*, op. cit., p. 222.
11. *Sachar Committee Report*. 153.
12. Ibid., p. 157.
13. Sumon Kumar Bhaumik and Manisha Chakrabarty, 'Earnings Inequality. The Impact of the Rise of Caste- and Religion-based Politics?', in Basant Rakesh and Shariff Abusaleh (eds), *Handbook of Muslims in India*, op cit., p. 239.
14. Jeemol Unni, 'Informality and Gender in the Labour Market for Muslims', in Basant Rakesh and Shariff Abusaleh (eds), *Handbook of Muslims in India*, op. cit., p. 228.
15. Sonia Bhalotra and Bernarda Zamora, 'Social Divisions in Education in India', in Basant Rakesh and Shariff Abusaleh (eds), *Handbook of Muslims in India*, op cit., p. 167.
16. The Muslims of India also have the lowest rate of 'pacca' housing (23.76%, compared to an average of 34.63%) (*Report of the National Commission for Religious and Linguistic Minorities* (Hereafter Mishra Commission Report), vol. 1, New Delhi, Ministry of Minority Affairs, 2007, p. 23).
17. *Mishra Commission Report*, vol. 1, op. cit., p. 84.
18. *Mishra Commission Report*, vol. 2, p. 41 and p. 43.
19. *Sachar Committee Report*, op. cit., fig. 4.25, p. 97.
20. Ibid.
21. *Mishra Commission Report*, vol. 1, op. cit., p. 150.
22. Ibid., pp. 152–153.
23. See the special issue of *The Organiser*, the RSS's mouthpiece entitled 'Shrinking Space of the Hindu—Sachar to Ranganath' (vol. LXI, no. 30, January 2010) and especially the editorial (R. Balashankar, 'Hindus: Deprived, Discriminated and Robbed', pp. 6–7) and the following articles: Dr. J.K. Bajaj, 'A period of minority assertion, Hindu subjugation', pp. 20–21; and Joginder Singh, former director of CBI, 'How long and how far? End this appeasement', pp. 27–28.
24. Manas Dasgupta, '15 points in 90 districts', *The Hindu*, 26 December 2010.
25. Shabnam Hashmi, Harsh Mander and Ram Puniyani (eds), *In defence of democracy*, New Delhi: ANHAD, 2007, pp. 65–67.
26. Shabnam Hashmi (ed.), *What it means to be a Muslim in India Today. A combined report of People's Tribunal on the Atrocities Committed against the*

NOTES

Minorities in the name of Fighting Terrorism and National Meet on the Status of Muslims in Contemporary India, New Delhi: ANHAD, 2011, p. 12.

27. Christophe Jaffrelot with Virginie Dutoya, Radhika Kanchana and Gayatri Rathore, 'Understanding Muslim voting behaviour' *Seminar*, no. 602, 2009, pp. 43–48.
28. Iqbal A. Ansari, *Political Representation of Muslims in India (1952–2004)*, Delhi: Manak, 2006, p. 370.
29. Mushirul Hasan, *Legacy of a Divided Nation*, op. cit., pp. 194–195.
30. C. Jaffrelot, 'The Muslims of India: Towards Marginalisation?', in C. Jaffrelot (ed.), *India since 1950. Society, Politics, Economy and Culture*, New Delhi: Gatra Books, 2011, pp. 564–580.
31. Marc Gaborieau, *Un Autre Islam. Inde, Pakistan, Bangladesh*, Paris: Albin Michel, 2007, p. 291.
32. Zoya Hassan, *Politics of Inclusion. Castes, Minorities and Affirmative Action*, Delhi: Oxford University Press, 2009, p. 165. See also Violette Graff, 'Muslims and Polities', in C. Jaffrelot (ed.), *India since 1950*, op. cit., pp. 581–609.
33. For a recent, unsystematic, survey of the diversity of Indian Muslims, see Vinod K. Jairath (ed.), *Frontiers of embedded Muslim communities in India*, New Delhi: Routledge, 2011.
34. The conformity of Indian Muslims' patterns of social organisation to a 'caste' system has been a matter of debate among anthropologists since the 1960s. For a reappraisal of these debates, in the context of Hyderabad, see Syed Ali, 'Collective and Elective Ethnicity: Caste among Urban Muslims in India', *Sociological Forum*, 17 (4), Dec. 2002, pp. 593–620.
35. Marc Gaborieau, *Un Autre Islam.*, op. cit., pp. 204 sq. and 'The Muslims of India. A Minority of 170 Million, in C. Jaffrelot (ed.), *India since 1950*, op. cit., pp. 533–557.
36. The Ashraf/Ajlaf cleavage is more pronounced among the Muslims of North India than among their co-religionists of the south and the east; for an overview of these regional variations, see Mattison Mines, 'Muslim Social Stratification in India: The Basis for Variation', *Southwestern Journal of Anthropology*, 28 (4), Winter 1972, pp. 333–349.
37. Zarina Bhatty, 'Status and Power in a Muslim Dominated Village of Uttar Pradesh', in Imtiaz Ahmad (ed.), *Caste and Social Stratification among Muslims in India*, Delhi: Manohar, 1978, pp. 207–224.
38. Individuals can make a claim to higher social status by changing their occupation, and entire castes can make attempts at upward social mobility by claiming foreign ancestry and by emulating the behaviour of upper castes, so as to claim Ashraf status—a process known as 'Ashrafization'.
39. Syed Ali, 'Collective and Elective Ethnicity', art. quoted, p. 614.
40. Margrit Pernau, 'Middle Class and Secularization: The Muslims of Delhi in the

Nineteenth Century', in Imtiaz Ahmad and Heimut Reifeld (eds), *Middle Class Values in India and Western Europe*, Delhi: Social Science Press, 2001, pp. 21–41.
41. Syed Ali, 'Collective and Elective Ethnicity', art. quoted.
42. Satish Saberwal, 'On the Making of Muslims in India Historically' in Basant Rakesh and Shariff Abusaleh (eds), *Handbook of Muslims in India.*, op. cit., p. 57.
43. As exemplified, for instance, by Maulana Ashraf Ali Thanawi's *Bahishti Zewar* (Heavenly Ornaments), published in 1905.
44. Barbara Metcalf, *Islamic Revival in British India. Deoband, 1860–1900*, Princeton: Princeton University Press, 1982, p. 245-246.
45. Shail Mayaram, *Resisting Regimes, Myth, Memory and the Shaping of a Muslim Identity*, Delhi: Oxford University Press, p. 245.
46. Satish Saberwal, 'On the Making of Muslims in India Historically', op. cit., p. 58.
47. On this organisation and more generally on 'Dalit Muslims', see Yoginder Sikand, *Islam, Caste and Dalit-Muslim Relations in India*, Delhi: Global Media Publications, 2004.
48. Yoginder Sikand, *Muslims in India since 1947*, London/New York: Routledge-Curzon, 2004, p. 111; S. Ubaidur Rahman, *Understanding the Muslim leadership in India*, Delhi: Global Media Publications, 2004, pp. 71-74.
49. Cited in L. Jenkins, 'Caste, class and Islam: boundaries of backwardness in India', *The Eastern Anthropologist*, vol 53, no. 3-4 (2000), p. 330.
50. Sampradaan, *Giving and Fund Raising in India. Religious Philanthropy and Organized Social Development Efforts in India*, Delhi: Sampradaan, Indian Center for Philanthropy, 2001.
51. The JI-H always had a policy of restricted membership. But if the 'full-fledged members' (*arkan*) were only 4,776 in 2000, the number of 'workers' (*karkun*) was much higher and estimated at 270,246; cf. Irfan Ahmad, *Islamism and Democracy in India. The Transformation of Jama'at-e-Islami*, Princeton: Princeton University Press, 2009, appendix 1, p. 240.
52. HWF, Vision 2016. Creating Partnership with the Needy, Delhi, n.d, p. 13.
53. NSS 55th Round, July 1999–June 2000 cited in the Mishra Commission Report, vol. 1, op. cit., p. 25.
54. These ten-year-old figures have been reconfirmed in 2004–05 by another survey, the All India Head Count. It has shown that 'SCs/STs together are the most poor [sic] with a Head Count Ratio (HCR) of 35 percent, followed by the Muslims who record the second highest incidence of poverty with 31 percent people below the poverty line. Incidence of poverty among Muslims in urban areas is the highest with HCR of 38.4 percent. The Hindu (general) is the least poor category with an HCR of only 8.7 percent and the OBCs are at intermediary level of HCR of 21 percent, close to the all India average'. Cited in the Mishra Commission Report, vol. 1, op. cit., p. 107.
55. Abusaleh Shariff, 'Spiritual Capital and Philanthropy among Muslims', in Basant Rakesh and Shariff Abusaleh (eds), *Handbook of Muslims in India*, op. cit., p. 255.

NOTES

56. Ibid., p. 263.
57. In Delhi, for instance, the Vishva Hindu Parishad protested the lease of 123 proprieties to the local Waqf board for a period of 99 years. Finally, no specific body was formed to supervise the retrocession of these proprieties to the Waqf board and encroachments continued; cf. Muhammad Arshad, 'Azad Hindustan main Auqaf ki Surat-e-Hal' (Urdu) [The Situation of the Auqaf in Independent India], in Pervez Rehmani and Muhammad Arshad (eds), *Hindustani Musulman. Musulman-e-Hind ki Qadim o Jadid Tarikh aur Mojudah Surat-e-Hal ka ek Jaezah* (*Urdu*) [Indian Muslims. A Study of the Ancient and Modern History and of the Present Condition of the Muslims of India], Delhi: Dawat Publications, 2001, p. 94.
58. The only two Waqf boards administered by Shias are situated in Bihar and Uttar Pradesh. In all other provinces, the proprieties of the Shia Auqaf are administered by Sunni Auqaf boards; ibid., p. 95.
59. Mohammad Rizwanul Haque, 'Waqf Experience in India', in Syed Khalid Rashid (ed.), *Awqaf Experiences in South Asia*, Delhi: Institute of Objective Studies, 2002, p. 125.
60. On the waqf issue and the reform, *see Parliament of India—Rajya Sabha, Ninth report of joint parliamentary on waqf*, New Delhi: Rajya Sabha Secretariat, 2008, p. 286.
61. Loïc Wacquant, *Urban Outcasts. A Comparative Sociology of Advanced Marginality*, Cambridge: Polity Press, 2008, p. 9.
62. Many studies mistakenly take cities as relevant units of analysis when, in fact, localities within these cities are at the right level. See Christophe Jaffrelot's review of Ashutosh Varshney, 'Ethnic conflict and civic life: Hindus and Muslims in India', *Perspective on Politics*, vol. l, no. 3, 2003, pp. 636–637.
63. Loïc Wacquant, *Urban Outcasts*, op. cit., p. 8. The author is here referring to the ghettos of French and American cities.
64. Finbarr B. Flood, *Objects of Translation. Material Culture and Medieval 'Hindu-Muslim' Encounter*, Princeton: Princeton University Press, 2009.
65. Jackie Assayag, *At the Confluence of Two Rivers. Muslims and Hindus in South India*, Delhi: Manohar, 2004.
66. Sunil Kumar, *The Emergence of the Delhi Sultanate*, Delhi: Permanent Black, 2010, p. 100.
67. Ibid., p. 128.
68. Often credited with the diffusion of Islam in the Indian subcontinent, Sufi missionaries were not always men of peace and sometimes excelled in the arts of war as well; in the case of Bijapur, see Richard M. Eaton, *Sufis of Bijapur, 1300–1700*, Princeton: Princeton University Press, 1978.
69. On the circulation of Muslim elites to and within the Deccan during the medieval period, see Richard M. Eaton, *A Social History of the Deccan, 1300–1761: Eight Indian Lives, The New Cambridge History of India*, vol. 1, no 8, Cambridge: Cambridge University Press, 2005.

NOTES

70. Sanjay Subrahmanyam, 'Iranians Abroad: Intra-Asian Elite Migration and Early Modern State Formation', *Journal of Asian Studies*, 51 (2), May 1992, p. 342.
71. After his victory over the Lodhi sultans at Panipat in 1526, Babur skipped Delhi and established his capital in Agra. His son Humayun returned to Delhi, before fleeing to the Afghan highlands and Iran following Sher Shah's revolt, finally returning in Delhi in 1556. Akbar, for his part, made Delhi his capital for only eight years, preferring Agra. Jehangir spent most of his reign in Lahore and it is only under Shah Jahan that Delhi regained its imperial glory.
72. *Tuzuk-i-Jahangiri*, translated by Alexander Rogers, edited by Henry Beveridge, Delhi: Munshiram Manoharlal Publishers, 1978, p. 3.
73. J.E. Richards, *The Mughal Empire*, *The New Cambridge History of India*, 1.5, Cambridge: Cambridge University Press, 1996, p. 12.
74. Iranian migration to Hyderabad stopped in the early 1950s except for a handful of political refugees and a small number of women married to third- or fourth-generation 'Iranis'; cf. Vinod K. Jairath and Huma R. Kidwai, 'We are different from Shias here; we are different from Iranians there: Irani Shias in Hyderabad', in Vinod K. Jairath (ed.), *Frontiers of Embedded Muslim Communities in India*, Delhi: Routledge, 2010, p. 54.
75. C.A. Bayly, *Rulers, Townsmen and Bazaars. North Indian Society in the Age of British Expansion*, Delhi: OUP, 1992, p. 348.
76. Mushirul Hasan, *From Pluralism to Separatism. Qasbas in Colonial Awadh*, Delhi: Oxford University Press, 2004, p. 16.
77. Justin Jones, 'The Local Experiences of Reformist Islam in a "Muslim" Town in Colonial India: The Case of Amroha', *Modern Asian Studies*, 43 (4), 2009, pp. 871–908.
78. Mushirul Hasan, *From Pluralism to Separatism*, op. cit., p. 17.
79. This genre found its roots in Persian and Turkish poetry and started developing in India in the twelfth century, around poets such as Masud bin Sad Salman (d. 1116) and later on, Amir Khusrau (d. 1324). It gradually gave shape to 'a style of poetry in which there were light-hearted descriptions of the beauty of young boys in the various professions, and praise or disparagement of a city or its residents'; Satish Chandra, 'Cultural and Political Role of Delhi, 1675–1725', in Robert Frykenberg (ed.), *Delhi through the Ages. Selected Essays in Urban History, Culture and Society*, Delhi: OUP, 2006 [1986], p. 118, note 32.
80. Ayesha Jalal, *Self and Sovereignty. Individual and Community in South Asian Islam Since 1850*, Delhi: OUP, 2001, p. 11.
81. Quoted in Khurshidul Islam and Ralph Russell, *Three Mughal Poets. Mir, Sauda, Mir Hasan*, Delhi: OUP, 2006 [1969], p. 260.
82. Ayesha Jalal, *Self and Sovereignty*, op. cit., p. 13.
83. Ibid., p. 10.
84. See the analysis of Jurat's 'Mukhammas-i-Shahr Ashob', in Frances W. Pritchett,

NOTES

'The World Turned Upside Down: Sahr-Asob as a Genre', *Annual of Urdu Studies*, vol. 4, 1984, p. 39. On the anti-plebeian bias of the *shahr ashob*, see also Ishrat Haqe, *Glimpses of Mughal Society and Culture*, Delhi: Concept Publishing Company, 1992, p. 71 sq.

85. As Janet Abu-Lughod has shown, the model of the Islamic city was coined by Orientalists on the basis of a limited sample of primarly North African cities, and many other cities of the Muslim world were at odds with this model. Nonetheless, Abu-Lughod concedes that legal disctinctions between believers and non-believers, leading to their physical estrangement, as well as the imperative of sexual segregation and the autonomy by default of residential neighbourhoods did make an imprint over most cities of the Muslim world. And however mythical it may have been, the idea of the Islamic city proved to be and has remained an important source of inspiration for Muslim architects and town-planners; cf. Janet L. Abu-Lughod, 'The Islamic City: Historic Myth, Islamic Essence and Contemporary Relevance', *International Journal of Middle East Studies*, 19 (2), 1987, pp. 155–176.

86. Xavier de Planhol, *The World of Islam*, Ithaca: Cornell University Press, 1966, p. 9.

87. For a reappraisal of the 'Islamic City' model in the study of the cities of Mughal India, see Eckart Ehlers and Thomas Krafft, 'Islamic Cities in India? Theoretical Concepts and the Case of Shajahanabad/Old Delhi', in Eckart Ehlers and Thomas Krafft (eds), *Shajahanabad/Old Delhi. Tradition and Colonial Change*, Delhi: Manohar, 2003, pp. 11–27.

88. Charles Lindholm, 'Caste in Islam and the Problem of Deviant Systems: A Critique of Recent Theory', in T.N. Madan (ed.), *Muslim Communities of South Asia. Culture, Society and Power*, Delhi: Manohar, 2001 (1976), p. 490.

89. Stephen P. Blake, *Shahjahanabad. The Sovereign City in Mughal India 1639–1739*, Cambridge: Cambridge University Press, 1991, p. 35.

90. Eckart Ehlers and Thomas Krafft, 'Islamic Cities in India?', art. quoted, p. 19.

91. James L. Wescoat Jr., 'Gardens, Urbanization and Urbanism in Mughal Lahore: 1526–1657', in James L. Wescoat Jr. and Joachim Wolschke-Bulmahn (eds), *Mughal Gardens. Sources, Places, Representations, and Prospects*, Washington: Dumbarton Oaks, 1996, pp. 139–170.

92. Although the access to most Mughal gardens was restricted to the nobility, some were open to the general public (such as, with restrictions, the garden of the Taj Mahal); cf. Irfan Habib, 'Notes on the Social and Economic Aspects of Mughal Gardens', in James L. Wescoat Jr. and Joachim Wolschke-Bulmahn (eds), *Gardens*, op. cit., p. 135 sq.

93. Stephen P. Blake, *Shahjahanabad*, op. cit., p. 49.

94. Sunil Khilnani, *The Idea of India*, London: Hamish Hamilton, 1997, p. 110.

95. C.A. Bayly, *Rulers, Townsmen and Bazars*, op. cit., chap. 6.

96. Ibid., p. 234.

97. Ibid., p. 440.

NOTES

98. Ibid., p. 439.
99. Ibid., p. 447.
100. Ibid.
101. Sunil Khilnani, *The Idea of India*, op. cit., p. 109.
102. C.A. Bayly, *Rulers, Townsmen and Bazars*, op. cit., p. 450.
103. Christophe Jaffrelot, *La démocratie en Inde. Religion, caste et politique*, Paris: Fayard, 1998.
104. C.A. Bayly, *Rulers, Townsmen and Bazars*, op. cit., p. 450.
105. Ibid., p. 456.
106. David Gilmartin, *Empire and Islam. Punjab and the Making of Pakistan*, Delhi: OUP, 1988, p. 213.
107. C.A. Bayly, *Rulers, Townsmen and Bazars*, op. cit., p. 456.
108. Sunil Khilnani, *The Idea of India*, op. cit., p. 124.
109. This continuity is made explicit in the opening chapter of the novel, where Ali quotes the verses of Mir Taqi Mir reproduced above, which he recited on his arrival in Lucknow in 1782.
110. Ahmed Ali, *Twilight in Delhi*, New York: New Directions Publishing, 1994 [1940], p. 4.
111. Anita Desai, *In Custody*, Delhi: Random House, 2007 [1984].
112. For a critical discussion of *In Custody*, see Amina Yaqin, 'The Communalization and Disintegration of Urdu in Anita Desai's *In Custody*', in Ather Farouqui (ed.), *Redefining Urdu Politics in India*, Delhi: Oxford University Press, 2010, pp. 108-127.
113. Sachar Committee Report, p. 14.
114. Loic Wacquant, *Urban Outcasts*, op. cit., p. 8.
115. Ibid., p. 49.
116. Louis Wirth, *The Ghetto*, Chicago: Chicago University Press, 1964 [1928], p. 285.
117. A point also made by Didier Lapeyronnie, *Ghetto urbain. Ségrégation, violence, pauvreté en France aujourd'hui*, Paris: Robert Laffont, 2008, p. 12.

1. 'UNWANTED IN MY CITY'—THE MAKING OF A 'MUSLIM SLUM' IN MUMBAI

1. All the names used here are pseudonyms.
2. According to the 1901 Census, these areas were Chakla, Umarkhadi, Kharatalao, Nagpada, Mandvi and Dongri, which still have a significant proportion of Muslims.
3. The spatial concentration of Muslims, commonly referred to as the *mohalla*, was a term introduced by the Mughals for an administrative division of the city and has since been associated with Muslim neighbourhoods. The Marathi words *wada* and *wadi* were used in reference to Hindu localities and *chawl* referred to working-class neighbourhoods. See Masselos (2007a) and Chandavarkar (1994).

NOTES

4. Entire *mohallas* were identified (for certain parts even within 1901 Census data) with specific, at times occupational, groups—business communities like Khojas, Memons, Bohras, Ansari weavers, Qureshi butchers and so on.
5. See Chandavarkar (1994).
6. It is probably important to note that despite the communalisation of city politics in the 1940s, there was no mass exodus of Muslims from Bombay to Pakistan after 1947. For a detailed discussion see Hansen (2001a).
7. For a detailed account of the birth and rise of the Shiv Sena, see Gupta (1982), Heuze (1995), Lele (1995), Sen (2008) and Eckart (2003).
8. Here I draw from the work of Foucault, which is filled with implications and insights concerning spatiality (Crampton & Elden 2007). Foucault (1984) describes the control of space as central to the exercise of power. Elsewhere he emphasises that the space which we live in is not void but is a heterogeneous space in history/time, defined by a set of relations. See Foucault (1986).
9. Based on his critical analysis of urban reality and everyday life, Lefebvre (1991) maintains that spaces comprise spatial practices and representations that are influenced by hegemonic ideological imaginations. Space is made up of spatial practices (buildings and actions), representations of space (conscious theories and figures) and representational spaces (imaginations, experiences).
10. For the worst affected areas in the city during the 1992–93 riots, see the Srikrishna Commission report (1998) and the report of the Indian People's Human Rights Tribunal (1994).
11. In 1968, when the Shiv Sena won forty-two seats in the corporation elections, it had the largest number of representatives in the corporation after the Congress. This considerably eased the tasks and increased the efficiency of the *shakhas* across the city. See Gupta (1982).
12. A study conducted by YUVA (1996) traces the concentration of Muslims over a period of two decades in a progressively shrinking settlement now surrounded by Hindu settlements. Drawing municipal ward boundaries between the exclusive Hindu and Muslim areas has institutionalised this division.
13. http://www.topmumbai.com/corporators.htm (Accessed in November 2010).
14. http://twocircles.net/2010nov21/cong_cuts_muslim_representation_new_maha_cabinet.html (Accessed in November 2010).
15. The residents have to pay a rent of Rs. 300 and the rent for commercial establishments is Rs. 400 now. Earlier, it was 15–25 rupees for housing and 55 rupees for commercial establishments.
16. However, this is illegal since the residents do not have ownership of the land and are themselves tenants.
17. This is with reference to the areas between the square-shaped plots that were allotted to those resettled.
18. The other affected areas were slums such as Kherwadi (in Bandra), Majaswadi (in Jogeshwari) and Cheetah Camp (in Mankhurd).

NOTES

19. The rights-based approach to development (or rights discourse in development) refers to the shift in the develoment perspectives of INGOs emphasising development as a right of citizens that has to be claimed from state. The rights-based approach followed by NGOs is criticised by Marxist scholars as a process that de-politicises development, where increased emphasis is put on elite advocacy rather than on social movements. Supporters of INGOs and NGOs, on the other hand, argue that they re-politicise development by bringing it to the centre of citizens' politics.
20. The percentage of slum population in M (east) is 77.55% and is higher than the city average of 54.06%. See the Mumbai Human Development Report (2009).
21. These pieces of information are provided by local NGOs and elected representatives in the area. Official sources do not give segregated data based on religion or language.
22. This is again based on unofficial estimates.
23. There are fourteen parallel roads that cut across the entire area. A fifteenth one is being planned between the garbage dump and settlement area.
24. Fieldnotes, 13 May 2010. One particular house that I visited was spacious but minimal. There was a large iron bed in a corner. Above the bed was the television, which was showing a cricket World Cup match. The room had two windows and a bathroom. There was a loft above that served as another bedroom with a double bed placed there and a sari that served as curtain to allow the privacy of a separate room.
25. 'Unauthorised' or 'illegal' status is defined by the Slum Rehabilitation Act (1995) as those slum settlements that have been built after January 1995. The date was extended to January 2000 by the Congress-led government in June 2009 just before the assembly elections in order to fulfil an election promise made in 2004.
26. Through the intervention of a local NGO, the demolition of some houses was prevented as Muslim slum-dwellers had documents to prove their existence before 2000.
27. This pattern of consumption is imitated in the M ward itself where, according to BMC's official documents, the major consumers of water are industries such as Bharat Petroleum Corporation Limited (BPCL), Hindustan Petroleum Corporation Limited (HPCL), Pepsi, Dukes, the slaughterhouse and the Rashtriya Chemicals and Fertilizers (RCF) colony.
28. Shivaji Nagar is described as one of the hotbeds of crime in the city by Shaban, A., *City, Crime and Space: A Case of Mumbai Megapolis*, Tata Institute of Social Sciences, Centre for Development Studies, Mumbai: Tata Institute of Social Sciences, 2006.
29. Interview with Ramzan ji, 25 November 2009.
30. Shields (1991), drawing largely from the work of Lefebvre, Bourdieu and Foucault, theorises social spatialisation as a social construction of the spatial and its imposition and enactment in the real topography of the world.

NOTES

31. Similar connotations have been made to racial and ethnic ghettos in the west that effectively lead to their production as socio-spatial solutions meant for ethno-racial closure or control by the dominant mainstream. See Wacquant (2008).
32. Emma Tarlo (2003) describes a similar collective silence and the deliberate loss of official memory articulated through the experiences and memories of the poor and marginalised who were targeted in the mass slum clearance and sterilisation drives ubiquitous in Delhi during the Emergency.

2. FACING GHETTOISATION IN 'RIOT-CITY': OLD AHMEDABAD AND JUHAPURA BETWEEN VICTIMISATION AND SELF-HELP

1. The authors are most grateful to Abida Desai for her so precious help in the field.
2. On the web site of the Municipal Corporation, the first sentence reads: 'Ahmedabad, better known as "Amdavad", is initial "Karmabhumi" of Mahatma Gandhi, Sardar Vallabhbhai Patel, Vikram Sarabhai and Abdul Kalam in western part of India' (http://www.amcgujarat.com/ amc_web/ ahd/ah_city.htm, accessed on May 2010). Born in Tamil Nadu, Abdul Kalam, who has worked at Ahmedabad as a scientist and was President of India in 2002–07, is the only Muslim element in this introductory sentence where the first name, Ahmed, is downplayed and the Hindu notion of 'Karmabhumi' highlighted.
3. *Jizya* is a tax that non-Muslim people had to pay the rulers.
4. A. Varshney, *Ethnic conflict and civic life, Hindus and Muslims in India*, New Haven/London: Yale University Press, 2002, p. 7.
5. Most of the city wall was demolished in 1924 to make the expansion of the city easier (Kenneth L. Gillion, *Ahmedabad: A Study in Indian Urban History*, Berkeley and Los Angeles: University of California Press, 1968, p. 150 and p. 170).
6. Harish Doshi, 'Traditional Neighbourhood in Modern Ahmedabad: The Pol' in *Reader in Urban Sociology*, 1991, p. 179. See also, Harish Doshi, *Traditional neighbourhood in a modern city*, New Delhi: Abhinav Publications, 1974; and Jan Hesselberg, *Issues in urbanisation: study of Ahmedabad city*, Jaipur: Rawat, 2002.
7. Ornit Shani, *Communalism, caste and Hindu nationalism*, Cambridge: Cambridge University Press, 2007, p. 33.
8. Darshini Mahadevia, 'Changing economic scenario. Informality and increased vulnerability', in Amitabh Kundu and Darshini Mahadevia (eds), *Poverty and vulnerability in a globalising metropolis: Ahmedabad*, New Delhi: Manak, 2002, p. 36.).
9. Ornit Shani, *Communalism, caste and Hindu nationalism*, op. cit., p. 43.
10. On the inclusive power of this 'legendary Trade Union', see Ashutosh Varshney, op. cit., pp. 232–234.

NOTES

11. Howard Spodek, 'From Gandhi to Violence: Ahmedabad's 1985 Riots in Historical Perspective' in *Modern Asian Studies*, vol. 23, no. 4, 1989, p. 779.
12. Jan Breman, *The making and unmaking of an industrial working class: sliding down the labour hierarchy in Ahmedabad, India*, New Delhi: Oxford University Press, 2004, pp. 143–145.
13. D. Mahadevia, 'Changing economic scenario', op. cit., p. 50.
14. O. Shani, op. cit., p. 34.
15. Sujata Patel, 'Urbanization, Development and Communalisation of Society in Gujarat' in T. Shinoda (ed.), *The Other Gujarat*, Mumbai: Popular Prakashan, 2002, p. 213.
16. The growth of the city over one century has been dramatic, from 5.72 sq km in 1872 to 98.15 sq km in 1981.
17. See K.M. Kulkarni, *Geography of crowding and human response: a study of Ahmedabad city*, New Delhi: Concept, 1984.
18. O. Shani, op. cit., p. 36.
19. Ibid., p. 46.
20. Ibid.
21. The famous painter, Toofan Rafai, told us that he had to move from the Old City to Juhapura, not only because the local Hindus objected to the drawing lessons he gave to the local girls, but also to his meat-eating habits (Interview with Toofan Rafai, 25 February 2010, Juhapura).
22. R. Jasani, 'A potted history of neighbours in Ahmedabad', op. cit.
23. Ibid., p. 9.
24. Xavier de Planhol, *The World of Islam*, Ithaca: Cornell University Press, 1966.
25. Gujarat Census office (Gandhinagar).
26. Sujata Patel, 'Urbanization, Development and Communalisation of Society in Gujarat', op. cit., p. 210.
27. On the Hindu traditionalist leanings of Patel and Munshi, see C. Jaffrelot, *The Hindu nationalist movement in India*, New York: Columbia University Press, 1996, respectively pp. 84–90, 99–101, 84–85, 182, 194, 198, 287–289, and 304.
28. See Ghanshyam Shah, 'Communal riots in Gujarat: report of a preliminary investigation', *Economic and Political Weekly*, vol. 5, no. 3, pp. 187–200; and Howard Spodek, 'From Gandhi to Modi: Ahmedabad, 1915–2007', in E. Simpson and A. Kapadia (eds), op. cit., p. 139.
29. Justice P. Jaganmohan Reddy, *Inquiry into the communal disturbances at Ahmedabad and other places in Gujarat on and after 18th September 1969*, Ahmedabad: Government of Gujarat, 1970, pp. 179–182.
30. Ashutosh Varshney, *Ethnic conflict and civic life: Hindus and Muslims in India*, New Haven: Yale University Press, 2002, chap. 10.
31. Such as: 'Every Muslim is a traitor, send him to Pakistan' (Justice P. Jaganmohan Reddy, op. cit., p. 58).

NOTES

32. Ibid., pp. 151–166.
33. Megha Kumar, op. cit., p. 98. Another survivor similarly remembers: 'These people who killed my father and attacked my mother and sister were ghar ke hi log [members of the family]' (ibid., p. 107).
34. O. Shani, op. cit., p. 123.
35. Ibid., p. 113.
36. Ibid., p. 118.
37. Ibid., p. 117.
38. Dave Commission report cited by O. Shani, op. cit., p. 88.
39. Megha Kumar, op. cit., pp. 147–148.
40. O. Shani, op. cit., p. 109.
41. Shahabuddin, Aman Chowk Relief Camp, 1/6/1985, recorded in Achyut Yagnik's 1985 documentary, 'The 1985 riot in Ahmedabad', SETU Archives, Ahmedabad.
42. Megha Kumar, op. cit., p. 150.
43. For more details, see C. Jaffrelot, 'The 2002 Pogrom in Gujarat: The Post-9/11 Face of Hindu nationalist Anti-Muslim Violence' in J. Hinnels and R. King (eds), *Religion and violence in South Asia*, London/New York: Routledge, 2006, pp. 173–192.
44. Ahmedabad and Godhra saw the most serious clashes, with 350 and 100 victims respectively in early March, according to official statistics. After these two cities came Mehsana (50 dead) and Sabarkantha (40 dead).
45. The VHP president in Gujarat in fact stated that the Muslim shops in Ahmedabad were divided up the morning of 28 February. He added that the most active thugs in the violence were Waghri untouchables—the 'payoff' came in the form of looting Muslim shops (rediff.com, 12 March 2002).
46. R. Robinson, *Tremors of violence. Muslim survivors of ethnic strife in Western India*, New Delhi: Sage, 2005, p. 58.
47. For more details see the section 'Gujarat, a laboratory for Hindu nationalism', of C. Jaffrelot, 'The BJP at the Centre: a central and centrist party?', in T.B. Hansen and C. Jaffrelot (eds), *The BJP and the compulsions of politics in India*, Delhi: Oxford University Press, 2001, pp. 316–369.
48. In the words of Jan Breman, 'Dalits have lost their "beyond the pale" classification and are supposed to pay for their acceptance within the Hindutva fold by joining the hunt against the excluded minority made to live at the margins of society as a new category of untouchables' (Jan Breman, *The making and unmaking of an industrial working class*, op. cit., p. 289).
49. Ward Berenschot, *Riot politics: Hindu-Muslim Violence and the Indian State*, London: Hurst, 2011, p. 152.
50. Ibid., p. 153.
51. D. Gupta, 'Citizens or victims?', *Seminar*, No. 602, 2009, p. 50.
52. Amnesty International, *Abuse of law in Gujarat: Muslims detained illegally in*

NOTES

Ahmedabad, http://web.amnesty.org/library/Index/ENGASA200292003?pen&of=ENG-IND, cited in Rowena Robinson, *Tremors of violence*, op. cit., p. 246.
53. Interviews with M.M. Tirmizi on 26 February 2010 in Ahmedabad, and with Abrar Ali Saiyed on 27 Feb. 2010 in Ahmedabad.
54. Asghar Ali Engineer, *Muslim Communities of Gujarat: An Exploratory Study of Bohras, Khojas and Memons*, Delhi: Ajanta Press, 1989.
55. Suchitra Sheth and Achyut Yagnik, *Shaping of modern Gujarat*, Delhi: Penguin, 2005.
56. Interview with Shafi Maniar, 30 March 2010 in Ahmedabad.
57. Interview with Raju Biman, 6 March 2010 in Ahmedabad.
58. Primary Census data accessed at the Gujarat Census Office (Gandhinagar).
59. http://dawoodi-bohras.com/about_us/people/engineer/ (Accessed on May 2010).
60. Interview with J.S. Bandukwala, 2 March 2010 at Baroda. Prof. Bandukwala, who taught physics at the MSU (Baroda) for decades, has given up any hopes of reforming the Bohra community from the inside after the 1972 events in Udaipur. He had been one of the targets of the Hindu nationalist militants in 2002.
61. *Times of India*, 23 February 2009. Available at http://articles.timesofindia.india-times.com/2009-02-23/india/28035897_1_narendra-modi-mufti-shabbir-ahmed-siddiqui-muslim-votes (accessed 24 March 2011).
62. *Times of India*, 19 January 2001. Available at http://timesofindia.indiatimes.com/ india/New-Deoband-chief-lauds-Modis-Gujarat/articleshow/7315607.cms (accessed 24 March 2011).
63. Interview with Farooq Sheikh, 31 March 2010 in Ahmedabad.
64. Interview with Sabir Khabi, 2 April 2010 in Ahmedabad.
65. In 2002 rioters did not go to the Muslim areas. They only attacked Muslim pockets in majority areas.
66. http://www.visionjafri.org/webpages/pg_ahsanjafri.html (accessed on May 2010).
67. The personal secretary of Chief Minister Narendra Modi had been informed of these developments by a senior police officer, Sanjeer Bhatt (who was suspended in August 2011) (*Tehelka*, 19 February 2011, p. 34).
68. Jafri was a Bohra and the reactions of this community to his death are very revealing of its inner divisions. 'While there was no comment on the conservative leaders' side, a web site of the Dawoodi Bohras, the best organised and wealthiest of the community, launched a forum called 'Progressive Dawoodi Bohras'. The discussion on Jafri was initiated by 'Awarebohra' who posted a very interesting piece of writing called 'A valiant Bohra family's battle against Modi' where one could read: 'If you happen to talk to the Muslims (not Bohras) [sic], who survived the fateful day, they address Ahsan Jafri as 'shaheed' [martyr] Ahsan Jafri, whereas you talk to any other Dawoodi Bohra who happened to be present there on that day (there are quite a few who survived, in fact Ahsan Jafri was the only Dawoodi Bohra to have laid down

NOTES

his life that day, all the remaining 54 or so who died in Gulberg society were Muslims), they don't even seem to acknowledge the great act this gentlemen [sic] succeeded in putting off' (http://dawoodi-bohras.com/forum/viewtopic.php?f=l&t=5025 (accessed on May 2010)). Approving of this message, several Bohras attacked the 'Adbes' and their leader the 'Syedna'. Not only do Bohras not look at themselves as Muslims (as evident from Awarebohra's formulas), but they are deeply divided.

69. See also, in a less dramatic vein the social work of Bombay-based Muslim mafiosi as described by Naipaul in the first chapter of *India, a million mutinies now*, New York: Penguin, 1990.
70. O. Shani, op. cit., p. 117 and p. 121.
71. P. Swami, 'The arms smugglers', *Frontline*, 12 January 1996, p. 45.
72. Some Muslim monuments have been restored by foreigners but the municipal corporation and the state government concentrate on the Hindu heritage, like the Maratha Badhra Fort.
73. J. Breman, 'Ghettoization and Communal Politics: the dynamics of inclusion and exclusion in the Hindutva landscape' in R. Gupta and J. Parry (eds), *Institutions and inequalities*, New Delhi: Oxford University Press, 2004.
74. Arvind Rajagopal, 'Special political zone', op. cit., p. 542.
75. Ibid., p. 533.
76. R. Jasani, 'A potted history of neighbours and neighbourliness in Ahmedabad', op. cit., p. 157.
77. 'Special political zone: urban planning, spatial segregation and the infrastructure of violence in Ahmedabad', *South Asia History and Culture*, 1:4, October 2010.
78. Jan Breman, op. cit., p. 229.
79. R. Jasani, 'A potted history of neighbours and neighbourliness in Ahmedabad', op. cit., p. 164.
80. E. Field, M. Levinson, R. Pande and S. Visaria, 'Segregation, Rent Control, and Riots: The Economics of Religious Conflict in an Indian City', *The American Economic Review*, vol. 98, no. 2, May 2008, p. 7.
81. 'Because property rights were based on employment history, they were not transferable on the informal market. Hence, workers and ex-workers remained in more integrated neighbourhoods even as the distaste for, or fear of, living among other religions rose on account of external events. We show that, for a given level of religious diversity, violence was twice as likely in mill neighbourhoods. Further, this violence was predominantly directed against members of the minority group', ibid., pp. 3–4.
82. Rajagopal points out that as early as the 1970s, 'Muslims were (...) obliged to live together in ghettoes with little class distinction; auto-mechanics and bootleggers resided amidst clerics and dentists, journalists and teachers' (A. Rajagopal, op. cit., p. 542).

NOTES

83. R. Jasani, 'A potted history of neighbours and neighbourliness in Ahmedabad', op. cit., p. 164.
84. Darshini Mahadevia, 'A city with many borders—beyond ghettoisation in Ahmedabad', in Annapurna Shaw (ed.), *Indian cities in transition*, Hyderabad: Orient Longman, 2007, p. 376.
85. Ibid., p. 377. This—still incomplete—homogenisation process is largely due to the influx of Muslims, but it is also marginally due to the outflow of members of the Hindu minority, in 2002, hundreds of families of milkmen went out for instance (Nirenda Dev, *Godhra. A journey to mayhem*, New Delhi: Samskriti, 2004, p. 44).
86. 'The Integrated Urban Development Project-Ahmedabad', document given by Kirtee Shah, founder and honorary director of Ahmedabad Study Action Group (ASAG), extract from a seminar on Public/Private Sector Partnerships for Urban Infrastructure and Service Delivery, Seoul, Republic of Korea, 2–4 April 2002.
87. Other public and private agencies were involved. Houses were financed through a group loan and flood relief subsidies from the government of Gujarat or the British NGO Oxfam.
88. Interview with Yaqub, 22 April 2010 in Ahmedabad.
89. Ibid.
90. Nowadays, only a handful of the original resettled people still live in Juhapura. The majority left around the beginning of the 1920s to go back to their native place, on the banks of the Sabarmati River.
91. Interview with A.S. Sayed, 22 March 2010.
92. A case in point is R.A. Kadri, retired Assistant Commissioner of Police of Ahmedabad whose brother has migrated to the United States but also owns a house in Juhapura and contributes to philanthropic work in the area.
93. Interview with Nadeem Jaffa, 24 March 2010.
94. Interview with Ghazala Paul, 9 April 2010.
95. Ibid.
96. Interview with Mr. Gena, 19 March 2010. Bukari Fakuna, who shifted in 2008—note that the migration flows continue—from Gujarat College to Juhapura, thinks that 'the previous area was better [...] Juhapura is peaceful but still its far and not so well developed', (interview with Bukari Fakuna).
97. The wall is located between Vasna and the eastern part of Juhapura. However, the two areas are not totally separated since this is not a continuous wall and connections still exist via the main road, Sarkhej Road, and few secondary ones.
98. D. Mahadevia, 'A city with many borders', op. cit., p. 378.
99. In July 2010, Amit Shah, the MLA of Sarkhej-Lambha and until then Gujarat Minister of State for Home was put under judicial custody. He is one of the prime suspects in the Sohrabuddin Sheikh-Kausar Bi murder case.
100. The only Muslim MLAs are elected in the Old City (in Jamalpur, Kalupur

and Shahpur) and cannot do anything for Juhapura. They focus on their constituency anyway.
101. In July 2010, around thirty people were affected by contaminated water in Sankalit Nagar (see http://www.dnamdia.com/mdia/report_2–taken-iU-in-juha-pura-after-using-contaminated-water_1412138).
102. Interview with Dr. Kherala, 15 April 2010.
103. Ibid.
104. Ibid.
105. Samerth is a secularist NGO founded in 1992 and run by Muslim people.
106. Data kindly transmitted by Ghazala Paul, founder and director of Samerth; extract from a survey conducted by the NGO on the state of educational needs in Juhapura.
107. Harsh Mander, 'Inside Gujarat's relief colonies. Surviving state hostility and denial', *Economic and Political Weekly*, 23 December 2006, pp. 5235–5239.
108. 332 families and 1,745 people, data for 2007 according to 'The Uprooted, Caught Between Existence and Denial', Centre for Social Justice and Anhad, 2007.
109. Name changed.
110. Since the rehabilitation phase got over at the end of 2002, secularist NGOs have been in charge of the advocacy part while Islamic trusts have managed to provide daily needs in the relief colonies. For that reason, today they are not at all involved in the relief colonies.
111. Interview with Rachida, 17 April 2010.
112. T.B. Hansen, *Wages of violence: naming and identity in post-colonial Mumbai* Princeton: Princeton University Press, 2001, see chap. 6, 'In the Muslim Mohalla.'
113. R. Jasani, 'Violence, Reconstruction and Islamic Reform—Stories from the Muslim "Ghetto"', op. cit., p. 4.
114. Ibid., p. 11.
115. According to one of R. Jasani's informants (ibid., p. 15).
116. Ibid., p. 25.
117. C. Jaffrelot, 'Cinq années amères dans la démocratie indienne. Après les pogromes du Gujarat', *Esprit*, July 2007, pp. 53–66.
118. Interview with Alamder Bukari, 9 February 2010.
119. Interview with A.S. Sayed, 22 March 2010.
120. Interview with A.A. Khan, 20 April 2010.
121. Interview with Bukari Fakuna, 20 February 2010.
122. Rizwan Kadri, a famous architect, president of the Sunni Muslim Waqf Committee and member of the Crescent Education and Medical Trust, told us that after the riots, the upper layer of the Muslim community realised that 'zakaat was not enough. Education and livelihood were needed too' (Interview with Rizwan Kadri, 25 January 2010).
123. Interview with Javed Sayed, 7 April 2010.
124. Interview with Gena M. Husain, Juhapura, 25 February 2010.

NOTES

125. Interview with Asifkhan Pathan, 25 January 2010.
126. M. Thapan, 'Imagining citizenship: being Muslim, becoming citizen in Ahmedabad', *Economic and Political Weekly*, 16 January 2010, Vol. XLV, no. 3, p. 49.
127. Interview with N. Jaffri.
128. Ibid.
129. For example, associations pay for books, uniforms, fees, etc. They also give free tuitions after school, professional classes such as computer, sewing, preparation to administration entrance examinations, etc.
130. Interview with Shafi Maniar, 30 March 2010.
131. Yasmine, the wife of a well-off businessman, decided to get involved in the NGO Samvad after the 2002 events (Interview with Yasmine, 3 March 2010).
132. Interview with Alamder Bukari, joint editor of the Gujarati newspaper *Gujarat Today*, 9 February 2010.
133. Interview with Imamkhan Pathan, 26 March 2010.
134. Interview with Javed Sayed, businessman and honorary worker in the NGO Gujarat Sarvajanik Welfare Trust, in charge of education, 7 April 2010.
135. In addition, a lot of them have been killed or arrested by the authorities since the pogroms of 2002.
136. Interview with Karim Lakhani, op. cit.
137. S. Sheth and N. Haeems, 'Sisters under the skin: events of 2002 and girls' education in Ahmedabad', *Economic and Political Weekly*, Vol. XLI, no. 17, p. 1709.
138. Ward Berenschot, *Riot Politics*, op. cit., p. 97.

3. RAMGANJ, JAIPUR: FROM OCCUPATION-BASED TO 'COMMUNAL' NEIGHBOURHOOD?

1. An occupational group refers to both Hindu and Muslim caste groups practising the same profession.
2. This phrase refers to the fusion of the two main rivers Ganga (Ganges) and Yamuna, where Ganga represents the Hindu community and Yamuna refers to the Muslim population.
3. *Mushtarka* (common, in Urdu) refers to the shared traditions of Hindus and Muslims.
4. During the Gulf war in 1991 Muslim migratory labourers in the Gulf had to return which led to a fall in remittance. It also led to a fall in jewellery export destined for gold souks in the Gulf countries. Local jewellery-makers told me that they lost orders and it had a direct impact on the workforce in this industry.
5. Boileau estimated the size of the population on the basis of 5 members per family. He reported a total number of 80,000 houses in the city. See A.H.E. Boileau, *Personal Narrative of a Tour through the Western States of Rajwara in 1835*, Calcutta, 1835.

NOTES

6. Robert W. Stern, *The Cat And The Lion: Jaipur State in the British Raj*, Netherlands: E.J. Brill, Leiden, 1988, p. 56.
7. As recorded in the caste-based Census carried out by the Jaipur State.
8. Kavi Jaan (ed.), *Kyam Khan Rasa*, Jodhpur: Dasrath Sharma. The book records the conversion of important Rajput clans such as Bhatis and Kyam Khani Chauhans of the Shekhawati region, which constitutes the modern districts of Jhunjhunu and Churu. They were converted to Islam during the reign of Feroz Tughlaq (1351–88). See Sunita Budhwar (Zaidi), 'The Qayamkhani Shaikhzada Family of Fatehpur-Jhunjhunu', *Proceedings of the Indian History Congress*, 39th Session, Osmania University, Hyderabad, 1978.
9. Vibhuti Sachdev, Giles Henry Rupert Tillotson, *Building Jaipur: The Making of an Indian City*, London: Reaktion Books, 2002, p. 50.
10. Topkhana Hazuri Chowkri was originally designed to host artillery for the king and was later occupied by artisans engaged in *gota* making (silver and gold border). Currently, these artisans are engaged in *nagina* (semi-precious stone) polishing work. See Surjit Singh, 'Segregation of Population in Jaipur City: The Past and Present', *Working Paper*, Institute of Development Studies, Jaipur, 2003.
11. For the Kanpur incident see Lavan Spencer, 'The Kanpur Mosque Incident of 1913: The North Indian Muslim Press and Its Reaction to Community Crisis', *Journal of the American Academy of Religion*, Vol. 42, No. 2, June 1974, pp. 263–279.
12. His victory is also attributed to his moderate stand. He intervened to prevent a communal conflict following the slaughtering of some cows by Muslim butchers. He publicly defended Muslims by stating that the entire community cannot be punished for the wrongs of one person. See Mayaram Shail, 'Violence and Survival' in *Creating a Nationality: The Ramjanmabhumi Movement and Fear of the Self*, New Delhi: OUP, 1998, p. 127.
13. The riots started after the victory procession of BJP candidate Girdhari Lal Bhargava entered the already sensitive area of Ramganj, in a deliberate act of provocation.
14. For a detailed account of these episodes of communal violence, see Shubh Mathur, *The Everyday Life of Hindu Nationalism. An Ethnographic Account*, Delhi: Three Essays Collective, 2008, chap. 5.
15. Ibid.
16. Jaipur Municipal Corporation website, http://www.jaipurmc.org/Cdp/02-Chap-ter-2.pdf. (Accessed on June 2009).
17. Data collected from the website of Rajasthan Government [http://www.dop.raj-asthan.gov.in/civillist/cug_civillist_query.asp?svalue=civil]
18. I draw here specifically on my findings from fieldwork conducted during July-September 2009 and July-August 2010 in the Ramganj area of Jaipur. I conducted in-depth interviews with thirty-two people. The interviews were mainly in Hindi and a few in English. Notes were later transcribed and translated

into English. Respondents were located through snowball sampling methods whereby those interviewed were asked for referrals to other potential informants. Some informants were paid, on the basis of 100 Rs per family, to be introduced to other Muslim families. In doing so I made an effort to avoid over-sampling from a particular social network by limiting the number of referrals from any snowball chain and continuing to recruit participants from other sources to expand the range of sample, especially in terms of socioeconomic status as well as levels of participation in Muslim organisations and groups. The interviewees ranged in age from 20–80, and they included approximately equal numbers of women and men.

19. The ward numbers and the population figures mentioned here have been taken from the Contingency Plan 2006 of the Ramganj Police Station, Jaipur City, North. It should be noted that the wards have been reorganised since and the current ward numbers do not correspond to those used here.
20. The 'Ashrafisation' of the Julahas (weavers) was set in motion by the census operations of the British in the 1930s, a fact unknown to the great majority of weavers; on the census as an 'instrument of mobility' of this community, see Vasanthi Raman, *The Warp and the Weft, Community and Gender Identity among Banaras Weavers*, Delhi: Routledge, 2010, p. 64.
21. Rehmanis trace their origin to Abdul Rehman ibn Awf who lived in Saudi Arabia some 1400 years ago and is said to be one of the first eight people to have accepted Islam.
22. On this process of ashrafisation among the butchers of Delhi, see Zarin Ahmad, 'From Tanzeem to Taaleem, Tanzeem and Tijaaraat: the Changing Role of the All India Jamiat-ul-Quresh', in Vinod C. Jairath (ed.), *Frontiers of Embedded Muslim Communities*, Delhi: Routledge, 2011.
23. The Rangrez are further divided into two subgroups: Rajawatis and Shekhawatis, each having a separate *biraderi*. Here, I refer to the Rajawati Rangrez *biraderi* of 4,500 people.
24. *Biraderi* means brotherhood, or extended clan comparable to a Hindu endogamous caste in its traditional occupation.
25. The Silawatan group specialised in stone inlay work (*pachekari*). Most families migrated to Pakistan at the time of independence. As per the respondent at present there are only 3 to 5 Silawatan families in Ramganj.
26. Very colourful handmade shoes with embroidery and sequin work made by the Muslim mochi community of Jaipur.
27. According to residents, Mirza Ismail notified the neighbourhood as a legal settlement before Partition. The neighbourhood has a predominant Muslim and Dalit population.
28. Facts and figures have been crosschecked with the Adarsh Nagar SHO, national daily, *The Hindu* and the local Hindi daily *Dainik Bhaskar* of 21 February 2008.
29. Formed in October 1992, RAF is a paramilitary force that deals with riots and related unrest.

NOTES

30. The term *'miyan'* (sir) is a mark of respect in Urdu but has become a derogatory term in India.
31. 'Non-Muslim' (*ghair mazbabi, ghair musalman*) is a phrase used to distinguish anything Muslim from other religious groups but mainly refers to Hindus.

4. A MINORITY WITHIN A MINORITY: THE SHIAS OF KASHMIRI MOHALLA, LUCKNOW

1. There were and still are other Kashmiri Mohallas in other cities of Uttar Pradesh, due to the massive exile of qualified Pandits from Kashmir. Kashmiri Mohalla in Lucknow had the largest Kashmiri Pandits population in pre-Independent India, after Kashmir.
2. Though Shias were holding the upper-ranks of the states administration, some of the highest officials were Sunnis. Sunnis were also well represented in the middle and lower ranks of the administration.
3. Along with the Shia aristocrats from Kashmir came various groups of Kashmiri Bandhs (folk theatre performers), invited to the Court by Nawab Asif udDaula (1775–97).
4. See Mushirul Hasan, *From pluralism to separatism: Qasbas in colonial Awadh*, Oxford: Oxford University Press, 2004.
5. Veena Talwar Oldenburg, *The Making of Colonial Lucknow, 1856–1877*, Princeton, N.J.: Princeton University Press, 1984
6. The Kaisar-i-Hind was a medal awarded by the British Crown between 1900 and 1947 to civilians who rendered distinguished services in the advancement of the interests of the British Raj.
7. 1 bigha equals 27,830 square feet, or 2,585 square meters.
8. South of Kashmiri Mohalla.
9. Interview conducted in Kashmiri Mohalla, on 24 April 2010.
10. Former capital of the Shia Awadh dynasty.
11. Interview with the author, Kashmiri Mohalla, 24 April 2010.
12. We can mention here Pandit Rameshwar Nath Kao, founder of R&AW, Pandit Bishan Narain Dar, Congress President in 1911 or Kailash Nath Wanshoo, former Chief Justice of Rajasthan and Supreme Court Judge. All hailed from Kashmiri Mohalla, Lucknow.
13. In a fragmented polity, the majoritarian 'first past the post' electoral system does have the effect of dispersing the minorities.
14. In these elections, the Congress won 21 seats with 18.25% of the vote share, while the Bharatiya Janata Party obtained only 10 seats with a 17.5% of the vote share.
15. The current Mayawati-led Government counts five Muslim members, out of a total of 52 members.
16. The 1999 Samajwadi Party Cabinet—counting eighty-nine members—did not have a single Muslim Minister.

NOTES

17. Sachar Committee Report, p. 275.
18. No census data was made available at the Census Bureau of the Uttar Pradesh Government.
19. These early episodes of Sunni-Shia violence have been dealt with in detail by Mushirul Hasan, 'Traditional Rites and Contested Meanings: Sectarian Strife in Colonial Lucknow' in Violette Graff. (ed.) *Lucknow, Memories of a City*, Delhi: OUP, 1997, pp. 114–135.
20. A Shia doctrine preaching disassociation from the 'enemies' of the 'house of the Prophet' (*ahl-al-bayt*). In practice, a ritual denigration of the first four Caliphs (Abu Bakr, Omar, Usman and Muawiyah).
21. A linking artery between Kashmiri Mohalla and Rustom Nagar bears today the name of the boys—Mohammad Abbas alias 'Babbu' and Yusuf Bhopalo—who sacrificed their lives for the cause of the processions.
22. The Muslim Personal Law Board and the Shia Personal Law Board are institutions that aim at regulating aspects of the civil life of Muslims (such as marriage contracts, or *Nikahnamas*, or inheritance rights). The Shia Personal Law Board announced the creation of a new *Nikahnama* in May 2006. It was made official during the Board General Assembly in Mumbai in November of the same year.
23. Interview with Ibne Hassan, advocate and political activist, at his house in Kashmiri Mohalla, 28 April 2010.
24. 'The House of Peace'.
25. Interview with the author at his constituency office, 26 April 2010.
26. Interview with the author at Unity College, Lucknow, 30 April 2010.
27. The author could not find specific socio-economic surveys pertaining to the area considered in the present research. The Chief Engineer of the Lalbagh Municipal Corporation told him that the municipality had never conducted such studies. Furthermore, the author was chastised by the same engineer for conducting an 'anti-secular kind of research', a posture which did not facilitate further data collection from the municipality.
28. Interview with Ibne Hassan.
29. Interview with Syed Kazim Zaheer, at his residence, on 15 October 2010. The organisation that was the most often referred to was the Nadwat ul-Uloom.
30. A theologian and logician born in Harran (now in Turkey), quoted as a source of the founders of Wihabbism.
31. Interview held in Lucknow with a close associate of the Shia Personal Law Board.
32. These accusations are in complete contradiction to the Iranian affinities of some Shia clerics in Lucknow. It is worth noting that the Shia enclave of Lucknow started to grow at the moment of the Shia revolution in Iran. Though disconnected, the events of the Iranian revolution certainly gave Shias a sense of confidence and assertion, and a greater legitimacy to their religious leaders, some of whom travel frequently to Iran.
33. During the last fieldwork conducted for the present chapter, in November 2010,

NOTES

violence erupted in Nakhas the day before Eid-ul-Azha (Bakri-Eid), when two prominent Shia clerics—Maulana Kalbe Jawad and Maulana Agha Roohi—were preventively arrested on the District Magistrate's order, after he declared his intention to organise a demonstration against the Board of the Shia College. The Board had been indefinitely postponing its internal elections in order to prevent the empowerment of clerics within the institution.

34. Source: Office of the Chief Engineer of Lalbagh Municipal Corporation.
35. Observation drawn from fieldwork and local interviews.
36. Father of Maulana Kalbe Jawad, *Imam-e-Juma*. (leader of the Friday prayers) at the Shahi Asafi Mosque in Lucknow and leader of the Waqf Movement (or *Tehreek-e-Awqaf*) in Lucknow.
37. The amount of 40% of the World Bank's total grant was often verbally quoted to the author.
38. Interview with Anwar Abbas, writer and head of the Archaeological Survey of India task force for Uttar Pradesh.
39. Interview with Sibtey Hasan Naqvi, former founder and President of the Anjuman-e-Zardozan (Embroiderers' Association).
40. It is worth noting that the leadership of the Anjuman-e-Zardozan ensured a parity of representation to both communities. If the President was a Shia, the General Secretary would be a Sunni, and vice-versa. The unity of the organisation was preserved despite the riots that shook the city in the 1970s.
41. It is estimated that around 50,000 Sunnis from Lucknow are currently employed in the Arabian Peninsula.
42. Interview with Kulsum Mustapha, journalist.
43. In 1991, Muslim representation in the police in Uttar Pradesh accounted for 4.6% of the total forces. Quoted in Mushirul Hasan, *Legacy of a Divided Nation*, Delhi: OUP, 1997, p. 294.
44. Interview with Kulsum Mustafa.
45. Interview conducted in Kashmiri Mohalla, April 2010.

5. ALIGARH: SIR SYED NAGAR AND SHAH JAMAL, CONTRASTED TALES OF A 'MUSLIM' CITY

1. The author would like to express her gratitude to Pr. Nadeem Ali Rezavi from the Centre of Advanced Study, Department of History, Aligarh Muslim University and to Salim Zaweed, Fazeela Shahnawaz, Enayat Ullah Khan, Pr. M.K. Pundhir, Mum-taz Alam, Afshan Majid, Asghar Raja, Habib Manzer and Adil Zubair for their so precious help in the field.
2. The Doab designates the alluvial area between the Ganges and Yamuna Rivers. It used to be a central location in the Vedic age. It is divided between the Upper Doab, the Lower Doab and the Central or Middle Doab. This last part comprises the districts of Etah, Aligarh, Agra, Hathras, Firozabad and Mathura.

NOTES

3. The Mohammedan Anglo-Oriental College was founded in 1875 with the aim of providing a modern education to the Muslim community of India. It further developed into the Aligarh Muslim University (AMU) in 1920. The university and with it the whole city of Aligarh became a crucial symbol of Muslim identity in post-independence India (Wright, 1966). The Muslims represent 18% of Aligarh district's population. They are a highly urbanised community as 62% of them live in urban areas. They are largely concentrated in the cities of Aligarh, Atrauli and Khair (Shahid, 2007).
4. Twenty-five semi-directive interviews were conducted in Upar Fort, twenty-five in Shah Jamal and fifteen in Sir Syed Nagar. Interviews were also conducted in the Hindu dominated areas of Cyan Sarowar (in the Civil Lines, five interviews) and Sasni Gate and Khirni Gate (in the Old City, fifteen interviews). At last, Muslim MLAs, MLCs and main politicians of the town were interviewed. In the subsequent pages, the anonymity of the respondents is preserved (all the names have been changed), except for these public personalities.
5. In recent elections and with the view to occulting the Muslim history of the city, some Hindu communalist groups tried to assert that Aligarh was actually the distorted pronunciation of 'Harigarh' ('Hari' being the other name of Vishnu and Krishna). But this claim met little support among the population (Interview with Aligarh's Assistant Election Commissioner, 26 July 2010, Election Office, Civil Lines, Aligarh).
6. In the 1960s, Aligarh became once again the focus of a national debate that reinforced its 'Muslim image'. As a university founded by a Muslim leader for the educational advancement of the Muslim community, the AMU used to fall under the article 30(1) of the Constitution, which affirmed its minority character: 'All minorities, whether based on religion or language, shall have the right to establish and administer educational institutions of their choice'. In 1965, after the Vice-Chancellor of the AMU, Ali Yavar Jung, was grievously assaulted, the Government of India decided to reduce the autonomy of the University Court and declared in a sworn affidavit that Aligarh Muslim University is an institution established, not by a minority community so as to attract the provisions of Article 30(1) of the Constitution of India, but by the Central government' (Noorani, 2002: 21). The Muslim character of the AMU was formally denied. Even today the AMU is still pushing demands to have its minority status restored. (For a detailed report and historical account of this issue, see the *First Annual Report of the Minorities' Commission*, 1979 and Graff, 1990).
7. The 2008 Annual Report of the AMU shows that out of 20,875 students, 12,343 came from Uttar Pradesh, 4,235 from Bihar, 994 from Jharkhand, 608 from West Bengal, 572 from Uttarakhand, 546 from Jammu-and-Kashmir, 132 from Kerala etc. I am most grateful to the Public Relations Officer of the University, Dr Rahat Abrar, for providing me with this information.

NOTES

8. Phapala, near the railway station, used to be such a mixed locality. Hindu families who used to live in Upar Fort gradually sold their houses: some of my oldest respondents had memories of Hindu neighbours who left after the riots.
9. These colleges are still affiliated to the Agra University today.
10. On most recent but similar tensions in the Old City, see Rizvi (2006), where the author relates how the 2006 Aligarh riots erupted and how Muslims were incited to leave their *mohallas*.
11. On these riots, see the much furnished report of the Minorities' Commission (1979).
12. This situation was to change in the post-Independence period, particularly after the 1970s.
13. Brass has taken an inventory of the teaching staff listed in the telephone directory of the AMU in 1997: it contained around 1,075 names from which he managed to identify 130 Hindu names only (and six uncertain, Brass, 2003: 439).
14. The Koil constituency has long been reserved for SCs.
15. It is to be mentioned that the Hindus who were interviewed were also characterised by this growing political apathy.
16. Mann for instance refers to a mosque in Upar Fort, established by *zat* Muslims who prevented low status Muslims from entering 'their' mosque (Mann, 1992: 148).
17. One should recall however, that in the Civil Lines, we also find very poor and backward localities such as Jivangarh, Jamalpur or Maulana Azad Nagar. The construction of the Civil Lines as a purely educated part of the city is therefore largely a myth.
18. The current MLA, Zamir Ullahisan, example of such residential mobility: a man of the Old City, he eventually bought a big house in the Civil Lines, a shift which has been resented by the residents of the Old City.
19. Last but not least, the Muslim elite itself is far from monolithic. In particular, within the AMU, the opposition has been historical between Communists and Communalists, (Brass, 1965: 99–100), Leftists and Rightists, Progressives who promote modernisation and Conservatives who swear by formal Islam. Theodore Wright, considering the issue of the minority character of the AMU, has brilliantly highlighted different orientations among the Muslim elite: traditional, fundamentalist, modern and secular (Wright, 1966).
20. It is noteworthy indeed that Peter de Ruiter chose, between others, the locality of Shah Jamal in Aligarh as a case study for his book *A World for Children—Growing up without child labour*, Amsterdam: KIT Publishers, 2009.
21. I am most grateful to the draftsman of the Municipal Corporation for providing me with the detailed maps of the wards 54 and 62.
22. See Christophe Jaffrelot and Charlotte Thomas (chapter 2 in this volume). The migration of middle class Muslims to the locality of Juhapura fostered the

NOTES

self-development of the area. This is not yet the case in Shah Jamal, though successful businessmen are progressively settling private schools in the *mohalla*, such as the Glorious Public School.

23. This expression is borrowed from a book by William Julius Wilson, *The Truly Disadvantaged: The Inner City, the Underclass and Public Policy* (1987) dedicated to the conditions of the Black underclass who remained stuck in ghettos while the Black middle class experienced upward social mobility. The truly disadvantaged were the Black poor who cumulated race and class disadvantages over the years.
24. Pierre Bourdieu, *Homo Academicus*, Paris: Les Editions de Minuit, 1984.
25. Sir Syed Nagar was only affected by the great riots of 1990–91. While the experience of curfew left its mark on the residents, very few were killed in the area.
26. For many respondents, this unregulated multiplication of flats indicates that the mafia is involved. The multi-storeyed buildings that damage the grounds are normally unauthorised.

6. BHOPAL MUSLIMS: BESIEGED IN THE OLD CITY?

1. The authors are most grateful to Ira Saraswat for her precious help in the field.
2. P.N. Shrivastav and S.D. Guru, *Madhya Pradesh District Gazetteers. Sehore and Bhopal*, Bhopal: Directorate of gazetteers—Department of culture, Madhya Pradesh, 1989, p. 49.
3. See Shaharyar Khan, *The Begums of Bhopal. A Dynasty of Women Rulers in Raj India*, London: I.B. Tauris, 2000. Shaharyar Khan, who became the Foreign Secretary of Pakistan in the 1990s, was the grandson of the Nawab of Bhopal, which is his birthplace.
4. Ibid., p. 39.
5. Ibid., p. 84.
6. Shah Jahan Begum cited in ibid., p. 85.
7. Kamla Mittal, *History of Bhopal State. Development and Constitution, Administration and National Awakening, 1901–1949*, Delhi: Munshiram Manoharlal, 1990, p. 21.
8. Ibid.
9. Ibid., p. 58.
10. Ibid., p. 56.
11. Ibid., p. 195. For a more positive view of the Hindu-Muslim relations before Independence see S. Ashfaq Ali, *A Guide to Bhopal*, Bhopal: Jai Bharat Publishing House, 1987, pp. 92–96.
12. *Bhopal in 1937–38*, Bombay: Government of Bhopal, 1940, p. 8.
13. *Bhopal in 1936–37*, Bombay: Government of Bhopal, 1939, p. 9.
14. See the 'Epilogue' of Shaharyar Khan, *The Begums of Bhopal. A Dynasty of Women Rulers in Raj India*, New York: I.B. Tauris, 2000.
15. *Bhopal in 1936–37*, Bombay: Government of Bhopal, 1939, p. 8.

NOTES

16. *Kamla Mittal, History of Bhopal State*, op. cit., p. 170.
17. P.N. Shrivastav and S.D. Guru, *Madhya Pradesh District Gazeteers. Sehore and Bhopal*, op. cit., p. 80.
18. *Bhopal in 1937–38*, Bombay: Government of Bhopal, 1940, p. 60.
19. Inayatullah Khan Tarzi Mashriqi had been expelled from Bhopal for his nationalist leanings (*Madhya Pradesh Vidhan Sabha sadasyon ka sankshipt parichay*, 1972, Bhopal: Madhya Pradesh Vidhan Sabha sachivalay, 1972, p. 12).
20. On this specific feature of Bhopal politics, see Rajendra Verma, *The Freedom Struggle in the Bhopal State, New Delhi:* Intellectual Publishing House, 1984, p. 50.
21. See V.P. Menon, *The story of the integration of the Indian states*, Calcutta: Orient Longman, 1961, p. 59.
22. Durga Das, *India from Curzon to Nehru and after*, London: Collins, 1969, p. 242.
23. Naresh Kumar Jain (ed.), *Muslims in India. A bibliographical dictionary*, vol. II, Delhi: Manohar, 1983, p. 190.
24. S.P. Singh Sud and A. Singh Sud (eds), *Indian Elections and Legislators*, Ludhiana: All India Publications, no date, p. 290.
25. Similar forms of religious toleration were seen in the neighbouring villages where some forms of syncretism were evident: 'Once every year a fair is held in the village Kulhari of Tahsil Icchawar. About 400–500 people from nearby villages assemble there near a *dargah* (tomb) of a Pir (a person who has attained divine power). A few legends are associated with the Pir. Hindus and Muslims alike hold him in respect' (P.N. Shrivastav and S.D. Guru, *Madhya Pradesh District Gazeteers. Sehore and Bhopal*, Bhopal: Directorate of Gazetteers, 1989, p. 133).
26. Ibid., p. 567.
27. Ibid., p. 83.
28. Chandralekha Lehri, *Socio-demographic profile of Muslims. Study of Bhopal city*, New Delhi and Jaipur: Rawat Publications, 1997.
29. P.N. Shrivastav and S.D. Guru, *Madhya Pradesh District Gazeteers. Sehore and Bhopal*, op. cit., p. 98.
30. Ibid., p. 91.
31. Ibid., p. 95.
32. Ibid., p. 187.
33. Recently, a special issue of the RSS mouthpiece, *The Organiser* declared: 'This great King was the founder of Bhopal, which is unfortunately today called the city of the nawabs and the real history of Bhopal is deliberately brushed under the carpet' (Sangeet Verma, 'How Bhojpal became Bhopal', *Organiser*, Varsha Pratipada Special, vol. LXI, no. 47, 21 March 2010, p. 8).
34. Nasir Kamaal, 'Why just three buildings, Gaur Sahib!', *The Telegraph*, 10 April 2010.
35. The BJP has also attacked the Urdu Academy that had been created in 1976. Aziz Qureshi, a Bhopal-based lawyer who had been elected on the Congress

NOTES

ticket MLA from Sehore in 1972 and MP from Satna in 1984 before becoming chairman of the Urdu Academy, emphasised that, while Congress Chief Ministers like Arjun Singh and Digvijay Singh made a point to protect the Academy, the BJP Chief Minister, Sunderlal Patwa (1990–92) wanted to shift the Academy to a much smaller building, a decision which was strongly resisted by the Muslims of Bhopal. (Interview with Aziz Qureshi, 20 February 2004, Bhopal. See also *Parliament of India. Eighth Lok Sabha Who's Who*, New Delhi: Lok Sabha Secretariat, 1985, p. 233).

36. *Bhopal riot: a report, Bhopal and Delhi:* Sanskritic Morcha and PUDR, 1993, p. 4.
37. *National Mail*, 15 December 1992.
38. *Bhopal riot: a report*, op. cit., p. 6.
39. *Dainik Bhaskar* (Hindi), 7 and 8 December 1992.
40. Interview in Bhopal, 19 February 1994.
41. *National Mail*, 15 December 1992.
42. *Bhopal riot: a report*, op. cit., p. 11.
43. *National Mail*, 25 December 1992.
44. Ibid., 26 December 1992.
45. Ibid., 19 December 1992
46. *The Statesman*, 10 December 1992.
47. *Bhopal riot: a report*, op. cit., p. 41.
48. *National Mail*, 10 December 1992.
49. Ibid., 26 December 1992.
50. Ibid., 27 December 1992.
51. Frank Moraes (ed.), *The Indian and Pakistan Year Book & Whos' Who, 1952–1953*, vol. XXXVII Bombay: Times of India, 1950, p. 501.
52. P.N. Shrivastav and S.D. Guru, *Madhya Pradesh District Gazeteers. Sehore and Bhopal*, op. cit., p. 331.
53. The first college was established in 1946 and Saifia College—the first good one—was founded by Mullah Sajjad Husain in 1956. It was not meant for Muslims only, but since it had been founded by a Muslim and was located in the Old City, it became, de facto, the main place of higher education for the Muslims of Bhopal.
54. Zahid Malik, *Dr. A.Q. Khan and the Islamic bomb*, Islamabad: Hurmat, 1992.
55. Chandralekha Lehri, *Socio-demographic profile of Muslims*, op. cit., p. 40.
56. Ibid., p. 87.
57. http://reliablegroup.org/about-us.html (accessed on May 2010).
58. Sikandar Haziz Khan has been honoured by the Makkah Chamber of Commerce of the country for promoting 'fruitful and constructive cooperation aimed at development of trade exchange between India and Saudi Arabia' (ibid.).
59. Interview with Retd Professor Afaq Ahmed, Barkatullah University, Bhopal, 25 January 2010.
60. Interview with Rajendra Kothari (PHD Chamber of Commerce and industry), Bhopal, 28 January 2010.

NOTES

61. Bar Association List obtained from the District Court Bhopal.
62. Website of the district court of Bhopal: http://www.bhopal.nic.in/dcourt/SUB-ORDINATE.htm
63. *Central Chronicle*, 24 January 2010, p. 2.
64. Hamidullah expired in 1960 without taking part in politics and his daughter, Begum Sajida Sultan, who became Nawab in 1962, did not join politics either. Her son, Mansoor Ali Khan Pataudi, the 9th Nawab of Bhopal until 1971, when India abolished royal entitlements through the 26th Amendment to the Constitution, was less interested in politics than in cricket—he was the captain of the national team in 1962.
65. *Parliament of India, Rajya Sabha, Who's Who*, New Delhi: Rajya Sabha Secretariat, 1982, p. 309.
66. *Madhya Pradesh Vidhan Sabha sadasyon ka sankshipt parichay*, 1967, Bhopal: Madhya Pradesh Vidhan Sabha sachivalay, 1970, p. 139; and *Madhya Pradesh Vidhan Sabha sadasyon ka sankshipt parichay*, 1972, Bhopal: Madhya Pradesh Vidhan Sabha sachivalay, 1972, p. 155.
67. *Madhya Pradesh Vidhan Sabha sadasyon ka sankshipt parichay*, 1977, Bhopal: Madhya Pradesh Vidhan Sabha sachivalay, 1977, p. 83.
68. *Parliament of India ninth Lok Sabha, Who's Who*, New Delhi: Lok Sabha Secretariat, 1992, p. 28.
69. *Madhya Pradesh Vidhan Sabha sadasyon ka sankshipt parichay*, Bhopal: Madhya Pradesh Vidhan Sabha sachivalay, 1985, p. 265.
70. *Madhya Pradesh Vidhan Sabha sadasya parichay 1990*, Bhopal: Madhya Pradesh Vidhan Sabha Sachivalay, 1991, p. 2.
71. Interview with Naser Islam, Bhopal, 27 January 2010.
72. Interview with Ghufran Azam, Bhopal, 25 January 2010. Educated at Saifia college and Hamidia college, Azam followed a route similar to those of the MLAs mentioned above: he has first been a student union leader and then a Congress youth leader (he occupied many posts at the local and state levels within the Youth Congress between 1963 and 1974). Subsequently he was given increasingly important responsibilities within the party apparatus from President of Bhopal District Congress Committee to General secretary of the MP Pradesh Committee in 1977–80. In 1980 he was given a Lok Sabha ticket and became MP of Betul (one of the few Lok Sabha constituencies Muslim candidates have won repeatedly in Madhya Pradesh). He joined the Rajya Sabha in 1989 before being appointed at the helm of the Waqf Directorate. See also Parliament of India, Rajya Sabha, *Who's Who 1990*, New Delhi: Rajya Sabha Secretariat, 1990, p. 31.
73. Interview with Yassir Hasnat, Bhopal, 27 January 2010.
74. 'Madhya Pradesh Who's Who' in *Reference Madhya Pradesh*, Raipur, Deshbandhu Publication Division, 1997, pp. 475–608.
75. *Parliament of India, Tenth Lok Sabha Who's Who*, New York: Lok Sabha Secretariat, 1992, pp. 338–339.

NOTES

76. This estimate has been made through the voters list obtained from the Councillor of the area, Rizwan Oureishy.
77. The words of Farhan Alam, 26 years, auto dealing business, Jahangirabad.
78. The loans were organised through family members. There were very few who had taken loans from the Bank.
79. The majority of the inhabitants of Ibrahimpura and Jahangirabad are upper caste Muslims who do not benefit from any social benefit or development schemes run by the government. Had they been OBCs, they would have qualified for the various government programmes that have been set up and would have probably interacted more with the state. Most of them were unaware of the financial aid schemes of the government for education in general and girls education in particular.
80. The words of Sheikh Zahoor, butcher, Jahangirabad.
81. This view of the BDA is not contradicted by the website of this institution: 'Today, the old city of Bhopal, clumped together on one side of the lake, meets the modern one across the bridge. The former, with its cramped pathways, deteriorating, neglected structures and admirable mosques, is a complete contrast to the fast and developing New Bhopal, which has wide, clean, well-lit roads and well maintained architecture. A visit to the bazaars or markets of Old Bhopal includes a visit to the popular silver market, which is said to have the cheapest silverware in the country, and also to the art galleries, which hold exhibitions of the works of many modern Indian artists and sculptors. On the other side of the bridge, New Bhopal is known as one of the greenest cities in India and is impressive with its exquisite parks and gardens, broad pathways and contemporary establishments', http:// bdabhopal.org/bhopal.html#2 (accessed on March 2010).
82. Interview with Retd Professor Afaq Ahmed.
83. The decline or Urdu poetry has been well captured by the film, based on Anita Desai's novel, *In Custody*, which was partly shot in the ancestral house of Javed Akhtar in Bhopal (a place where he studied)—and where Akhtar's wife, Shabana Azmi, plays a leading part (incidentally, her father was an Urdu poet too).
84. *Census of India 2001, District Census Handbook. Part XII-A&B. Village and town directory. Primary Census Abstract*, Bhopal, Directorate of Census operations, n.d., p. 395.
85. Interview with Farhan Ansari, Bhopal, 25 January 2010.

7. MUSLIMS OF HYDERABAD—LANDLOCKED IN THE WALLED CITY

1. Bharati Ray, *Hyderabad and British Paramountcy, 1858–1883*, New Delhi: Oxford University Press, 1988, p. 2.
2. Syed Abid Hassan, *Whither Hyderabad?*, Madras: B.N. Press, 1935, pp. 2–3.
3. Sarojini Regani, *Nizam-British Relations, 1724–1857*, Secunderabad: Swarajya Printing Works, 1963, p. 185.

NOTES

4. The Nizam's government prohibited the formation of any organisation 'so named or so constituted and the Hyderabad State Congress, is, if formed, declared to be an unlawful association under Public Safety Regulations'. See, N. Ramesan (ed.), *The Freedom Struggle in Hyderabad, Vol. IV*, Hyderabad, 1966, pp. 185–186. According to P. Sundaraiah, the Indian National Congress, in response, did not encourage popular struggle which was therefore endorsed by Hindu nationalists who were to form the backbone of the local Congress. (P. Sundaraiah, *Telangana people's struggle and its lessons*, Calcutta, 1972, p. 75).
5. Like in Bhopal, Muslims almost monopolised the army and the police (where they were 54,288 out of 60,217 in 1930) as well as the bureaucracy (they were 60,229 out of 76,323) (*The Tribune*, 5, 6, and 7 June 1939). See also Ian Copland, 'Communalism in princely India: the case of Hyderabad, 1930–1940', *Modern Asian States*, 22 (4), 1988.
6. S.R. Ante, *Bhaganagar struggle*, Poona: Sadashiv Peth, 1970.
7. Narendra Luther, *Hyderabad—A Biography*, New Delhi: Oxford University Press, pp. 221–223.
8. P.V. Kate, *Marathwada under the Nizams, 1724–1948*, Delhi: Mittal Publications, 1987, pp. 64–65; Narendra Luther, *Hyderabad*, op. cit., OUP, p. 221.
9. For the Intelligence Bureau's assessment of the threat posed by the Ittehad, see M.K. Sinha, Deputy Director, Intelligence Bureau, 18 Nov. 1947, NAI, Ministry of States, f.136 PR, 1947; cited by Sherman C. Taylor, 'The integration of the princely state of Hyderabad and the making of the postcolonial state in India, 1948–56', *Indian Economic Social History Review*, Vo. 44, No. 4, 2007, pp. 489–516.
10. Wilfred Cantwell Smith. 'Hyderabad: Muslim Tragedy', *Middle East Journal*, Vol. 4, 1950, pp. 27–51; see specially, p. 44, cited by Sherman Taylor, 'The Integration...', art. quoted; see also P.V. Kate, *Marathwada under the Nizams, 1724–1948*, op. cit., pp. 64–65.
11. Swamy Ramananda Tirtha, *Memoirs of Hyderabad Freedom Struggle*, Bombay, 1967, pp. 83 and 179.
12. Hyderabad State Congress, *The Nizam Disowned*, Hyderabad, no date, pp. 8–14.
13. S.N. Prasad, *Operation Polo: The Police Action Against Hyderabad*, New Delhi, 1972, pp. 29–39, cited by Sherman Taylor in 'The Integration...', art. quoted.
14. V.H. Desai, *Vandemataram to Janaganamana: Saga of Hyderabad Freedom Struggle*, Bombay: Bharatiya Vidya Bhavan, 1990, p. 143.
15. B.K. Narayana, *Finances and Fiscal Policy of Hyderabad State (1900–1956)*, Hyderabad, 1973, p. 4; N. Ramesan, *The Freedom Struggle*, op. cit., p. 290.
16. On 1 November 1956, the map of India was redrawn into linguistic states, and Hyderabad state was divided between Andhra Pradesh, Bombay State (present-day Maharashtra), and Mysore state (present-day Karnataka). Hyderabad and the surrounding area were added to Andhra Pradesh on the basis of its Telugu linguistic majority, and Hyderabad became the capital of the state.

17. Ibid., p. 29.
18. Ratna Naidu, *Old City, New Predicament: A Study of Hyderabad*, New Delhi: Sage Publications, 1990, pp. 98–100.
19. Omar Khalidi, *Muslims in Indian Economy*, New Delhi: Three Essays Collective, 2006, pp. 149–150.
20. Ibid.
21. Iqbal Masood, *Dream Merchants, Politicians and Partition: Memoirs of an Indian Muslim*, New Delhi: HarperCollins, 1997, pp. 58–59; and 'India's No. 1 Tax Target', *Business Week*, 20 September 1958, p. 151, cited by Omar Khalidi, *Muslims in Indian Economy*, op. cit., pp. 150–151.
22. Figures based on Osmania University Diary, 1990 and 1997 as cited by Masood Ali Khan, 'Education of Muslims in AP', 143, in AWB Qadir, et. al (ed.), *Education and Muslims in India Since Independence*, New Delhi: Institute of Objective Studies, 1998. *Siasat*, 9 September 2004, internet edition.
23. http://www.osmania.ac.in/Teachers%20Profile/ (Accessed in October 2010).
24. The fact that Hyderabad is regarded as a symbol of Muslim separatism and even a den of 'fifth columnists' is evident from the explanation Swami Aseemanand gave to the Indian police for justifying the Mecca Masjid blast in 2007: '...at the time of independence the Nizam of Hyderabad decided to go with Pakistan, so they should also be taught (a lesson)...' (See English translation of the confession of Swami Aseemanand on the website of *Economic and Political Weekly*, associated to the following article: C. Jaffrelot, 'Paradigm shift by the RSS ? Lessons from Aseemanand's confession', *EPW*, vol. 46, no. 6, 5 February 2011.).
25. Ratna Naidu, *Old Cities, New Predicaments: A Study of Hyderabad*, op. cit., pp. 20–21.
26. Ibid.
27. Ibid., p. 21.
28. Ibid., p. 23.
29. Ibid., p. 29.
30. The last Nizam had already shifted the seat of his administration from Purani Haveli to a new location, north of the Musi River. Subsequently, the Municipal Corporation and then the Police Commissioner's Office have been shifted. Now, the High Court of the state has applied to be relocated in the new city.
31. Geoff Noriss, *Urban Deprivation and the Inner City*, Taylor & Francis, 1979, p. 17.
32. The Multiple Deprivation index is based on six indicators: Income Deprivation, Employment Deprivation, Health Deprivation and Disability, Housing Deprivation, Education, Skills and Training Deprivation, Geographical Access to Services: see http://www.northdevon.gov.uk/append6-2.pdf; Also see Ratna Naidu, *Old Cities*, op. cit., pp. 15–16.
33. Ratna Naidu, *Old Cities*, op. cit., pp. 15–16.
34. Ratna Naidu, *Old Cities*, op. cit., pp. 98–100.

NOTES

35. Mohammad Shaquzzaman, *Problems of Minorities' Education*, Hyderabad: Book-links, 2001.
36. Osmania University, *Report on Socio-Economic Survey of Minorities in AP, 1998*, sponsored by AP Minorities Commission (Hyderabad, 1989). This mimeographed pamphlet of a bare seventeen pages is a summary of the survey conducted in 1989. Mirza Ansar Baig, the then Chairman of the Commission, who holds the voluminous report claims that since the Report has not been placed in the AP Legislature, it cannot be made public. Cited by Omar Khalidi. *Muslims in Indian Economy*, op. cit., pp. 156–157.
37. *Backward Classes Commission Report*, Government of Andhra Pradesh, 2007.
38. Omar Khalidi, 'Muslim ministers in the state cabinets: the cases of Karnataka and AP (1956–2000)', *Radiance*, 16–27 October 2001, pp. 16–17.
39. Ratna Naidu, *Old Cities*, op. cit., pp. 82–84.
40. Ibid. p. 84.
41. Rekha Pande, 'Women and children workers in the Old City of Hyderabad', *Intersections: Gender and Sexuality in Asia, and the Pacific*, Issue 17, July 2008; http://intersections.anu.edu.au/issue7/pande.html
42. Jeremy Seabrook, *Notes from Another India*, London: Pluto Press, 1995, see the chapter 'The Lacquer Bangle Makers of Hyderabad', pp. 176–182.
43. Rekha Pande, 'Women and children workers in the Old City of Hyderabad', art. quoted.
44. Zahed Farooqui, 'Neglect of education in Old City of Hyderabad', March 17, 2008, http://www.siasat.com/discussions/viewtopic.php?t=874&postdays=0&posterder=asc&star t=0
45. Ibid.
46. Ibid.
47. Interviews with Confederation of Voluntary Associations (COVA) and interviews with Naandi Foundation, a Hyderabad-based NGO staff working in the Old City schools.
48. COVA (Confederation of Voluntary Associations) is a national network of voluntary organisations in India dedicated to the issues of social harmony, peace and justice. The prime focus of COVA is on citizenship rights and on perspective building for harmony and peace in South Asia. Through direct programmes and by networking with other CSOs, COVA directly works with the slum communities in the Old City of Hyderabad through different programmes catering to women, youth and children. COVA-Kasturba Gandhi Peace Centres now work in Hyderabad and Jammu and Kashmir to address issues related to women's rights in these regions and to propagate values of peace and harmonious coexistence. On the education problem in Hyderabad, among girls especially, see 'Hyderabad', in Zoya Hasan and Ritu Menon, *Educating Muslim Girls. A Comparison of Five Indian Cities*, New Delhi: Women Unlimited, 2005, pp. 83–113.

NOTES

49. For our survey, we participated in a transect walk in this locality and conducted interviews as well as group discussions with the residents of the locality. Apart from this we also conducted interviews and group discussions with various stakeholders such as volunteers from COVA from the Old City, women working in the bangle business, local leaders, senior citizens, members from the Arab community who are the descendants of people brought from Yemen during the Nizam's rule and also local journalists.
50. Syed Habib Qadri, a resident of this locality, who is working as sub-editor of the Urdu daily *Rahnuma-e-Deccan*, said that this area is the epitome of deprivation in civic amenities and children loiter here without education. 'Parents don't have awareness and show no interest in sending their children to schools'.
51. As per the Waqf Survey Commissioner's report in 2001, there are 35,613 Waqf institutions in the state comprising 3,632 mosques, 1,600 *dargahs* (Sufi shrines), 11,373 *ashurkhanas* (Shia shrines), 7,380 *chillas*, 8,371 graveyards, 1,122 *idgas*, 359 *panjas* and 1,776 miscellaneous properties. All in all, these properties are worth 1,385 crore rupees! But they are in an utter state of neglect. More than half of the properties are under illegal occupation, one of the culprits being the government itself. (A.P. State Waqf Board, *Annual Report for years 1997–2000*, Hyderabad, 2000; and an unpublished document entitled 'Hon'ble CM Review Meeting on 18 October 2004 at 12.30 pm', given by S. A. Huda, Officer on Special Duty, in Hyderabad December 2004; 'More than half Waqf land is encroached', *Deccan Chronicle*, 23 September 2001, Internet Edition). Sultan Oman in his thesis claimed an even higher figure of waqf properties, see 'Public policy towards Muslims: a case study of Hyderabad', M. Phil Dissertation, Dept. of Political Science, OU, 1980, p. 154. He lists 42,341 properties as opposed to 35,613. Either he counted differently or was supplied with different figures by the Waqf Board (1980) or the properties were sold away illegally between the two decades. Cited by Omar Khalidi, *Muslims in India*, op. cit., pp. 164–165.
52. Ibid.; see also the interviews with the residents of the two localities we visited.
53. Interview with Mr. Zahed Ali Khan (Editor of *Siasat*, Urdu daily, Hyderabad) in November 2010.
54. Fieldwork interview with a retired government employee, Mr. Masood Ali Khan, an Old City resident, 12 October 2010.
55. 'Communal riots in Hyderabad: understanding the causes', *Economic and Political Weekly*, vol XLV, no. 17, April 24, 2010, pp. 14–16.
56. http://www.ghmc.gov.in/tender%20pdfs/election_wards.pdf
57. Interview with Mr. Yousufuddin, a private employee and a resident of Tolichowki, on 3 November 2010.
58. Omar Khalidi, *Hyderabad in Indian Economy*, op. cit., p. 163.
59. Syed Majeedul Hasan, 'Indian Muslims and foreign exchange remittances: a sample survey', *Journal Institute of Muslim Minority Affairs*, vol. 1, 1980, pp. 89–97.

NOTES

60. M. A. Siraj, 'Hyderabad Muslim economy from penury to opulence', *Islamic Voice*, November 1991, p. 20.
61. For details see, Afzal Shariff, *Indian Muslim Labour*, New Delhi: Anmol, 1998.
62. Syed Riazuddin and Amani M. Ameeruddin, *Deccan Business Directory*, Urdu Market Research and Advertisers, Hyderabad, 2001. Cited by Omar Khalidi, *Muslims in Indian Economy*, op. cit., p. 164.
63. 'Figs from barkas tickle palates in Europe', *Deccan Chronicle*, 5 September 2004, Internet Edition.
64. *Deccan Business Directory*, compiled by Syed Riazuddin and Amani M. Ameeruddin, Urdu Market Research and Advertisers, Hyderabad, 2001.
65. 'Charminar chief banked on his clout', *Deccan Chronicle*, 26 February 2002, Internet Edition.
66. It is a business where medical professionals and doctors from the US outsource transcription work to India. This industry provides lucrative employment.
67. IBNLive at 01:31 PM, 16 September 2010; http://ibnlive.in.com/conversations/thread/165443.html

8. SAFE AND SOUND: SEARCHING FOR A 'GOOD ENVIRONMENT' IN ABUL FAZL ENCLAVE, DELHI

1. This study would not have been possible without the hospitality and friendly guidance of my *ustad*, Maulana Wali Sheikh [not his real name]. I would also like to thank my colleagues at CSH, Veronique Dupont and Marie-Helene Zerah, for guiding me through the maze of Indian urban studies. Yoginder Sikand and Usha Sanyal provided valuable comments on a preliminary version of the text. Last but not least, my gratitude also goes to Chakraverti Mahajan for assisting me in my last batch of interviews in AFE in October 2010, and for inviting me to sharpen my analysis of the theme of 'security'.
2. Mohammad Abul Fazl Farooqi, *Nasheb-o-Faraz: Savaneh Hayat* (Urdu), Delhi: Applied Publications, 2003, pp. 60–61. In the excerpts reproduced here, I have followed Rizwanullah's translation for the English edition of the text (*Ups and Downs: An Autobiography*, Delhi: Pharos, 2006). The pagination, however, is that of the original Urdu version.
3. The JI-H always had a policy of restricted membership. But if the 'fully-fledged members' (*arkan*) were only 4,776 in 2000, the number of 'workers' (*karkun*) was much higher and estimated at 270,246; cf. Irfan Ahmad, *Islamism and Democracy in India: The Transformation of Jamaat-e-Islami*, Princeton: Princeton University Press, 2009, Appendix l, p. 240.
4. This expression is derived from Richard Banegas and Jean-Pierre Warnier, 'Nouvelles figures de la réussite et du pouvoir', *Politique Africaine*, no. 82, June 2001, p. 12, who in the context of contemporary African societies talk of a 'war of competing moralities' (*une guerre de moralités concurrentes*).

NOTES

5. Nida Kirmani, 'Competing constructions of Muslim-ness in the south Delhi neighbourhood of Zakir Nagar, *Journal of Muslim Minority Affairs*, 28, 3, 2008, pp. 355–370; Khan Tabassum, *Emerging Muslim Identity in India's Globalized and Mediated Society: An Ethnographic Investigation of the Halting Modernities of the Muslim Youth of Jamia Enclave*, New Delhi: PhD dissertation (Mass Communication), Ohio University, 2009, chap. 4.
6. Quoted in C.M. Nairn, 'Ghalib's Delhi: a shamelessly revisionist look at two popular metaphors', *Annual of Urdu Studies*, vol. 18, 2003, p. 7.
7. For an account of Delhi's place in Indo-Muslim power politics and social imagination across the centuries, see the introduction to this volume. From two million at the death of Aurangzeb (1707), Delhi's population declined to 200,000 by the time the British took it over from the Marathas (1803); by the time of the 1857 uprising, this population had declined to 160,000; ibid., pp. 7–8 and Mushirul Hasan, 'Imaging the 1857 Rebellion', in Colonel A.R.D. Mackenzie, C.B. Honorary A.D.C. to the Viceroy, *Mutiny Memoirs*, M. Hasan (ed.), Delhi: Niyogi Books, 2009, p. 28.
8. R.E. Frykenberg, 'The Study of Delhi: Analytical and Historiographic Introduction', in R.E. Frykenberg (ed.), *Delhi Through the Ages: Essays in Urban History, Culture and Society*, Delhi: OUP, 1986, p. xxvi.
9. Eckart Ehlers and Thomas Krafft, 'Islamic Cities in India? Theoretical Concepts and the Case of Shajahanabad/Old Delhi', in Eckart Ehlers and Thomas Krafft (eds), *Shajahanabad/Old Delhi. Tradition and Colonial Change*, Delhi: Manohar, 2003, pp. 11–27.
10. Stephen P. Blake, *Shahjahanabad: The Sovereign City in Mughal India 1639–1739*, Cambridge: Cambridge University Press, 1991, p. 67.
11. Samuel V. Noe, 'What happened to Mughal Delhi: A Morphological Survey', in R.E. Frykenberg (ed.), *Delhi Through the Ages*, op. cit., p. 237.
12. Delhi's population only regained its pre-Mutiny level in 1872.
13. Mushirul Hasan, 'Imaging the 1857 Rebellion', art. quoted, p. 28.
14. Tai Yong Tan and Gyanesh Kudaisya, *The Aftermath of Partition in South Asia*, London: Routledge, 2000, p. 198.
15. Syed Shahabuddin, *Demography of Muslim India: An Analysis of 2001 Census Data*, Delhi: Indian Institute of Minority Affairs, 2005, p. 8, table V-4.
16. Ibid., tables VIII, IX and X, pp. 30–33.
17. Percival Spear, 'Ghalib's Delhi', in Ralph Russell (ed.), *Ghalib: The Poet and his Age*, Delhi: OUP, 2005 [1997], p. 49.
18. Gopal Krishna, 'Communal violence in India: a study of communal disturbance in Delhi', *Economic & Political Weekly*, 20 (3), 19 January 1985, pp. 117–131.
19. Tai Yong Tan and Gyanesh Kudaisya, *The Aftermath of Partition in South Asia*, op. cit., p. 1999; Vazira Fazila-Yacoobali Zamindar, *The Long Partition and the Making of South Asia: Refugees, Boundaries, Histories*, Delhi: Viking Press, 2008 [2007], p. 21 and note 13, p. 248.

NOTES

20. See for instance the account of Muslim metal workers quoted in Anis Kidwai, *In Freedom's Shade*, Delhi: Penguin, 2011 [1974], p. 45.
21. Tai Yong Tan and Gyanesh Kudaisya, *The Aftermath of Partition in South Asia*, op. cit., p. 199.
22. Anis Kidwai, *In Freedom's Shade*, op. cit., chap. 15, 'Mosques and mazars'.
23. These were to be located in Pahari Imli, Pul Bangash, Phatak Habash Khan and Sadar Bazar; Vazira Fazila-Yacoobali Zamindar, *The Long Partition*, op. cit., p. 29.
24. Veronique Dupont, 'Spatial and Demographic Growth of Delhi since 1947 and the Main Migration Flows', in Veronique Dupont, Emma Tarlo and Denis Vidal (eds), *Delhi: Urban Space and Human Destinies*, Delhi: Manohar, 2000, p. 230.
25. Ashutosh Varshney, 'Ethnic Conflict and Civil Society: India and Beyond', in Steven I. Wilkinson (ed.), *Religious Politics and Communal Violence*, Delhi: OUP, 2005, table 7.1, p. 192.
26. *Walled City Riots: A Report on the Police and Communal Violence in Delhi 19–24 May 1987*, Delhi: People's Union for Democratic Rights, 1987.
27. Nida Kirmani, *Questioning the Muslim Woman: The Narration of Multiple Boundaries in Zakir Nagar*, PhD dissertation (Sociology), University of Manchester, 2008.
28. Rowena Robinson, *Tremors of Violence: Muslim Survivors of Ethnic Strife in Western India*, Delhi: Sage, 2005, p. 61.
29. Sanjay Kumar, 'Changing Face of Delhi's Politics: Has it Changed the Face of the Political Representatives', in Christophe Jaffrelot and Sanjay Kumar (eds), *Rise of the Plebeians? The Changing Face of Indian Legislative Assemblies*, Delhi: Routledge, 2009, p. 424.
30. Lalit K. Jha, 'Muslims in Delhi: a divided lot', *The Hindu* (online edition), 24 April 2004.
31. Sikhander Bakht (1918–2004) was elected from Chandni Chowk under the Janata Party banner. This success was that of a highly atypical 'Muslim' politician, who married a Hindu woman and joined the BJP in 1980.
32. With 17,804 votes, the Congress arrived in third position, behind the RJD (23,394 votes) and the BSP (18,387 votes).
33. Omar Khalidi, *Muslims in Indian Economy*, Delhi: Three Essays Collective, 2006, p. 61.
34. Ibid., p. 63.
35. K.G. Munshi, *Socio-Economic Profile of Indian Muslims: A Case Study of Delhi*, Delhi: Institute of Objective Studies, 1996, pp. 41, 141.
36. Jagmohan—who would later on become Lt. Governor of Delhi—was committed to preventing the Muslims of Old Delhi from creating 'another Pakistan' and was instrumental in the Turkman Gate massacre of 19 April 1976, which cost at least twelve lives; cf. Emma Tarlo, *Unsettling Memories. Narratives of India's Emergency*, Delhi: Permanent Black, 2003, p. 39. The same Jagmohan tried to halt the

development of AFE and became the *bête noire* of Abul Fazl Farooqi and his brother Faznullah.
37. Gopal Krishna, 'Communal Violence in India', art. quoted, p. 121.
38. On Old Delhi's Qassai community, see Zarin Ahmad, *'Taleem, Tanzeem aur Tijaarat*: the Changing Role of the AIJQ' in Vinod C. Jairath (ed.), *Frontiers of Embedded Muslim Communities in India.*, Delhi: Routledge, 2011, pp. 158–173.
39. Omar Khalidi, *Muslims in Indian Economy*, op. cit., p. 65.
40. Delhi High Court Bar Association, *Members Directory, 2005–06*. I am grateful to Karuna Nundy for her help in accessing this directory.
41. Source: http://delhihighcourt.nic.in
42. Only Haryana and Bihar have a smaller share of Muslims in their police force; see Rowena Robinson, *Tremors of Violence*, op. cit., table 3.7, p. 92.
43. See the data given for area 2 (including AFE) and 26 (172 and 145 households respectively) in K.G. Munshi, *Socio-Economic Profile of Indian Muslims*, op. cit., pp. 53–62.
44. Declared a Central University in 1988, Jamia Millia was initially established in Aligarh in 1920 in the wake of the non-cooperation movement. It moved to the Karol Bagh area of Delhi in 1925, and later to Okhla in 1935. Since its creation, Jamia Millia has primarily catered to the educational needs of Muslim students (currently 60% of the total number of students) who feared that they would not gain admission anywhere else. However, the recent upgrading of the university makes it increasingly inaccessible to Muslims; see Khan Tabassum, *Emerging Muslim Identity in India's Globalized and Mediated Society*, op. cit., p. 75.
45. Aanchal Bansal, 'Civic role ends where Jamia Nagar begins', *ExpressIndia.com*, 19 November 2008. This estimation of Jamia Nagar's population is only tentative and does not match the data given by the Census 2001 for South Delhi (314,015 Muslims for the whole district, including Nizamuddin).
46. According to the principal of the Jamia Ahl-e-Bait, located in Shaheen Bagh, this Shia population would comprise 7,000 to 10,000 individuals for the whole of Jamia Nagar (1.8 to 2.6% of the total population).
47. In analysing the formation of AFE through its politics of story-telling, I draw inspiration from Ruth Finnegan, *Tales of the City: A Study of Narrative and Urban Life*, Cambridge: Cambridge University Press, 1998.
48. Parvez Hashmi was elected in the Okhla constituency in Delhi's first legislative election, in 1993. He remained undefeated until 2008 and only resigned from this post after being elected to the Rajya Sabha in 2009.
49. Syyed Mansoor Agha, *Abul Fazl Enclave at a Glance*, n.d., p. 5.
50. Interview, 18 November 2009.
51. The acting chairman of the RWA (who also occupied this post from 1984 to 1987) told me that the authors of the booklet analysed here were 'mad' (*pagal*) and he vehemently criticised their attempt to deny AFE its religious outlook; interview, AFE, October 2010.

NOTES

52. Syyed Mansoor Agha, *Abul Fazl Enclave at a Glance*, op. cit.
53. Ibid., p. 23.
54. For more details on Abul Fazl Farooqi's life trajectory, cf. Laurent Gayer, 'I never held money with my teeth: constructions of exemplarity in Abul Fazl Farooqi's *Nasheb-o-Faraz*', *SAMAJ*, 4, December 2010.
55. Mohammad Abul Fazl Farooqi, *Nasheb-o-Faraz*, op. cit., p. 63.
56. Ibid., pp. 63–64.
57. Interview with Syyed Mansoor Agha, AFE, November 2009.
58. Ibid.
59. Interview with Maulana Shafi Moonis, AFE, October 2010.
60. Interview with Zafarul Islam Khan, AFE, October 2010.
61. Conversation with the *mali* (gardener) of Dawat Nagar, November 2009.
62. Interview with the editor of *Radiance Weekly*, Ejaz Ahmed Aslam, Dawat Nagar, November 2009.
63. This hospital was due to open in 2010 with fifty beds before expanding to 200. Generally, the JI-H is reluctant to conduct philanthropic activities in AFE, as it fears that it would be perceived as an opportunistic ploy by local residents, who in any case are considered by Jama'at cadres to be less in need than other Muslims of India; interview with Ejaz Ahmed Aslam, Dawat Nagar, November 2009. Most of the JI-H social work (including the construction of the aforementioned hospital) is supervised by the Human Welfare Foundation (HWF); see HWF, *Vision 2016: Creating Partnership with the Needy*, Delhi, n.d.
64. Personal observation, Dawat Nagar, November 2009.
65. Interview, AFE, November 2009.
66. I am well aware of the distinction between *din* (religion) and *iman* (faith) in Islam, the former being related to the outward dimension of religion whereas the latter qualifies its inward expression. My emphasis on the *dini* dimension of Islam is not a matter of personal choice but an attempt to account for my respondents' own perspective on their religious values and aspirations.
67. Margrit Pernau, 'Middle Class and Secularization: The Muslims of Delhi in the Nineteenth Century', in Imtiaz Ahmad and Heimut Reifeld (eds), *Middle Class Values in India and Western Europe*, Delhi: Social Science Press, 2001, pp. 21–41.
68. On the history, sociology and politics of SIMI, see Irfan Ahmad, *Islamism and Democracy in India*, op. cit. On the controversy regarding SIMI's possible shift to terrorism since its interdiction in 2001, see 'The SIMI Fictions', *Tehelka*, 16 October 2008.
69. Mukulika Banerjee (ed.), *Muslim Portraits. Everyday Lives in India*, Delhi: Yoda Press, 2008, p. xv.
70. Not his real name.
71. Not his real name.
72. Although we can suppose that the majority of AFE residents are Barelwis, their institutional presence remains limited in the neighbourhood.

73. Interview, AFE, October 2010.
74. Tablighis control the Bilal Mosque in AFE I, administer a *madrasa* for girls in Shaheen Bagh (the Zayed Women's College) and are currently constructing a mosque in the vicinity of the former.
75. Luise White, *Speaking with Vampires: Rumour and History in Colonial Africa*, Berkeley: University of California Press, 2000, p. 64.
76. Christiane Brosius, *India's Middle Class: New Forms of Urban Leisure, Consumption and Prosperity*, Delhi: Routledge, 2010, p. 94.
77. Interview, AFE, October 2010.
78. Interview, Dawat Nagar, November 2009.
79. Interview, AFE, November 2009.
80. Conversation, AFE, October 2010.
81. Not his real name.
82. Conversation, Zakir Nagar, November 2009.
83. Conversation, September 2010.
84. Conversation, November 2009.
85. Interview, October 2010.
86. Khan Tabassum reaches the same conclusion in her ethnography of media consumption among Jamia Nagar's middle-class youths; see her *Emerging Muslim Identity in India's Globalized and Mediated Society*, op. cit., pp. 70, 86.
87. Minna Saavala, *Middle Class Moralities: Everyday Struggle Over Belonging and Prestige in India*, Delhi: Orient Blackswan, 2010, p. 12.
88. On the appeal of 'moral achievement' over South Asia's new middle classes, see Laurent Gayer and Ingrid Terwath, 'Introduction: modelling exemplarity in South Asia', *SAMAJ*, 4, 2010.
89. Interview with the teaching staff of Jamiat-ul Bannat al-Islami, AFE, October 2010.
90. 'Gulhae-e-akhlaqiyat' (Urdu) [The Flowers of Ethics], *Rafiq-e-Manzil*, January 2005, p. 5.
91. On the literary and social trajectory of the notions of *akhlaq* and *adab* in India, see Mushirul Hasan, *A Moral Reckoning: Muslim Intellectuals in Nineteenth-century Delhi*, Delhi: Oxford University Press, 2007 [2003], p. 2, and Barbara D. Metcalf (ed.), *Moral Conduct and Authority: The Place of Adab in South Asian Islam*, Berkeley/Los Angeles: University of California Press, 1984, which shows that the notion of *adab* was historically more encompassing than its modern association with *sharif* culture tends to suggest.
92. Although I am yet to meet such families in AFE, Craig Jeffrey's work points in that direction; Craig Jeffrey, Patricia Jeffery and Roger Jeffery, 'Karate, computers and the Quran Sharif: Zamir', in Mukulika Banerjee (ed.), *Muslim Portraits*, op. cit., p. 72. The role of *madrasas* in the development of their students' *akhlaq* and *adab* is studied in detail in Arshad Alam, *Inside a Madrasa: Knowledge, Power and Islamic Identity in India*, Delhi: Routledge, 2011, Chapter 6.

93. Pradip Datta, Biswamoy Pati, Sumit Sarkar, Tanika Sarkar, Sambuddha Sen, 'Understanding communal violence: Nizamuddin riots' *Economic & Political Weekly*, 10 November 1990, p. 2491.
94. I borrow this notion of 'choiceless decision' from Begonia Aretxaga, *Shattering Silence. Women, Nationalism and Political Subjectivity in Northern Ireland*, Princeton: Princeton University Press, 1997, p. 61.
95. Interview, AFE, October 2010.
96. A similar observation was made by Nida Kirmani in the neighbouring locality of Zakir Nagar; 'Competing Constructions of Muslim-ness in the South Delhi Neighbourhood of Zakir Nagar', art. quoted, p. 360.
97. On the influence of national and global media on the middle class Muslim youth of Jamia Nagar, see Khan Tabassum, *Emerging Muslim Identity in India's Globalized and Mediated Society*, op. cit.
98. See the results for area 2 (covering AFE, Naibasti, Zakir Bagh & Okhla) in K.G. Munshi, *Socio-Economic Profile of Indian Muslims*, op. cit., p. 59, which shows that the heads of 149 of the 172 surveyed households worked away from home, probably with a substantial part employed outside AFE, considering the limited economic opportunities available locally.
99. Interviews at the (Shia) Jamia ahl-e-Baith and the (Deobandi) Jamiat-ul-Banat al-Islami, October 2010.

9. MARGINALISED IN A SYNCRETIC CITY: MUSLIMS IN CUTTACK

1. As per the 2001 Census, Muslims constitute barely 2.07% of Orissa's population, which is overwhelmingly Hindu (94.35%); Christians, with a population of 2.44%, are numerically the largest minority in Orissa.
2. This may explain why Andrew Sterling, the British administrator-cum-historian of Orissa, called his work *An Account (Geographical, Statistical and Historical) of Orissa Proper or Cuttack*.
3. Subhas Bose was born in Oriya Bazar where Muslims lived in large numbers. He left for Calcutta after completing his school education at Cuttack. Incidentally, when Bose visited the city in 1939, Amin welcomed him on behalf of 'The Cuttack City Sirajud-Daula Memorial Committee'. Cuttack's nationalist Muslims considered the Battle of Plassey (1757) as the first battle for Indian independence.
4. At times there have been violent clashes to gain control over a mosque or a Waqf property. See http://mdiamediacentre.com/2009/12/10/legal-restriction-vacated-from-indian-mosque/ (accessed on August 2011).
5. Personal communication with some Muslim youths of Oriya Bazar.
6. A Muslim leader disclosed during the interview that his son is married to a Brahmin girl. Initially the parents of the girl were opposed to the marriage and even lodged a complaint with the police, but the relationship between the two families

NOTES

became extremely cordial soon after the marriage. He had full admiration for his daughter-in-law for her adaptability. In another interview, a young Muslim political leader, who is married to a Hindu girl, fondly talked about the complete cultural compatibility in his married life, thereby suggesting the similarities of culture between the two communities.

7. Cuttack's aversion towards communal riots partly goes with the thesis of Ashutosh Varshney.
8. Interview with Muhammad Ayub, Corporator, Cuttack Municipal Corporation. Ayub has a doctorate in Oriya literature and is the founder of the Oriya Gazal Academy.
9. http://orissa.gov.in/cadre/cadrelist.htm & www.orissa.gov.in/revenue/gradation/Final_gradation, (accessed in August 2011).
10. Interview with Dr. Sayed Mustaq Ali.
11. Swarna Jayanti Sahai Rojgar Yojna (Golden Jubilee Urban Employment Plan) is a unified Central Government-sponsored scheme for urban poverty alleviation.
12. Interview with Ata Mohiuddin, Secretary, Orissa Madrasa Education Board, Bhubaneswar.
13. The promotion of *madrasa* education by the West Bengal government of the Left Front came at a price, that of their secularisation, which has brought the 500 'High *Madrasas*' funded and administered by the public Board of Madrasa education on par with national standards of education but which has also robbed them of their special characteristics, a trend denounced by some Bengali Muslims (Gupta 2010).
14. Interview with Md. Yakub, teacher, Madrasa-i-Sultania, Cuttack. Under this scheme, the Orissa Madrasa Board has received an annual grant of 10,872,000 rupees. This grant enabled the board to appoint 302 teachers in 151 *madrasas* with a monthly salary of Rs 6,000 per teacher. Proposals to appoint teachers in another 99 *madrasas* are at the planning stage. Interview with Ata Mohiuddin.
15. Interview with Sajida Begum, Headmistress in-charge, Urdu Girls' High School, Cuttack.
16. Not far from this mosque is Oriya Bazar Mosque, the headquarters of the Deobandis.
17. Interview with Md. Abdul Ahad, Dewan Bazar, President/Secretary of Anjuman (1996–2010).
18. Interview with M.Q. Khan at Cuttack. Khan, who taught English and was the former Vice-Chancellor, has been actively taking up community issues.
19. Interview with Dr Syed Mustaq Ali, Chairman of the Trust, Cuttack. Ali and his family members, who are all doctors, run a private nursing home in the city. An ardent nationalist, Ali, who played Ranji Trophy cricket, strongly advocates modern education for Muslim children. He publishes small booklets such as 'Aaiye English Sikhen' to teach English to *madrasa* students.
20. Interview with the butchers/labourers of Bounsagali.

NOTES

21. Under the Orissa Prevention of Cow Slaughter Act, 1960, killing cows is totally prohibited. It is a recognisable offence and carries penal provision of imprisonment up to a maximum of two years or a fine up to Rs 1,000 or both. While the slaughter of a heifer or a calf is prohibited, that of a bull or bullock is allowed on the production of a fit-for-slaughter certificate if the animal is over fourteen years of age or has become permanently unfit for breeding.
22. Interview with Md. Arif Faimeed, former corporator (Congress), Oriya Bazar, Cuttack.
23. Personal communication with a young Muslim activist of Bounsagali.
24. Interview with Sheikh Muntaqueen Buksh.
25. Similar trends have been noticed in Hyderabad (Ali, 2002) and in Delhi (Ahmad, 2011).
26. Interview with Hussain Rabi Gandhi, President, Orissa Sahitya Academy.

10. KOZHIKODE (CALICUT)'S KUTTICHIRA: EXCLUSIVITY MAINTAINED PROUDLY

1. A book was aptly titled, *Cities of Kerala: Actually Small Towns*, Natarajan, Baiju (ed.), Mumbai: Marg Publications, 2007.
2. Due to Kerala's undulating terrain and it being a narrow land strip nudged between the Western Ghats and the sea.
3. 819 sq km, *District Handbooks of Kerala: Kozhikode*, Department of Information and Public Relations, Government of Kerala, 2003.
4. The addition of three *panchayats*, Beypore, Cheruvannur and Elathur, is expected to raise the population to nearly 6 lakhs and the area to 118.2 sq km (two more are on the cards).
5. Headquarters of important Malayalam dailies like *Malayala Manorama*, *Madhyamam* and *Chandrika*.
6. Regional trade centre/wholesale bazaars for products like copra and rice.
7. The term Mappila is a contraction of the words *maha* (great) and *pilla* (child), and was initially an honorific title among the Nairs of Travancore, later extended to early Christians and Muslims. Although this term is sometimes applied to the whole Muslim population of Kerala, it more specifically refers to Malabar Muslims.
8. The KNM was founded in 1950 but was the emanation of the Ilahi reformist movement that took off in Kerala in the 1920s; on Muslim reformist currents in Kerala, see Filippo and Caroline Osella, 'Islamist and social reform in Kerala', *Modern Asian Studies*, 42 (2/3), March-May 2008, pp. 317–346.
9. Mattison Mines, 'Muslim social stratification in India: the basis for variation', *Southwestern Journal of Anthropology*, 28 (4), Winter 1972, p. 336.
10. Ibid.
11. K.C. Zachariah and Irudaya, Rajan, *Kerala Migration Survey*, Thiruvananthapuram: Centre for Development Studies (CDS), 2007.

NOTES

12. According to Indian embassies in the GCC states, more than 50% of Indian migrants are of Kerala origin.
13. Harish Damodaran, *India's New Capitalists: Caste, Business, and Industry in a Modern Nation*, Delhi: Permanent Black, 2008, p. 305.
14. Ibid., p. 306.
15. A religious sub-group in Kerala (referred to as Thiyyas in northern parts), forming about 25% of the population. They were among the most seriously backward communities until advances were achieved by the Sree Narayana Dharma Paripalana Yogam social reform movement in the late nineteenth and early twentieth centuries.
16. For example, the National Youth Meet organised by the IUML in February 2010 showcased its political empowerment model in front of Muslim youths from other Indian states.
17. The IUML has some presence in other states like Tamil Nadu, unlike the All India Majlis-i Ittihad al-Muslimin, whose presence is limited to Andhra Pradesh's Hyderabad constituency.
18. U. Mohammed, *Educational Empowerment of Kerala Muslims. A Socio-Historical Perspective*, Calicut: Other Books, 2007, p. 20.
19. Other ancient Kerala ports are Muciri, Ezhimala, Tondi, Kollam and Vizhinjam.
20. Sanjay Subrahmanyam, *The Career and Legend of Vasco Da Gama*, Cambridge: Cambridge University Press, 1997, p. 104.
21. Today's city-centre, *Mananchira*, stands in the place of the destroyed royal palace, courtyard and pond.
22. Arabs from the Gulf region, mostly Yemenis, as well as some Persians.
23. Such as the 1,100 year-old Muccinti mosque and the 1,000 year-old Jama Masjid.
24. Matrilineal practice among the Hindus—particularly those of the Nair caste—which was discontinued during the 'modernisation' phase of the twentieth century.
25. In old age, it would seem the husband is generally staying permanently with the wife's family.
26. Recently dismantled and rebuilt as numerous individual houses for members within the compound. Part of *waqf* trust, it has a rice mill at the entrance.
27. Each house usually has a well with surprisingly clear, drinkable water, considering the locality's proximity to the sea.
28. Filippo Osella, personal communication.
29. Kozhikode is said to be 'the second Mecca for football in India', after Calcutta. Muslims have a noticeable presence in the local sport scene.
30. www.thekkepuram.org.
31. Harish Damodaran, *India's New Capitalists*, op. cit., p. 305.
32. V.K. Shashikumar, 'Here come the pious', *Tehelka*, 9 October 2010.
33. This consists of spoken Malayalam written in the Arabic script; it was widely practiced among Malabar Muslims until the reform movements of the

NOTES

nineteenth/early twentieth century. Makhti Thangal was the first Muslim to write in Malayalam around 1912. Still popular, *Mappilapattu* song and the Oppana dance are examples of the blending of Arab and local influences.

34. Affiliated to the IUML, it has branches in all GCC nations plus the UK. It has eight district and eight area committees.
35. Filippo and Caroline Osella, 'Muslim Entrepreneurs in Public Life between India and the Gulf: Making Good and Doing Good', in Filippo Osella, Benjamin Scares (eds), *Islam, Politics, Anthropology*, Oxford: Blackwell, 2010, p. 195.
36. Kerala has a literacy record but it is limited to primary education. Higher education is predominantly a system of caste/community-managed private institutions, some of which are supported by the government (which meets the salary expenses of the teaching and non-teaching staff) whereas others are entirely self-financed.
37. Filippo Osella and Caroline Osella, 'Migration, money and masculinity in Kerala', *The Journal of the Royal Anthropological Institute*, 6(1), Mar. 2000, pp. 117–133.
38. Chavakkad in Thrissur (know as *'Mini-Gulf'*) and Malappuram have the highest proportion of Gulf expatriates. Also worth being mentioned is Ponnani, in Malappuram, the cultural and religious capital of Kerala Muslims.
39. Filippo and Caroline Osella, 'Muslim Entrepreneurs in Public Life between India and the Gulf', art. quoted, p. 195.
40. Al Umma was implicated in an attack against an office of the RSS in Chennai in 1993, during which 11 RSS workers were killed.
41. V.K. Shashikumar, 'Here come the pious', art. quoted.
42. A. Abdul Salim, P.R. Gopinathan Nair, *Educational Development in India: The Kerala Experience since 1800*, New Delhi: Anmol Publications Pvt. Ltd., 2002.
43. A few episodes in the period of Portuguese attacks (1498) and subsequent 'pepper politics', in the reigns of Mysore (1782–92) and Great Britain (1792–1947), and in the phase of the Mappila tenant revolt (1821–1921), have affected Hindu-Muslim relations in Kozhikode and the Malabar region at large along the centuries.
44. U. Mohammed, *Educational Empowerment of Kerala Muslims: A Sociohistorical Perspective*, Calicut: Other Books, 2007, p. 24.

11. MUSLIMS IN BANGALORE: A MINORITY AT EASE?

1. My heartfelt thanks to Maqbool Siraj, Hussain Saheb and Biju Abdul Qadir for helping me meet the 'right' people.
2. In South Asia, Muslims, taking into account the Islamic numerology, often use 786 as a substitute for 'Bismallah al-Rehman al-Rahim'. But this practice is not universally accepted by all Muslims.
3. Men are allowed to have up to four wives in Islam.
4. Bangalore was then known as Bengaluru. The name was changed to Bangalore during colonisation, and again to Bengaluru in 2005.

NOTES

5. See Richard Eaton, *The Sufis of Bijapur 1300–1700: Social Roles of Sufis in Medieval India*, Princeton: Princeton University Press, 1978.
6. On Tipu, see Mohibbul Hasan Khan, *History of Tipu Sultan*, Calcutta: The Bibliophile, 1951; and Kate Brittlebank, *Tipu Sultan's Search for Legitimacy*, Delhi: OUP, 1997.
7. Janaki Nair, *The Promise of the Metropolis: Bangalore's Twentieth Century*, Delhi: OUP, 2005; Smriti Srinivas, *Landscapes of Urban Memory: The Sacred and the Civic in India's High-Tech City*, Minneapolis: University of Minnesota Press, 2001.
8. Cosmopolitism is defined here as the coexistence in a given city or locality of groups from various ethnic and religious backgrounds.
9. Aurélie Varrel, 'Back to Bangalore': *Etude géographique de la migration de retour des Indiens très qualiés à Bangalore*, PhD Dissertation, 2008, p. 77.
10. Janaki Nair; op. cit., p. 246.
11. http://www.languageinindia.com/dec2002/urduinkarnataka.html
12. Jackie Assayag, *At the Confluence of Two Rivers: Muslims and Hindus in South India*, Delhi: Manohar, 2004, p. 222.
13. K. Rahman Khan, *Report of High Power Committee on Socio-Economic and Educational Survey—1994 of Religious Minorities in Karnataka*, Karnataka State Minorities Commission, Bangalore, 1995.
14. This rank is based on lifestyle and consumption habits of the people. The survey was conducted by the Nielson Upper Middle and Rich (UMAR).
15. Omar Khalidi, *Muslims in Indian Economy*, Delhi: Three Essays Collective, 2006, pp. 186–187.
16. Established in 1868, the entrance fees were 10 lakhs in August 2010.
17. The Al-Ameen movement was founded in 1966 by Mumtaz Ahmed Khan to provide educational banking and health facilities for under-privileged sections of the Bangalorean population, especially Muslims.
18. Janaki Nair, op. cit., p. 51.
19. Prophet.
20. I mean here not the type of burqas worn by 'born-again' Muslims (abaya and so on).
21. Muslim-ness includes here both the people (who happen to be Muslim) and the area (Muslim-dominated).
22. In India, pharmacies are frequently opened near a clinic in order to attract the patients going to that clinic.
23. Byrasandra Tavarekere and Madivala Layout, a neighbourhood of Bangalore.
24. Smriti Srinivas, op. cit., p. 35.
25. It does not however make its way through Shivaji Nagar.
26. Among others, see Didier Lapeyronnie, *Ghetto urbain: ségrégation, violence, pau-vreté en France aujourd'hui*, Paris: Robert Laffont, 2008.
27. In fact, it is usually more 'food-based' than religion-based as such (cf. food restrictions of Brahmins and other communities).

28. See in particular, Loïc Wacquant, *Pariahs Urbains: Ghetto, Banlieues, Etat*, Paris: La Découverte, 2006; and Sudhir Venkatesh, *Off the Books: The Underground Economy of the Urban Poor*, Cambridge: Harvard University Press, 2006.
29. The notion of 'ghetto' implies the idea of a forced relegation owing to poverty, discriminatory policies, state violence and so on.
30. Hira has appointed a social worker who identifies the basic needs of the most underprivileged populations, and, with the money collected from donors, directly pays for their hospital and educational fees, their groceries and medicines and so on.
31. See Robert Hayden, 'Antagonistic tolerance: competitive sharing of religious sites in south Asia and the Balkans', *Current Anthropology*, 43(2), April 2002, pp. 205–219.
32. James Jasper, *The Art of Moral Protest: Culture, Biography and Creativity in Social Movements*, Chicago: University of Chicago Press, 1997.
33. Srinivas, op. cit., p. 117.
34. Janaki Nair, op. cit., pp. 274–275.
35. http://www.languageinindia.com/dec2002/urduinkarnataka.html
36. *The Hindu*, 19 August 2009.

CONCLUSION: 'IN THEIR PLACE'? THE TRAJECTORIES OF MARGINALISATION OF INDIA'S URBAN MUSLIMS

1. On the most successful Muslim-owned companies of India, see Harish Damodaran, *India's New Capitalists. Caste, Business, and Industry in a Modern Nation*, Delhi: Permanent Black, 2008, pp. 302–306.
2. Ansaris currently occupy a central position in the power looms of Maharashtra (Bhiwandi, Malegaon) and recently made inroads in the handloom industry of Uttar Pradesh. Some Qureshis, for their part, have made the transition from meat sellers to owners of integrated abattoirs-cum-meat-processing-plants (the most notable example in this regard is that of Sirajuddin Qureshi of Hind Agro); ibid., p. 304.
3. Some Silawats of Rajasthan have become successful builders, whereas the Malis of Maharashtra occupy some key positions in the retail trade and distribution; cf. Asghar Ali Engineer, 'Muslim middle class and its role', *Secular Perspective*, 16–31 May 2001; and Omar Khalidi, *Muslims in Indian Economy*, Delhi: Three Essays Collective, 2006, p. 1999.
4. Vasanthi Raman, *The Warp and the Weft. Community and Gender Identity among Banaras Weavers*, Delhi: Routledge, 2010, p. 241.
5. On the global expansion of Al Kabeer, see Preeti Chamikutty, 'The growth of Al Kabeer', *The Economic Times*, 3 October 2007.
6. Karen Isaksen Leonard, *Locating Home. India's Hyderabadis Abroad*, Delhi: Oxford University Press, 2007, p. 207.

NOTES

7. Filippo Osella and Caroline Osella, 'Migration, money and masculinity in Kerala', *The Journal of the Royal Anthropological Institute*, 6(1), March 2000, pp. 117–133.
8. Satish Saberwal, 'On the Making of Muslims in India Historically' in Basant Rakesh and Shariff Abusaleh (eds), *Handbook of Muslims in India. Empirical and Policy Perspectives*, New Delhi: Oxford University Press, 2010, p. 47.
9. Francis Robinson, *Separatism Among Indian Muslims. The Politics of the United Provinces Muslims, 1860–1923*, Delhi: Oxford University Press, 1997 [1975], p. 44.
10. See Mushirul Hasan, *Legacy of a Divided Nation. India's Muslims since Independence*, London: Hurst, 1997; and Yoginder Sikand, *Muslims in India since 1947*, London/New York: Routledge/Curzon, 2004.
11. For a panorama of Indian Muslims' economic activities across India, see Omar Khalidi, *Muslims in Indian Economy*, op. cit.
12. Muhammad Hanif, 'Azad Hindustan mein Musulmanon ki Mu'ashi Surat-e-Hal' (Urdu) [The Economic Situation of Muslims in independent India], in Pervez Rehmani and Muhammad Arshad (eds), *Hindustani Musulman. Musulman-e-Hind ki Qadim o Jadid Tarikh aur Mojudah Surat-e-Hal ka ek Jaezah* [Indian Muslims. A Study of the Ancient and Modern History and of the Present Condition of the Muslims of India], Delhi: Dawat Publications, 2001, pp. 75–79.
13. These trading castes are generally descendants of Hindu converts from trading communities of Sindh and Gujarat, such as the Lohanas.
14. Asghar Ali Engineer, *The Bohras*, Delhi: Vikas Publishing House, 1993 [1980].
15. Bimal Prasad, *The Foundations of Muslim Nationalism*, vol. I, New Delhi: Manohar, 1999, p. 127.
16. A few other cases of successful Muslim industrialists worth mentioning are Adam-jee Haji Dawood—a Memon from Gujarat—who built an industrial empire in the 1920s and 1930s, as well as Ahmed Ebrahim Bawani, another Jetpuri Memon who also started his industrial activities in Burma in the 1930s, before moving to his native Junagadh after the Second World War.
17. D.E.U. Baker, *Changing Political Leadership in an Indian Province: the Central Provinces and Berar, 1919–1939*, New Delhi: Oxford University Press, 1979, p. 117 and p. 129.
18. If we go by this work, Delhi may be the place where Sunni businessmen have been the most influential, especially in Sadar Bazar (Narayani Gupta, *Delhi Between Two Empires, 1803–1931. Society, Government and Urban Growth*, New Delhi: Oxford University Press, 1981, p. 54 and p. 61).
19. Claude Markovits, 'Businessmen and the Partition of India', in Dwijendra Tripathi (ed.), *Business and Politics in India: A Historical Perspective*, New Delhi: Manohar, 1991, p. 291.
20. Omar Khalidi, *Muslims in Indian Economy*, op. cit., tables V and VI, pp. 45–46.

21. Pt. Umer Hayat Khan Ghauri, *Hindustan Mein Milli Masail* (Urdu) [National Problems in India], Delhi: Hindustan Publications, p. 154. Let us underline that the writer is close to the Jama'at-i-Islami Hind (JIH) and that his rather extreme views are more representative of those of this Islamist organisation than of Indian Muslims at large.
22. Sonia Bhalotra and Bernarda Zamora, 'Social Divisions in Education in India', in Rakesh Basant and Abusaleh Shariff (eds), *Handbook of Muslims in India*. op. cit., p. 192.
23. Imtiaz Ahmad, 'Muslim educational backwardness: an inferential analysis', *Economic & Political Weekly*, 16 (36), 5 September 1981, p. 1460.
24. Francis Robinson, *Separatism among Indian Muslims*, op. cit., p. 39.
25. Imtiaz Ahmad, 'Muslim educational backwardness', art. quoted, p. 1457.
26. On Muslim girls' education, see Zoya Hasan and Ritu Menon, *Educating Muslim Girls. A Comparison of Five Indian Cities*, Delhi: Women Unlimited, 2004.
27. On the current transformation of Indian *madrasas*, see Yoginder Sikand, *Bastion of the Believers. Madrasas and Islamic Education in India*, Delhi: Penguin, 2005, in particular Chapter 5.
28. See for instance Waris Mazhari, 'Dini Madaris ke Nisab-o-Nizam Mein Tabdili ka Masla' (Urdu) [The Issue of Change in the Curriculum of Madrasas], in *Da'wat-e-Fikr-o-A'mal* [Invitation to Thought and Action], Delhi: Foundation for Islamic Studies, 2009, pp. 12–20.
29. Yoginder Sikand, *Bastion of the Believers*, op. cit., p. 203.
30. Patricia Jeffery, Roger Jeffery and Craig Jeffrey, 'The First Madrasa: Learned Mawlawis and the Educated Mother', in Jan-Peter Hartung and Helmut Reifeld (eds), *Islamic Education, Diversity, and National Identity*, Delhi: Sage, 2006, p. 229.
31. Indeed, for the teaching staff of *madrasas* as well as for the families of their *tuleba*, the pedagogical project of these institutions is not limited to imparting religious education but also rules of civility (*akhlaq o adab*). This emphasis on proper behaviour and etiquette can be supplemented by 'technical' training aiming to transmit practical skills to students so that they can have access to a wider array of job opportunities in India or abroad (especially in the Gulf). As Arshad Alam shows in his recent ethnography of a Barelwi *madrasa* of Eastern UP, Quranic schools can therefore become vectors of extraversion for poor Muslim students, while providing them with some social and cultural capital, 'which in effect give them some degree of mobility'. Arshad Alam, *Inside a Madrasa*, op. cit., p. 203,
32. Ibid., p. 94, 203.
33. Craig Jeffrey, *Timepass. Youth, Class, and the Politics of Waiting in India*, Stanford: Stanford University Press, 2010, p. 85.
34. R. Jeery and P. Jeery, *Population, Gender and Politics*, Cambridge: Cambridge University Press, 1997.
35. In most of the cases, 'testing' consists in sending the same CV with a Brahmin

NOTES

name, with a Dalit name and with a Muslim name in response to some job advertisement and to compare the number of invitations for interviews in different categories.

36. S.K. Thorat and P. Attewell, 'The legacy of social exclusion', *Economic and Political Weekly*, Vol. 42, No. 41, 13–19 October 2007, pp. 4143–4144; and S.K. Thorat and Katherine S. Newman, 'Caste and economic discrimination: causes, consequences and remedies', ibid.
37. Sonal Desai and Veena Kulkarni, 'Unequal Playing Field. Socio-religious Inequalities in Educational Attainment', in Rakesh Basant and Abusaleh Shariff (eds), *Handbook of Muslims in India*, op. cit.,p. 285.
38. Vani K. Boorooah, 'On the Risks of Belonging to Disadvantaged Groups', in Rakesh Basant and Abusaleh Shariff (eds), *Handbook of Muslims in India*, ibid., p. 213.
39. For instance, out of 1,026 dead in the Bhagalpur riot (1989), 876 were Muslims (see Asghar Ali Engineer, *Communal Riots in Post-independence India*, Delhi: Orient Blackswan, 1991.
40. In the case of Hyderabadis, for instance, see Karen Isaksen Leonard, *Locating Home, op. cit.*
41. And even—unofficially—cities, since Hindu nationalists call Aligarh, 'Harigarh', Ahmedabad, 'Karnavati', Bhopal, 'Bhojpal', and so on.
42. In the case of Abul Fazl Enclave's RWA, for instance, the production of a de-Islamised narrative of the locality was primarily the result of a lobbying strategy aimed at the regularisation of the colony, which saw class markers as a more efficient resource than religious ones for interacting with political and judicial institutions.
43. Rubina Jasani, 'Violence, reconstruction and Islamic Reform: stories from the Muslim "Ghetto"', *Modern Asian Studies*, 42 (2/3), March-May 2008, pp. 431–456.
44. Anna Bigelow, *Sharing the Sacred. Practicing Pluralism in Muslim North India*, Oxford: Oxford University Press, 2010.
45. Jeremy Seabrook and Imran Ahmed Siddiqui, *People without History. India's Muslim Ghettos*, Delhi: Navayana, 2011.
46. For long, urban sociologists—and in particular those of the 'Chicago School'—failed to make a distinction between ghettos and enclaves, but the two concepts have acquired a life of their own in recent years; see for instance Ceri Peach, 'The Ghetto and the Ethnic Enclave' in David P. Varady, *Desegregating the City. Ghettos, Enclaves, and Inequality*, Albany: State of New York University Press, 2005, pp. 31–48.
47. This notion of 'choiceless decision' is borrowed from Begonia Aretxaga, *Shattering Silence. Women, Nationalism and Political Subjectivity in Northern Ireland*, Princeton: Princeton University Press, 1997, p. 61.
48. Jeremy Seabrook and Imran Ahmed Siddiqui, *People without History*, op. cit.

NOTES

49. A recent study by the National Council of Applied Economic Research shows that only 2.1% of the Muslim population of West Bengal (25.2% of the total population of the province, which includes 12 of the 90 'minority-concentrated' districts in the country) has government jobs, way behind a supposedly communally-tainted state such as Gujarat, with its 9.1% Muslim population and 5.4% share in public offices; cf. 'Bengal worse than Gujarat for Muslims?', *The Times of India Online*, 23 March 2011.
50. Alain Corbin, *Le Miasme et la jonquille. L'odorat et l'imaginaire social, XVIIIe-XIXe Siècles*, Paris: Flammarion, 2008 (1982), pp. 210–211.
51. Partha Chatterjee, 'Are Indian Cities Becoming Bourgeois At Last?', in *The Politics of the Governed*, Delhi: Permanent Black, 2004, p. 132.
52. For an illustration of the pressures exerted by Hindu nationalists on practising Muslims in Indian cities, see the case of Rohini in Delhi, where pro-Hindutva residents have been preventing local Muslims from constructing a mosque; cf. Mumtaz Alam Falahi, 'Rohini Mosque: undeterred by Hindutva pressure Muslims building it brick by brick', *twocircles.net*, 11 July 2009, URL: http://twocircles.net/2009julll/rohini_mosque_undeterred_hindutva_pressure_muslims_build-ing_it_brick_brick.html.
53. The urge to regroup in enclaves manifests itself also in localities where insecurity has not been directly experienced by Muslims but who know about the way coreligionists living in mixed areas have been attacked by Hindus elsewhere (see the impact of the assassination of Ehsan Jafri on the Muslims of Aligarh and Bangalore). The impact of violence inflicted by Hindu mobs on other religious minorities should also be accounted for (see the impact of the anti-Sikh pogrom of 1984 on Delhi Muslims, for instance).
54. Quoted by Rowena Robinson, *Tremors of Violence. Muslim Survivors of Ethnic Strife in Western India*, Delhi: Sage, 2005, p. 244.
55. This judgment concerned a Parsi Housing Society of Mumbai, which claimed to have the right to reserve membership to Parsis only. The Court invoked the freedom of association to justify its decision.
56. For the case of Mumbai, see Rowena Robinson, *Tremors of Violence*, op. cit., p. 43.
57. Dionne Bunsha, 'Ahmedabad's ghettos', *Frontline*, 27 September 2003.
58. Although such 'borders' do exist in other cities, they are yet to take such a formal shape. On these 'borders', see Darshini Mahadevia, 'A City with Many Borders—Beyond Ghettoisation in Ahmedabad', in Annapurna Shaw (ed.), *Indian Cities in Transition*, Delhi: Orient Longman, 2007, pp. 341–389.
59. Rowena Robinson, *Tremors of Violence*, op. cit., p. 49.
60. Sameera Khan, 'Negotiating the Mohalla: exclusion, identity and Muslim women in Mumbai', *Economic and Political Weekly*, 28 April 2007, p. 1529.
61. Rowena Robinson, *Tremors of Violence*, op. cit., p. 59.
62. Rowena Robinson, *'Nata, Nyaya:* Friendship and/or Justice on the Border', in

NOTES

Vinod K. Jairath (ed.), *Frontiers of Embedded Muslim Communities in India*, Delhi: Routledge, 2010, p. 243.
63. Sachar Committee Report, op. tit., p. 242.
64. On the role of these *mohalla* committees, see Sushobha Barve, *Healing Streams. Bringing Back Hope in the Aftermath of Violence*, Delhi: Penguin, 2003.

ANNEX: HINDU/MUSLIM RIOTS IN POST-INDEPENDENCE INDIA

1. Varshney, Ashutosh, Wilkinson, Steven, Varshney-Wilkinson dataset on Hindu-Muslim violence in India, 1950–1995, Version 2. [Computer file]. ICPSR04342–vl. Ann Arbor, MI: Inter-university Consortium for Political and Social Research [distributor], 2006–02–17. doi:10.3886/ICPSR04342. Based on the archives of the *Times of India* from January 1950 to December 1995. http://dx.doi.org/10.3886/ ICPSR04342

BIBLIOGRAPHY

Books and book chapters

Ahmad, I., 'Recognition and Entitlement: Muslim Castes Eligible for Inclusion in the Category "Scheduled Castes"' in Ashfaq Husain Ansari (ed.), *Basic Problems of OBC & Dalit Muslims*, New Delhi: Serials, 2007.

Ahmad, L., *Islamism and Democracy in India: The Transformation of Jamaat-e-Islami*, Princeton: Princeton University Press, 2009.

Ahmad, Z., 'Talim, Tanzeem aur Tijaarat: the Changing Role of the AIJQ', in Vinod K. Jairath (ed.), *Frontiers of Embedded Muslim Communities in India*, Delhi: Routledge, 2011, pp. 158–173.

Ansari, I. A., *Political representation of Muslims in India, 1952–2004*, New Delhi: Manak Publications, 2006.

Appadurai, A., 'The production of locality' in R. Fardon (ed.), *Counterworks: Managing the diversity of knowledge*. London: Routledge, 1995.

Bahauddin, K.M., *Kerala Muslims: The Long Struggle*, Kottayam: Sahitya Pravathaka Cooperative Society, 1992.

Basant, R. and Sharif, A. (eds), *Oxford Handbook of Muslims in India: Economic and Policy Perspectives*, NewDelhi: OUP, 2010.

Bayly, C.A., *Rulers, Townsmen and Bazaars: North Indian Society in the Age of British Expansion, 1770–1870*, Cambridge: Cambridge University Press, 1983.

Brass, P., *Factional Politics in an Indian State: The Congress Party in Uttar Pradesh*, Berkeley and Los Angeles: University of California Press, 1965.

——— *Forms of Collective Violence, Riots, Pogroms and Genocide in Modern India*, Gurgaon: Three Essays Collective, 2006.

——— *The Production of Hindu–Muslim Violence in Contemporary India*, Seattle: University of Washington Press, 2003.

Certeau, M. D., *The Practice of Everyday Life*. (S. Rendall, Trans.) Berkeley and Los Angeles: University of California, 1998, Sage, 1992.

BIBLIOGRAPHY

Chandavarkar, R., *The origins of industrial capitalism in India*, Cambridge: Cambridge University Press, 1994.

Crampton, J. and Elden, S., *Space, knowledge and power: Foucault and geography*, Ashgate: Aldershot, 2007.

Dale, S.F., *Mappilas of Malabar 1498–1922: An Islamic society on the South Asian frontier*, Oxford: Clarendon Press, 1980.

Dhar, J.N., 'Lanes and Localities of Cuttack', in Karuna Sagar Behera, et al (eds), *Cuttack: One Thousand Years, Vol. I*, Cuttack: Cuttack City Millennium Committee, 1990. Section II, pp. 23–43.

Dupont, V. and Heuzé, D.G. (eds), *La ville en Asie du sud: analyse et mise en perspective*, Paris: Edition of the School for Higher Studies in Social Sciences (EHESS), Purusartha, 2007.

Eckert, J., *The charisma of direct action: power, politics and the Shiv Sena*, Delhi: Oxford University Press, 2003.

Foucault, M., 'Space, knowledge and power' in P. Rabinow (ed.), *The Foucault reader*, New York: Pantheon Books, 1984.

Benei, V. and Fuller, C. J. (eds), *The Everyday State and Society in Modern India*, London: Hurst & co, 2001.

Gangadharan, M., *Duarte Barbara's The land of Malabar*. Kottayam: MG University Publication, 2001.

——— *The Malabar Rebellion*, Kottayam: DC Books, 2006.

Govindan, P.K., *ICS Collectors of Malabar: Jottings from memory*, Calicut: Poorna Publications, 1995.

Graff, V., 'Religious Identities and Indian Politics: Elections in Aligarh 1971–1989', in Wink, A. (ed.), *Islam, Politics and Society in South Asia*, New Delhi: Manohar, 1991, pp. 133–178.

Gupta, D., *Nativism in A Metropolis: The Shiv Sena in Bombay*, New Delhi: Manohar, 1982.

Gupta, N., *Reading with Allah: Madrasas in West Bengal*, New Delhi: Routledge, 2010.

Hansen, T. B., 'Governance and Myths of State in Mumbai' in V. Benei and C. Fuller (eds), *The Everyday State and Society in Modern India*, London: Hurst & Co, 2001b.

——— *The saffron wave: Democracy and Hindu nationalism in Modern India*, New Delhi: Oxford University Press, 1999.

——— *Violence in Urban India—Identity Politics, Mumbai and The Post-colonial City*, New Delhi: Permanent Black, 2001a.

Hasan, M., 'Traditional Rites and Contested Meanings: Sectarian Strife in Colonial Lucknow' in V. Graff. (ed.), *Lucknow, Memories of a City*, Delhi: Oxford University Press, 1997b, pp. 114–135.

——— *From pluralism to separatism: qasbas in colonial Awadh*, New Delhi: Oxford University Press, 2004.

——— *Legacy of a Divided Nation: India's Muslims since independence*, Boulder, CO: Westview Press, 1997a.

BIBLIOGRAPHY

Hasan, Z. and Ritu M., *Educating Muslim Girls: A Comparison of Five Indian Cities*, New Delhi: Women Unlimited, 2005.

Hasan, Z., *Dominance and Mobilisation: Rural Politics in Western Uttar Pradesh*, New Delhi: Sage Publications, 1989.

——— *Politics of inclusion: castes, minorities, and affirmative action*, New Delhi: OUP, 2009.

Heuze, G., 'Cultural populism: The appeal of the Shiv Sena' in A. T. Sujata Panel, *Bombay — Metaphor for Modern India*, Delhi: Oxford University Press, 1995.

Hussain, A., 'Muslim Institutions of Cuttack Town: Past and Present' in Karuna Sagar Behera, et al (eds), *Cuttack: One Thousand Years, Vol. II*, Cuttack: Cuttack City Millennium Committee, 1990, pp. 30–36.

Ismail, E. and Kurup, K.K.N., *The Keyis of Malabar: A Cultural Study*, Calicut: Malabar Institute for Research and Development, 2008.

Jaffrelot, C., *The Hindu Nationalist Movement and Indian Politics 1925 to the 1990s*, London: Hurst, 1996.

Kothari, M., and Contractor, N., *Planned Segregation: Riots. Eviction and Dispossession in Jogeshwari East, Mumbai/Bombay, India*, Mumbai: YUVA, 1996.

Krishna Ayyar, K.V., *The Zamorins of Calicut*, University of Calicut: Publication division, 1999.

Kunhali, P., *Calicut in history*, University of Calicut: Publication division, 2004.

Kunhali, V., *Sufism in Kerala*, Calicut: Calicut University Press, 2004.

Kunju, I.A.P., *Mappila Muslims of Kerala: Their history and culture*, Trivandrum: Sandhya Publications, 1989.

Kurup, K.K.N. and Ismail, E., *Emergence of Islam in Kerala in 20th Century*, New Delhi: Standard Publishers, 2008.

——— *The Keyis of Malabar: A cultural study*, Calicut: Malabar Institute for Research and Development, 2008.

Kurup, K.K.N., *The Ali Rajas of Cannanore*, Calicut: Calicut University Press, 2002.

——— *The Legacy of Islam: A Study of e Mappilas of Kerala*, Kannur: Samayam Publications, 2006.

Lefebvre, H., *The Production of Space*, Oxford: Blackwell, 1991.

Lelyveld, D., *Aligarh's First Generation*, New Delhi: Oxford University Press, 2003, [1996], (First edition: Princeton University Press, 1978).

Madan, T.N. (ed.), *Muslim Communities of South Asia: Culture, Society and Power*, New Delhi: Manohar, 2001.

Maheshwari, A., *Aligarh Muslim University: Perfect Past and Precarious Present*, New Delhi: U.B.S. Publishers, 2001.

Makhdum, S.Z., *Tuhfat al-Mujahidin: A Historical Epic of The Sixteenth Century* (a translation from Arabic), Calicut: Other Books, 2006.

Mann, E. A., 'Religion, Money and Status: Competition for Resources at the Shrine of Shah Jamal, Aligarh' in Troll, C.W. (ed.), *Muslim Shrines in India: Their Character, History and Significance*, Oxford: Oxford University Press, 1989.

——— *Boundaries and Identities: Muslims, Work and Status in Aligarh*, New Delhi: Sage, 1992.

Masselos, J., 'Appropriating Urban space: Social constructs of Bombay in the time of the Raj' in Masselos, J. (ed.), *The City in Action: Bombay Struggles For Power*, New Delhi: Oxford University Press, 2007a.

——— 'Postmodern Bombay: Fractured Discourses' in Masselos, J. (ed.), *The City in Action*, op. cit.

Mehmood, T. (ed.), *Politics of Minority Educational Institutions: Law and Reality in the Subcontinent* (Gurgaon: Imprint, 2007).

Mehta, D. and Chatterji, R., 'Boundaries, names, alterities: A case study of a "communal riot" in Dharavi, Bombay' in V. Das, M.L.A. Kleinman, M. Ramphele and P. Reynolds (eds), *Remaking A World: Violence, Social Suffering and Recovery*, New Delhi: Oxford University Press, 2001.

Metcalf, B., *Islamic Revival in British India: Deoband, 1860–1900*, Delhi: Oxford University Press, 2002.

Miller, R.E., 'Mappila' in Bearman, P., Bianquis, T., Bosworth, C.E., Van Donzen, E. and Heinrichs, W.P. (eds), *Encyclopaedia of Islam* (*third edition*), Leiden, London: Brill, 2007.

———*Mappila Muslims of Kerala: A Study of Islamic Trends*, Chennai: Orient Longman (Rev. Ed.), 1992.

Mohammed Koya, S.M., *Mappilas of Malabar: Studies in Social and Cultural History*, Calicut: Sandhya Publications, 1983.

Mohammed, U., *Educational Empowerment of Kerala Muslims: A Socio-historical Perspective*, Calicut: Other Books, 2007.

Narayanan, M.G.S., 'Kozhikode: Yesterday and Today' in Natarajan, B. (ed.), *Cities of Kerala: Actually Small Towns*, Mumbai: Marg Publications, 2007.

——— *Calicut: The City of Truth Revisited*, University of Calicut: Publication division, 2006.

——— *Cultural Symbiosis in Kerala*, Trivandrum: Kerala Historical Society, 1972.

——— *Malabar*, Calicut: Malabar Mahotsav, 1993 [Souvenir, 1994].

Noorani, A.G., *The Muslims of India, a Documentary Record*, Oxford: Oxford University Press, 2003.

Oldenburg, V.T., *The Making of Colonial Lucknow, 1856–1877*, Princeton, N.J.: Princeton University Press, 1984.

Osella, F. and Osella, C., 'I Am Gulf: The Production of Cosmopolitanism Among the Koyas of Kozhikode, Kerala' (Chapter 9) in Simpson, K. (ed.), *Struggling With History: Islam and Cosmopolitanism in the Western Indian Ocean*, New York: Columbia University Press, 2008.

——— 'Muslim Entrepreneurs in Public Life Between India and The Gulf: Making Good and Doing Good' (Chapter 12) in Osella, F. and Soares, B. (eds), *Islam*,

BIBLIOGRAPHY

Politics and Anthropology, Chichester; Malden, MA: Wiley-Blackwell, 2010 (Also in Journal of the Royal Anthropological Institute, 15 (s1), 2009).

Punwani, J., '"My area, your area": How riots changed the city' in S. Patel and J. Masselos (eds), *Bombay and Mumbai: A City in Transition*, New Delhi: Oxford University Press, 2003.

Richard, E., 'Multiple lenses: Differing perspectives of Fifteenth-Century Calicut' (Chapter 3) in Richard, E. (ed.), *Essays on Islam and Indian History*, New Delhi: Oxford University Press, 2000.

Robinson, R., *Tremors of violence — Muslim survivors of ethnic strife in Western India*, New Delhi: Sage, 2005.

Sanyal, U., *Devotional Islam and Politics in British India: Ahmad Riza Khan Barelwi and His Movement, 1870–1920*, Delhi: Oxford University Press, 1996.

Sen, A., *Shiv Sena Women—Violence and Communalism in a Bombay Slum*, New Delhi: Zubaan, 2008.

Shaban, A., *City, Crime and Space: A Case of Mumbai Megapolis*, Tata Institute of Social Sciences, Centre for Development Studies. Mumbai: Tata Institute of Social Sciences, 2006.

Shahid, M., 'Representation of Muslims in Local Bodies — A Case Study of District Aligarh, Uttar Pradesh (UP.)' in Waheel, A. (ed.), *Muslims of Uttar Pradesh*, Aligarh: Centre for the Promotion of Educational and Cultural Advancement of Muslims of India (CEPECAMI), Aligarh Muslim University, 2007, pp. 201–213.

Sharar, A.H., *Lucknow: The Last Phase of an Oriental Culture* [translated by E. S. Harcourt and F. Hussain], Delhi: Oxford University Press, 1975.

Shariff, A., 'Spiritual Capital and Philanthropy among Muslims' in R., Basant and A. Shariff (eds), *Oxford Handbook of Muslims in India*, op. cit., pp. 254–268.

Shields, R., *Places On The Margin: Alternative Geographies of Modernity*, London: Routledge, 1991.

Siddiqui, J.M., *Aligarh District, A Historical Survey: From Ancient Times to 1803 A.D.*, Centre of Advanced Study in History, Department of History, Aligarh Muslim University, New Delhi: Munshiram Manoharlal Publishers, 1981.

Sikand, Y., *National Study on the Socio-Economic Conditions of Muslims in India*, Jahangirabad: Indian Social Institute, 2006.

Singh, B., *Gazetteer of India, Uttar Pradesh, District Aligarh*, Allahabad: Government Press, 1987.

Tarlo, E., *Unsettling Memories: Narratives of the Emergency in Delhi*, California: University of California Press, 2003.

Trivedi, M., 'A Genre of Composite Creativity: *Marsiya* and its Performance in Awadh' in M., Hasan and A., Roy (eds), *Living Together Separately: Cultural India in History and Politics*, Oxford: Oxford University Press, 2005, pp. 195–221.

Varshney, K., *Ethnic Conflict and Civil Life: Hindus and Muslims in India*, New Haven and London: Yale University Press, 2002.

BIBLIOGRAPHY

Wacquant, L., *Urban Outcastes: A Comparative Sociology of Advanced Marginality*, Cambridge: Polity Press, 2008.

Wilson, W.J., *The Truly Disadvantaged: The Inner City, the Underclass and Public Policy*, Chicago: University of Chicago Press, 1987.

Zaheer, S.K., *The Memoirs of Syed Ali Zaheer*, Delhi: Frank Bros & Co. Publishers, 2004.

Articles

Alam, J., 'The Contemporary Muslim Situation in India: A Long-Term View', *Economic and Political Weekly*, January 12–18, 2008, vol. 43, no. 2.

Ali, S., 'Collective and Elective Ethnicity: Caste among Urban Muslims in India', *Sociological Forum*, Vol. 17, no. 4, December 2002.

Appadurai, A., 'Spectral Housing and Urban Cleansing: Notes On Millennial Mumbai', *Public Culture*, 12 (3), 2000.

Asmer Beg, M., 'Uttar Pradesh: Signs of a Congress Revival?', *Economic and Political Weekly*, 26 September–2 October 2009, vol. 44, no. 39.

Chiriyankandath, J., 'Changing Muslim politics in Kerala: Identity, interests and political strategy', *Journal of Muslim Minority Affairs*, Vol. 16:2, July 1996.

Dale, S.F, 'Trade, Conversion and the Growth of the Islamic Community of Kerala, South India', *Studia Islamica*, no. 71, 1990.

DeVotta, N., 'Demography and Communalism in India', *Journal of International Affairs*, Vol. 56:1, Fall 2002.

Engineer, A.A., 'Bombay-Bhiwandi in National Political Perspective', *Economic and Political Weekly*, 19 (29), 1984.

——— 'Communal Riots, 2006', *Secular Perspective*, Bombay: Centre for Study of Society and Secularism, 2007, http://www.csss-isla.com

Farooqi, M.N. (interview), in 'The Aligarh Shock', *Frontline*, 22 December 1990–4 January 1991.

Foucault, M., 'Of Other Spaces' (Trans. Jay Miskowiec), *Diatrics*, 16 (1), 1986.

Gandhi, K., 'Aligarh Muslim University, Capitalising on Communal Violence', *Economic and Political Weekly*, June 9 1979, vol. 14, no. 23.

Gangadharan, M., 'Hadrami Sayeds of Mamburam: Defiance to Compliance', *Mappila Padhanangal*, Calicut: Vachanam Books, 2007 (published in Malayalam, and provided an English copy by the author).

——— 'Mappilas: The Kerala Muslims', *Mappila Padhanangal*, Calicut: Vachanam Books, 2007 (published in Malayalam, and provided an English copy by the author).

Graff, V, 'Aligarh's Long Quest for Minority Status', *Economic and Political Weekly*, August 11 1990, vol. 25, no. 32.

Hasan, M., 'The Muslim Mass Contact Campaign: An Attempt at Political Mobilisation', *Economic and Political Weekly*, vol. 21, no. 52, 1986.

Holston, J. and Appadurai, A., 'Cities and Citizenship', *Public Culture*, 8 (2), 1996.

BIBLIOGRAPHY

Kanungo, P., 'Hindutva's Entry Into A "Hindu Province": Early Years of RSS in Orissa', *Economic and Political Weekly*, 38(31), 2003.

Khan, M.Q., 'Cuttack—The Age Old City of Peace, Social Amity and Communal Harmony', *MEDICON 2004*, IMA Souvenir, Cuttack: IMA House, 2004.

Kirmani, N., 'Competing Constructions of "Muslim-ness" in the South Delhi Neighborhood of Zakir Nagar', *Journal of Muslim Minority Affairs*, vol. 28, no. 3.

Masselos, J., 'Power in The Bombay "Mohalla", 1904–15: An Initial Exploration Into The World of The Indian Urban Muslim', *South Asia*, 1977.

McGilvray, D.B., 'Arabs, Moors and Muslims: Sri Lankan Muslim Ethnicity in Regional perspective', *Contributions to Indian Sociology*, no. 32, 2, 1998.

Minault, G. and Lelyveld, D., 'The Campaign For A Muslim University, 1898–1920', *Modern Asian Studies*, vol. 8, no. 2, 1974.

Osella, F. and Osella, C., 'Globalisation Is Ruining Us: Neo-liberal Capitalism, Islamic Reform and Business in Kozhikode (Calicut), South India', *Tapasam, Journal for Kerala Studies* (Issue on 'History, Representation and Ambivalence'), October 2010.

——— 'Islamism and Social Reform in Kerala, South India', in *Modern Asian Studies*, 42, (2–3), 2008.

——— 'Muslim style in South India', *Fashion Theory*, Vol. 11, Issue 2/3, 2007.

Rizvi, H.A., 'What Really Happened in Aligarh', *The Mill Gazette*, 16–31 July, 2006.

Sharma, M., Sharma, H. and Naqvi, T.F., 'Survival of Aligarh Lock Manufacturing Industry', *Economic and Political Weekly*, September 24–30 2005, vol. 40, no. 39.

Shahabuddin, S., 'Demography of Muslim India: An analysis of 1991 census data', *Jounal of Muslim Minority Affairs*, Vol. 18:2, October 1998.

Varshney, A., 'Ethnic Conflict and Civil Society: India and Beyond', *World Politics* 53, 2001.

Wacquant, L., 'Getto', *International Encyclopedia of the Social and Behavioral Sciences*, Elsevier, 2004.

Wright, T.P., 'Muslim Education in India at the Crossroads: the Case of Aligarh', *Pacific Affairs*, vol. 39, no. 1–2, Spring-Summer 1966.

Zaidi, S.A., 'Who is a Muslim? Identities and Exclusion—North Indian Muslims, c. 1860–1900', *Indian Economic and Social History Review*, 47(2), 2010.

Dale, S.F., 'Trade, Conversion and the Growth of the Islamic Community of Kerala, South India', *Studia Islamica*, no. 71, 1990.

Other References

Anjuman Islamia Ahle Sunnat-O-Jama'at, Orissa, *Souvenir, Golden Jubilee Celebration: 1953–2003*, Cuttack, 2003.

GoI-UNDP Orissa Project State Urban Development Agency SUDA, *City Development Plan for Cuttack* (Hyderabad: Administrative Staff College of India), www.scribd.com/doc/37169728/City-Development-Planfor-Cuttak

Human Development Report, *Mumbai Human Development Report*. United Nations Development Programme. New Delhi: Oxford University Press, 2009.

BIBLIOGRAPHY

Indian People's Human Rights Tribunal, *The Peoples Verdict: An enquiry into the December '92 and January '93 riots in Bombay*, Bombay: Indian Peoples Human Rights Commission, 1994.

Innes, CA (IAS). *Malabar Gazetteer*, Government of Kerala, 1905.

Justice K.K. Narendran Commission Report, Parts I & II, *Kerala Gazette Extraordinary* no. 269, Government of Kerala, February 2002.

Justice Ranganath Mishra Commission Report, National Commission for Religious and Linguistic Minorities (NCRLM), Government of India, May 2007.

Koya, S.P., 'The Koyas of Calicut: A distinctive Matrilineal social group', paper presented at *Seminar On Matriliny Among Malabar Muslims—Continuity and Change*, sponsored by the Indian Council of Social Science Research, in Calicut, February 10–11, 2007 (unpublished).

Logan, W., *Malabar Manual* (2 Volumes, Reprint Madras 1887 edn. 1989, 1995), New Delhi: Asian Education Services, 2000.

Minorities' Commission, *First Annual Report for the Year Ending 31st December 1978*, Manager, Government of India Press, New Delhi, 1979.

Mishra, R., *Report of the National Commission for Religious and Linguistic Minorities*, New Delhi: Ministry of Minority Affairs, 2007.

Nida-e-Sayeed-Seminary [The First Convention of The Old Boys' Association, Sayeed Seminary, Cuttack, 25 and 26 January 2009], Cuttack, 2009.

Prime Minister's High Level Committee (Sachar Committee), *Social Economic and Educational Status of the Muslim Community in India: A Report*, New Delhi: Cabinet Secretariat, 2006.

(Justice) Srikrishna, B.N., *Report of the Srikrishna Commission: An inquiry into the riots at Mumbai during December 1992 and January 1993*, Mumbai: High Court, 1998.

Waheed, A., *Project Report on Evaluating Area Intensive and Madrasa Modernization Programme and Evolving Future Strategies for Promoting Educational Advancement of Muslims in Tehsil Koil, District Aligarh*, Aligarh: Centre for the Promotion of Educational and Cultural Advancement of Muslims of India (CEPECAMI), Aligarh Muslim University, 2007.

Zachariah, K.C., Rajan, I.S. (eds), *Kerala Migration Survey*, Thiruvananthapuram: Centre for Development Studies (CDS), 2007.

INDEX

Index of places

Ahmedabad, 4, 43–54, 56–71, 77–79, 136, 153, 156, 158, 165, 171, 219, 231, 312, 319–321, 323–325, 341 n2, 343 n44/45, 380 n41
Amraiwadi, 47, 54
Asarwa, 46–47, 54
Astodia, 56–57
Bapunagar, 43, 47, 50, 54, 56
Behrampura, 54, 57, 63
Chamanpura, 54
Dagbarward, 55
Danilimbda, 57
Dariapur, 54–55, 57
Fatehvadi, 68
Fort Walls, 45–48, 50, 55–56
Gheetkanta, 57
Gomtipur, 46–47, 54, 56–57, 59, 63, 73
Gulberg, 47, 57–58, 65, 156, 323, 344 n68
Gyaspur, 68, 71
Indira Garibnagar, 44
Jamalpur, 43, 47, 54, 57, 63, 75, 346 n100
Juhapura, 43, 45, 47, 59, 63, 66, 68–79, 153, 319–320, 324–325, 342 n21, 346 n90/92/96/97/100, 347 n101/106/124, 355 n22
Kalupur, 47, 54, 56–57, 63, 67, 74, 346 n100
Karanj, 57
Khadia, 47, 54, 56–57, 59, 67
Khanpur, 54
Khokhra-Mehamdavad, 47, 54
Maktampura, 68, 70–71
Makaraba, 68
Mirzapur, 19, 51, 54
Maninagar, 54
Naginapol, 55
Naroda, 47, 54, 57
Narol, 54
Navangpura, 43
Okaf, 68
Palij Kuan, 67
Rakhial, 47, 54, 56–57, 63
Raipur, 54
Ramrahim Nagar, 79
Sarangpur, 54
Saraspur, 43, 46–47, 56–58
Sardarnagar, 54
Sarkhej, 66, 68, 71, 74, 346 n97/99
Shah Alam, 67, 70
Shah Vali, 71
Shahpur, 43, 47, 54, 57, 63, 168, 170, 184, 346 n100

INDEX

Shalam, 57
Vadigam, 55, 57
Vatwa, 54
Vejalpur, 68, 71, 76
Aligarh, 129–150, 152–158, 160, 162, 177, 313, 320, 323, 353 n2, 354 n3/5/6, 355 n10/12, 320 n44, 380 n41, 381 n53
   Aligarh Muslim University, 129, 132, 353–354
   Civil Lines, 129, 131, 134–136, 140, 144–149, 153–154, 156, 158, 166–167, 354 n4/5, 355 n17/18
   Jamalpur, 148, 166–167, 355 n17
   Jivangarh, 148, 355 n17
   Manik Chowk, 136
   Maulana Azad Nagar, 148, 355 n17Old City, 129–130, 134–136, 144, 146–150, 157–158, 354 n4, 355 n10/18
   Shah Jamal, 129–130, 141, 146–151, 153–155, 157–158, 354 n4, 355 n20/22Sir
   Syed Nagar, 131, 146, 148, 154–157, 313, 323, 354 n4, 356 n25
   Upar Fort (or Upar Kot), 130, 135, 138, 141, 146–147, 154, 158, 354 n4, 355 n8/16
Azamgarh, 221, 233
Bangalore, 287–298, 305–310, 312, 319–320, 322, 375 n4, 376 n17/23, 381 n53
   Benson Town, 295, 308
   Bharatinagar, 297
   BTM Layout, 300, 309
   Charminar Masjid, 298
   Cole's Park, 295, 308
   Cottonpet, 305
   Frazer Town, 295, 300, 308
   Jaymahal, 297
   Jaynagar, 295, 298
   Kambal Posh (Hazrat Sayyid Shah Mohiuddin), 297, 300, 305
   Koramangla, 295, 299
   Malleshwaram, 298
   Mysore Road, 295
   Rajajinagar, 298
   Richmond Town, 298
   Russell Market, 295, 297–298
   Sadaramangla, 300
   Srirangapattanam, 289
   Sultan Shah Masjid, 297–298, 304
   Tannery Road, 287, 295
   Ulsoor, 297
   WhiteFields, 300
Bhadrakh, 245
Bhopal, 158–187, 190, 193, 318, 357 n19/33/35, 358 n53, 359 n64/72, 360 n81/83, 361 n5, 380 n41
   Acharya Narendra Dev Nagar, 173
   Arera Colony, 166, 168, 170
   Bairagarh, 165–166, 171, 178
   Berasia, 163, 178
   Fatehgarh, 171
   Govindpura, 166–168, 172–173, 178, 185
   Habibganj, 167, 173
   Ibrahimpura, 159, 166–168, 175–176, 181–182, 184, 360 n79
   Idgah Hills, 166–167, 173, 183
   Indira Nagar, 173
   Jahangirabad, 159, 165–168, 170, 172, 177, 181–182, 184, 360 n77/79/80
   Koh-e-Fiza, 173, 183–185
   New Market, 166–168
   Piplani, 166, 172
   Maharana Pratap (M.P.) Nagar, 166–167, 170
   Shah-i-Khas, 163, 165, 170
   Shahjahanabad, 166–167, 171
   Taj-ul-Masjid, 163, 165

INDEX

Tatya Tope (T.T.) Nagar, 168, 170, 183
Bombay, 26, 177, 207, 219, 306, 308, 314, 339 n6, 345 n69, 361 n16
Calcutta, 321, 371 n3, 374 n29
Chikmagalur, 295
Cochin, 265, 267
Cuttack, 237–246, 248–252, 254–258, 260, 312, 319–320, 322, 324, 371 n3, 372 n7
    Alamchand bazaar, 241
    Anjuman Islamia Ahle Sunnat-o-Jama'at, 254
    Baloo Bazar, 239
    Bibi Alam, 241
    Bounsagali, 255–256, 258–260, 373 n20/23
    Bukshee Bazar, 239
    Dewan Bazar, 238, 254, 372 n17
    Gunga Manzil, 239
    Hazrat Bokhari Baba, 241
    Jallaupoor, 239
    Kafeelah Bazar, 239
    Kuddumrasool, 239
    Madrasa-i-Sultania, 250–251, 253–255, 372 n14
    Mastan Dargha, 241
    Qadam-i-Rasul, 241
    Sayeed Seminary, 251–252, 255
    Sheikh Bazar, 253
    Sutahat Masjid, 242
    Telingah Bazar, 239
    Urdu Girls High School, 252, 372 n15
    Urdu Secondary Training School, 253
Delhi, 5, 8, 14–17, 20, 81, 87–88, 105, 125, 127, 131, 148, 156, 165, 177, 189, 213–233, 235–236, 238, 257, 292, 303, 314, 318–319, 323, 335 n57, 336 n71, 341 n33, 366 n7/12, 367 n36, 368 n44/45/48, 378 n18, 381 n52/53
    Abul Fazl Enclave, 213, 225–226, 319, 323, 368 n49, 369 n52, 380 n42
    Babarpur, 220
    Ballimaran, 220
    Batla House, 221, 223
    Bilal Masjid, 228
    Chandni Chowk, 20, 220, 239, 367 n31
    Chitli Qabr, 226
    Dawat Nagar, 227–228, 369 n61
    Ghaffar Manzil, 223
    Gumbad Wali Masjid, 227
    Jamia Ahl-e-Bait, 230, 232, 368 n46
    Jamiat-ul Bannat al-Islamia, 370 n89
    Jamia Millia Islamia, 214, 223, 226, 235
    Jamia Nagar, 215, 219, 221–223, 230–232, 368 n45/46, 370 n86, 371 n97
    Karol Bagh, 220, 368 n44
    Matia Mahal, 220
    Mustafabad, 217
    Nizamuddin, 217, 231, 368 n45
    Noor Nagar, 223, 232
    Okhla, 217, 220–221, 223–224, 368 n44/48, 371 n98
    Paharganj, 220
    Pahari Imli, 367 n23
    Phatak Habash Khan, 367 n22
    Pul Bangash, 367 n23
    Qarawal Nagar, 220
    Qasabpura, 217
    Rohini, 230–231, 381 n52
    Sadar Bazar, 218, 367 n23, 378 n18
    Seelampur, 217, 220, 222–223
    Shaheen Bagh, 223, 230, 232–233, 368 n46
    Shahjahanabad, 17, 20, 216–217

INDEX

Zakir Bagh, 232, 371 n98
Zakir Nagar, 219, 221, 223, 230
Dubai, 66, 175, 274
Gujarat, 2, 5, 10, 21, 43–44, 46, 50–53, 57, 59, 60–65, 72–74, 76–77, 79, 157, 200, 219, 289–290, 295, 309, 314, 318–319, 322–325, 328, 343 n45, 346 n87/96/99, 348 n132/134, 378 n13/16, 381 n49
Gulf (Persian), 2, 14, 93, 95, 126, 128, 209–211, 248, 266–267, 271, 273–278, 284, 300, 312–313, 316, 320, 348 n4, 374 n22, 375 n35/38, 379 n31
Hyderabad, 6, 15–16, 81, 87, 119, 136, 158–160, 165, 179, 189–195, 197, 199–211, 219, 252, 274, 282, 318, 320, 333 n34, 336 n74, 361 n4/16, 362 n24, 363 n48, 373 n25, 374 n17
    Baraks ou Barkas, 195, 198, 205
    Chandrayangutta, 198, 204–205
    Damika Bagh, 195
    Dar-us-Salaam, 193
    Gowlipura, 195
    Hafeezbaba Nagar, 205
    Hussaini Alam, 195
    Jagdish Huts, 195
    Mecca Masjid, 195, 200, 362 n24
    Shah Ali Banda, 195
    Tolichowki, 199, 207–208, 211, 364 n57
Jaipur, 81–87, 89–91, 94, 98–100, 102, 312, 320, 323, 325–326, 349 n18, 350 n26
    Amritpuri, 88, 91, 99
    Bhatta Basti, 87, 89
    Chandpur, 89
    Char Darwaza, 87–88, 91–92
    Ghat Darwaza, 83, 89
    Haji Abdul Rehman Colony, 87
    Hameed Nagar, 89
    Hasanpura, 87, 89
    Jalupura, 89
    Johari Bazaar, 83, 85–86, 91
    Karbala, 87
    Kidwai Nagar, 82, 87–88
    Madeena Masjid, 87
    Mansarovar, 82, 88
    Modi Khana, 83
    Noorani Masjid, 99
    Purani Basti, 83
    Ramchandraji, 83, 92
    Ramganj, 82, 86–89, 91–93, 96, 98, 101–102, 320, 349 n13/18, 350 n25
    Ramnagar, 89
    Rishi Ghalav Nagar, 86–87
    Shastri Nagar, 86–87, 89
    Sikar House, 87, 89
    Sita Rampuri, 87
    Topkhana, 83, 89, 92, 94, 96, 349 n10
    Visheshwarji, 83
Kandhamal, 243, 328
Kannur, 264–266, 271–272, 276, 278
Kasargod, 264–266, 278, 283
Kendrapada, 245
Kollam, 283, 374 n19
Kozhikode, 263–270, 272–273, 275–285, 312, 319, 322, 374 n29, 375 n43
    Idiyangara, 269
    Kampuram, 277
    Kappakkal, 277
    Kundungal, 269
    Kuttichira, 263, 267, 268–269, 271–274, 277, 279, 282–285
    Madrasatul Mohammadiya High School, 276
    Miskal mosque, 269, 284
    Mugadhar, 269
    Pallikandi, 269, 277

INDEX

Parappil, 269
Valiyangadi, 269
Vattampil, 269
Lakshadweep islands, 271
Lucknow, 16, 105–111, 115–117, 119–124, 126, 128, 192, 313, 318, 320, 322, 325, 338 n109, 351 n1/12, 352 n32, 353 n36/41
   Dargah, 106, 118
   Hasanpuria, 106
   Kashmiri Mohalla, 105–106, 108–110, 117–119, 122–124, 126–128, 325, 351 n1/8/12, 352 n21/23
   Kazmein, 106
   Najaf, 106
   Noor Bali, 106
   Rustom Nagar, 106, 352 n21
   Tapewali Gali, 106
Mahe, 271
Malappuram, 264–266, 268, 274–276, 375 n38
Malerkotla, 319–320
Mangalore, 265, 278, 310
Marad, 278, 281–282
Meerut, 127, 136, 219
Mumbai, 21, 24–27, 29–30, 33–34, 37–38, 40–42, 45–46, 57, 59, 62, 65–67, 72, 93, 136, 140, 175, 199, 274, 309, 312, 319–321, 324–326, 352 n22
   Outside Mumbai: Ayodhya, 25, 57, 136, 172–173, 197, 199
   Andheri, 26
   Baba Nagar, 39
   Bandra, 28, 39, 339 n18
   Bhendi Bazar, 25
   Byculla, 26
   Deonar, 30, 37
   Dharavi, 25, 32
   Gautam Nagar, 36
   Ghatkopar, 32
   Govandi, 26
   Indira Nagar, 35
   Jogeswari, 26
   Kamla Raman, 39
   Kidwai Nagar, 26
   Kurla, 26, 37
   Lokhandwala, 26
   Madanpura, 25
   Mahalaxmi, 28
   Millat Nagar, 26
   Mira road, 26
   Mohammed Ali Road, 26
   Mumbra, 26
   Nagpada, 25, 338 n2
   Padma Nagar, 30, 35
   Rafi Nagar, 35, 39
   Raman Mama Nagar, 39
   Sanjay Nagar, 35
   Shastri Nagar, 36
   Sewri, 28
   Sion, 31
   Wadala, 26
   Worli, 28, 39
   Zakir Husain Nagar, 39
Mysore, 98, 265, 289–291, 295, 361 n16, 375 n43
Oman, 267, 277
Palakkad, 264–266
Ponnani, 271, 375 n38
Rourkela, 242
Salepur, 245
Saudi Arabia, 155–156, 274, 281, 350 n21, 358 n58
Thalassery, 271–272
Trivandrum, 265, 278, 283
UAE (United Arab Emirates), 267, 274, 313
Varanasi, 312
Vijayanagar, 289

INDEX

Index of names

Abdul Wahab, P.V., 267–268, 313
Ahmed, Mateen, 220
Ahmed, Syed Mustafiz, 247
Al Kabeer, 312, 377 n5
Alam, Zafar, 140, 143–145, 153
Ali, Haider, 289
Ali, Mir Laiq, 192
Ali, Moulvi Sayeed Mukkaram, 252
Ali, P. Mohammed, 267, 313
Ali, Sheikh Matlub, 247
All India Muslim Personal Law Board, 121
Alladin, 192
Andhra Mahasabha, 190
Ansari (caste group), 88, 123, 339 n4
Ansari, Farhan, 185, 360 n85
Aqueel, Arif, 172, 180
Arya Samaj, 138, 145, 190–191
Aurangzeb, 190, 238, 289, 366 n7
Awadh, 15, 105, 108–109, 351 n10

Babri Masjid, 9, 21, 25, 29, 30–32, 57, 86, 172, 181–182, 194, 198–199, 214, 280, 295, 309
Badajena, Brajanath, 239
Bahuguna, H. N., 117
Bahuguna, Rita, 116
Baig, Arif, 178
Baig, Roshan, 294, 297, 301, 303–305
Bajaj, Vithal Das, 162
Bajrang Dal, 173, 182
Bakht, Sikander, 220, 367 n31
Bandukwala, J.S., 344 n60
Barbosa, 268
Barelwis, 100, 241–242, 254, 290, 369 n72
Batuta, Ibn, 268
Beg, Sal, 240
Bhanja, Upendra, 239
Bhatt, Ashok, 56–57

Begum, Mumtaz, 294, 304
Bohras, 61–62, 83, 174, 195, 314, 322, 339 n4, 344 n54/68
Biman, Raju, 61, 344 n57
Burhanuddin, Sayyidna Muhammad, 62
Bux, Allah, 251

Charminar Cooperative Urban Bank, 209
Currimbhoy Ebrahim, 314

Das, Akhilesh, 116
Dasussalam Cooperative Bank, 209
Deobandis, 231, 241–242, 290, 372 n16
Deva, Mukunda, 238
Dey, Samir, 244

Faizabad, 105
Fakhruddin, Muhammad, 252
Faridi, Abdul Jaleel, 112
Farooqi, Mohammad Abul Fazl, 138, 213, 225–227, 231, 368 n36
Fayaz, Koli, 306
F.D. Education Society, 74–75

Gandhi, M.K. (Mahatma), 51, 53, 59, 341 n2
Gandhi, Indira, 53, 79, 177, 222, 224
Gandhi, Sonia, 79
Gaur, Babulal, 171, 173
Golwalkar, M.S., 53
Gowda I, 289
Gowda, Kempe, 289
'Guddu', Tanveer Hussain, 123
Ghufar, Azam, 179
Gujarat Sarvajanik Welfare Trust, 348
Gupta, Chandra Banu, 117

Hajee, V.K. Moidu, 267

INDEX

Hakeem, C. Abdul, 252
Haleem, Khwaja, 142, 145
Hanif, Mohamad, 247
Hashmi, Parvez, 220–221, 224, 368 n48
Hasnat, Yassir, 179, 359 n73
Hassan, Adil, 222
Hassan, Javad K., 267
Heptullah, Najma, 177, 180
Hindu Mahasabha, 138, 161–163, 178, 190–191
Huan, Ma, 268
Huda, S.A., 252, 364 n51
Husain, Basharat, 110, 118

Ibrahim, Dawood, 65–66, 78
Indian Mujahideen, 221
Iqbal, Shoaib, 220
Islam, Aminul, 241
Islamic Relief Committee, 73

Jama'at-i-Islami, 10, 73, 213, 280, 290, 298, 306
Jamiat-e-Ulema-e-Hind, 73
Jafri, Ahsan, 64–65, 156, 344 n68
Jana Sangh, 54, 56, 85–86, 145, 168, 178
Jawad, Maulana Kalbe, 117, 352 n33, 353 n36
Jilani, Zafaryab, 280
Jinnah, Mohammed Ali, 132
Jung, Bahadur Yar, 191

Kabli, Shabir, 63
Kararani, Sulaiman, 238
Karkare, Hemant, 40
Khalaji, Bakhtiyar, 238
Khalik, Abdul, 142, 145
Khan, Ahmad Raza, 241
Khan, Alivardi, 238
Khan, A.Q., 174
Khan, Asif Mohammad, 221

Khan, Aslam Sher, 180
Khan, Babu, 192
Khan, Habibullah, 247
Khan, Hamidullah, 161
Khan, K. Rahman, 294, 376 n13
Khan, M.Q., 252, 372
Khan, Maulavi Abdus Sobhan, 247
Khan, Muhammad Taqi, 238
Khan, Mumtaz Ali, 294, 304
Khan, Muzzafar Hussain, 247
Khan, Obeidullah, 174
Khan, Shakir Ali, 162, 177–180
Khan, Sikander Hafiz, 175, 358 n58
Khan, Sultan Mohammad, 177
Khan, Tughan, 238
Khan, Zahed Ali, 206, 364 n53
Khurana, Madan Lal, 232

Lal, Bhure, 136, 138
Latif, Abdul, 65–66, 78

Madhani, Abdul Naser, 278
Madhok, Balraj, 54
Majid, Abdul, 239, 252
Malhotra, Jagmohan, 222
Malviya, Chatur Narayan, 162–163
Malis (caste group), 312, 377 n3
Maniar, Shafi, 61, 75–77, 344 n56, 348 n130
Mashriqi, Inayatullah Khan Tarzi, 162–163, 177, 180, 357 n19
Mather, Rafi, 267
Maulavi, Wakkom, 283
Mayawati, 117, 351 n15
Meeran, M.E., 267
Meraj, Jaffar Hussain, 207
Mishra, Mahima, 243
Modi, Narendra, 344 n67
Moily, Veerapa, 4, 291
Moonis, Maulana Shafi, 226–227, 369 n59
Munshi, K.M., 51

INDEX

Nagri resolution, 313
Naqvi, Zafar Ali, 115
Navman, K.K., 139
Nazar, K.V. Abdul, 267
Nehru, Jawaharlal, 177

Osmania University, 160, 193
Osatullah, S.M., 252
Owaisi, Abdul Wahed, 193
Owaisi, Akbaruddin, 205

Pachori, Suresh, 185
Pandya, Haren, 60
Patel, Sardar, 161
Patel, Vallabhbhai, 51, 341 n2
Patnaik, Biju, 243–244

Qazmi, Subi, 123
Qudsia Begum, 160, 165
Qumruddin, 251
Qureshi (caste group), 51, 96, 99, 145, 259, 299, 307, 312, 339 n4, 377 n2
Qureshi, Aziz, 177, 357 n35
Qureshi, Hamid, 178

Rafai, Toofan, 342 n21
Rahman, Maulavi Latifur, 247
Ram Janmabhoomi, 21, 219, 231
Ray, Radhanath, 239
Razaak, Abdur, 268
Razakars, 191
Razmi, Saidullah Khan, 162
Razvi, Kasim, 191
Razzaq, Irfan, 294
Reliable group, 175
Rizvi, Maulana Athar, 120
Rizvi, Sayyid Abid Hasan, 209
Roy, Akshoy Kumar, 251

Sadi, Shaikh, 240
Sadiq, Maulana Kalbe, 119

Saifullah, Dr., 252
Sait, Ahmed Usman, 267
Samajwadi Party, 6, 34, 114, 143–144, 153, 351 n16
Sayeed, Mohammad, 251
Senapati, Fakir Mohan, 239
Shah Jahan, 17, 20, 216, 336 n71
Shah Jahan Begum, 160, 165, 356 n6
Sharieff, Jaffer, 294
Sharma, Shankar Dayal, 163, 177
Sheikh, Arif, 39–40, 222
Sheikh, Farooq, 63, 344 n63
Shia Personal Law Board, 118, 120–121, 352 n22/31
Shias, 12, 34–35, 44, 83, 91, 105–106, 108–110, 115–126, 128, 192, 195, 298, 302, 322, 325, 335 n58, 351 n2, 352 n32
Shiv Sena, 25–26, 29–30, 34, 36, 38, 339 n7/11
Shukla, Shyam Kishore, 116
Siddiqi, Taab, 222
Siddiqui, Hasnat, 178–180
Sikandar Begum, 160
Silawats (caste group), 312, 377 n3
Singh, Digvijay, 179, 358 n35
Singh, Lal, 162
Sinha, Sushil Kumar, 252
Sir Syed Ahmad Khan, 131–132
Solanki, Madhavsinh, 54–55
Sultan, Jahan Begum, 160–161, 165, 175
Sultan, Mainmoona, 177, 180
Sultan, Mohammad, 250
Sultan, Tipu, 289
Sunnis, 12, 35, 83, 91, 99, 106, 115–122, 125–126, 128, 195, 241, 280, 298, 302, 314, 325, 351 n2, 353 n41
Syed Maratib Ali, 314

Tablighi Jama'at, 73, 100, 230, 242, 244, 290, 298

INDEX

Tirtha, Swami Ramananda, 190–191, 361 n11
Toor Baitulmal, 209
Tughluq, Firuz, 238
Tyabji, Camar, 192

Uddin, Suja, 238
Unani medicine, 312
Ullah, Zamir, 143–145, 154, 355 n18
Urs, Dev Raj, 291

Vaghela, Shankar Sinh, 58
Varshney, Ashutosh, 53, 144, 335 n62, 341 n4/10, 342 n30, 367 n25, 372 n7, 382 n1
Vastanvi, Ghulam Mohammad, 62

Wahab, P.V. Abdul, 267, 313
Wodeyar, Chikka Deva Raja, 289

Yadav, Mulayam Singh, 114
Yusuf, Harun, 220–221
Yusufali, M.A., 267

Zaheer, Syed Ali, 115
Zuberi, Roohi, 145, 153

Index of acronyms

ABVP (Akhil Bharatiya Vidyarthi Parishad), 55
AMU (Aligarh Muslim University), 129, 131–134, 137–140, 146–149, 154–158, 320, 353 n1, 354 n3/4/6/7, 355 n13/19
AMWA (Ahmedabad Muslim Women Association), 77
ATS (Anti-Terror Squad), 200

BJP (Bharatiya Janata Party), 3, 5, 25–26, 30, 44, 56–57, 62–65, 75, 85, 99, 114–116, 121, 139, 142–145, 153, 159, 171, 173, 177–181, 183, 194, 199, 232, 244, 247, 260, 283, 288, 294, 302–304, 309, 318, 324, 349 n13, 351 n14, 357 n35, 367 n31
BMC (Brihanmumbai Municipal Corporation), 26, 28–29, 33, 35, 39
BPO, 210, 278
BSP (Bahujan Samaj Party), 6, 53, 112, 114, 116, 123, 142–144, 259, 367 n32

CBI (Central Bureau of Investigation), 200, 332 n23
CIESCO (Citizens' Intellectual Educational Social and Cultural Organization), 273, 275
CPI (M) (Communist Party of India–Marxist), 267–268

GSWT (Gujarat Sarvajanik Welfare Trust), 74, 348 n134

IML (Indian Muslim League), 280
IPS (Indian Police Service), 4, 69, 77, 141, 199, 248, 252
ISI (Inter Services Intelligence), 199
IT (Information Technology), 201, 208, 251, 267, 312
IUML (Indian Union Muslim League), 6, 264, 267–268, 280, 282–283, 374 n16/17, 375 n34

JDA (Jaipur Development Authority), 87, 89
JI-H (Jama'at-i-Islami Hind), 213–214, 221, 224, 226–229, 234–235, 334 n51, 365 n3, 369 n63, 379 n21

KHAM (Kshatriya, Harijans, Adivasis, Muslims), 55

INDEX

KNM (Kerala Naduvathul Mujahideen), 265, 280, 373 n8

LDF (Left Democratic Front), 267–268

MIM (Majlis Ittehadul-Muslimeen), 6, 179, 189–191, 193–194, 197, 205, 207, 210–211, 318
MES (Muslim Educational Society), 283–284

NDF (National Democratic Front), 278, 280, 283
NGO (Non Governmental Organisation), 68, 72, 77, 185, 340 n26, 346 n87, 347 n105/106, 348 n131/134, 363 n47

PAC (Provincial Armed Constabulary), 136
PFI (Popular Front of India), 278, 280– 281

RAC (Rajasthan Armed Constabulary), 86
RAS (Rajasthan Administrative Service), 90
RPS (Rajasthan Police Service), 90
RSS (Rajasthan Secretariat Service), 90, 375 n40
RSS (Rashtriya Swayamsevak Sangh), 53–54, 58, 63, 136, 199, 218, 242–243, 357 n33

SIMI (Student Islamic Movement of India), 221, 229, 231, 369 n68

TDP (Telugu Desam Party), 194, 206
TLA (Textile Labour Association, Ahmedabad), 46

UDF (United Democratic Front), 112, 267–268

NOTES ON CONTRIBUTORS

Qudsiya Contractor is currently a doctoral candidate at the Tata Institute of Social Sciences, Mumbai. She has previously worked as a researcher and human rights activist.

Juliette Galonnier is a PhD student at the Observatory for Social Change (OSC), Sciences Po, Paris. She studies the way stigmatized minorities relate to the city and how ethnic violence impacts urban space. Her fields of interest cover Hindu-Muslim riots in India and ethnic conflict in general, Muslim politics in India, residential segregation, ethnic identity and minority elites.

Radhika Kanchana is a PhD student at the Center for International Studies and Research, Sciences Po (CERI), Paris. Her doctoral research is titled 'Taking stock of the guest-worker migration policies: the Arab-Gulf countries and the Indians'. She holds a previous degree in International Relations from Syracuse University, USA.

Pralay Kanungo is Professor and Chairperson, Centre for Political Studies, Jawaharlal Nehru University, New Delhi. He taught at Delhi University and was Fellow at the Nehru Memorial Museum and Library. He is the author of *RSS's Tryst with Politics: From Hedgewar to Sudarshan* (Manohar 2002) and has co-edited *Cultural Entrenchment of Hindutva* (Routledge 2011) and *Public Hinduisms* (Sage, Forthcoming). He has written several articles on Hindutva and the Sangh Parivar.

Aminah Mohammad-Arif is a research fellow at CNRS (Centre national de la recherche scientifique) and the Deputy Director of the Centre for South Asian Studies (CEIAS, Paris). She has published *Salaam America: South Asian Muslims in New York* (Anthem Press, 2002) and has co-edited

NOTES ON CONTRIBUTORS

(with J. Schmitz) *Figures d'islam après le 11 septembre: disciples et martyrs, réfugiés et migrants* (Karthala, 2006), and (with C. Jaffrelot) *Politique et religions en Asie du Sud: le sécularisme dans tous ses états?* (Purushartha, EHESS, 2012). She is the co-founder and the co-editor of the *South Asian Multidisciplinary Academic Journal* (SAMAJ). She is presently working on Muslims in Bangalore.

Neena Rao, PhD, is currently working as Director Business Development and Policy Advocacy at the Centre for Climate Change and Environment Advisory, DR MCR HRD Institute of AP. She has a blend of an interdisciplinary academic training, implementation (practical experience) and passion that is necessary to be effective in developmental work such as Natural Resource Management, Rural Livelihoods, Inclusive & Sustainable Development, and Environmental Justice. Specifically, she has a rather unique combination of interdisciplinary training, spanning Economics and History, and a PhD in Natural Resource Management & Environmental Policies. As National Director, Livelihoods Programme with Naandi Foundation, Hyderabad, India, she has worked with women's self-help groups in Nagaland, the Andamans and around 50,000 farmers (farmers' cooperatives) in AP, India. She has authored the book *Forest Ecology in India: Colonial Maharashtra 1850-1950* (Cambridge University Press) and several papers on this topic.

S. Abdul Thaha, PhD, is an Assistant Professor at the Centre for the Study of Social Exclusion and Inclusive Policy, Maulana Azad National Urdu University, Hyderabad, India. He has published a book, *Forest Policy and Ecological Change in Hyderabad State* (Cambridge University Press, New Delhi, 2009). He has also published several articles and research reports in the field of history and social development issues. He is currently working on the issues of poverty and social exclusion of Muslims in India.

Charlotte Thomas is a PhD student at the Center for International Studies and Research, Sciences Po (CERI), Paris, and affiliated with the Institute of Strategic Research of the Military School (IRSEM) in Paris. She studies the Muslim community in Ahmedabad after the 2002-pogrom with a specific focus on the ghetto of Juhapura.

Gilles Verniers is a PhD candidate at the Center for International Studies and Research, Sciences Po (CERI), Paris, and a PhD Affiliate at the Centre de Sciences Humaines, New Delhi. His research focuses on the Samajwadi

NOTES ON CONTRIBUTORS

Party and Electoral Politics in Uttar Pradesh, and more broadly on political mobilization and representation dynamics in north India. Based in New Delhi since 2005, he also serves as Sciences Po Representative to India.

Shazia Wülbers did her M.Phil in European Studies from the Jawaharlal Nehru University and her PhD in Political Sciences at Sciences Po Paris. She is currently a lecturer and researcher at the Institute for Political Science, University of Hamburg where she is working on her Habilitation on Norm Diffusion from the EU and the US to India. Her latest publications include 'A Comparison of Indian Muslims and the Muslims Living in the European Union', in B. Krishnamurthy and Geetha Ganapathy-Doré, eds, *India, EU and US: A Trialogue*, (Shipra Publishers: New Delhi), *The Paradox of EU-Indian Relations: Missed Opportunities in Politics, Economics, Development Cooperation and Culture* (Lexington: Maryland) and *EU India Relations: A Critique* (Academic Foundation: New Delhi).